SUJIT SARAF is a novelist and playwright who lives in San Jose, California. His other works include *The Peacock Throne*, short-listed for the Encore Award in London, and *The Confession of Sultana Daku*, which has been optioned for film rights.

He is the founder and artistic director of Naatak (www.naatak.org), the largest Indian theatre company in the USA, for which he writes and stages plays and musicals.

He holds a Ph.D. in engineering from the University of California, Berkeley, and has been, in his day jobs, a space scientist for NASA and Lockheed Martin, a professor at IIT Delhi, and an entrepreneur in Silicon Valley. He now runs a software company in California.

PRAISE FOR SUJIT SARAF

The Peacock Throne

'One of the best novels I have read this year...a novel distinguished by the writer's capacity to tell a powerful and ambitious story'—Tabish Khair, *New Statesman*

'Gripping...the characters are...captivating...[Sujit Saraf] recreates the chaos, violence and stench of Indian urban life with enormous skill and fidelity'—*Independent*

'Teems with memorable characters and historical figures...enthralling'—*Daily Mail*

'[Sujit Saraf's] cast of characters is large, various and skillfully drawn and the chaotic life of the city is brilliantly evoked. He is also very funny.'—*Sunday Telegraph*

'Brings the sights, sounds and smells of Delhi right off the page...enlightening and entertaining...a fascinating read'—*Daily Express*

'An enormous novel in every sense...with every face and voice beautifully distinct'—*The Times,* London

'Bleak and shocking as well as entertaining and comical, Sujit Saraf's intelligent novel is a remarkable feat'—*The Sunday Express*, UK

'There have been very few novels about contemporary politics so far which have been written with the same depth and verve. It soaks in the smells and tastes of Chandni Chowk—and the vast sweep of events and characters is ever more interesting as the author has been able to inject a wry humour into his writing... [an] enjoyable, intricately woven expanse of a novel on modern India'—*Indian Express*

'Does for Delhi and democracy what Vikram Chandra's *Sacred Games* does for Bombay and organized crime'—*Time*

'He pulls his narrative off with considerable style and élan...an astonishing book'—*Hindustan Times*

'A gripping story'—*Literary Review*

Riveting...irreverent, farcical and entertaining'—*Good Books Guide*

'Saraf is a natural storyteller...an ornate, beautifully written tale'—*Sydney Morning Herald*

'A majestically sprawling fable'—*Big Issue*

The Confession of Sultana Daku

'[The] novel bowls along, carrying you effortlessly with it...a really good and unusual read'—Gillian Wright, *India Today*

'[A] tour de force'—*Deccan Herald*

Harilal & Sons

SUJIT SARAF

SPEAKING
TIGER

SPEAKING TIGER PUBLISHING PVT. LTD
4381/4 Ansari Road, Daryaganj,
New Delhi–110002, India

ISBN: 978-93-86050-75-5
eISBN: 978-81-933073-1-1

10 9 8 7 6 5 4 3 2 1

For sale in the Indian subcontinent only

Typeset in Sabon Roman by SÜRYA, New Delhi
Printed at Replika Press Pvt. Ltd.

To
Hiralal Saraf,
trader and traveller,
1880–1960

Contents

Family Tree *viii*

1. RAMPURA, 1899 1

2. CALCUTTA 63

3. BOGRA 149

4. WATSONGANJ 415

5. RAMPURA, 1972 483

Author's Note 515

Acknowledgements 517

Harilal Tibrewal (*b.*1887)

m. Parmeshwari in 1899

↓	↓	↓
Gopi Chand (*b.* 1906)	Durga Prasad (*b.* 1908)	Tribhuvan Lal (*b.* 1909)
m. Sharda	*m.* Gayatri	*m.* Kusum

Harilal Tibrewal (*b.*1887)

m. Manki in 1916

↓	↓	↓	↓	↓	↓
Garib Das (*b.* 1921)	Fakir Chand (*b.* 1925)	Shanti (*b.*1927)	Kaushalya (*b.*1929)	Ishwar Das (*b.* 1933)	Mohan Lal (*b.*1934)
m. Sumitra	*m.* Lajwanti	*m.* Nagar Mal	*m.* Jodh Raj	*m.* Nirmala	*m.* Radha

I

RAMPURA, 1899

1

Sand and sky were white. Another dry day. Eyes scoured the bowl above, seeking a wrinkle. July and not a wisp of cloud, nor a drop of rain. The young could not recall a summer so stark, the old spoke of the Bhaiya and Saiya famines of fifty-five years ago. In the evenings, at hushed gatherings on sand dunes under a lonely moon, they told stories. 'We remember such times in our youth. We have felt the sun singe our cheeks, seen withered stalks of bajra stretch into the distance, picked our way through dunes littered with dead goats and camels, watched the sand shift over the horizon, wept over the deceitful play of light against dust that creates the illusion of an impending rainstorm.'

Furrows of bajra lay untouched, and those that had been ploughed showed no signs of sprouting. Inside their homes women sighed daily, staring at images of Hanuman in their temples. 'Of all the creatures made by Raamji, why were we chosen to live in this cruel Shekhavati, this land of scrub and sand and khejra leaves where nothing but the poor bajra grows begrudgingly? What curse pushed the water so deep into the earth that even in the best of times a hand must deal out a hundred lengths of rope before the bucket strikes water? And if this crop should fail—as it surely will if the earth sees no drop for another week—who will feed whom in the gloomy winter? What milk shall we squeeze out of our starving cows? And where can we go when the camels that must carry us are dead themselves? Ah, how have we been negligent? Have we not recompensed the pandits, built poorhouses, erected temples? Is not the earth our mother, and is it not a mother's duty to provide? We hear daily of this Bengal, a thousand miles to the east; we are told it is lush, rich and overrun with mango orchards; we hear a hard-working man in Bengal may coax not one but three crops out of the land in a single year. Who in Shekhavati ever saw a mango?'

Already, bajra was six rupees to a munn, but the price carried no meaning: even if every beggar were to throw six silver rupees in every bania's face, there was no bajra to be had. A child cannot eat a silver rupee, even one with the face of the English queen on it. How long could one live on tamarind seeds ground into flour? How long on a gruel of tamarind water and jowar grains? How long on tamarind flowers, the bark of khejra trees, leaves and shoots? There would be no animal fair in Nagaur this year, no buying of cows or camels. Who would sell what, and to whom? To what purpose? 'We will remember this year forever,' said the young and the old, 'the year of the Chhappaniya famine, the famine of the year fifty-six. Our children will speak of it to their children, if the Chhappaniya lets them live long enough to beget any.'

Every day brought new tales, new fears, new agony. A Jatni had sold three sons for a bag of bajra. Wild dogs had been seen feeding on the long-dead bodies of beggars. Shopkeepers had stocked rooms with mounds of bajra, gwar and barley from previous years, and were now biding their time through the months of Saavan and Bhadwa, making daily offerings to Hanuman inside their homes, praying it would not rain. When Bhadwa had passed and the price of bajra had reached ten rupees to a munn, they would throw open their stores.

'It is true,' said the young, 'that a bania is born to gorge on the blood of innocents. Look at his quivering belly, filled with stolen grain! Look at the bags of salt in his kitchen, stolen from the mouths of hungry children! But let his bajra rot in his house.'

'We remember the Saiya and Bhaiya,' said the old. 'Ah, how we paid back the banias then!'

There were reports of a Bhil uprising in the south. Bhils had abandoned their villages, come out of their mountains and forests, blocked roads and robbed grain carts. They had nothing to eat, so they drank Mahua, danced under its sweet spell and burned down every shop they could find. Let the banias deal with that!

They said that the Thakur of Nawalgarh had commissioned a road to be built all the way to Jaipur, perhaps even to Delhi. For a day of work, he would pay five paisa for a man and four for a woman. Payment would be in bowls of bajra. But whoever heard of a road built through sand? The tibbas of Shekhavati were not ordinary desert dunes; they were known to shift daily, hourly, even by the minute. A man might sit down to rest under one and get up to find the tibba half a kos away. It was foolhardy, this road. The tibbas would obliterate it faster than it could be laid, and the men would all be dead from hunger before the thakur could bring out the first bowl of bajra. Where would the bajra come from anyway? Which bania would supply it? If he could sell to the Thakur of Nawalgarh, why would he not sell it to others in Jaipur at a higher price?

Every night, parties set out over the cool sand, bound for the great cities of Delhi, Bombay and Calcutta, hoping to cross the desert before the sun rose the next morning. They walked on foot, goading their remaining cows, tending to the camels that carried women and children, clothes and pots and pans. They walked east, finding their way by the light of the moon, preparing for the dreadful dawn, passing tibbas littered with camel carcasses, and sometimes humans they dared not identify. They watched with sinking hearts the glow in the east, and then the ascent of the great ball of fire. They watched their cows lie down in the scrub, never to get up. They saw their camels sit—front feet first, hurling women to the ground—and lay tired faces in the sand, still chewing on the remains of khejra leaves. Some collected their belongings and plodded forward, never to be seen again. Some returned to their desolate villages, defeated by the Chhappaniya.

Lines and ropes had grown long at wells. Women brought their men along to haul up the buckets. There were quarrels, even among neighbours. Six years ago in the village of Rampura—across the dry riverbed from Nawalgarh—there had been a great celebration when a well had been sunk. Being a brahmin, Master Bholaram had drawn the first water. Everyone had taken a sip, and everyone had remarked that it tasked like amrit, the nectar drunk by the gods themselves. Women had sat up all night, singing the Peepli. Mornings and evenings, children had run riot round the well, bathing, splashing, coming in the way of women who approached with their pots. That was six years ago. In this, the year of the Chhappaniya, no one spoke of the taste of water. Men watched the rope that snaked down the well, counting knots placed six feet apart, gasping when the fiftieth knot had passed from view, waiting for the inevitable day when no length of rope would strike water. Women, who could not count numbers so large, turned to their men and asked, 'How many knots? How many knots?'

The answer meant nothing to them, except that the well was nearly as dry as the tibbas.

There was a dam six kos away—made of earth, not brick or concrete—but families had already staked out spots around it to slurp the last few drops it still held in its reservoir. When a man jumped into the water, the women of Rampura cursed him—may Raamji bring down his wrath on the fool who bathes at a time like this!

Half a kos from the dam, a dozen men entered the house of Duli Chand Tibrewal, whose shop had been closed for days. 'Give us your bajra!' they demanded. 'Open your stores and let us have your mounds of grain! We have heard of spells cast by you. We know of the idols you have buried under your floor to ward off rain!'

Duli Chand was resting on a string-bed, laid inside a double-ceiling to the right of the door. The double-ceiling had been installed a few months ago at a height of five feet. A ladder had been placed against it. Even in the hot, dry afternoon, it was cool inside the ceiling. Duli Chand had had the servant lay a carpet of sand and sprinkle it with water—a few drops taken surreptitiously from his wife's kitchen.

When he saw the mob enter, he sat up on the cot but did not come down from the double-ceiling. Because he was in the dark, the men could not see him. He heard them fling abuse and smash pots. He knew they were digging up his kitchen floor, looking for the idols he had buried. *It is not wise to confront men ruled by passion*, he told himself as he waited for their anger to spend itself. Hearing a rustle under him, he crawled to the edge of the double-ceiling and peered down. His son Harilal stood there.

'They have found three idols and want to speak to you,' said the boy.

Now they will not go away easily, thought Duli Chand. He descended from his perch and walked into the kitchen, where he was immediately surrounded.

'Give us your bajra!'

'Raamji sees everything, Duli Chandji!'

'A bania feasts on the blood of children!'

Duli Chand sighed. 'I will organize a great Panchijarnya yagya,' he told the men, 'the largest puja anyone has seen in Rampura, even in all of Shekhavati. A hundred brahmins. They will chant for seven days to melt the heart of Indra. I promise you rain in four weeks.'

'Remember your promise,' the men warned as they left.

Harilal looked at his father in admiration. 'So you will bring rain to Shekhavati!'

'The gods are not fools,' Duli Chand replied bitterly, 'and Indra is their king. His law is unchanging—the bania's belly shall always be full, while he who smashes pots will forever be hungry.'

'The men said it was you who had pushed up the price of bajra.'

Duli Chand sighed. 'That is the way of the world—it wants the bania to suffer in good times and bad. When Indra sends down rain and bajra sways in the fields, a munn can be had for less than a rupee. Who suffers? The bania. Now, when bajra is scarce and the price is six rupees, who must suffer? Why, the bania. But how will a man recoup his expenses if not from customers? How will he pay for robberies and thefts, and the rotting mountains of barley from three years ago?' Duli Chand pointed to the mound of debris the men had left in the kitchen. 'The digging of my floor will merely raise the price further—an adhela for every munn.'

'They found no bajra in the house,' Harilal pointed out.

Duli Chand brought out a bag of cloth from the double-ceiling. 'The wise do not keep grain in the house; they store seed. This little bag contains a whole field!'

'Whom will you give it to?'

'To the man who can pay. Now or later. To a hard-working man who understands that even the earth must be paid for her bounty.'

'But I saw sacks of bajra in the store yesterday.'

'They are now in the railway yard at Jaipur. Waiting to be taken all over Shekhavati. To towns that offer better rates than Rampura.'

'But what of us? We have no grain tonight.'

'Come with me.'

Duli Chand slipped on a kurta, shook the dust from his dhoti, pressed a turban on to his head and set out with Harilal.

Rampura was deserted. Hari anxiously scanned the bleak desert sky.

'I see no clouds anywhere.'

Duli Chand said, 'If it does not rain by the second day of the second fortnight in the month of Aashaadh, says the farmer, break your plough and use it for fuel, and chew on the seed you would have planted, because the land will offer nothing. Today is the first day.'

Hari looked at the sky again. 'What if it does not rain tomorrow?'

'What if it does not? We are not farmers. No matter how stingy Indra Bhagwan is with his rain a bania will not go hungry, as long as he has a shop where he may buy cheap and sell dear.'

They walked in silence to the school, and then to a room behind it, where Master Bholaram sat smoking on a cot. On seeing Duli Chand he rose, opened a cupboard and threw two gunny bags on the floor.

'These do not look like bajra bags,' Harilal said.

'This is rice,' Duli Chand said with pride, 'and the second bag is wheat, fit for the Maharaja of Jaipur himself.'

'Bajra is for Jats,' Master Bholaram added.

Harilal studied the bags. 'English markings?'

Master Bholaram brought out spectacles and read aloud, 'American Methodists for Famine Relief, United Presbyterian Mission: for distribution in the Shekhavati region of Rajputana. Not for sale. Transferred to the Jaipur depot, June 14, 1899'.

Harilal quickly added up the years in his head, using the tables Master Bholaram had taught him. 'This is fifty-seven years old.'

'They give us rotten wheat!' Duli Chand exclaimed. 'No one in England will eat this, so they send it to us.'

Master Bholaram laughed. 'Your boy has a good head for arithmetic, Duli Chand Babu. He can add and subtract inside his head, but that is the English date, not ours. This wheat is no more than a month old.'

Chastened, Duli Chand busied himself in a careful examination of the bags.

'Where do the sahibs get grain at a time like this?' asked Harilal, awed.

Master Bholaram took off his spectacles. 'No one knows. They hand out rice and wheat when even the Thakur of Nawalgarh has to run around arranging for bajra. And how do they transport it when all the camels are dying?'

'Trains,' Duli Chand said dismissively. Then a frown clouded his brow. 'Who knows which hands have touched this? Christian? What might they have mixed in it?'

Master Bholaram shook his head. 'I spoke to the sahib who distributes these. The rice is from Bengal.'

'But who packed it? The sahib would not know—he would not have squatted on the threshing floor to fill bags. Bengal has Musalmans.'

'You will wash it carefully, of course,' said Master Bholaram.

Duli Chand picked up the bags.

'I had to pay the railway guard at Jaipur,' Master Bholaram said softly. 'He said these bags were bound south, towards Sirohi.'

Duli Chand considered this. 'Add it to my account.' He unwrapped his turban, rolled it again, tightly, pushed it firmly down on his head, loaded both bags on his head and turned to leave.

'You cannot be seen like this in daylight,' Master Bholaram warned. 'There will be a riot. Come back late in the night and take the bags.'

'What will my wife cook this evening?'

'Take a handful.'

Duli Chand set the bags on the ground, tore a seam, scooped up handfuls of grain into his dhoti and tied two knots, one for rice and one for wheat; these he tucked into his waist. Then he carefully sealed the bag with string. 'I do not want you to open these in my absence.'

Master Bholaram turned the face of a martyr on him. 'We have known each other for twenty years, Duli Chand Babu. Have I ever stolen from you?'

Duli Chand shook his head in embarrassment and walked out of the school, Harilal in tow.

'Why did you send our bajra to Jaipur, if we had no food at home?'

'The rate was good.'

'But now you have to pay Masterji.'

'He gets it free from English sahibs. And he knows that I know. He cannot charge more than half-price.'

They took a circuitous path home to avoid being seen, staying close to the dry riverbed beyond which lay the town of Nawalgarh, 10 miles away. A gazelle lay on its side in the bed, dead. Where the river veered north, away from Rampura, they walked along the boundary wall of Seth Daulatram's new mansion. Harilal rarely came this way, fearing wild animals. No one lived in the haveli; jackals could be heard howling in its vast grounds all night. In Rampura, they had a name for the building—Daulatram's Tomb.

'This man was a banker to princes,' Duli Chand said to his son. 'Every month, his firm still sends fifty thousand bales of jute to England. But look at his haveli: not yet four years old, and the plaster is peeling off the walls. It is true: the higher you rise, the greater your fall.'

'Does he not live in it any more?'

'He never lived in it, never even saw it. This is what happens when one overreaches. He had the silver—a bania always has silver if he is careful—but he overlooked the wrath of Raamji. A man may not build a monument to himself. He must collect his wealth discreetly, almost surreptitiously, looking this way and that, making every effort to hide his good fortune. Instead he chose to flaunt it. Why did he need a whole haveli? This is why I have installed the double-ceiling near our door. Our ceilings are 10 feet high. Once I sit down on my cot, I need no more than 5 feet of air. What will I do with the extra space above my head? And will it break my back to bend over just a little when walking under the double-ceiling? The more you bend, Hariya, the more you endear yourself to Raamji.'

'But I am tall, babuji. You yourself say so. In a year to two, I will bump my head against that ceiling.'

Duli Chand smiled. 'And that will remind you, again and again, that pride robs you of wealth, in this world and the next. Daulatramji died the day after his haveli was completed. Some say it was the haveli that took him. Now its plinth is sinking. The paintings on its walls have faded. In a few years, it will become one with the tibbas. True, a man must live where his shop is, or he will lose both his home and his customers.'

'Where is his shop?'

'He has hundreds, in Kalkatta, Kanpur, Assam, Bombay. His head-accountant, Khemchand Biyani, looks after them.'

'Did Daulatramji not have sons?'

'Three, but a dozen daughters are better than such sons. The oldest retired to Benares in his youth, the second lives like a fakir in Brindavan. Only the third ever earned anything, but he nearly brought his father's firm to ruin. Fortunately for him, Khemchand Biyani is a wise and thrifty man. As long as he lives, Daulatramji's firm will go on. After his death, who knows? Much money can be made in Kalkatta, but it is lost as easily.'

'Where is Kalkatta?'

'In Daulatramji's time, the journey took months. He had to go by camel to Jaipur, then walk to Mirzapur from where he took a boat down the Ganga to Kalkatta. Now, you reach Delhi in a day or two, then sit in a train that takes you to Kalkatta in two days.'

'I would like to see a train,' Harilal said. 'Master Bholaram says it runs without camels and its whistle can be heard for miles.'

'There are dozens in the Jaipur yard,' said Duli Chand.

'Did Daulatramji have one?'

Duli Chand laughed. 'The sahibs own them all. But Daulatramji's sons could buy one if they wanted.'

From where they stood, they had a clear view of the whole boundary wall, until it ended and turned sharply towards the riverbed. From this angle, Hari thought he could see a giant red snake lying across the wall. This was the faded fresco his father had referred to—a train, full of strange faces that peered out of a hundred windows. The colours had nearly vanished, and one had to stand at a certain angle to notice the painting.

'Will you spend your day gazing at walls, Hariya? Let us go.'

Hari turned to his father. 'Why does anyone live in Rampura at all? Why not take the train to Kalkatta?'

Duli Chand sighed. 'A man needs two sons so one may go to Kalkatta. Not everyone is thus blessed.'

Hari pointed to the smoke drifting out of a window high in the wall of the mansion. 'That's a kitchen. Someone lives inside this haveli.'

'That is Hemraj, son of Khemchand Biyani. Works in Kalkatta, earns seventy-five rupees in a month. When he comes to Rampura, he stays in the haveli. In a few days he will return to Kalkatta to join his father.'

'Should we talk to him?' Hari asked, excited.

'Why? Idle chatter befits Jats. It is not proper to talk to someone unless there is business to be discussed.'

As they walked home, Duli Chand admonished his son. 'Do not keep looking back. No one yet knows we have rice with us, but you will surely give us away.'

But Hari had turned to look at the haveli, and the smoke drifting from its kitchen. What did Hemrajji look like? A man who had walked in Kalkatta and earned seventy-five rupees every month!

When they reached home, Hari's mother ran to the door, almost spilling the water she had brought for Duli Chand. She was crestfallen to see them empty-handed. 'You said Masterji would give you rice.'

'I cannot be seen with a sack in daylight,' said Duli Chand, loosening the knots in his dhoti. 'Have Muniya bring a plate, and don't spill a grain!'

He sprinkled water on his feet, taking care not to waste a drop, placed a foot on the ladder near the door and disappeared into the double-ceiling.

That night, Hari had the first of three dreams he would have about the haveli. He stood on a riverbank, watching the dry bed and the dead gazelle, and before him rose a mansion. It was not the one Daulatramji had built. Its wall was painted with a great fresco that rose thirty feet high and stretched for a kos. A black-headed snake lay across the earth, stretching from mountain to plain, over rivers and bridges and canals, its body broken into red boxes, each sitting on wheels that ran on black lines in the ground. A plume of smoke emerged from the head and blackened the sky above, watched by a man smoking a strange bidi, adding a puff to the great cloud above. Then Hari noticed that the red boxes were full of holes, and the men and women who sat inside were pale sahibs. They wore hats and coats and their yellow hair flew in the wind. A tall, bearded sahib with flowing hair sat atop the red box, taking no notice of the robe that fluttered about him in the wind. Hari recognized him right away: this was Jisu, the god of the sahibs. In one hand he held a bidi, and the other seemed to be waving. And who should he be waving at but Krishna and Radha, seated in a chariot—the type owned by the Thakur of Nawalgarh—which flew above the snake on a pair of wings! Hari took a step back to see the whole snake, but it stretched too far in either direction. He was woken by his mother's voice, calling softly.

'Hariya's father! Draupadi has a fever. Could you send for the ojha?'

She stood outside the double-ceiling. Hari felt the warmth of Draupadi's body crushed against his. *Perhaps I have a fever too*, he thought. *Why else would Raamji send down such a dream?*

'Harilal will fetch the ojha,' replied Duli Chand.

Hari felt the hand of fate on his head. He now knew what the dream meant. Drawing his mother into the room—away from his father—he whispered, 'Where is the silk kurta you bought me last year? The one with brocade.'

'You need not dress up to see an ojha.'

'I am twelve,' he said with dignity.

His mother laughed. 'All right.'

In his brocaded kurta, Hari ran to the ojha's house. As a child, he had feared the man who brought smoke and medicine into the house. Now the ojha was in his seventies, deaf and nearly blind. Hari shouted into his ear.

'Pranaam!'

The ojha started. 'Whose son are you?'

'Shri Duli Chand Tibrewal.'

'The one whose son was taken by the pox?'

'Do you not remember me?' Hari asked. 'I am the one who had the pox. You took it away.'

'Raamji gives and Raamji takes away.'

'My sister is not well. Babuji has asked you to come.'

'Whose son are you?'

Hari told him everything again, helped him off the cot, dispatched him with his tools, and made his way to the dry riverbed. He walked by the outer wall of Daulatram's haveli, found the door and ran into a courtyard. A servant was drawing water from a well and another was sweeping, sending up clouds of dust. The yard was decrepit: peeling plaster, moss on the walls, soot-blackened ceilings.

'Pranaam,' Hari said, 'Where is Hemrajji?'

The servants ignored him. He passed through a door into a second courtyard that was also lined with rooms. At the far end, he saw a light in one and peered inside. A lantern cast a yellow arc on the wall. A mattress lay in the centre. Seated on it, bending over a red-bound book, was a man whom Hari recognized instantly, not because he had seen him before but because he wore a foreign wristwatch. On hearing Hari's footsteps, Hemraj Biyani flicked a switch and pointed a bright circle of light at him. An English light, no doubt. Silk kurta, pleated dhoti. Kalkatta!

'Pranaam,' said Hari, bringing his hands together. He squatted at the door and waited. Having seen him in the circle of his English light, Hemraj went back to his papers. After what seemed like an eternity he asked, 'Whose son are you?'

'Shri Duli Chand Tibrewal.'

Hemraj nodded. Hari squirmed his way into the room, still squatting. The stone floor was cool. He stopped far from the mattress, and suddenly his situation became clear to him. In his haste to reach the haveli, he had given no thought to what he would say to Hemrajji. And now he must come up with something! He lied.

'My father has sent me.'

'Yes?'

'He asks if you would agree to take me to Disavar.'

'Where in Disavar?'

'Kalkatta.'

Hemraj looked hard at Hari. 'How old are you?'

'Twelve.'

'I was your age when I went to Kalk...Calcutta. Fourteen years ago.'

This gave Hari hope. He inched closer. 'My father said, "Ask Hemrajji if he needs a servant or a munim."'

'Do you understand account books?'

'Yes. And multiplication tables for one-and-a-quarter, one-and-a-half, one-and-three-quarters, two-and-a-half.'

'Who taught you?'

'Master Bholaram.'

'Can you read letters?'

'Yes.'

'In Hindi?'

'Modhiya.'

Hemrajji held out paper and a pencil. 'Write something in Modhiya.'

Hari had used nothing but slate and chalk in school. He placed the paper carefully on the floor and wrapped his fingers around the pencil, marvelling at the extravagance—a whole sheet of smooth paper was to be wasted for a few scrawls in Modhiya. But Hemrajji was watching. His hand trembled. Master Bholaram's passion was arithmetic, not language, so Hari's training in Modhiya consisted wholly of one essay, dictated by Masterji once a week and written repeatedly by his students until it had been committed to memory. Slowly and painfully, Hari formed the words.

The Rigved says she is mother to the eleven rudras, daughter to the earth, space, ether, fire, wind, sun, moon and stars, sister to Vishnu ...

He handed back the paper. Hemrajji stared at it and asked, 'Who is?'

Hari had written and erased those lines so many times on his slate, remembering only Master Bholaram's adverse comments on his handwriting and spelling, that they had lost all meaning. With some difficulty, he remembered. 'The cow.'

'Ah. The cow.'

Hari wondered if the essay had been insufficient.

'Do you have brothers?' askd Hemrajji. Hari shook his head. Hemrajji appeared surprised. 'I will need to talk to your father.'

'He is not well,' said Hari. 'The shop has been closed for days.

Bajra is six rupees to a munn in the Chhappaniya. Even jowar is climbing. No one has seen rice for months. If my father were to keep his shop open all night, no one would come to buy. How will a man recoup his expenses if not from customers?'

Hemrajji appeared amused. 'Do you sit behind the cash box with your father?'

'All day, as soon as I return from Master Bholaram's school.'

Hemrajji nodded approvingly but went back to his books. After a while, Hari asked, 'Should I tell my father you have agreed?'

'Come back tomorrow.'

Hari rose and bowed. Hemraj placed a mango in his hands, 'Tell your mother this is from Bengal.' Hari gasped: a perfect mango, small, smooth, yellow and firm! 'And tell your father that Khemchandji Biyani remembers him.'

Long shadows lay across the dunes when Hari emerged from the haveli. He turned to look at the wall, half expecting a red snake drawn across it, but it was the same as before: blank and grey. He walked home, mango in hand. The sky was clear. The night would be cold.

The ojha had arrived and was squatting next to Draupadi, his blindness nearly complete in the dim glow of a lantern. A bronze pot of water lay before him. His knives were arrayed on the mud floor. Red chillies crackled in a censer. Hari's mother sat in a corner, a shawl over her face. Holding Draupadi's arm up in the air, the ojha blew weakly into the censer and chanted. Smoke filled the house, and the smell of chillies wafted on it. Draupadi coughed. Leaning forward to look into the censer, Hari coughed too. Duli Chand scolded him.

'Step back!'

The ojha drew a knife from the pot of water and peered into Draupadi's half-closed eyes. 'Why have you come here, when the Chhappaniya is among us?' he asked softly.

'It is hot,' Draupadi replied.

'Go away. Leave the poor child alone!' he commanded,

brandishing the knife over the girl, describing ever widening arcs in the air, taking care to drag the blade across the earth in the lower half of its trajectory. Hari leaned closer, listening. He could not understand the chants. In Sanskrit, perhaps. Master Bholaram had been very strict about this. 'Arithmetic above all,' he had said. 'Multiplication tables. Accounts. Then some Modhiya. Perhaps Hindi when you are fifteen. For the very brightest among you, some English.' No Sanskrit. 'A bania must learn numbers, not words. When he needs to read the Shastra, he will pay a brahmin to do it. Does Rampura not have pandits that a bania must waste his time learning Sanskrit?' *Just as well*, thought Hari. He would not need Sanskrit in Kalkatta.

The ojha tied a talisman around Draupadi's arm. She would not stop coughing. Hari was troubled. It was inauspicious that Draupadi should suffer so on the day he had met Hemrajji of Kalkatta. Perhaps the Chhappaniya did not want him to go? What would a boy do if fever visited him in Disavar? Did they have ojhas in Kalkatta?

His mother rocked Draupadi in her arms. Gradually, the fumes dissipated and the coughing died down. The girl drifted into a troubled slumber and the ojha rose to go. 'It will leave the child before the sun rises tomorrow,' he predicted. Hari's mother signalled to Rukmini, his oldest sister. She handed the ojha a coconut. His half-dead eyes gradually found their focus. Even in the dark he had seen what Hari held in his hands. 'If Duli Chandji so wishes, I will have the mango.'

Suddenly, all eyes were on the fruit. Hari had forgotten about it.

'Where did you get that?' Duli Chand asked sharply.

'In the dunes,' he lied. 'On the large tibba beyond the river.'

The ojha mumbled. 'Raamji has sent us the Chhappaniya. Now he seeds the sand with mangoes.'

'It isn't yet ripe,' Hari sputtered.

'The fever has not left the child,' the ojha said darkly, 'and may choose to linger for another day.'

Duli Chand sighed. 'Give it to him.'

The ojha fondled the mango and laid a trembling hand on Hari's head. 'You will see pools of water full of lilies, my son.'

As soon as the ojha had left, Duli Chand turned angrily to Hari. 'Where did you find the mango?'

'It is a gift from Hemrajji. A servant delivered it.'

'Was there a message?'

'Yes,' said Hari. 'Hemrajji needs a munim, someone to do his accounts. He has asked if he may take me to Disavar with him.'

Duli Chand was taken aback. 'He asked for *you*? How does he know of you?'

'The message said Khemchandji Biyani remembers you well. "Get me Duli Chandji's son," he said. "A boy from that family can be trusted."'

Duli Chand's face softened. 'Khemchandji is a rare man. Never forgets a favour. Even now, when he sits with English sahibs and sells a thousand bales of jute every day.'

'Do I have your permission?'

'My son will not be anyone's servant.'

'A munim, an accountant, not a servant.'

'A man who leaves his own shop to serve in someone else's is a fool. However small my shop may be, you are its master. Khemchandji will give you a salary, no more. You will help multiply his capital.'

'As soon as I have learned the ways of Disavar, I will leave his shop and open my own.'

'Look at this boy,' Duli Chand said, turning to Hari's mother. 'His pride knows no bounds. Speak softly, my son, or the gods will hear you!'

She took a step forward and removed the shawl from her face. 'When a man like Khemchandji asks for your son, you should hand him over without asking. Who knows when one might need a favour from such a man?'

'Hari's mother!' Duli Chand replied irritably. 'This is not a matter for women.'

'No one has heard of the Chhappaniya in Bengal,' Hari pleaded. 'There are a hundred ways for a bania to earn money. What is there to do in our Shekhavati? It gives us nothing but famine.'

'Do not speak thus of Shekhavati,' replied Duli Chand. 'We lived through the Saiya and Bhaiya famines; we will live through this Chhappaniya.'

'What of the others that will follow?' Hari demanded.

Duli Chand squatted on the floor and mumbled, 'Only twelve, and look how he talks back. Who will look after your sisters after I am gone? You have four.'

'If Harilal's brother had lived ...' Hari's mother began.

'It was Raamji's wish to take him away!' Duli Chand said sharply, cutting her short.

Hari fell silent, suddenly guilty. There stood Rukmini and Jasoda, looking at him, awaiting his answer. And there lay Draupadi, sleeping fitfully. What lack of sense he had displayed in going to the haveli! A boy could not be heedless of his obligations. 'I am already twelve,' he said aloud, 'not a child who chases fantasies. What more do I need when I already have a shop?'

Duli Chand looked away.

'Who knows what a man eats in Disavar?' Hari continued. 'What kind of flour do they put into his rotis? Where do they grind his grain? Which water does he drink? How does he know it is clean? Only the reckless leave home to go to faraway lands full of Musalmans, Bengalis and English sahibs.'

Duli Chand rose. 'The sun has set. Do not forget to feed the animals, Harilal.'

Hari went outside, threw khejra bushels at the camel, fed the cows and poured water—very little—into the tank. He looked away as the cows chewed, hoping not to confirm what he had sensed as he approached: one of the cows, a brown Nagauri whom Rukmini called Tara, was missing. He had heard horrid tales: a passing butcher would see the emaciated beast, note its pitiful ribs and sunken eyes, and approach the master. A silver rupee would change hands. The butcher would untie the cow and lead it away. Not a word would be exchanged.

He knew many people who had thus given away camels, but a cow! And to hand it to a Musalman butcher! Everyone knew what such men did with the animals ... but surely his father would not allow such a thing. Tara had perhaps wandered off. His father would soon send him after her.

They shared Master Bholaram's grain that night.

'We eat rice in the Chhappaniya,' Hari's mother said gratefully. 'We must not forget what Raamji has sent us.'

'I am still hungry,' Jasoda complained.

'Eat lightly,' her mother admonished, 'or your brother will go hungry.'

Hari did not want to eat at all. He was thinking of Calcutta. Everyone in Rampura, they said, could be accommodated into one building in Kalkatta, and there were thousands of such buildings. There were mangoes, cucumbers and bags of rice. There was so much water that people bathed their cows. The crowds were such that a man from Rampura would find himself bumping into someone at every step. There were officers, sahibs and memsahibs ...

'I am not hungry,' Rukmini said. 'Hariya can have my rice.'

Hari's mother regarded her oldest daughter indulgently. Already fifteen: her in-laws would send for her any day now. There would not be much to give her when she left, but a girl had to be thankful for what she could get.

'Your mother-in-law is a kind woman,' she said to Rukmini. 'Speaks softly. Not one to torment a little girl. She will be to you as I am: a mother.'

Rukmini tossed her head in disagreement. Jasoda laughed. At eleven, she had at least four years in her mother's home before her in-laws asked for her. She had peeked at her husband during the wedding, and knew him to be a good-looking boy. 'When my warrior comes for me,' she said, 'I will refuse to go.'

Her mother patted her absently, looking at Muniya: eight,

recently engaged to the son of a bania from Mukundgarh. For Draupadi, who was now four, they would look for a boy in a larger town like Sikar or Jhunjhunu. It was difficult for a fourth daughter, especially when there was only one brother to shoulder the burden of four weddings. If Harilal's brother had lived ... Then she turned her eyes on Hari. It was time to marry off the boy. He had already been engaged for four years. Perhaps next year, when the Chhappaniya would have passed.

'A married girl does not speak thus of her husband,' Rukmini scolded Jasoda. 'You do not belong to this house. When he comes for you, you will go.'

Hari drew Muniya aside. 'Have you seen Tara today?'

'Babuji gave her to Nanuram,' she said. 'His children need milk.'

Hari knew that could not be true. Tara was too old to give milk and Nanuram had no children, but Muniya was too young to know that.

'Go to sleep, all of you,' Hari's mother said. She unfolded an old bajra roti and placed it carefully on a brass plate with some rice, an onion, salt and khejra pickle. With the plate and a pot of water, she approached the double-ceiling and called softly, 'Hariya's father.'

Duli Chand reached out and took the plate from her. Hari approached his father.

'I did not see Tara when I fed the animals.'

'It is dark, Harilal. Your eyes have deceived you.'

'It was still light when I went outside.'

'She may have wandered off.' Hari could not see his father's face in the double-ceiling. 'Tomorrow I will gift her to a goshala, where they will take good care of her until she dies.'

'A goshala gives nothing for an old cow.'

'This is not a question of money, Harilal. What is money? The dirt on one's palm. Comes off as easily as it comes on.'

Hari's mother had overheard. 'Is Tara lost?' she cried.

'Calm down, Hariya's mother. Tara has run off in the tibbas. Hariya will bring her back tomorrow morning.'

'The night will be cold! She will shiver.'

'There is nothing a boy can do in the dark,' Duli Chand said. 'Now go to sleep, Harilal. At dawn, I want you to lay out your mother's pots on the roof.'

'Do you think it will rain tomorrow?'

'No. But one must be prepared.'

Hari lay down next to Draupadi, who was now sound asleep. The ojha's talisman was doing its work. Rukmini came and sat next to him.

'Why do you want to go to Disavar?' she asked.

'I don't,' he said, 'but Hemrajji has asked for me.'

Hari shut his eyes, wondering why Daulatramji had walked 500 miles through the tibbas to get to Mirzapur. Why did a boy go to Kalkatta? Was it the Chhappaniya, the dry riverbed, the dusty lanes, the dunes beyond the town? And Tara lay on the ground somewhere in a shed, her legs tied, eyeing the butcher's knife. But the world was full of butchers. Who could keep watch over all of them? Who could dictate what such men did inside their homes? When a man did something sinful, the sin accrued to his account, not Hari's. He had loved Tara as one loved a mother, and still did.

He drifted into sleep.

Early the next morning, he stepped outside and looked up. The sky was ashen and clear. Undeterred, he placed a ladder against the wall, climbed to the roof and swept it clean. Rukmini stood at the base of the ladder and handed him every pot they could find in the kitchen, one by one. Hari arranged them neatly on the roof. Every drop Indra Bhagwan chose to send down that day would be captured.

Lying down next to the bowls, he thought of Calcutta again, the great Kalkatta of his imagination. Dark clouds massed above him. Thunder rolled. He would soon be drenched! What had the ojha said? Pools of water full of lilies …

'Harilal!' Rukmini called. 'Come down from the roof! Babuji wants to speak to you.'

Inside his double-ceiling, Duli Chand coughed to indicate that

Hari was to climb in. He did, and sat down on the cool carpet of sand at the foot of his father's bed.

'The month of Aashaad will end soon,' said Duli Chand. 'If it has not rained until the eleventh day of the second fortnight, the Chhappaniya will last all summer.'

'Yes,' said Harilal, knowing his father had not summoned him merely to talk of famine. 'I have laid out the pots on the roof.'

'What took you so long?'

'I was looking for clouds.'

'In Disavar, a boy must leave his bed before dawn so he may start the day's business. Is this how you prepare for it?'

Hari gasped. What had wrought this change? Which goddess had found in her heart the grace to listen to his appeals? He wanted to cry and lay his head at his father's feet, but Duli Chand continued to regard him sternly.

'Hemraj leaves in a few days. Go see if your mother is done with puja. You must tally the inventory in the shop today.'

Hari climbed down from the double-ceiling. Rukmini was waiting. 'What did he say?'

'Mark an ojha's words,' Hari told her. 'They always come true.'

Two days later, Master Bholaram arrived on hearing the news. 'Harilal is a thrifty boy,' he said to Duli Chand, 'he will earn much in Disavar.'

'Raamji will protect him,' Duli Chand replied.

Master Bholaram—who was also the postmaster of Rampura—withdrew a postcard from his satchel. 'There is a letter for you from Narayan Dasji,' he said.

On hearing Narayan Das's name, Hari's mother came and stood at the door, a corner of her shawl pulled low over face.

'Read it, Masterji,' Duli Chand said.

Master Bholaram admonished him. 'Harilal should read it—he needs to practise his Modhiya.'

Duli Chand smiled. 'He is shy, and you are his Guruji: he will not come into the house when you are present.'

'It is not as if Narayan Dasji writes in Hindi,' protested Master Bholaram. 'Why must Harilal hesitate to read before me?'

'You think of his education, I think of propriety,' Duli Chand said sharply. 'I cannot ask the boy to read a letter from his own father-in-law!'

Chastened, Master Bholaram put on his spectacles and read aloud. 'Narayan Das Nangaliya from Chirawa says Raam Raam to Shri Duli Chand Tibrewal in the auspicious town of Rampura. Master Bholaramji has informed me that Chiranjeev Harilal is to go to Disavar with the son of Shri Khemchandji Biyani. Given the expense of the journey, I understand that Harilal will not return for at least three years, so it would be improper to delay the wedding any longer. The period of engagement has lasted six years. Chiranjeev Harilal is already twelve, and the eleventh is upon my daughter. What Raamji has begun we should complete while it is affordable. In ten days the period of chaumasa will begin, when a wedding would be inappropriate. Our pandit says that Aashaadh sudi dashmi, four days before the chaumasa begins, is auspicious. Although the Chhappaniya has sent bajra to six rupees, we have found a supplier in Mukundgarh. I have also arranged for water.The rest is in the hands of Raamji, on this Aashaadh sudi chauth in the Vikram Samvat year of one thousand nine hundred and fifty six.'

'Today is the fourth!' Duli Chand exclaimed. 'How can I arrange a wedding in six days?'

Master Bholaram shrugged. 'Once the chaumasa begins, Harilal cannot be married off for four months.'

'But Hemraj wants to leave for Kalkatta in three days—it is improper to travel during the chaumasa.'

'Ask him to postpone his trip,' said Master Bholaram. 'For one anna, a pandit will remove the obstacle to travel, but no pandit will dare preside over a wedding during the chaumasa. And who knows what will follow the Chhappaniya next year? What if bajra goes even higher?'

Duli Chand sighed. 'I have only one son, and he has the

misfortune to come of age during a famine. You may tell Narayan Dasji that Aashaadh sudi dashmi is acceptable to us. We will bring no more than eighty guests.'

Master Bholaram objected. 'You must take everyone in Rampura. Harilal is your only son.'

'Where will I find the camels to carry them?' demanded Duli Chand. 'Those still living are too weak to go fifty miles among the tibbas.'

'Some guests could go on cycles.'

'A cycle cannot cross shifting dunes. It is the English sahib's vehicle, meant for streets, not tibbas. For us, there is the camel.'

'A cycle does not chew on khejra bushes as it goes,' responded Master Bholaram. 'Two years ago, Nanuram was thrown when his camel stopped to eat khejra leaves on a tibba.'

'Nanuram is a munim: he understands accounts, not camels.' Saying this, Duli Chand raised his voice and turned slightly towards the door, where he knew his wife stood, listening.

'Hariya's mother, do you hear me? Harilal's wedding has been fixed for dashmi, six days from now. You must start the songs tomorrow.' Turning to the kitchen door, behind which Hari stood, ears cocked, Duli Chand said, 'Go to the shop. Tell Nanuram to shut down for the day and come here.'

Hari rushed out of the house, eager to be alone so he could consider this sudden turn of events. He knew he was too old to remain unmarried, and an engagement that lasted this long always raised questions about the fitness of the bride or groom. Yet he had not expected a wedding to intrude into his reverie. How was he to think of Kalkatta now that he had to contend with a bride?

Nanuram laughed on hearing the news. He was a slight, thin man who had been hired by Duli Chand's father when a child of seven, fifteen years ago. He had attended Duli Chand's wedding and watched his children grow. As a child, he used to call his master Duliya, but this had changed to the more formal 'Duli Chand Babu' with time. No such formality attended his relations with Hari, whom he now lifted in his arms and taunted. 'You will soon have a new master.'

'Have you seen this girl?' Hari asked anxiously.

Nanuram lied. 'Yes, and she has a sharp tongue!'

'I know her name—Parmeshwari.'

'Do not let it pass your lips before the wedding. That is inauspicious.'

'I am the groom, not the bride.'

'Is that what Master Bholaram teaches you? That a groom may freely utter his bride's name?'

'Take me to Chirawa tomorrow so I may get a glimpse of her.'

Nanuram laughed again. 'A groom may not see the bride before his wedding. Indeed, you will not leave your house after they bathe you tomorrow. Now let us go to your father. I have much work to do so you may bring home his daughter-in-law. '

The next morning, Harilal sat on a wooden stool while his sisters smeared turmeric paste on his feet, knees, hands, shoulders and cheeks. Women took turns rubbing the paste into his skin, giggling, daubing his cheeks playfully with clumps of duub grass and painting henna patterns on his palms.

'There is no water,' Hari's mother told Duli Chand. 'How do we bathe the groom?'

'Run a damp towel over his face. Raamji will understand.'

After his toilet, Harilal was given a pink shervani that came down to his ankles, and adorned with pearl earrings, silver bangles and a necklace. Duli Chand approached his son with an iron rod that looked like an umbrella stick.

'This is a chitiya,' he said. 'Keep it with you at all times; lay it by your side when you go to bed: there are spirits about, ready to snatch a bridegroom.'

Nanuram spent the next seven days spreading the word in Rampura—two men from every family were invited to the wedding. Hemraj Biyani sent a messenger expressing his inability to attend. Duli Chand sighed. 'I am only a shopkeeper. No one from Daulatramji's family will come to my son's wedding.'

It was not easy to find camels at a time like this. Nanuram sought them in Nawalgarh—beyond the riverbed—and even as far as Sikar and Jhunjhunu. The beasts he found were emaciated, perhaps unequal to the burden of a 50-mile journey in the heat. Charged with arranging for forty, he was able to find only twenty-five.

'A mere fifty guests,' Duli Chand thought gloomily. 'That is how I marry off my only son.'

'I have rented a chariot for Harilal,' said Nanuram. 'The bullocks are free but we have to pay for fodder.'

Duli Chand wondered if they should do without the chariot. A camel could take care of itself in the tibbas, but Nagauri bullocks would need to be fed, and they ate much more. Yet it was heartless to suggest that his son go to his wedding on a camel, so he said vaguely, 'We will make arrangements.'

'In Chirawa, the responsibility for fodder will fall on the bride's father,' Nanuram pointed out.

This soothed Duli Chand. 'Have you consulted the pandit about our departure?'

'Yes. We must leave the house in the middle of the first prahar, at ten-thirty in the morning,' said Nanuram. 'The hours after that are inauspicious.'

'But we cannot ride in the scorching heat. I had hoped to travel by night.'

'Let us pass through your door at ten-thirty and wait outside Rampura all afternoon. We can start for Chirawa early in the evening. That will satisfy both the pandit and the sun.'

On the day of departure, Nanuram herded the guests to Duli Chand's house early in the morning, afraid to miss the auspicious hour. Hari was roused, bathed sparingly under the hand pump and dressed in a red tunic embroidered with gold thread. A red turban was pressed on his head, a pink sash wrapped round his waist and a coconut stuffed into it. A sword—sheathed in a scabbard lined with velvet—was hung from the sash. A fresh pattern of henna was painted on his palms and darkened through repeated scrubbings of lemon juice.

Half an hour before the auspicious moment, the men had all

gathered outside the house. A mare had been rented. It stood in silver blinkers and tasselled reins, and a silk shawl was thrown over the saddle. Known to be the strongest man in Rampura, Master Bholaram lifted Harilal in his arms and deposited him into the saddle, keeping an arm round his waist lest he fall off. Inside the house, women began to sing.

'The moment has come,' Duli Chand announced.

On his cue the women sang louder, and the mare was led away, trailed by the whole procession and Master Bholaram walking alongside, an arm still round Hari's waist. On reaching the dunes outside Rampura, the mare was dispatched and everyone rested under a peepul tree. The guests dispersed to go home and pack for the trip to Chirawa.

Master Bholaram and Nanuram unrolled blankets and served dried bajra seeds to those who remained. Nanuram looked at Hari's clothes with concern. He had rented the tunic from a Nawalgarh shopkeeper on the promise of a bag of bajra. If its gold threads were to suffer damage the rate would certainly increase, and Duli Chand would have to contend with an irate shopkeeper.

Hari lay wearily under the tree, choking under his turban, feeling the coconut dig into his waist but afraid to remove it because that would invite a rebuke from his father. He whispered to Nanuram, 'Could I return home for the afternoon? You could have me fetched when you set out for Chirawa.'

Nanuram laid an affectionate hand on his head. 'Once the groom has passed his doorstep, he may not return without his bride.'

Hari dreaded the long journey to Chirawa. The roasted bajra grains had served to increase his thirst. He was afraid to drink too much water, knowing his father would disapprove. Thus worrying, he fell asleep.

He was woken four hours later. Twenty-five camels had massed around the peepul tree, snorting, chewing on khejra bushels, covering the whole area with their droppings. They were loaded with bedding rolls and pots of water. Each had two chairs strapped on its back, one in front of the hump and one behind. There was much shouting and joking as the guests mounted, two to each beast, and called to each other to hand over pieces of luggage. Nanuram had brought a chariot drawn by two caparisoned bullocks. Hari climbed into it, pressed his body against a cushion and dozed off again. Duli Chand climbed in after him, followed by Master Bholaram and two elderly men.

Everyone was mounted by early evening. Nanuram gave the word and they set out in a long, slow-moving caravan that cut across the desert. Duli Chand saw the fading sun sink to the dunes and shook his son awake.

'This is your wedding procession. You must not sleep through it. Tomorrow, you will be a married man, and hopefully a responsible one.'

Hari chewed on grams and watched the line of camels. They moved lazily, biting into khejra bushes on either side. The guests had all slumped in their chairs, after tying themselves to their camels' humps so they would not roll off when asleep. The coconut seemed to have grown in the last hour—it felt like a giant melon wedged above his hip—and his shervani was too warm for such a day.

'Do not look so gloomy, Hariya,' said Master Bholaram. 'Boys have been married off in worse times.'

'He broods too much,' Duli Chand said of his son. 'A boy should use his time productively. Perhaps you could give him a last lesson, Masterji. Who knows when we will reach Chirawa.'

'I have not brought my slate and chalk,' Hari said. That was a relief, because he did not want to put his mind to multiplication tables in his present state.

Master Bholaram said, 'That is just as well, because you are no longer a student. Your last lesson is written in the Shastra, which I hope you will read in Disavar.'

Hari nodded vaguely, noting the contradiction he dared not mention—Masterji had told him a hundred times that a bania who wished to read the Shastra should employ a brahmin to do so, because his own time was better spent earning the brahmin's wages than in mastering Sanskrit.

'A boy may not choose how he spends his time,' Masterji continued. 'His tasks are prescribed for him in the Shastra. He passes through four stages, depending on his varna—in your case, that of a bania—and his ashrama, or his station in life.'

'I understand,' said Hari, having heard this before.

'You have completed Brahmacharya, the stage of study and celibacy. The second, that of Grihasthi, requires that you marry, beget children, enjoy material comforts—in moderation, of course—and fulfil obligations such as pujas and charitable works. Your father is a Grihastha.'

Hari chuckled. The thought of children, *his* children, was absurd.

'I can read your face,' Masterji said. 'You are only twelve, but your father was only seventeen when his boy was born.'

This reference to his first son—Hari's older brother, snatched away by the pox—caused Duli Chand to look away. Masterji continued.

'When you have married off your children and seen the faces of your grandchildren, you advance to the third stage, Vanaprastha, that of retirement and detachment.'

Hari burst out laughing. His grandchildren!

'Finally, you pass into Sannyas, the stage of renunciation, when you give up all possessions and attachments, and prepare for the end.'

At this point, Duli Chand interposed. 'Let the boy dwell on his wedding, Masterji. He has no conception of Vanaprastha or Sannyas.'

'Those stages come faster than you think,' said Master Bholaram, who himself had never married and was, therefore, stuck in Brahmacharya. 'When they do, one is never prepared.'

'What of you, Masterji?' Duli Chand asked playfully. 'When do you plan to pass into the next stage?'

The two elderly men travelling with them giggled toothlessly.

Master Bholaram was embarrassed. 'I go where Raamji leads me ...'

They travelled all night, stopping twice to rest and feed the bullocks. It was still dark when the caravan entered Chirawa and made its way to the Hanuman temple, where Narayan Das Nangaliya and a dozen men greeted them with jaggery, grams and water.

'This is not how I had hoped to welcome guests to my daughter's wedding,' he said to Duli Chand, 'but this is the will of the Chhappaniya.'

A weary and sleepy Duli Chand nodded to show that he understood. They walked to a public house adjoining the temple, where arrangements had been made for their stay. The men of Rampura laid out their bedding in the rooms and fell asleep, while a man hired by Narayan Das sat outside the house, should they need any assistance.

Late in the morning, the men rose and went to the dunes for their toilet. Duli Chand and Master Bholaram walked with Hari concealed carefully between them, to prevent the urchins of Chirawa from getting a good look at the groom. On returning, they found buckets of cool water awaiting them, arranged by Narayan Das. Each had a blissful bath. Hari used a full bucket of water, and leaned over it when turning the pot over his head so the overflow could be used a second time. He had not bathed so generously in weeks.

Master Bholaram studied the board hanging outside the public-house, listing recent weddings for which guests had spent the night there. Picking up a lump of coal, he added his own entry to it: 'On this Aashaadh sudi dashmi in the Vikram Samvat year of one thousand nine hundred and fifty six, the year of the great Chhappaniya, 121 guests arrived from the auspicious town of Rampura for the wedding of Harilal Tibrewal (may he live long), son of Duli Chand Tibrewal, grandson of Laduram Tibrewal, to the daughter of Narayan Dasji Nangaliya (may Raamji keep her husband safe), and stayed for four days.'

Master Bholaram did not know the exact number of guests. He had heard Nanuram say there were fifty, but he felt that 121 was a more appropriate number. He also knew they would stay for only two days because of the Chhappaniya, not the four that would be usual for guests invited by a man of Narayan Das's standing, but the board would hang here for a long time, announcing these details to other wedding guests. When one wrote for eternity, it did not help to be fussy. On further consideration, the date troubled him. It would announce itself to future generations, who would perhaps speak Hindi, or even English. Did they not say that children in Jaipur no longer counted days using the Vikram Samvat? It did not behoove him to make a display of ignorance when he was, after all, the only man in Rampura who understood the English calendar. Marking out a rectangular box above the Vikram Samvat date, he wrote neatly, 'on the English date of Tuesday, July 18, 1899'.

After their baths, some men put on silk dhotis and kurtas, tied red turbans round their heads and went to tour the town of Chirawa. Some accompanied Duli Chand and Nanuram to discuss arrangements with Narayan Das, others played cards and board games. All day, Hari sat in his red tunic with three boys, the chitiya by his side, windows shut lest someone in the village sneak a peek at the groom. At six in the evening, Duli Chand returned to say that the hour of dhukaav—Hari's entry to the bride's house—had arrived.

'The pandit has determined that the last moment of the fourth prahar—a few minutes before nine in the evening—is the best time.'

There was much confusion at the announcement. The men found last-minute wrinkles in their kurtas. One of the dhotis was declared to be shabby, so the wearer was impelled by general opinion to ask for a loan. The sun had disappeared behind the dunes when they emerged from the public-house. A man deposited Hari on a mare; musicians with sarangis and drums surrounded him. In panic, Hari looked over his shoulder to find his father and Nanuram busy with arrangements, and the three boys who had come from Rampura busy devouring sweets piled on a platter. He was alone. The musicians set up a boisterous tune. The procession began to advance, increasing in size as the people of Chirawa joined it.

Narayan Das's house sat no more than 200 feet from the Hanuman temple, so the dhukaav soon found itself at the gates. The mare was brought to an abrupt stop. Someone handed Hari a branch of neem, and a barber held up a plate of wood decorated with the figures of birds. Hari turned nervously to Nanuram. 'What do I do?'

Nanuram pointed to the plate. 'That is the toran. Strike it with the branch.'

Hari raised an arm and tried to rise in the saddle, but lost balance and fell forward. A ripple of laughter ran through the guests.

'The toran is too far for the boy!' someone called out.

Another scolded the barber. 'Why must you hold it so high?'

A guest from Rampura taunted the barber, who had been engaged by Narayan Dasji. 'Have there been no weddings in Chirawa before this?'

'Hurry up,' Duli Chand said. 'The women have begun to sing.'

Laughing, Master Bholaram pulled Hari off the mare and raised him high in the air. Thus suspended, Harilal feebly raised the branch again. A few leaves grazed the toran, and a cry of relief went up.

'It is done!' Duli Chand declared.

The women continued to sing; the barber was dispatched; Master Bholaram deposited Harilal on a squat wooden stool. He stood quivering, exhausted by the toran effort.

'Do not shake so much,' Nanuram whispered. 'The bride's aunt is laughing.'

Hari sought out the giggling form—it was covered in a pink shawl. Another woman, her face hidden behind a sequined veil, raised her arm—he stood taller than her because of the stool—and daubed vermilion on his forehead.

'Stand still!' Nanuram mumbled into his ears. 'That is your mother-in-law.'

With trembling hands, she reached up and placed a coconut on his head. There was much laughter when it rolled off.

The toran ceremony over, the guests entered the house and were seated on mats in the courtyard, sipping cool water spiced with cumin and raw mangoes. Hari was taken by Nanuram into a small room, where the three boys sat in a circle around him.

Duli Chand asked Master Bholaram, 'Where in Shekhavati did Narayan Dasji find mangoes?'

'He perhaps knows someone in Disavar.'

They sat all evening in the courtyard, awaiting the hour fixed by the pandit for the wedding. It was almost midnight when Duli Chand came into the room to fetch a drowsy Hari.

'Stand up straight,' he scolded his son. 'This is your wedding!'

A bamboo pavilion had been erected in the courtyard. It was festooned with paper blossoms—flowers were in short supply, given the times—and a fire pit stood ready in the centre. Led by Duli Chand, Hari walked unsteadily to the pit, gathered the hem of his tunic—Nanuram had rented the wrong size—and lowered himself next to the fire pit.

The pandit was chanting. He interrupted himself to admonish the groom. 'Move to your left! The bride must sit on the right.'

Grains of rice were thrust into Hari's hands. Water was sprinkled on a pile of coconuts. The pandit continued to mumble. Hari stole glances to his right. Where was the bride? Had something gone wrong? After what seemed like an hour to him, he heard a rustle of silk. It was the aunt, not the bride. He looked up and there she was: Parmeshwari, fast asleep in her aunt's arms. Almost eleven, thought Hari impatiently, yet she cannot stay up past midnight. He studied her through the corner of his eye: red skirt and matching blouse trimmed with piping; a thin shawl through which he could see the braids in her hair; silver bracelets on her ankles; earrings that looked like gold. There was a large ring in her nose, too. In the dim glow of lanterns, he could not see the face clearly.

The aunt settled down next to Hari with the bride in her lap.

Someone scolded. 'Cover her face!'

The aunt pulled the shawl over Parmeshwari's head, and the face of his bride was obscured from Hari's gaze. He turned his attention to the pandit, who was now directing him to pour a ladle of ghee into the pit. Fire lit up the pavilion, causing the sequins on Parmeshwari's shawl to shimmer. At a word from the pandit, Hari was raised to his feet. The aunt stood up with Parmeshwari in her arms. They circled the fire seven times, with the aunt leading for the first three rounds, Hari for the last four. *I am being married off to an old hag*, he thought.

The wedding lasted all night. In the faint light of dawn, Parmeshwari was taken away by her aunt and Hari brought back to the public-house near the temple. He fell asleep immediately.

That evening, Narayan Das invited all his guests to a feast of bajra, rice, daal, sweets cooked in ghee, and fritters fried in sesame oil. Hari was given the first bite. While they ate, women from Narayan Das's family sang from behind a curtain.

After the feast, Narayan Das's men unfolded a silk sheet and invited Duli Chand to sit on it. A scroll was read out by Narayan Das, listing the gifts he had given to his daughter's new family: turban and shervani for Hari, shawl for Hari's mother, silk kurta and dhoti for Duli Chand, silver bracelets for Hari's sisters, tiny anklets for his cousins. Each guest received a silver rupee, some grains of rice and a spot of vermilion on the forehead.

'It is not much,' Narayan Das said. 'But at a time like this ...'

Duli Chand made a dismissive sound to accept the apology, even as he tried to hide his disappointment. Had not Narayan Das received a coconut and eight annas from everyone in Chirawa, so he could give proper gifts to the groom's family? Going by the size of tents, the arrangements in the public house and the decorations at the ceremony, the wedding would have cost about five hundred rupees: admittedly a large amount, but why else did a man hoard his money if not for his daughter's wedding? And why else did a man raise a daughter, if not to give her away with much more than he could afford? It is the Chhappaniya, he consoled himself, and it would not last forever. Perhaps the gifts that came with the festival of Gangaur would be more generous. And the gifts for Diwali would have to outshine the ones for Gangaur. A man who was tight-fisted in his daughter's wedding had no dearth of opportunities to compensate for his thrift.

It was time for the guests to say farewell and return to Rampura. The chariot was brought to Narayan Das's house. Duli Chand noted with concern that the Nagauri bullocks looked exhausted, as if they had not been fed properly—someone in Narayan Das's family had neglected his duties. Hari climbed in, one hand steadying the turban and the other holding the sword attached at his waist. Narayan Das turned to his wife impatiently.

'Where is the nevgan?'

Before a summons could be sent, the barber's wife appeared at the door with Parmeshwari in her arms, asleep.

'Wake her up,' Narayan Das said to the nevgan. Turning to his wife, he whispered, 'Did you not tell her what is to be done at the doorstep? It looks odd if a girl shows no feeling when leaving her father's house.'

Shaken awake, Parmeshwari moaned in protest.

'Ah,' said Narayan Das appreciatively. 'She weeps.'

Seeing Parmeshwari stir, her mother set up a terrible wail, and the women of Chirawa joined in. Tears flowing, they sang songs of separation and corralled the barber's wife, blocking her path to the chariot.

Our daughter leaves her home. When shall we next hear her laugh? Our daughter leaves her home. Block her path, my sisters!

Amidst the singing and crying, Narayan Das gently nudged the nevgan toward the chariot, pushing aside the women of Chirawa with a heavy heart, seeming to apologize for his heavy-handedness.

'The girl does not belong to us,' he kept saying. 'Her family awaits.'

Being a brahmin, Master Bholaram climbed the chariot

in the front to sit with the driver. In the back, the nevgan laid Parmeshwari on a soft mattress next to Hari. As she prepared to mount, Narayan Das's wife pulled her close.

'Listen, nevgan! Be careful when taking off my daughter's mangtika: she cries if her hair gets entangled in it. Do not let her eat too many sweets and keep her away from toys—it would not be proper in her father-in-law's house—and see that she does not push too hard on the swing, if they have one outside the house in Rampura.'

Master Bholaram directed the driver to use his whip, and the bullocks started. The nevgan sobbed loudly. Women scrambled after the chariot, singing and wailing.

Someone peeked in to get a glimpse of Parmeshwari—her face hidden behind a corner of her shawl—and called, 'Look how she sobs!'

'Do not forget your sisters in Chirawa when you get to Rampura!'

Narayan Das took off his turban, wiped his eyes clean, and walked with Duli Chand, Nanuram and the fifty guests to the public-house, where they supervised the loading of the camels.

'It is still early in the evening,' he said, looking up at the sky. 'You will be in Rampura before the sun rises.'

The guests mounted and the caravan set off.

Meanwhile, the chariot was followed by the wailing women all the way to the dunes outside Chirawa. Once the last house had been passed, the women fell back; their singing died down. Parmeshwari's mother brushed away the last tears from her swollen eyes and declared, 'She cried a lot.'

'We have seen a dozen weddings, but never have we seen a girl sob like this.'

Then the women returned to their homes.

The chariot picked up speed after Master Bholaram took the whip from the driver and used it freely on the bullocks. Hari sat on a velvet cushion in the corner, watching the sleeping form of his bride cradled in the arms of the nevgan, who had dozed off.

He noticed that the barber's wife was laden with jewellery, like the bride herself, but hers was silver while the bride wore gold. It was a clear night. A waxing moon bathed the desert; the dunes glistened like silver. Gently, Hari pushed aside the shawl covering Parmeshwari's face. A tear had dried on her cheek. They should not have woken her for the leave-taking ceremony, he thought. A large red bindi obscured much of her forehead; the pendant in her nose ring had been crushed under a cheek; the mangtika had slipped from its place in her hair and flapped loosely against her ears with the rolling of the chariot. He gazed in wonder—look how the moon dwells on her face!

They reached Rampura at dawn, and the guests went to their homes. Hari slept through the morning while Parmeshwari sat in a room, surrounded by Hari's sisters. He was not allowed inside. All afternoon, the women of Rampura came in droves to see the bride. They lifted the shawl from her face, held up their lanterns to get a good look, and paid her for the privilege. Some gave a pie, some a paisa, some an adhela and some a full anna. When someone gave more than an anna, there were gasps and laughter. All day long, there was singing.

In the evening, Rukmini drew Hari aside, handed him a velvet purse and said, 'You may go in now.'

'Why?' he asked nervously. 'This is a matter for women.'

'Do you not want to see her?'

Hari thought of the shadows dancing on Parmeshwari's face among the tibbas. He could not, of course, tell his sister that he had already seen his bride's face. Holding up the purse, he asked, 'How much?'

'A rupee. You are the groom. You cannot give your bride an adhela.'

He stuffed the purse into his waistband—the tunic had been returned but the sash was his to keep, and he was still dressed as the groom—pushed open the door and entered the room. Parmeshwari sat on the bed in a filigreed silk skirt. A shawl with silver embroidery was thrown over her shoulders; it was wrapped over her head and pulled low over the face. He knew he was supposed to lift the shawl from her face and present the purse, but was aware that his sisters were watching through cracks in the door, giggling. He sat down on the floor.

Parmeshwari stirred. She seemed to be looking at him through the shawl. He wondered if it was proper to speak to her. Would he be scolded? He wanted to assure her that his sisters meant well—no doubt their giggling had intimidated her—but they would certainly overhear whatever he said. Perhaps he could whisper or speak in signals... No, he would wait them out. Sooner or later, his mother would find them stuck to the door and peel them away. Waiting, he fell asleep: he was tired, having stayed up all night during the ride through the desert.

An hour later, the nevgan quietly entered the room, gathered Parmeshwari in her arms—she, too, had fallen asleep—and took her away.

The next day, Nanuram took Parmeshwari and the nevgan back to Chirawa, in the same chariot that had brought them to Rampura. He carried a letter from Duli Chand to Narayan Das, written by Master Bholaram.

'Duli Chand Tibrewal from Rampura says Raam Raam to Shri Narayan Das Nangaliya in the auspicious town of Chirawa. As promised, Chiranjeev Harilal's mother has kept the girl for a day, not the two that she had wanted. I am sending her back with my munim Nanuram, a man I trust completely. Harilal will leave for Disavar with Hemraj Biyani, son of Khemchandji Biyani, in two days. The chaumasa will begin tomorrow, but our pandit says that a trip to Disavar is permitted during the chaumasa months if matters of business are pending. The rest is in the hands of Raamji, on this Aashaadh sudi dwaadashi in the Vikram Samvat year of one thousand nine hundred and fifty six.'

On the day Hari was to set off with Hemraj, his mother packed three kurtas, a pyjama and two cotton dhotis in a tin box. From the double-ceiling, Duli Chand addressed his son:

'You must remember why a boy goes to Disavar: to work

hard so he may earn a little. Avoid idle chatter or gossip; get by on as little as you can; do not waste money on shows and dances, of which there are many in Disavar; rise early; go to bed late; do not buy clothes—your mother can send them to you; speak little—the wise do not make flowery speeches but seek profit in the price of jute; speak respectfully to your elders; say pranaam to Khemchandji Biyani; touch his feet when you see him; sit far from him; do not blow your nose in his presence; show deference to Hemraj too: he is young, but he earns seventy-five rupees in a month.'

Later that morning, Master Bholaram brought a letter for his nephew in Jorhat in Assam. 'Perhaps Harilal could post this from Kalkatta?'

'He will,' said Duli Chand. 'Why waste money on postage from Shekhavati?'

Master Bholaram shook his head. Being the postmaster of Rampura, he was an authority on postal rates. 'Whether you post it from Shekhavati or Kalkatta, it will cost a paisa. But it will reach Jorhat faster if Harilal posts it from Kalkatta.'

Duli Chand turned to his son. 'Mark Masterji's words. There is much wisdom in them.'

Pleased at his success, Master Bholaram continued. 'Never attach a reply postcard, because you get no discount—it costs another full paisa. And if your letter weighs more than one-and-a-half tola, send a parcel instead. You can put twenty tolas in it for two annas.'

'The boy's mother wants him to pack his trunk, Masterji,' Duli Chand said impatiently.

But Master Bholaram held up the postcard, beckoned Hari and had him count the number of lines in the message.

'Thirty-five,' Hari reported. Master Bholaram beamed with pride. He was known for his fine hand: he could squeeze more than five hundred words on to a small postcard using a reed pen. When people in Rampura had long letters to send, they paid Master Bholaram a pie to squeeze their message on to a single postcard, rather than spend a paisa on a second one.

'Study this letter carefully,' he admonished Hari. 'When you write from Disavar, I shall count your words!'

'Write down a message for me,' Duli Chand said to Master Bholaram. 'I am told Khemchandji has failing eyesight, so do not print small letters.'

Master Bholaram pulled out his pad and a pencil, and Duli Chand spoke:

'Duli Chand Tibrewal from the town of Rampura says Raam Raam to Shri Khemchand Biyani in the auspicious town of Kalkatta. I have sent my son with yours. Treat him as you will. Should he prove to be lazy, punish him as you would your own son. Should he prove himself useful, find something suitable for him to do in Kalkatta, or anywhere else in Disavar.

Bajra is quoted strong at six rupees to a munn because of the Chhappaniya, but business is not good because no one has the money to buy. It is piling up in the rail yards of Jaipur, bound for the east and the south, where grass still grows. There is no profit in jowar this year, and a man in your position knows that no one in Shekhavati wants to deal in afeem. The rest is in the hands of Raamji, on this Aashaadh sudi teras in the Vikram Samvat year of one thousand nine hundred and fifty six.'

'Khemchandji has been in Disavar for twenty-five years,' said Master Bholaram. 'Should I add the English date?'

Duli Chand nodded irritably. Bholaram scribbled in his fine hand: July 21, 1899.

At the appointed time—the pandit had said nine in the morning—Duli Chand handed Hari a packet bearing his letter to Khemchand Biyani, Master Bholaram's letter to his nephew and other messages to relatives in Bengal and Assam. Six silver rupees had been sewn into a pocket inside his kurta. They sat against his chest. His mother gave him a bundle—to be tied round his waist—stood him so he faced east, daubed red paste on his brow, sprinkled rice over his head and placed a lump of jaggery coated in curd on his tongue.

Hari patted the coins at his chest. 'How will I pull them out when I need to buy food?'

'Why must you buy food at all?' Duli Chand demanded. 'Your mother has given you rotis for three days.'

'The journey could take longer.'

'Make the rotis last. Take small bites if you know you will be delayed.'

'Do I not share my food with Hemrajji?'

'He earns seventy-five rupees in a month and lives in Disavar. Surely he is not reckless enough to travel without food.'

'The coins will dig into the flesh when I go to sleep.'

'Why must you sleep at all?' Duli Chand asked. 'Stay alert until you reach Disavar, and beware of pickpockets.'

Hari's sisters watched from inside the room—they were hesitant to say anything in Duli Chand's presence. He looked once at Rukmini, touched his parents' feet and stepped out of the house, then ran all the way to Seth Daulatram's haveli, bearing his tin box and the bundle round his waist, where Hemraj Biyani was waiting impatiently.

'I hope you slept well last night,' he said to Hari, 'because there is no rest for a bania in Disavar.'

Without a word—he knew no response was expected—Hari handed over his box to be loaded on the camel. They climbed into the saddle—two chairs tied around the hump—with Hemraj in front. At Hari's prodding the camel stood up, front feet first. Hemraj lost his poise, and would have fallen to the ground if Hari, sitting behind the hump, had not held him in place with both hands. He laughed.

'You have spent too many years in Disavar, Hemrajji!'

Hemraj turned and nodded, and Hari was overjoyed at this acknowledgment. *Once we reach Delhi*, he told himself, *I will be Hemrajji's ward, but as long as we are in Shekhavati it is I who will teach him how to ride, and how to avoid treacherous dunes.*

The camel ambled out of Rampura under a scorching August sun, past dry wells and fallow fields. Most in Rampura still hoped that the month of Saavan would bring a few showers. Once planted, bajra could sprout in five days, but it was clear that the crop would not reach full height by the end of Kartik, when it would have to be cut. A few men had stubbornly run their camels over the land, ploughing dry furrows and throwing seed—bajra, cucumber, melon, barley—as if the mere act of sowing would reap a harvest.

Around them, khejra trees rose like monsters among the dunes, their lumpy branches, shorn of leaves, looking like gnarled fingers. Having passed the peepul tree to the north, Hari shut his eyes. 'I am going to Disavar,' he told himself, 'where no one has seen a tibba or chewed on khejra leaves. In Bengal, they feed bajra to cattle.'

They headed north-east towards the plains of Delhi, eyes anxiously scouring the horizon for a caravan: it was safer to travel in groups, especially in such times. Cattle carcasses littered the countryside. A dead camel lay directly in their path. Vultures hovered over it, flying off at their approach. Hemraj watched the half-eaten flesh in disgust as they circled it. Hari said soothingly,

'A few drops in the month of Saavan, and the tibbas will turn green. It is not too late to plant the bajra.'

'For a boy of twelve, you talk a lot.'

Subdued, Hari said nothing for a mile, watching Hemraj's head bob up and down, and the tail of his kurta flying in the wind. Finally he could not contain himself.

'Is everyone in Disavar very rich?'

'Only those who work hard and watch their expenses.'

'Is your father rich?'

Hemraj turned around to face Hari. 'Do not speak thus of my father. He rises early and goes to bed late. The whole firm rests on his shoulders.'

'What do you do?'

'I buy and sell jute, worth a thousand every day.'

Hari set his mind to calculate what this meant, using the tables Master Bholaram had taught him. He had bought kites—adheliyas for half-anna and aanal for an anna. Two adhela kites would cost an anna; sixteen annas made a rupee; a thousand rupees would buy 32,000 adhela kites and 16,000 aanal ones!

They rode all day, stopping whenever they found a well so the camel could drink. Hari noticed that Hemrajji suffered much under the sun, especially because, unlike Hari, he did not wear a turban. Bypassing the town of Jhunjhunu—going through it would have required a detour—they headed straight for Chirawa, which was reached late in the evening. This was Hari's second visit to Chirawa in three days. He wished they could go to Narayan Dasji's house—being the son-in-law, he would be welcomed—but knew he would be scolded for the breach of propriety.

Hemraj decided to skirt the town, saying he wanted to avoid beggars, of whom there were too many because of the Chhappaniya. Hari pointed out that it was almost midnight, but Hemraj said, 'Hunger keeps them awake and on the lookout for travellers. In any case, going through the town will certainly cost something, while the tibbas never ask for silver.'

Not wishing to seem importunate, Hari did not press the point. They rested for a few hours under a peepul, then continued eastward at dawn. Hari watched the sunrise with growing excitement. Every step the camel took brought them closer to Loharu, which lay beyond Shekhavati.

Late in the morning, they reached a dry riverbed. In normal times, they would have taken a boat across the river, but now the camel was able to walk across. When it climbed up the other bank, Hari looked back at the shore they had left behind. He was in Loharu, no longer in Shekhavati. He thought, 'I will never see the ruins of the Chhappaniya again.'

Indeed, the Chhappaniya seemed to know that the river, even when dry, was not to be crossed. On its eastern bank, the scrub was greener. Hari saw tongas and buggies, and once an English sahib on a horse. Later that day, when they were a few miles from Delhi, Hemraj sold the camel to a burly tonga driver, who drove them to Delhi railway station in his tonga. Hari sat spellbound, thinking nervously about the precarious balance of the two-wheeled tonga, watching red-brick buildings and wide streets, and crowds larger than any he had seen. This was Delhi, where in an instant his eyes swept over the whole population of Rampura. And Kalkatta was far larger!

Late in the night, the tonga pulled up in the Delhi railway station yard, which was littered with sleeping forms. Dark men swooped down on them, offering to carry their luggage. Hemraj waved them away.

'I hope that is not too heavy,' he said, pointing to Hari's box. 'We cannot waste money on coolies.'

Placing his steel trunk on his head, he slung a bundle from his shoulder and set off. Hari did likewise. The station was quiet. They crossed railway tracks and climbed on to a platform which, like the yard outside, was full of sleeping men. Hemraj found a clearing. They set down their trunks, opened their bundles and ate bajra rotis with onions and salt. Having drunk water from a hand-pump on the platform, they fell asleep, arms wrapped around their boxes to ward off thieves. As sleep claimed him, Hari recalled how the hand-pump had gurgled with water, and how any coolie could have drunk as much as he wanted, and how it leaked and no one cared.

A whistle woke them up. The sun was up and the station was bustling. Men stood around them, and the platform was busy with bundles and pots. A black locomotive wheezed and hissed nearby, pulling a long line of red cars and screeching as it came to a stop. Smoke blanketed the sky. Hemraj turned to Hari with a fatherly smile.

'That is a train.'

'I know,' said Hari. He had recognized it right away, but the snake in his dream had been full of English sahibs.

'Where have you seen one before?' demanded Hemraj, annoyed.

Hari did not answer. Here was the snake; he must touch it. He must see what it looks like inside! But Hemraj remained as he was, squatting comfortably on the ground.

'It has begun to move!' Hari cried.

'That one goes to Punjab. Our train will start in the afternoon.'

Hari nodded, confused, wondering why this one could not take them to Bengal. Hemraj began to fold their sheets and Hari sprang to help. They took turns visiting the latrines; the other stood guard over the luggage. Hari had never been to a latrine before—in Rampura they simply went to the tibbas. He was horrified by the filth but pretended not to notice. After they had washed at the hand-pump—Hemraj cleaned his teeth with a stick of babool, Hari merely rinsed his—Hari expressed a desire to see the Qutub Minar. Hemraj firmly turned down the idea. 'It is in Mehrauli, outside Delhi.'

'We have all morning.'

'No tongawala will go that far for less than eight annas.' This defeated Hari. He could not allow Hemrajji to think he was careless with money. 'Besides,' added Hemraj, 'you are going to Disavar to work, not to see buildings and towers.'

Hari sighed. The trip felt too long already. 'How long before our train gets to Kalkatta?'

'Two days and two nights.'

'Why waste money on a train?' Hari asked, incredulous. 'In two full days, even a camel could get us there.'

Hemraj chuckled. 'Calcutta is not Sikar or Jhunjhunu. Let me show you how far it is.' He took Hari to the station lobby and showed him a map mounted on the wall.

'Is this a picture of Kalkatta?'

'This is Hindustan,' said Hemraj. 'Here is Delhi, in its very heart. Do you see the red-brown region to the west? That is Rajputana—all twenty-two states—and here is its greatest city, Jaipur. The region above it is our Shekhavati. You can see Jhunjhunu and Sikar, and the dot between them is Nawalgarh, though no train passes through it.'

'Where is Rampura?'

Hemraj laughed. 'This map was drawn by English sahibs in London. They have not heard of Rampura.' His hand traced a long arc, west to east, to a green patch on the right. 'This is Disavar: Bengal and Assam and all the great cities in the plains.

Do you see how far it is from Shekhavati? And do you see how green it is, even in a map? And this,' said Hemraj, letting his finger rest on a web of lines and tracks, 'is Calcutta, the greatest city in Hindustan. The city of sahibs. The home of the Lat Sahib.'

'And the Queen?'

'She lives in England, but the Lat Sahib is her chief munim, as Nanuram is your father's.'

Awed, Hari studied the shades of green, yellow and blue around the confusion of Calcutta. 'Are those rivers?'

'The Hooghly, which springs from the Ganga herself.'

'Can you see buildings in this map?'

'We must rest now. There will be no sleeping on the train.'

Hemraj bought tickets. Hari wondered if he should extract the coins sewn into his kurta, but Hemraj did not ask him for money. This gesture seemed especially generous, but he was too intimidated to express gratitude. They spent the morning lying in a corner of the station platform, watching the rush of travellers amidst the whistling of locomotives billowing smoke. Early in the afternoon, a train pulled up. Men peered out of every window, called to each other and leaned far out to catch their breath. Those on the platform hurled themselves against the windows and sought openings in the mass of limbs. Hemraj and Hari joined the rush. A few English sahibs and memsahibs made their way to the cars in the front, trailed by coolies and bearers with umbrellas. The crowds there were thinner, and the windows had glass panes. Hemraj noted Hari's gaze and scoffed. 'Those are European cars. Who do you think you are, a sahib?'

Hari looked in dismay at the human parts spilling out of windows—elbows, feet, sometimes whole torsos. It was impossible for anyone to board the carriage. Perhaps they would have to wait for another day. 'When does the next train start?'

'Why wait for the next one when you have one before you?' said Hemraj.

Pulling Hari roughly after him, he positioned the boy near a train window. From inside, a dozen faces regarded them with hostility. Hari was lifted off the ground and thrust through the opening, landing on a lattice of limbs that gave way and allowed him to descend until he was part of the structure. His box and bundle flew in after him. Grabbing both, he found crevices into which to squeeze them. In a moment of panic, he wondered if this was all part of Hemrajji's plan: to trap him in a crowded car and send him to Disavar all by himself! Whom would he talk to? Which language would he speak there? How would a boy get by in Kalkatta with six rupees? But then he saw Hemrajji sail into the car through the same opening, with a trunk and bundle, forcing his way through resisting hands.

Suspended in the mass of limbs, they waited. Early in the evening, a whistle was heard and the train inched forward. As they pulled out of Delhi, Hemraj cleared a little space on a bench—just sufficient for their buttocks—and they squeezed themselves into place, boxes on their laps. Hari breathed deeply and surveyed the carriage for the first time. Three benches ran the length of the car, two along the sides and one in the centre, on which they were seated. The central bench carried two rows of people with their backs to each other. Whenever Hari bent forward, the man behind him leaned back to take the available space, forcing him to sit hunched until he managed to recover the lost territory by pushing back resolutely. A narrow shelf ran along each wall near the top. It was stacked with trunks and bundles, but there was little hope of finding space for their trunks on it. Dust swirled through the open windows—they had no bars, no shutters—and the stench of latrines at either end of the car mixed with the perspiration of men squeezed together in the heat.

'We should have brought fans with us,' Hari said.

'I told you there would no sleeping on the train.'

'How did you climb in through the window by yourself?'

'I hired a coolie,' said Hemraj. 'He took an anna and pushed me through. That is the only way to enter the carriage—the men inside will never open the door.'

Hari looked around and wondered how the others had

managed to get inside. Had each hired a coolie, or were they born inside the train? Did they live here?

'If we had not come in through the window,' Hemraj said with the assurance of someone who knew, 'we would have waited for the next train, which will start tomorrow. We would have run out of bajra. Do you know how much rice costs at the station?'

'Could we have travelled another class?'

'Everyone goes third-class, even rich banias who have been to Disavar many times and built large havelis in Shekhavati. Had he come to Rampura to see his haveli, Daulatramji himself would have travelled third-class. Why pay one-and-a-half times the fare for a mere two-day journey? Will inter-class get you to Calcutta faster? Will the Howrah Bridge look more beautiful through inter-class windows? Bengalis travel inter-class, even those deep in debt—that is why they are in debt. And the only ones who sit in second-class are government officers and big zamindars, paying four times as much. Such men do not understand the value of money. They spend it on comfort.'

'Isn't there a first-class?'

'Your mind wanders where it should not. First-class is for judges, barristers, civil surgeons, colonels in the military. And English sahibs.'

'But how will we sit like this for two days?' asked Hari, heart sinking. Was this what Disavar would be like?

'We will adjust,' said Hemraj confidently, adding, 'Bring out your rotis and eat them now. Once the sun sets, you won't be able to see much.'

They opened their bundles using their boxes as tables on their laps. Hari looked at his dinner—bajra rotis, balls of fried dough, salt, jaggery, grams, pickled mango, saangar pickle made from khejra leaves, and sweet, fried bajra powder. The rotis were now stale. 'Perhaps we could buy something for an anna at the next station.'

'You cannot trust station food, even from a Hindu stall. They put onions and garlic in everything, sometimes even eggs. And you never know who has cooked it, and who served it to you. Is he a brahmin? Is he even a Hindu? It is all right for Musalmans to accept food from us—we cannot accept it from them.'

Reluctantly, Hari chewed on his roti, drank from the bottle he had filled at the station, tied the remaining rotis back into the bundle and leaned back forcefully, reclaiming the air above the bench from the man behind him. Shortly after, his bowels began to trouble him. He nudged Hemraj and asked where a person might relieve himself on a train.

'There are latrines at either end,' said Hemraj. 'Take some water with you: there are no taps there.'

Bottle in hand, Hari rose from his bench, and Hemraj immediately placed his bundle there to block the space. Hari pushed his way through to the end of the carriage. The latrine was a small room with an opening in the floor. The stench was overpowering. He was revolted. After stepping over two men asleep on the floor outside, he peered into the hole. In the fading light of day, he saw tracks and the sleeper planks laid across them, and swooned. The hole seemed large enough to swallow him. Trembling, he placed a foot on either side and squatted, desperately clutching a metal bar that was perhaps installed for this very purpose. At least I have water to wash myself, he thought.

On emerging from the latrine, he felt that the crowd was not as oppressive as he had imagined. Their smells were not intrusive, their bodies not intimidating. Indeed, now that he was outside the latrine, he was not sure he could smell anything at all. Emboldened, he leaned against the door. It flew open and nearly hurled him on to the tracks. Hands flew out of the train and pulled him back to safety, and he was scolded for his rashness. He took comfort in the thought that Hemrajji could not have seen this from where he sat.

He made his way back. Another long journey, another struggle, but he had learned how to cut a passage through unyielding human flesh. When he saw Hemrajji on the bench guarding his spot, he went to a window, thrust his head through over the shoulders of protesting men, and inhaled the evening air. 'It is only a boy!' someone called. 'He looks no more than ten. Let the boy breathe!' a voice commanded, and a little space was created for him. He leaned far out. Smoke stacks lined the horizon. Giant banyans seemed to rotate as the train passed them. Pools of water ran along the tracks. Between them, bullocks were digging long furrows in dark soil. Here and there he saw huts, drying dung cakes, smoke from cooking fires and cows returning home, kicking up dust against the setting sun. There was no Chhappaniya here.

I am already in a land that lives, he thought, his heart pounding, and we have only begun! No dunes, dust-storms, camels dying by the tibbas or lonely footprints in the sand. Look at those pools of water! And that tree is no miserable khejra bush with its prickly leaves and gnarled trunk. Could those be mangoes? No, we are still far from Bengal. But if the land is so rich just east of Delhi, how green will it be in Bengal?

He leaned even further out. By twisting his neck, he could see the funnel of smoke that emerged from the locomotive, but not the beast itself. Then the train rounded a curve and he saw it clearly—a black camel charging relentlessly forward, turning its many wheels and flailing the arms between them, hauling more people than lived in the whole town of Rampura. Then a sharp pain forced both his eyes shut. Blinded, he ducked back inside and slowly peeled grains of coal from his eyelids. They must have flown back from the locomotive. The man next to him chuckled. 'That is what happens to the boy who leans too far out of a train.'

His tears gradually washed the soot away. He set his face and leaned out of the window again, careful not to look toward the front of the train. It was nice to let the wind ruffle his hair.

Late that night they stopped at Tundla, where many more passengers streamed in through the windows. Hemraj stoutly resisted all attempts by the newcomers to encroach on their territory on the bench. A man wearing a turban and dhoti touched him on the shoulder.

'Are you from Shekhavati?' he asked in Marwari.

Hemraj brightened. 'Rampura, near Nawalgarh.'

'Sikar,' said the man. 'Raam Raam.'

'Churu,' said his companion.

The two were on their way to Calcutta, having come from Jaipur to Tundla, where they had changed trains.

'It is better to start from Delhi,' Hemraj told them. 'Then you don't have to switch from metre-gauge to broad-gauge.'

'Ah, but it is cheaper to start from Jaipur and switch at Tundla.'

Defeated, Hemraj turned defensive and pointed to Hari. 'I have a boy with me. He will not be able to switch trains.'

The men nodded. They eventually found themselves places on the bench, opened their bundles and brought out bajra rotis, and Hari felt at home. They asked Hemraj if Hari was his son.

'My sons are in Kalkatta. I have been in Disavar for ten years.'

'What do you deal in?'

'Jute. Cotton. A little opium,' Hemraj said.

'Which firm?'

'Daulatram Gulabchand.'

The men nodded knowingly. 'Which office?'

'5 Amherst Row,' replied Hemraj.

'That is the head office,' the men observed.

'My father is the chief munim.'

'Are you Khemchand Biyani's son?' the men asked, surprised.

Hemraj nodded, and the two men expressed great pleasure at the coincidence. 'Tell your father that Nathmalji from Andrew Yule & Company remembers him well!'

'Andrew Yule? There is no money in jute gunny any more,' observed Hemraj.

The men shrugged, neither confirming nor denying the claim, and continued their meal. Hari had been watching them carefully. They lived in Disavar, yet their clothes were shabby—only the poor in Rampura wore such threadbare kurtas. He asked them, 'Is your Andrew Yule sethji very rich?'

The men exchanged glances and laughed. 'Our master is the richest seth in the world.'

'Is he from Rampura?'

'His Rampura is beyond the seven seas, in England. Have you ever seen a sahib?'

Hari nodded. When Maharaja Madho Singh of Jaipur had passed through Rampura, a sahib in military uniform had been seen in his entourage. Everyone in Rampura had gathered round him but Hari had kept his distance, not forgetting his father's warning about such people. 'My babuji says that sahibs eat with their left hands.'

'It does not matter which hand he eats with: a sahib is a good bania,' the man said sternly. 'He does not let a paisa slip through his fingers, and he never pays an anna more than he must.'

'Send this boy to Andrew Yule & Company,' the second man said to Hemraj, 'and we will show him how a sahib keeps his shop.'

'He will work at Daulatram Gulabchand with my father,' Hemraj said.

The next day, the train stopped at Kanpur. Those near the windows repulsed every attempt by others trying to enter the carriage. In the evening, at Allahabad station, Hemraj and Hari squeezed their way out—the traders from Andrew Yule saved their spots for them—and found a Hindu stall, where Hemraj bought a pitcher of tea, which held as much as two cups but cost only a paisa, slightly more than a cup.

'You should always buy your tea in Allahabad,' Hemraj said, 'because it is mid-way between Delhi and Calcutta. Had we drunk it in Kanpur, we would need another cup before reaching Calcutta—a paisa wasted.'

Hemraj drank first and handed the pitcher to Hari, who drained it and threw it on the tracks, amused at the thought of the train crushing it when it started. They reclaimed their space, and the two traders from Shekhavati now proceeded to go and get their own tea while Hari and Hemraj saved their spots.

That night the train passed Mughalsarai and entered Bengal. Raniganj was crossed in the morning. As they ploughed eastward, a sense of accomplishment and relief settled on the carriage. They had sat on wooden benches for a day and two nights. When tired, they had dozed with hands clutching their bundles, backs propped against the backs of those behind them, sometimes tumbling on each other to wake up and resume their upright naps. From time to time they cast glances at their steel trunks lying wedged between others on the shelves above. When hungry, they opened their bundles and chewed on bajra seeds. Hari had discovered that the central bench—while far from the sights offered by window benches and stiflingly hot by day—was sheltered from biting wind at night and the ravages of flying coal dust. The latrines had gradually become dirtier, but the smell had become one with the air and no longer troubled Hari. Although no passengers had left the train, the carriage seemed to have expanded to accommodate its load, and they were now wedged comfortably in the mass like pieces in a jigsaw puzzle.

They passed low-lying hills that were impossibly green. Between the heads and shoulders of others Hari caught glimpses: bamboo thickets, palms, coconut groves, ploughed fields, mango trees, bullock carts, and many, many people, even in what looked like remote villages. *These are Bengalis*, he thought with mounting excitement. *Do they remember, on waking every morning, how close they are to Kalkatta and Dhaka and Jorhat?* They could jump on to a train and be in Kalkatta in a few hours. Why, then, did they not all go there? Why live in these fields when you were so close to the great city? Did the Bengali know what famine was? He would certainly laugh if Hari were to mention the Chhappaniya. At this very moment in Rampura, men stood among caked furrows, looking at the clear sky and praying for rain; here, even on a hot day such as this dark clouds had massed above, and were of no interest to the Bengalis from the way they went about their fields. Should a few drops fall before the month of Saavan in Rampura, children would run to the dam to study water levels and come home with tall tales.

Sometimes, as the train rounded a hillock, an entire plain would be revealed, dotted with huts, smoke and cows, and paddy fields submerged in water. Women with saris pulled up to their waists stood in pools along the tracks, fishing with small nets. This brought tears to Hari's eyes. What had the ojha said? 'Pools of water full of lilies ...'

'Get that boy away from the window,' someone called. 'His eyes are watering again.'

Hari remained where he was. Hemraj came and stood by him just as the train rumbled on to a bridge. The ground fell away, revealing a vast river, the widest expanse of water Hari had ever seen. The riverbed that separated Rampura from Nawalgarh was a mere creek against this.

'This is the Ganga,' Hemraj said, folding his hands.

Hari pointed to the men at the nets under the bridge. 'These people eat fish.'

Hemraj made a sound of disgust. 'They eat worse things. Those nets are for crabs, mussels, shellfish—things one should never touch.'

'How do you know?' Hari asked in wonder.

'When you have been with Bengalis for years you learn their ways,' said Hemraj, adding quickly, 'of course, no one from Shekhavati would think of touching such things, no matter how long he may live in Calcutta.'

As the hours passed the forest grew denser, punctuated by rivulets and bridges, wild pomelo and swaying bamboos, and the dark green of mangoes. The trees were so close together that they formed a wall on either side, with creepers jumping from branch to branch. Sometimes, screeching langurs and monkeys scampered up the branches to escape the train. Dirt trails ran next to the track, busy with bullock carts piled with hay and women with baskets of plantains on their heads.

They stopped at Burdwan station, where Hemraj grudgingly bought a golden pomelo and a dozen bananas for an anna, but only after the woman who sold it had agreed to throw in a custard apple for free. The two traders from Andrew Yule ate a banana each, and bought four coconuts in return. They drank coconut water to offset the heat, then ate the white jelly inside the shell.

After Burdwan, the train took a sharp turn to the right and ran south. The clouds finally burst into thunder and rain. Hari leaned out of the window, felt the drops on his face and gasped.

'We are just north of Calcutta now,' said Hemraj. 'Two more hours.'

Fields gave way to factories with long sheds, under which men seemed busy with thousands of whirring spindles and bobbins.

'Jute,' Hemraj said. 'They are weaving strands into hessian, which they will turn into sacks. Do you see those bales stacked on bullock carts? Those may have come from the firm of Daulatram Gulabchand. We sell 1,500 such bales every day.'

'Does Daulatram Gulabchand own a jute factory?'

'Factories belong to English sahibs. We sell them their jute,' said Hemraj. 'They send most of it to Dundee.'

Hari did not know where Dundee was but did not ask. He was breathless with excitement, conscious of being connected to Calcutta, Bombay, England and the whole world through Daulatram Gulabchand. What a glorious firm, and what good fortune to be working for it! When they got to Kalkatta, he would ask Khemchandji Biyani—after he had touched his feet, of course—to put him to work right away. I have not come to while away my time watching sights, he would say. Give me work! And he would do anything that was asked: wait on English sahibs, run errands for Hemrajji, count bales lying in yards, tally up sales and inventory, apply discounts, weigh out merchandise. Why, he would even carry those bales on his own shoulders if Khemchandji should ask!

After the factories had been passed, the tracks began to multiply. Another train passed them, going in the opposite direction, seemingly empty. *No one wants to leave Disavar*, thought Hari. Hazy buildings had appeared in the distance. They slowed down and braced for the final approach. Hari leaned far out and saw Howrah Station before the train itself did.

'Kalkatta!' he yelled. The men around him looked up in surprise.

It was all a blur—wires and poles, tracks and carriages and engines and smoke and, of course, men. This was not Rampura! He held his breath when the train glided along a platform filled with thousands of red-shirted coolies, men and women with umbrellas, bundles and beddings. Coolies ran alongside. Everyone was looking at them; Howrah Station had been awaiting their arrival. Finally, after much hissing and screeching, they were still. The uproar on the platform suddenly drowned all sounds inside the train.

The carriage emptied out quickly. The two traders from Andrew Yule took their leave. With boxes and bedding, Hemraj and Hari fought their way to the door. On the platform, they were immediately accosted by coolies. Hemraj waved them away. Walking out of the station in a river of men—ten bananas from Burdwan swinging by a string at Hemraj's side—they took a horse-drawn tonga after some negotiation with the tongawala. The horse went round a curve and trotted down the approach to the river Hooghly, and Harilal had his first view of Calcutta.

They neared a long bridge whose metal arches gave way to a flat, unsteady stretch of road, full of tongas, carts and goats.

'Howrah Bridge,' Hemraj said as the tonga entered the metal arches and struggled up the steep slope. 'The river is in tide.' They passed the arches, then sped through the flat, open expanse of the bridge, where Hari saw a sea of black umbrellas. On the other shore of the Hooghly was Calcutta, with the largest buildings Hari had ever seen rising above thousands of little dots, each a house. A hundred chimneys belched smoke and blackened the sky. He peered down at the river and was alarmed to see boats lined up under them. 'Won't they collide with the pillars?'

'This is a pontoon bridge. It floats on boats.'

The river was dotted with white sails. A lonely steamer approached from the right, sending a black whirl of smoke upward. Hari pointed to the buildings on the other shore. 'Which seth can afford a haveli that large?'

'Those are offices for English sahibs.'

It was not clear to Hari what business of the sahibs would require so many offices. And what did these Bengalis, walking briskly along the bridge in their dhotis and kurtas, eat? Where were the fields of bajra that would feed them? Where were the shops to employ all? He thought it prudent not to ask—he would have time to find out for himself. Hemraj seemed to sense the question, because his hand traced an arc from left to right, covering the Hooghly, the boats, the steamer, the thousands of men and carts and goats on the bridge, and the buildings on the other side. 'This is Kalkatta. All of India is ruled from here. One ward in this city holds more people than all of Shekhavati.'

Having crossed the bridge, the tonga trotted into Harrison road where, in the sea of dhotis, Hari saw a few sahibs in suits and topis. Once he even saw a memsahib but pretended not to notice. It would not do to make too much of these things in Kalkatta. Much more awaited him, and he must not appear over-enthusiastic. He studied the shops they passed—clothes, shoes, brass-bands with tubas on display, musical stores. The footpaths were choking with people—men who wore their dhotis oddly and women in saris, not the skirts of Rampura. Almost everyone had an umbrella tucked under the armpit—did it rain all the time? As if in answer, a few drops fell from above. Garbage lay strewn all over the street. The tonga made its way through slush, swerving to avoid horse-drawn carts that ran on rails.

'Trams,' Hemraj said, without explanation. Then they turned left. 'Machua, vegetable market.'

Hari was shocked to see mountains of refuse, banana peels, pineapple cores, mango stones and rotting apples. So much food, so many people, so much water! Hemraj had noticed his disgust. 'This is Ward Seven, Bara Bazar. You might think the stalls in Machua are dirty, but each sells fruit worth two hundred every day. You cannot expect to find the dry, bare markets of Rampura here.'

The tonga turned into a narrow lane, almost bumping into

oncoming traffic, drawing retorts from passers-by, skirting mounds of oranges, apples, watermelons and bananas. Men were urinating in full view. Bales of jute lay piled three high on the side, along with rolls of cloth spread out on tarpaulins. The stench of drains was everywhere. Tall buildings rose to the left and right, shutting out sunlight. From the walls on either side—so close that they could almost be touched at the same time—pipes protruded into the lane, dripping. Hari brushed off a drop and wondered what it was. People in balconies leaned over steel rails to look down at them. A man was transferring steel rods from the top shelf in his shop to the bottom one. Whenever he pulled out a rod, it extended all the way across the lane and traffic came to a stop, waiting until the rod had been inserted into its new location. The tonga continued, now bumping along cobblestones, splashing through puddles, and nearly colliding with three men with baskets on their heads. An altercation followed between the tongawala and the men, in Bengali—Hari did not understand a word.

As they emerged from the lane, the sidebars of the tonga caught a man's umbrella and sent it flying across the road. He scrambled after it, pulling up his dhoti in a vain attempt to keep it dry. The umbrella was broken, so he demanded compensation. Already annoyed at the previous collision and delay, Hemraj ordered the tongawala to continue. The umbrella-man muttered 'Marwari!' and walked away.

'Is that a Bengali man?' Hari asked.

'Yes. Not just any Bengali but a bhadralok.'

Hari did not understand.

'A gentleman,' said Hemraj. 'A man who can read a newspaper.'

'He called you a Marwari. Does he not know you are from Shekhavati?'

'We are all Marwaris here.'

'He does not like us.'

'No,' chuckled Hemraj. 'But he will be in the offices of Daulatram Gulabchand tomorrow, to pawn his wife's gold bracelet for six rupees.'

They turned into Amherst Row. Hemraj leaned forward and spoke to the tongawala. 'Stop at Lalgodam, number 5.'

They arrived at a three-storeyed building. Hemraj paid the tongawala, who protested earnestly at the amount. Hemraj's reaction was equally strident; the tongawala withdrew. They entered an arch displaying the names of firms located in the building—the largest said 'Daulatram Gulabchand'. In a room to the left, a flour mill churned noisily. Flour dust hung like mist over the whole area. The gateway opened into a court surrounded by galleries on the second and third floors, their arches separated by dark wooden columns. Dhotis and kurtas were hung out to dry on iron railings, which had the curlicue patterns Hari had seen in Daulatramji's haveli in Rampura. Some of the balconies were boarded up, some covered with wooden blinds. From the inside, the building looked like a haveli in Shekhavati: a dirtier haveli with much water and little sun.

A single staircase spiralled upward in a corner. They went up to the third floor, where Hemraj led him into a room. Men sat cross-legged on mattresses covered with white sheets, poring over red-binders, of which stacks lay strewn about. Pictures of old seths looked down from the walls, marigold garlands hanging from the frames indicating they were dead. Seated behind a wooden cash box at the far end, a frail old man looked up at their approach.

Hemraj kicked off his slippers—adding them to a pile on the linoleum near the door—put down his trunk and bundle, advanced over the mattress, knelt, touched the man's right foot with both hands, and ran his palms over his head. Khemchand Biyani, head clerk and chief accountant of Daulatram Gulabchand, muttered a blessing and asked, 'How is bajra quoted in Shekhavati?'

'Six rupees to a munn,' said Hemraj, 'because of the Chhappaniya.' He placed the bunch of bananas on the mattress. 'I bought these at Burdwan Station. A dozen for three paisa, including a pomelo and a custard apple.'

Hari was quite certain Hemrajji had paid an anna—four paisa—and not the three he claimed, but decided not to interrupt.

It was quite understandable for a man who earned seventy-five rupees in a month to forget such small amounts.

'You were wise to buy these in Burdwan,' said Khemchand Biyani. 'Here, the thieves in Machua charge twice as much.' Then his eyes fell on Hari. Hemraj beckoned him and bade him touch Khemchandji's feet.

'This is Harilal, son of Duli Chandji Tibrewal of Rampura.'

Hari tore open the seams of his kurta, withdrew his father's letter and laid it at the old man's feet. Khemchandji said to Hemraj. 'Read it.'

'But it is in Modhiya,' Hemraj replied.

He has trouble reading Modhiya, thought Hari with some surprise and disappointment. No wonder he had made no comment on his essay about the cow in Rampura.

Khemchand Biyani studied Hari carefully through his spectacles and asked Hemraj, 'How much was the boy's train ticket?'

'Nine rupees, eight annas, two paise and two pies.'

'Add it to his account. Then show him some bills from two years ago and ask him to calculate the amounts receivable.'

2

CALCUTTA

1

The firm of Daulatram Gulabchand took up the whole third floor at 5 Amherst Row. The building, named Lalgodam, had been erected during the opium boom, when the firm traded in opium futures worth lakhs of rupees. Three years ago, Seth Daulatram had died unexpectedly while seated at his cash box on the first floor. On the advice of an astrologer, the first two floors were let out to smaller businesses and the firm confined itself to eleven rooms on the top floor, arranged on three sides of a balcony overlooking the central courtyard.

The flour mill at the main gate operated for much of the day. Its motor began humming at six in the morning and stopped at midnight. All day long its flywheel turned, pulling at a noisy, flapping belt, spraying flour dust. Tenants on the lower floors had become accustomed to the permanent fog of flour. Workers near the gate were usually coated in white flour dust, and the smell of flour penetrated deep inside the building, rising as high as the third storey.

The eleven rooms of Daulatram Gulabchand had linoleum floors, soft mattresses covered with white sheets, and cash boxes in the corner. Each room dealt with a different line of business—jute, cotton, wool, bills of exchange, insurance or opium. Clerks toted up sales, amounts receivable and liabilities every day. In the evening they sat down to tally their accounts in red binders with Khemchand Biyani, who was the head munim—manager and accountant—of the Calcutta branch, and therefore, of the whole firm, because the Calcutta branch was the centre of operations. Every two months, he set out on a month-long tour that took him to the far-flung branches of Daulatram Gulabchand: Ratlam and

Indore in the Central Indian Agency, Nagpur and Chhindwara in the Central Provinces, Amritsar in Punjab, Jhunjhunu in Shekhavati, Bhiwani on the way to Delhi from Jhunjhunu, Kanpur in the United Provinces, Malwa in the opium belt, Patna and Bhagalpur in Bihar, Jorhat and Goalpara in Assam, Murshidabad and Mymensingh in Bengal. These branches reported to the Calcutta branch. He travelled by rail, except where no other means but bullock cart or camel cart were available, and spent much time in Kanpur, where the firm had moved its Mirzapur office ten years ago because Kanpur lay on the main railway route between Delhi and Calcutta. When the river Ganga had been the chief artery into Bengal, Mirzapur had been easily accessible—the railway line had reduced its importance.

This vast empire was said to have been built by Seth Daulatram in response to a childhood insult. His father had died during the Saiya famine of 1844, which, following the Bhaiya famine of the previous year, had devastated Shekhavati. Still unmarried at ten, he found employment in a jeweller's shop in Sikar. The jeweller taught him how to measure the purity of gold by rubbing it on a kasauti stone. Within a year, Daulatram could confidently price silver bricks and gold ingots, and even old ornaments that people brought—these had to be melted in a clay crucible before being evaluated, because the skin had impurities that the bulk did not.

One day he was sent to accept a consignment of gold biscuits from a supplier, who made him a proposition. 'Listen carefully, Daulatiya. I want you to certify my gold as one-anna-khaad.'

'Is it?' Daulatram asked. One-anna-khaad would make the gold 93.75 per cent pure, which he saw rarely in his dealings with suppliers.

The man shrugged. 'It may be one-thirteenth khaad.'

'That is not one-anna-khaad. And which impurity is it? Silver?'

'Copper or zinc.'

'My master prefers silver.'

'Who can tell?' asked the man.

'I can. My master can, too—he keeps samples with different types of impurities. He can compare them.'

'But you are the one who will certify it. Say one-anna-khaad when asked, and you may ask me for three rupees the next time I see you.'

'I will not cheat the jeweller,' Daulatiya replied. 'He feeds both my mother and me.'

He took the gold to the jeweller's store and ran it across a kasauti stone, then poured nitric acid on the resulting golden scratch and rubbed it vigorously with his finger. The scratch turned dark red. Daulatiya turned to his master. 'This is two-anna-khaad, 87.5 per cent. And the mix is copper.'

'Return it,' the jeweller ordered. 'I have no use for such gold.'

Daulatiya turned the gold ingot in his hand, fascinated that an imperceptible purity could devalue it so. Now it was gold, now a worthless piece of metal ...

'Do not eye it like a greedy dog,' the jeweller scolded. 'Your father was a fool to name you Daulatram—calling a boy wealthy does not make him so.'

Daulatiya was stung. He looked at his fingertip—blackened from a year of rubbing nitric acid on kasauti stones—and took a vow. On his next visit to the supplier he said, 'I will certify your next gold as one-anna-khaad.'

'I knew you would come around,' the supplier said, 'but I can only spare two rupees now.'

'Give me one,' said Daulatiya.

'Why?' asked the man, surprised.

'One rupee is all I need for a camel that will take me to Mirzapur.'

Daulatiya took the gold to his jeweller, certified it as one-anna-khaad, collected his one rupee from the supplier and left Rampura that very evening, carrying a brass pot, a rope, a blanket, and a bundle packed with cucumber, pickle and three cakes of bajra. His mother bid him a tearful farewell. It was the second fortnight of Kartik, three days after the festival of Diwali. A crop of bajra stood ready to be cut in the fields. Daulatiya's camel picked its way through the land and then among the tibbas. A sliver of the new moon appeared in the sky. Daulatiya rode all night, and the next day and night, to reach Jaipur in the morning, where he was told that camels could not go east beyond the borders of Jaipur State—the great desert of Shekhavati was both his home and his prison.

He walked 500 miles eastward, spending no more than half an anna every day on crushed grams and rice. Twenty days later, he rounded a hill and saw Mirzapur on the banks of the Ganga. On arriving in the town, he presented himself in the offices of the great firm of Sojiram Hardayal.

'Have you learned arithmetic?' asked Sojiram's old munim.

'I know multiplication tables for one-and-a-quarter, one-and-a-half, one-and-three-quarters and two-and-a-half.'

'Can you read and write?'

'A little, in Modhiya.'

'Deliver my crates to Kalkatta. I will pay food and passage,' said the munim.

Daulatiya drifted down the Ganga on a flotilla of boats belonging to Sojiram Hardayal, guarding crates of opium and keeping good accounts of spillage, and arrived in Calcutta six days later. Though only eleven, he began immediately as a gumashta—a clerk—in the Calcutta offices of the firm. Before long, he had opened his own hosiery business, starting with a small platform outside a shop in Cotton Street, then expanded into a cotton shop, then branched into opium. By the late fifties, with Sojiram Hardayal in decline after an unsuccessful attempt to corner the opium market, Daulatram Gulabchand—named after Daulatiya and his grandfather—was already one of Calcutta's leading firms, with offices in Farrukhabad, Mirzapur, Patna and Malwa. By the sixties, the firm had interests in opium, banking, gold wholesaling, wool export, cotton and insurance. It discounted bills of exchange issued by bankers in other towns, sold gold to Bengali retailers, issued insurance policies, collected commissions on bales of cotton, and speculated in jute, opium and government paper markets. In the eighties, it entered the jute business with the purchase of three jute presses.

Daulatram was not yet sixty-three when he died. His death was both sudden and inexplicable. He had bathed, finished his morning puja, opened a new account book and painted the swastika on its first page with his ring finger. Turning the page, he made the first entry in a small, neat hand—the expense for the puja in his newly completed haveli in Rampura. All subsequent expenses related to the haveli would be entered in this book.

Gumashtas were opening doors; servants were thrashing mattresses with bamboo brooms; a munim was bathing at the hand-pump in the courtyard, pumping it again and again, raising squeals of protest from its valves that could be heard all over Lalgodam. Daulatramji turned to a clerk.

'Who is that? Tell him not to waste water.'

The clerk stepped out of the office and saw that the offender was Khemchand Biyani, the head munim himself. Not wishing to pick a quarrel with his superior, the clerk returned to the office to placate his master. It was he who first saw Daulatramji slumped at the cash box.

No one was able to explain what had happened. A failure of the heart, the vaidya said, but it was generally agreed that the death had something to do with the new haveli in Rampura. Raamji would not tolerate such coincidence, if coincidence it was. There had been wide speculation about Daulatram's motives in building the Rampura haveli. It was clear that no one in his family would live in it, and Daulatramji was not given to vulgar displays of wealth that might have explained such profligacy. After the death, the name given to the haveli by the people of Rampura found its way to the Calcutta offices—Daulatram's Grave.

The folly of the great mansion failed to undermine Daulatram's prestige. It was accepted by the Marwaris in Calcutta, most of whom had dealt with the firm, that Daulatram's wealth was far exceeded by his humility. It had been a long time since anyone had laughed at his name, but he had continued to refer to himself by the humbler tag of Daulatiya, and no one who saw him would know that his firm did business worth many lakhs in a month. He died as he was born, in a cotton vest and cotton dhoti pulled high over his knees, though the wealthiest native businessman in all of Calcutta, and the first Marwari to import Manchester cotton directly from England.

In sons, Daulatram had been unfortunate. The oldest had been drawn to Shaivism and had removed himself to an ashram near the Ganga in Benares. Regretfully, Daulatram had settled an annuity on him. The second had initially shown promise: at twenty-five, he was already the banyan—chief native buyer and liaison—for the European firm of Kettlewell Bullen. However, on seeing his wife and son die in a train accident, he had turned to Krishna, and was reported to have become a fakir in Brindavan. His whereabouts were unknown. The third son, Jainarain, had been posted as the head munim in the Mirzapur branch, in preparation for his elevation to Calcutta. He failed to distinguish himself, partly because of the general decline in opium. He was brought back to Calcutta to replace his older brother as the banyan at Kettlewell Bullen. He did not made a favourable impression on the English sahibs at Kettlewell, so it was with relief that he took over the firm on his father's death. The absence of his brothers saved the firm from division. The banyanship of Kettlewell Bullen passed from the family, but it was merely a loss of prestige, not wealth, because Daulatram Gulabchand was then at the height of its prosperity.

Jainarain headed his father's firm for less than two years, during which he spent vast sums of money building temples and public houses in Haridwar and Benares. Where Daulatram had been measured in his charity, Jainarain's enthusiasm knew no bounds. Where Daulatram had cautiously entered the business of jute baling five years ago, Jainarain jumped into the jute futures market, which was the preserve of sahibs. He bought stakes in the Petroleum Company of Asia and the Burmah Oil Company, depleting the firm's capital to the extent that the opium trade had to be discontinued and the insurance business sold off. He did not, however, enjoy the moral authority of his father, and was prevailed upon by well-wishers to retire to Haridwar with his wife, where he received monthly accounts from the Calcutta office. That his marriage had yielded no children confirmed everyone in the belief that Daulatram's firm was not destined to end up in the hands of his sons.

The management of the firm fell to Khemchand Biyani, who had become the head munim four years before Daulatram's death. He was a grand-nephew of Daulatram, but far removed from the immediate family. A short, frail man of fifty-six—only ten years younger than Daulatram himself—he was rumoured to have accumulated a vast sum as the head munim, but nothing about his manner justified the tremendous hold he had on the imagination of everyone in Rampura. He was usually seated at the cash box in his corner of the gaddi, taking up one-eighth of one room, poring over accounts or talking to gumashtas in a soft, unassuming voice. No one would associate him with the great haveli of Seth Daulatram in Rampura which, although not owned by him, was in his care. It was said that he had a three-eighths of a per cent share in the profits of the firm, and Jainarain had such faith in him that he never once opened the monthly accounts sent to him. Khemchandji himself did not repose such trust in the clerks and munims of his branch or the other branches. He transferred them frequently, never letting a munim stay in one branch for more than two years. He varied the dates of his bi-monthly tour without notice, often arriving unannounced at a branch office and demanding to see the inventory register. The story of his ascent to the top of the firm—he was only a grand-nephew after all, and a distant one—was told over and over again in Rampura, together with the lesson that followed: any boy could become a head munim in Calcutta with the right application of thrift and prudence.

Hari was given a place next to Hemraj in one of the offices. On this first two days, he found the Lalgodam routine disorienting. The offices doubled as bedrooms. At night, the intense July heat and the snoring of fourteen gumashtas kept him awake. The men smoked endlessly. They coughed, cleared their throats and spat all the time. The pull punkah on the ceiling did not favour the far corner of the room—where Hari slept—and the servant assigned to tug at its cord usually fell asleep. A general hubbub woke everyone at six in the morning. There was a rush to queue for the latrines, of which there were three for eighty clerks, cashiers and munims in the eleven rooms. The lines were long and the men irritable. Before lining up, they would have run down to the hand-pump in the courtyard to fill a lota of water that they carried into the latrines: a single pot with which one had to both wash and flush. If anyone stayed inside for more than five minutes, those outside knocked impatiently. Jokes were made about their bowels, taunts flung for days afterward. Should the lota run out of water before all the shit had been flushed down, the next person would loudly announce the infraction. Used to the expanse of fields in Rampura, where a boy might relieve himself at leisure with nothing but sun and sand to watch him, Hari was dismayed. On his first morning, he nearly vomited because of the stench. The men did not seem to mind the smell, after having taken the precaution of tying handkerchiefs over their noses. At times, the latrine queue resembled a gang of masked robbers. Every morning, some of the men rose a few minutes before the others to beat the queue, and the smart ones had figured out who spent the most time inside the latrines, and therefore, which of the three queues to avoid. After brushing their teeth with sticks of babool, they took baths under the hand-pump next to the flour mill, where Hari found a coat of white powder on his body immediately after.

Their morning puja was perfunctory—joss sticks waved before images of Lakshmi, bhajans sung in muffled tones and tilaks imprinted on foreheads. Khemchandji discouraged any elaborate ceremony even as he demanded that they complete a puja before food or water passed their lips. The men then climbed to the rooftop, where a basa had been constructed for their meals. Two ovens, fired by wood and coal, sat next to each other, attended by a chef brought from Shekhavati to cook Marwari food. What he cooked, with his helpers, was a mishmash of Shekhavati and Bengali cuisine—rice, puri, mango pickle, daal-bati, and sometimes a sweet. Mats were laid out. The clerks sat in rows, ate in shifts, then trooped downstairs to their bedrooms, where servants would have dusted the mattresses and swept off the detritus of night. Cash boxes and ledgers were brought out, red-bound books were opened, swastikas were painted, and the day began with the addition of sales and purchases, a reckoning of the opening inventories, and an accounting of dispatches all over India. Those with debts to collect on, like Hemraj, waited for a few hours before starting their rounds of Bara Bazar with sheafs of bills. This was in deference to Daulatram Gulabchand's business associates—it was inauspicious for a trader to see a creditor in his gaddi early in the morning.

Hari found it disconcerting that he had nowhere to rest during the day, because all business was conducted on the mattresses which became available only after Khemchandji had locked the cash box—sometimes as late as eleven in the evening—and gone into the room where he slept. He lay awake at night, learning to identify men by the rhythm of their snoring, yearning for quiet, spacious and clean Rampura. There was one difference: plenty of water, as much as one could draw with the hand-pump. And no one even noticed. They had not heard of the Chhappaniya. If postcards from Shekhavati mentioned it, they probably forgot immediately after reading.

The men appeared to be in their twenties or thirties. Most were from Shekhavati—Rampura, Nawalgarh, Sikar or Jhunjhunu—three had come from Bikaner, and one from Jaipur. For the first two days, Hari spent all his time inside Lalgodam, shrinking from the latrines and the food, and looking about him for a place to sleep comfortably. The men tolerated his discomfort with good cheer, having gone through this 'settling down' when they had first come to Calcutta. They gave him tips on how to lie on the mattresses—always on your side with arms and legs wrapped round a thick bolster—how to secure his space—be the first to go to bed—and how to get ahead in the line for the latrine—wake up early. They laughed when he complained about the snoring. 'At least there are no mosquitoes in Kalkatta. Have you been to Jorhat in Assam? You will be sucked dry in one night if you sleep outside a mosquito net.'

'Latrines are the same all over Bara Bazar.'

'At least there *are* latrines. When Daulatramji first came to Disavar, he did not get to live in a building like Lalgodam.'

'He did not have a gaddi at all—just a wooden platform outside a shop.'

'It was years later that he bought a gaddi in Cotton Street.'

'There were no latrines there either, not even a place to piss. Everyone had to go to another gaddi, where the seth charged them—a pie for pissing in the drain, two for using the latrine.'

'I have seen the commissioner's bungalow in Patna,' said a clerk. 'There was one bathroom for him and another for his wife. Imagine that—a whole bathroom for one person. The floor was so clean that you could sleep on it; the commode sat in a far corner as if it were an after-thought.'

'What happened to the gaddi in Cotton Street?' Hari asked.

'Sold for a good price.'

'Did Daulatramji not want to keep his first office?'

'If you do no business inside it, it is just a room with a mattress. Only a fool is attached to bricks and linoleum.'

'But Lalgodam is so dirty,' said Hari, thinking of the white dust rising from the floor. 'The smell of flour ...'

'What flour?' the clerk asked.

On the second day, Hari was told that his father had been tardy in sending him to Disavar. 'A boy must learn to quote jute prices before he is ten if he wants to trade jute futures at fourteen. Daulatramji was eleven when he left Rampura, and you look like you are already fifteen.'

'I am twelve,' said Hari.

'You are tall for your age.'

Recalling what his father used to say, Hari responded, 'I have eaten Shekhavati bajra. Never been sick a day in my life.'

The clerk shook his head. 'They feed bajra to cattle here. Even the poor eat rice.'

On Hari's third day, Khemchandji asked to see his notes on the amounts receivable. Hari produced the piece of paper on which he had added up the numbers. Khemchandji studied it and said nothing. Later that day, a munim handed Hari a sheaf of bills, and a clerk told him how to make his way to Cotton Street and how to read a street address. A cashier handed him a few coins. 'Never leave Lalgodam without money,' he said. 'Three annas, one paisa and two pies entered into Harilal Tibrewal's account.'

Hari wrapped the coins in the large handkerchief his mother had given him, tied it round his waist, pulled his kurta down over it, went downstairs, ran across the courtyard, breathed flour dust and stepped into Amherst Row. It had just rained. He retraced his path from three days ago, heading back to Harrison Road, tripping over loose cobblestones and avoiding tongas. Passing the mounds of mangoes, oranges, bananas and apples in Machua, he held his nose and was again reminded of dry Rampura. On Harrison Road, trams rolled toward Howrah Bridge, pulled by horses that snorted and bucked when confronted with tongas that had strayed on to the rails. Hari considered climbing into a tram but was intimidated by the men who sat inside with umbrellas on their knees. Then he scolded himself for the indiscretion—his first foray into Bara Bazar, and he was already thinking of spending money.

He could not read the signs—in English and Bengali, he guessed—but found himself unable to overlook a pyramid of giant pineapples. The owner—Bengali, but dressed like an English sahib and certainly not a bhadralok—eyed him suspiciously, then sent a boy to shoo him away. Hari stood transfixed. Where in ragged Shekhavati would one see such pineapples? The boy made an impatient sound.

'Pineapple juice?' Hari asked in Hindi, hoping that would work because he did not know a word of Bengali.

The boy poured juice into a glass tumbler and extended it toward him. He studied the tumbler—his mother would have let him drink from clay, copper, brass or even steel, but never from unclean glass. Yet here was the boy with the tumbler and the juice had already been poured, so he owed money. Hopefully, the glass had been washed after it was last used—by a Musalman, for all anyone knew, or even a sahib, but sahibs would not come to a stall like this. With trembling hands, he accepted the juice and took a tentative sip. It sent a shiver of pleasure through his body. This Disavar was full of wealth. Look how full this tumbler was, and how rich this juice!

He drained the tumbler and set it down on the counter, afraid he had displayed too much enthusiasm. Everyone in Shekhavati knew that the prudent buyer is indifferent.

'Adhela,' said the boy.

Hari gasped. Half an anna for a glass of juice! He had been a fool. One should never buy before inquiring about the price, and then after a suitable degree of bargaining, depending on the temperament of the shopkeeper and the importance of the purchase. Why had he forgotten where he was? Perhaps he could bargain now. This was just a boy, not much older than him. He would start low and allow his offer to be raised until it stopped somewhere below half-anna. Even a paisa saved in this manner was a paisa that could be better spent elsewhere.

'Two pice?'

The boy seemed not to understand. He turned to the man inside the shop, who advanced to the counter sullenly. Hari lost his nerve. Unwrapping the handkerchief at his waist, he pulled out two one-paisa coins, handed them over and left shamefacedly. He could hear his father scold him—what kind of a boy buys pineapple juice from a stall when he can buy the pineapple and extract the juice himself for one-third the price? Well, at the very least he must now learn the correct price of juice on Harrison

Road. Hemrajji would know, if he had been foolish enough to ever buy juice from a stall. He would have to be discreet. It would not do to let anyone know that he had already bought juice without bargaining.

Leaving Harrison Road, he was able to locate 178 Cotton Street—a building much like Lalgodam—by asking shopkeepers. Around the courtyard, there were balconies with iron railings, as in Lalgodam. Climbing to the second floor, he entered a room covered with mattresses, with munims bent over red binders. Everything was as in Lalgodam. No doubt these were men from Shekhavati. After the harsh glare of Harrison Road, he was relieved to be among clerks and munims. He slipped off his chappals, sat down on a mattress and presented his bills to the nearest munim, who eyed him curiously.

'How old are you?'

'Twelve. The thirteenth is on me, to be completed on Phalgun sudi dwaadashi.'

'Khemchandji should not be sending young boys,' the munim grumbled as he placed the bills next to his cash box and went back to his binder. Not knowing what to do, Hari crawled to the edge of the mattress, sat cross-legged as the clerks in Lalgodam had taught him, and waited.

He sat for six hours, afraid to leave the room without permission but reluctant to ask for it. The pineapple juice seemed to expand against his belly until his bladder was bursting. In Rampura, he would have run out to the lane, squatted in the sand and relieved himself, but this seemed inconceivable on Cotton Street or Harrison Road. He made a mental note to never drink anything when setting out on important business. Who knew when he would next find a toilet?

At seven in the evening, when the gaddi was about to close, the munim called Hari to the cash box, had him sign the bill and counted out 125 rupees. Hari folded his handkerchief around the notes and tied it tightly around his waist, then walked down the staircase and into Cotton Street, his heart pounding. Here he was, with 125 rupees in his pocket! In Rampura, all the bajra in his father's store was worth less than that. Then awe turned to fear: what if someone should attack him? What if an English sahib or a police sergeant—was that not a sergeant in that topi?—should stop and search him? Would he have to answer in English? How would he explain where a boy like him got the money?

He walked carefully, silently, staying on the edge of the road, one hand always at the bundle on his waist. On Harrison Road, electric lights gleamed brightly on either side, mounted on poles he had not noticed during the day. He had been warned about these by a clerk in Lalgodam—a boy was not to touch the poles or he would be burnt to ashes. Only when he had turned left into Machua and the poles were far away did he feel safe. Even so, his hand stayed at his waist until he had crossed Machua, turned into Amherst Row and entered the courtyard in Lalgodam. There was comfort in the darkness of the building. Running up to the third floor he sneaked quietly into a latrine. Fortunately, it was dark. He lifted his dhoti carefully and urinated standing up—like a sahib—disgusted by the splash of urine but overwhelmed with relief. When he walked into Khemchandji's room, he saw a dozen flickering lanterns and the munims gathered around the old man. No one noticed him for a full fifteen minutes, until Khemchandji cast a glance his way through the munims. He handed over the money and the bills, hoping no one had seen him take everything into the latrine. Khemchandji studied the bills, counted the money and stowed it away in the cash box.

He walked out of the room, relieved and contented, and leaned against the iron railing on the balcony. He could hear the clatter of brass plates on the rooftop—the basa had opened for dinner—and smell the ghee that the cook had poured into a cauldron. The courtyard below was lit dimly by lanterns from the flour mill, which had shut down for the day; its flour dust had settled. A dog walked about, licking leftover rice and daal from plates of mango leaves lying in a corner. From Amherst Row, the din of tongas, the creaking of carts and the shouting of men invaded the courtyard, swirled around and rose to the third floor. *This is Kalkatta,* he told himself, *the greatest city in Disavar. This is where I will live, and this is where I will work. A boy must go where people live, because that is where the shops are. And where he finds shops, there he must get by, buying and selling and turning a profit.*

After a week of walking up and down Harrison Road and collecting on debts owed to the firm, Hari was told by Khemchandji that he would be paid ten rupees every month. He was overjoyed: it had not occurred to him that he was entitled to a salary. In Rampura, Master Bholaram perhaps earned five rupees in a month; here he was, in Disavar for a mere seven days, already earning twice as much. Even after subtracting the four rupees he would pay for his meals in the basa, he would have money left over to bank with Khemchandji. His father had been strict about this: money in excess of what was spent—and why would he need to spend on anything once the kitchen was paid up?—was to be banked with the firm.

Hemrajji was unimpressed when Hari gave him the news. 'The durbaan who guards the gate in Lalgodam gets ten rupees.'

This deflated Hari's spirits. The obvious question rose in his mind: if a guard earned ten rupees in a month, and if Hemrajji earned seventy-five as was rumoured in Rampura, what might Khemchandji's salary be? The question was impertinent but he asked anyway. Hemrajji hesitated.

'You must not think of him as a clerk with a salary. What he is paid does not matter because he has a share in the profits of the firm.'

Hari knew this, of course, including the number mentioned in Rampura—three-eighths of a per cent—but feigned ignorance. 'What per cent?'

'A young boy must not ask too many questions.'

In their train journey together, Hari had learned that Hemrajji could be free with information when excitement had loosened his tongue. Shrugging, he said, 'A salary of a few hundred, I suppose, not much more.'

Hemrajji lowered his voice. 'This is Kalkatta, where even a coolie knows how to speak with sahibs. Do you know how much the banyan of Kinsell and Ghose earns? Or the banyan of Ralli Brothers? Graham & Company? Thousands, perhaps tens of thousands.'

Hari's head swam with the numbers. 'Why doesn't Khemchandji become a banyan, then?'

'Not everyone has a banyanship in the family. Even if your father has been their banyan for twenty years, the English sahibs will not give you the banyanship unless they think well of you. It is not sufficient to know multiplication tables, and the sahibs do not care for Modhiya. A banyan must read and write in English, even speak a little of it. He must go to meetings at the Jute Balers' Association, where they discuss hessian rates in England and America. All in English.'

'Is Khemchandji a member of the association?'

'Daulatram Gulabchand is, and my father goes to represent the firm. But of course he says nothing there. What can he say, sitting with the Bara Sahib of Kinsell and Ghose? Even banyans hardly open their mouths in the presence of sahibs.'

Now Hari knew why he had come to Disavar. He must strive to become the head munim in Daulatram Gulabchand. Failing that, he must become a banyan, even if that meant learning some English. Quickly, he squelched the thought, afraid that Hemrajji would see it in his face. A boy who sees himself speaking to sahibs after seven days in Disavar comes to nothing, because he is all talk and no work.

In mid-November, a Lalgodam clerk who had returned from Shekhavati brought Hari a letter from his father, written in the neat, closely packed Modhiya of Master Bholaram.

'Duli Chand Tibrewal from the town of Rampura sends his blessings to Harilal (may he live long) in the auspicious town of Kalkatta. It has been four months since you left Rampura. The chaumasa months have ended: Saavan, Bhadwa and Ashwin came and went, and Kartik has almost passed. Not a single cloud appeared in the sky, not a drop of rain was seen. The brass pots you placed on the roof remained dry. By day, sand-storms swirled around them; by night, they stared at the moon. Master Bholaram organized many pujas, but Indra Bhagwan chose not to send rain. No one lit a lamp to celebrate Diwali this year—Rampura was as dark as the sky above it. The day after Diwali, those who had planted four months ago collected whatever they could find in the fields. It was a meagre harvest. The rate for bajra fluctuates, but what does a price mean when there is no grain to be had? Men starved with bags full of silver coins tied at their waists. Those living are willing to sell their ploughs, their clothes, the thatch of their houses, even their children, but no one will have them. Rampura is littered with the skeletons of cows, bulls, bullocks and camels. The only well-fed animals are dogs who feast on the bloated carcasses of dead children. Sevaramji's shop has shut down, and Tikamchandji passed away on the first day of Kartik, unable to bear the prospect of ruin. This is what Indra Bhagwan has decreed for our Shekhavati. I have asked Khemchandji to give you three rupees for Diwali. The rest is in the hands of Raamji, on this Kartik sudi saptami in the Vikram Samvat year of one thousand nine hundred and fifty six. Master Bholaram bids me add the English date—November 10, 1899—seeing that you have been in Disavar for four months, and wishes you to note the fineness of his hand.'

The letter depressed Hari. There was no word of his mother or sisters, and nothing about the shop. Had it shut down? Where was his father going to find three rupees to pay into Khemchandji's account in Rampura, for the unnecessary waste of paying him that amount for Diwali? What was he to do with the money anyway? He bought a postcard and wrote to his father.

> 'Harilal from the town of Kalkatta touches the feet of Shri Duli Chandji Tibrewal in the auspicious town of Rampura. I have not been able to find anyone going to Shekhavati because Diwali has just passed—festival

season is the busiest time for the firm, and no one wants to waste it on travel—so I will have to pay one-paisa postage for this letter. Please ask Masterji to disregard my poor hand: the message will not extend beyond the end of the postcard. Rains have now ended in Kalkatta, but Bara Bazar is still full of puddles of water, and the lanes are paved unevenly with cobblestones. People eat rice: they think bajra is coarse, and no one would ever think of eating gwar. I have no cause to complain of my time here. Khemchandji gives me ten rupees every month, of which I spend one rupee on milk. I think you will agree that milk is not an indulgence at my age. The basa costs four rupees. Once a week, they put ghee on my roti for a paisa. Twice a week I drink pineapple juice, spending a total of half an anna a month. Once a month, I eat a mango for two paise and some kachauris for a paisa. Mornings have now become chilly, so I have asked the servant for hot water for my bath. He takes a pie and provides a bucketful, but I am able to increase it by mixing cold water until it is just warm enough. Last month, I had a tailor make me a new kurta and bought a cotton dhoti for six annas, from a shop recommended by Hemrajji, who understands the rates in Kalkatta. In total, I am able to save eight annas every month.

I do not loiter outside Lalgodam, do not waste my time with Bengalis, and have not spoken once to an English sahib. I keep good accounts, obey Khemchandji, and show respect to all clerks and munims in Lalgodam. The rest is in the hands of Raamji, on this Kartik sudi teras in the Vikram Samvat year of one thousand nine hundred and fifty six. Please assure Master Bholaramji that I have made no attempt to learn English dates in Kalkatta.'

2

Hari soon discovered that a boy of twelve could do little but sit around the office and wait to be sent out on errands—a glass of rose sherbet for Khemchandji, a message to the durbaan at the door, a trip to collect rent from the flour mill. When he was dispatched to collect on debts, the amounts were small—125 was a pittance, he soon learned—and the payments involved no delays, because that would require some haggling over the interest rate with the debtor. However much his ten rupees had seemed at first, he was the lowest paid clerk in the office. The eight annas he had saved every month vanished as soon as winter required him to buy a muffler and a new pair of Nagra sandals. He kept scrupulous accounts, yet his earnings seemed to slip away and there was no prospect of accumulation.

Walking through the narrow, circuitous lanes of Bara Bazar, he shrank from the dirt and the rude crowds, the boys bathing at roadside pumps, the women cooking in a sea of slush, their pots and pans collecting splashes of water from tonga wheels. Then there was the problem of the fish market, which became impossible to avoid on his way to Cotton Street. There he saw goat carcasses, snails and fish that were still living, flailing when held by the tail, dripping blood on counters. When passing these, he longed for the open spaces of Rampura where a boy could wander in the fields and chew on bajra, or jump into the pond near the dam for an afternoon bath, without having to deal with Bengalis, crowds, English sahibs or tongawalas.

He had hoped this was to be a temporary situation that would enable him to start his own shop, as Seth Daulatram had done in Cotton Street, but where would he get the money for a shop, given that he had been unable to save even a few annas in nine months? Trade is in our blood, his father had told him, but that blood had to be sweetened with capital. No one would trust his money with a boy of twelve who knew nothing but arithmetic and Modhiya. Perhaps he could become a dalaal—a jute or opium under-broker; he could learn how to tell good jute from bad and arrange deals for Khemchandji. A good dalaal at a European firm could earn three hundred rupees in a month, but such firms employed experienced men who had already been brokers in Indian firms for years. The capital of a dalaal was his reputation and his word, and no one would trust the word of a boy. Besides, a dalaal had to know how to speak Bengali with Bengalis, a little Hindi, and perhaps some English when dealing with sahibs.

In June, eleven months after he had arrived in Calcutta, he asked the cashier in Lalgodam to show him his account. A red binder was produced and opened to a page that contained too few entries: his accumulated savings were three rupees and six annas.

Later that day, he walked down Cotton Street to collect on a bill. There was a letter from his father in his kurta pocket. Having received no news of home for seven months, and having sent none, lest his father—laid low by the Chhappaniya—be burdened with his misfortunes in Calcutta, he was afraid to read the letter. When did Raamji ever send good news from Shekhavati? June was the month of blistering heat in the tibbas, of preparation for bajra planting, of scanning the sky for wisps of cloud. Perhaps the Chhappaniya would return this year, as the Saiya famine had followed the Bhaiya. He sat on a bench and bought a glass of tea, knowing he should not drink anything when on an errand. With the tea calming his nerves, he opened the note.

> '... Rukmini is now sixteen, and her father-in-law has already asked thrice, "When will you send her to us?" I cannot delay her departure any longer, even if I am unable to buy the gifts that must go with her. Your mother has put together everything she could find in the house—after setting aside the gifts that must be given to Jasoda and Muniya when it is their time—but I do not know what I will give to her husband when he comes to take her away. Panditji has determined Aashaadh sudi dashmi—the day Raamji had chosen for your wedding

last year—as auspicious for Rukmini's departure. If you are able to, send a gold ring from Kalkatta. I have made enquiries, and gold has declined to twenty-four rupees in Kalkatta—some even quote twenty-three rupees, fifteen anna and a paisa for a tola, a rate I have not seen in fifteen years. Do not spend too much: a one-tola ring will be sufficient. You will find many men in Lalgodam leaving for Shekhavati in a week or two, before the chaumasa begins. Send the earrings with them ...'

Hari could read no more. He understood what the letter left unsaid—his sister Draupadi had not survived the fever that had attacked her a few days before his wedding. His father would not make the mistake of communicating such inauspicious news in a letter. Instead, he had named everyone but Draupadi, letting Hari divine the rest.

He wished he had never come to Disavar, and never believed those stories they had told him about Seth Daulatram. But for the Chhappaniya, he would be sitting in the shop with his father, weighing mounds of bajra and moth, gwar, cucumber and melons, bantering with customers, speaking of trips to temples in Sikar and Jhunjhunu. Why did anyone in Rampura have to step out of Shekhavati at all? 'There is much to buy and sell,' Hemrajji had said, 'and a hundred ways for a good bania to make money. Once a boy has learned the ways of Disavar, he starts out on his own.' Yes, but not a boy sent out before his time!

He could simply pack his trunk and return to Rampura. He would have to borrow money for the gold ring—Khemchandji would perhaps extend a loan. He would have to ask for more than twenty-four rupees: his father had not accounted for the cost of workmanship—two-and-a-half annas in a rupee. Excited, he stood up, then sat down immediately when reminded of the train fare. What would his father say about the waste? Ten rupees to go from Delhi to Calcutta, another ten to return, with nothing to show for the expense but a gold ring and a debt of thirty-five rupees! In any case, he could not return empty-handed. When someone—even a boy—returned from Disavar, he was expected to arrive with gifts for everyone, with stories of Kalkatta, English sahibs, trains, tongas and bales of jute. What stories would he tell?

Forlorn, he walked down Cotton Street, entered number 67 and took the staircase directly to the second floor, avoiding the crowded courtyard where a meeting appeared to be in session. As he had done hundreds of times, he slipped off his chappals, placed his bills respectfully before the munim at the cash box, and sat down cross-legged in a corner of the mattress to await his turn, knowing he would not be noticed until closing time three hours later, yet had to remain seated to be noticed at all. Had he arrived at closing time, they would have asked him to come the next day. Everyone wanted to avoid the ill omen of a creditor early in the afternoon, when three hours of business remained, yet no one wanted to see him at the end of the day. I am the agent of ill-luck, he told himself as he drifted into a waking slumber that he had mastered over a year of waiting in gaddis.

An hour later, his indiscretion with the tea returned to haunt him. He could not seek permission to go to the latrines. The munim would surely taunt, 'Have you come to collect money or piss in my building? Do they not have latrines in Lalgodam?' So he ignored the urge until he could bear it no longer. Gently, hoping the munim would not notice, he slid off the mattress, slipped on his chappals and walked out into the balcony. There seemed to be no latrine on the floor. He went upstairs; that floor, too, seemed to have nothing but offices. He climbed to the roof, thinking they might have built a latrine there. A thick pillar stood in the middle, supporting nothing, apparently part of an abandoned plan to add another floor to the building. Dark clouds hung overhead; a drizzle appeared imminent. Someone had thrown maize and bajra grains all over the roof. Hundreds of pigeons flapped about, feeding busily, trying to climb each other to get closer to the grain. Beyond the birds, a channel of concrete had been laid in the floor to collect rain water and direct it into a pipe that descended to the courtyard below. A boy slightly older than Hari was squatting on the channel, his dhoti pulled above his knees, urinating.

So they never built a proper latrine in this building, thought Hari.

He walked to the other end of the channel and squatted, taking care not to expose himself to the other boy, and began to urinate. The boy sprang to his feet, ran to Hari, pulled him up by the shoulders and dragged him behind the pillar. A storm of pigeons blinded them. Hari was terrified. Was this not a urinal? Had he not seen the boy squatting there? Before he could utter a word, however, the boy clapped a hand over his mouth and pointed to the stairwell.

Two men in turbans came up to the rooftop in great agitation. After looking anxiously at the sky, they bent over the concrete channel to study the stream of urine as it flowed and emptied into the drain. When the first drops spilled out of the pipe at the bottom, a cry went up in the courtyard below.

'Khaya! Khaya!'

The men on the rooftop frowned, scoured the sky again, held out their hands to catch imaginary raindrops and looked down at the channel in consternation, where the flow had now reduced to a trickle. They argued for a few minutes, then went downstairs. The boy released Hari and chuckled. 'How much did you wager?'

Hari did not understand. 'What is khaya?'

'Three for me,' said the boy. 'At seven to two.'

'What do you deal in?' asked Hari.

'What do *you* deal in?' the boy responded.

'I am a clerk with Daulatram Gulabchand in Amherst Row.'

'You look too young to be a clerk,' the boy said, though he himself was not much older.

'I started a year ago.'

'What are you doing on the rooftop? There are no gaddis here.'

'I drank too much tea ...' Hari said weakly.

The boy laughed. 'What is your name?'

'Harilal Tibrewal, son of Shri Duli Chand Tibrewal of Rampura in Shekhavati.'

The boy appeared surprised. 'Are you the son-in-law of Narayan Dasji Nangaliya of Chirawa?'

Hari nodded. The boy turned to face him, folded his hands and bowed. 'I would have touched your feet if you were older, but this will have to do.'

'Who are you?' Hari asked.

'Janardhan Kedia, son of Shri Sawarmal Kedia of Chirawa. I consider Narayan Dasji's daughters my sisters, so his son-in-law is my jija. Consider me your saalaa, jijaji.'

Hari was relieved: a boy from his wife's side of the family certainly had lower status—there was no reason to be intimidated by him. 'You have not told me what you deal in,' he said boldly.

Janardhan pointed to the sky. 'Rain.'

'That is not yours to sell.'

'Everything made by Raamji can be bought and sold if a bania knows how to price it,' Pointing to the concrete channel, Janardhan continued, 'This drains into a metal pipe, which flows straight down into rain-gauges on the ground floor.'

'I saw no gauges when I came up.'

'They are hidden in a double-ceiling to the left of the courtyard. Look down there, but keep your head out of sight.'

Hari peered over the steel rail into the courtyard. It was bustling with men, all shouting at the same time, right hands held up in the air, fingers dancing to flash secret signals to hidden partners.

'Those are all khayivals,' Janardhan said. 'They had bet that it wouldn't rain today, and have lost a lot of money because the odds of rain were only two to seven.'

'But it did not rain.'

Janardhan shrugged and looked at the channel, where the trickle of urine had disappeared. 'It did, at least three millimetres according to the Calcutta-mori rain-gauge that sits under this pipe. It would have been more had you been quicker to piss, or if I had remembered to drink tea this morning.'

'Is there a latrine here?' Hari asked, suddenly reminded of the pain in his bladder.

Janardhan laughed. 'Your piss is worthless now. Why give it away for nothing? Betting resumes tomorrow morning.'

He led Hari down to the ground floor where they found a latrine. After he had relieved himself, they went out to the courtyard. The cries of 'Khaya!' had died down and everyone was busy settling accounts. In the general melee, Janardhan approached a man, collected three silver rupees and slipped them into his pocket. Hari stared at the coins. Three rupees—eleven months of savings!

'This is your money too,' Janardhan said playfully as they walked out into Cotton Street. 'I did not invest in a glass of tea today. It was your bladder that took the gauge beyond two millimetres. Do you see now? Like rain, urine was made by Raamji, so it can be sold.'

'I want to deal in rain too,' Hari said eagerly.

'You are my jija. I cannot refuse you anything—my sister's happiness depends on you.'

He took Hari to a stall in Harrison Road, where they ordered pineapple juice. The shopkeeper handed them two glass tumblers filled to the brim.

'Give me steel!' Janardhan scolded.

'We do not have steel.'

'Brass will do,' he said grudgingly.

The shopkeeper brought out brass tumblers. Janardhan supervised the transfer to ensure there was no spillage, then upbraided him again. 'Fill them to the top.'

'These are larger than the glass tumblers.'

'I paid for two full tumblers, glass or brass.'

Disavar is a comfortable place after all, thought Hari as he drank the juice, if you know what to deal in, and how to deal with shopkeepers.

'Who brought you to Kalkatta?' Janardhan asked.

'Hemraj Biyani, son of Khemchandji Biyani.'

'I know him,' said Janardhan.

'He earns seventy-five rupees in a month,' said Hari impressively.

'He is a mere clerk, a gumashta, a man who fills out bills and quotes rates. Thirty a month, perhaps forty, unless Daulatram Gulabchand have forgotten how to do business. A beggar in Harrison Road earns half as much if he works hard. This is Kalkatta.' Janardhan pointed across the road, at shops stacked with bottles and cases marked with English labels. 'Limburger cheese, Dublin ginger ale, California Bartlett pears. You could easily spend forty rupees in that shop. And those are Harrison Road prices. The shops in Chowringhee charge twice as much. English sahibs who live there send their servants to Bara Bazar. "Go to Harrison Road," they say, "and we will pay half an anna for your tram fare." They know the servant will steal—indeed they call it a "squeeze"—and that the shopkeepers in Harrison Road are in league with servants to charge more when a sahib is buying, but they still save over buying in Chowringhee.'

Hari regarded Janardhan with wonder. What kind of a boy was this? He had just pocketed three silver rupees, thought nothing of Hemrajji, scolded Bengali shopkeepers, could read labels in English, and knew the ways of sahibs as if they were his neighbours. Would he now disparage Khemchand Biyani himself?

Janardhan had read Hari's mind. 'I speak to sahibs every week, sometimes every day.'

'Who taught you so much English?'

'No one; there was no need to. Sahibs are banias, not Bengali zamindars. They do not want to discuss the Ramayan with you. They want you to quote jute rates in English, read labels on boxes, and say "please", "thank you" and "Merry Christmas". A good Shekhavati bania can memorize that in a day.'

Hari was too awestruck to ask what kind of work this boy did that required him to speak to sahibs every day. The juice finished and they parted for the day.

'Come to 67 Cotton Street tomorrow morning,' said Janardhan.

Hari did not respond, his mind alive to wild possibilities in the company of this boy but also anxious about where they may lead.

That evening, Khemchand Biyani noticed that Harilal had not done his rounds for the day. Indeed, he had forgotten his bills with a trader in Cotton Street. 'I will disregard your first mistake,' he warned, 'but one cannot afford to be careless with paper.'

'Is there a jeweller who will make me a gold ring for two-anna to the rupee?' Hari asked.

Khemchand Biyani was taken aback by the directness of the question. 'Your father sent you in my care,' he said coldly. 'I see no need for you to buy a ring.'

'They are for my Rukmini Bai's muklava. It is time for her to go to her father-in-law's house. My father suggested a one-tola ring.'

Khemchandji appeared chastened. 'This is a good time to buy gold. It has fallen below twenty-four rupees. I will send you to a good jeweller who will not charge much for workmanship, but a one-tola ring will cost at least twenty-five rupees.'

'All right.'

Khemchandji waited for Hari to say more, then asked. 'Do you *have* twenty-five rupees?'

'I have saved,' he lied.

'That is a large amount for a boy of twelve to save.'

'I am thirteen; the fourteenth is upon me.'

'You have been here less than a year.'

'I have been frugal.'

'Where do you bank your savings? Did your father not tell you to maintain an account in the office?' Hari knew he had been caught. Not one to press an advantage, Khemchandji said, 'I could lend the money against your account.'

Hari shook his head. 'I already have eight rupees, to be given as advance to the jeweller tomorrow.'

'All right,' said Khemchandji, convinced the boy was up to no good but loath to spend time on an affair of little importance to the firm. 'The cashier will give you the jeweller's name and address.'

The next morning, Hari laid his first bet on rain. It was drizzling. He followed Janardhan into the courtyard at 67 Cotton Street, pushed through groups of khayivals arguing excitedly, and approached a man standing casually in a corner, murmuring 'Khayega? Khayega?' Indeed, Hari had seen him the previous day, but taken him to be a fruit-seller because he carried a basket of apples.

'Khaya,' Janardhan whispered, and handed him a rupee.

'How can you place a bet when it is already raining?' Hari asked.

'He is not taking morning bets,' said Janardhan. 'These will be settled by the afternoon.'

The man flashed a signal to Janardhan, who then led Hari to an unmarked, inconspicuous door that opened into a small room. Men were huddled together, watching a line of glass tubes standing in the centre of the room, each positioned under a pipe that emerged from the ceiling.

'These are lagayivals,' Janardhan whispered to Hari. 'They bet that it will rain this morning. Once the gauges show more than three millimetres, they make a 35 per cent profit on their capital. And if the level rises beyond six ...'

'We should have bet early in the morning.'

Janardhan shook his head. 'I have not won a morning bet since I stepped on broken glass when entering number 67 at dawn.'

'Was your one rupee for or against rain in the afternoon?'

'Only novices bet for or against—Bengalis, Biharis, banias recently arrived from Shekhavati. I once saw an English sahib here, who seemed quite confident it would not rain because it was April, as if Indra Bhagwan could read the English calendar. I am neither a lagayival nor a khayival—I deal in derivatives. As for you, do you think it will rain this afternoon?'

'Of course,' Hari replied. 'It is already raining.'

'But will it rain in the *afternoon*?'

'Yes.'

'Then you are a lagayival. Let us go to the fruit-seller outside. How much do you want to bet?'

'What are the odds for rain?'

'One One.'

Hari untied the handkerchief at his waist and placed three silver rupees and six one-anna coins on Janardhan's palm. 'Lend me ten annas,' he said. 'That will make it four rupees. I will return your ten annas next month at eight-anna-saikada interest.'

Janardhan frowned. 'Where did this money come from?'

'It is mine. I saved it.'

Janardhan picked three one-anna coins and returned the rest. 'Tuck these back into your waist.'

'But I need eight rupees. At odds of one one, I need to bet four.'

'Three annas,' Janardhan said firmly.

'The fruit-seller will laugh at me.'

'You are a bania, not a gambler. You need to please no one but Indra Bhagwan.'

A trickle had appeared at the mouth of one of the pipes. The lagayivals watched it anxiously, counting each drop as it splashed into the gauge below. When the eleventh drop had fallen, they cried in relief and rushed out of the room to flash signals to their associates, who immediately sought out the fruit-seller to settle their bets.

At noon, it stopped raining and the sky cleared. For five hours, Hari sat on the rooftop of 67 Cotton Street, watching the sky with a sinking heart. Afternoon was as sunny and clear as morning had been wet and overcast, almost as if Indra Bhagwan had shut a tap. Not a single cloud was to be seen anywhere. Hari fretted, reminded of the hours spent looking upward during the Chhappaniya. He should have been a natural khayival. How could a boy from Shekhavati—where sandstorms blew daily in his face—be so foolish as to bet that it would rain? His anxiety gave way to irritation and anger as the notion took hold in his mind that, somehow, someone had sabotaged the weather—Janardhan, or Khemchandji, or English sahibs. Did sahibs have the power to prevent rain?

At six, bets were settled. Hari stood quietly in a corner of the courtyard, head hung low. Janardhan put an arm around his shoulder. 'Three annas is not a large amount,' he said reassuringly. 'You will soon learn how to work with Indra Bhagwan. Believe me, he can be manipulated far more easily than some sahibs. He takes bribes, for one.'

Hari did not respond.

'You said you needed eight rupees,' Janardhan continued. 'Why?'

'It is time for Rukmini Bai, my sister, to go to her father-in-law's house. She is almost sixteen.'

'I will lend you the money, at the usual rate: eight-anna-saikada.'

Hari calculated: eight-annas to a hundred rupees, per month, was 6 per cent per annum as simple interest. Compounded monthly, it would be slightly higher. Daulatram Gulabchand charged traders in Cotton Street twice that rate for debts owed to the firm. Perhaps Janardhan's was being generous because of their family ties, but Hari shook his head anyway. 'I know there is no harm in taking money from my saalaa, or from anyone else in Chirawa. But it may only be accepted during the wedding, Holi or Diwali, or when the bride comes to her father-in-law's house. My father would not approve of this.'

'He will never know.'

'He will ask where I got the money.'

Janardhan shrugged. As they left the courtyard, he said 'You must not tell the munims in your office about what goes on at number 67.'

'Don't they all do it?'

'Everyone does it, but no one talks about it.'

The next day, Khemchand Biyani advanced Hari a loan of five rupees, to which he added his three rupees before depositing them with the jeweller as the first instalment for a one-tola gold ring.

Hari soon learned that Janardhan Kedia, who looked only slightly older than him, was almost seventeen. Short and thin, he was darker than Hari, and his spine was bent into a curve, which gave the impression that he was bowing in supplication even when he was shooing off a beggar. He had arrived in Calcutta three years ago with an uncle, hoping to set up a shop selling woollen clothes, which he planned to buy in Punjab once a month. He had not reckoned that Calcutta's warm weather could not support a thriving woollen goods market. Having lost some money, he began to arrange deals for bales of jute, eventually finding employment as the assistant to an under-broker in Andrew Yule & Company. He spent much of his time trudging up and down the jute warehouses on Chitpur Road, inspecting bales and striking deals for Andrew Yule, which shipped large quantities of jute: bales to Dundee, hessian and gunny to London. At other times, he tried to place cotton piece-goods produced by Andrew Yule's Bengal Cotton Mills with firms like Daulatram Gulabchand, which then sold them upcountry in cities like Kanpur and Delhi. None of this frenetic activity left a mark on his appearance. His hair was always well-oiled, his dhoti pleated, and his kurta pressed with its sleeves puffed.

For three years Janardhan had walked all over Ward 7, eaten at every stall in Bara Bazar and picked up much Hindi, some Bengali and a little English. He knew how to speak to beggars, shopkeepers, clerks, munims, tongawalas, Bengali bhadralok and English sahibs. He was on familiar terms with munims in dozens of gaddis, knew Bengali officers all over Ward 7, and boasted of a friendship with David Yule Sahib of Andrew Yule—this last was shared with Hari on the condition that it be kept confidential, for reasons Hari was not to know. Apparently, Janardhan was also well-known in 67 Cotton Street, where he had either earned or lost much money—so Hari judged from the reaction his name evoked. Meanwhile, his wife had come to live with his family in Chirawa, and he was eager to return to Shekhavati as soon as his stated goal—the accumulation of five hundred rupees—had been achieved.

'But you earn that much in a few weeks,' Hari said.

Janardhan sighed. 'Indra Bhagwan gives but He also takes. I will share a secret with you, and you must not ask how I know.' Pointing upward, he said, 'When you can afford to bet eight annas, he wants you to bet four.'

At first, Hari allowed Janardhan to lay his bets for him, restricting himself to a few annas, and winning or losing small amounts. He discovered that most betters relied on a rangbaaj—an expert at predicting rain—before they risked their money. With Janardhan as a reference, a rangbaaj agreed to give him tips in return for 25 per cent of the winnings. It was not long before Hari was almost a rangbaaj himself. That summer, it rained almost every day; therefore, men at 67 Cotton Street tended to be lagayivals, and most bets were either naali—betting that the drain would run—or khaal—betting that it would rain even more than that. Every morning, after an early lunch at the basa in Lalgodam, Hari idled on the rooftop, staring endlessly at the sky, trying to wring secrets from cloud patterns and separate naali from khaal in the humidity or the rain from previous days, until he thought he could penetrate the mind of Indra himself. There were days when he felt he could squeeze drops from the sky if he concentrated hard enough, or hold back its moisture through force of will. A bania knew a thing or two about rain, he told himself, especially one who had seen the Chhappaniya.

After he had presented his bills in gaddis near Cotton Street, he would run to number 67 to earn a rupee, then return to the gaddi to collect for Daulatram Gulabchand. He lost as often as he won, but the amounts he won were larger, and he watched his hoard build up. He did not share his secret with Khemchand Biyani, Hemraj, or anyone else at Lalgodam, assured that they were all part of the great game of Indra, in betting courts other than 67 Cotton Street where no one recognized them, and that a mention of the act would destroy its viability. It was comforting to know that no written record existed—all bets were placed verbally, all messages sent by hand-gestures.

He sensed disapproval in Janardhan's eyes when he bet large amounts, but he needed to pay the jeweller—the ring had been delivered and sent to Shekhavati, and the second instalment was due in a month. Should any money be left over after paying the second instalment, he told himself, he would look into renting a small platform in Cotton Street to start something—perhaps a hosiery business as Daulatramji had done …

Summer passed.

In October, he received a postcard from his father, their first communication in four months.

> '…Indra's heart has melted. This year has been as kind as the last was cruel. Early in the month of Saavan the sky shed its tears over Shekhavati. It rained so much that the dam overflowed. The bullocks and camels in Rampura are all dead—taken by last year's Chhappaniya—but men harnessed their own bodies to the plough and walked the furrows. And what a crop they have raised! Stalks of bajra are eleven feet high. There are rows of moth, moong, cucumber and melons, some even in places where no plough turned the earth, as if Mother Earth has provided out of the goodness of her heart. People eat the grain raw, right off the stalks, too impatient to cook or even thresh it. It flows down their gullets roughly and there are many stomach-aches in Rampura. But how sweet those aches are! The shop has overflowed with mounds of bajra and I have had to transfer stocks home, where a pile now sits in every corner. Its smell is everywhere. Even so, it has become difficult to turn a profit. When bajra was six rupees to a munn, there were no buyers. Now, a man can buy enough to eat three times a day, but I get no more than two rupees for a munn. Much of it will rot. Narayan Dasji Nangaliya sent a message asking when you would return from Disavar. Come back soon, but only if Khemchandji gives permission …'

Hari read the letter while sitting in the basa at Lalgodam. Slipping it into his kurta pocket, he looked at the sky—clear today—and thanked Raamji and Indra from the bottom of his heart, asking these two to include in his gratitude the names of gods he did not know. What a wonderful city this was, where a man could make money off Indra himself! And who knew, it may have been his tampering with the rain that had resulted in a lush crop in far-away Shekhavati! If a man could tame Indra, he could perhaps turn Shekhavati into Bengal ... There would be no need for a boy to leave home and go east to earn a few rupees.

That afternoon, 67 Cotton Street was deserted. Panicking, Hari located Janardhan in a Hanuman temple, sitting cross-legged, rocking to and fro while reciting Hanuman Chalisa. Seven flowers lay before him—five to the left and two to the right. Every time he finished the forty couplets he moved a flower, left to right, and began again. Hari waited a full hour for Janardhan to finish, then gave him the shocking news about number 67.

'Rain gambling ends with the rains,' Janardhan said. 'It will resume next June. That is why I am here: I close every season with seven recitations of Hanuman Chalisa.'

'What will I do all winter? I have been spending too much on tea and pineapple juice. And the kitchen adds ghee to my roti every day. How will I pay for all that?'

'Expenses must fall with a falling income, but never rise with it,' Janardhan declared.

'What do *you* do in winter?'

'I am Johnny K, protected by Andrew Yule & Company, which is protected by the Queen of England.'

Hari was horrified. 'You work for a sahib?'

'Why not? The banyan at Kinsell & Ghose is a Marwari, as are the banyans for half the European firms in Kalkatta.'

'What is a banyan?'

'Every English firm has one. The sahibs need someone who understands the market, who can guarantee the credit of buyers, and who can arrange for sellers with good rates. Who better than a bania from Shekhavati to become their banyan?'

'My father said sahibs do not wash before they eat.'

Janardhan laughed. 'How many sahibs has your father seen in Rampura? They are banias by blood. Would you like to meet one?'

'No sahib will agree to meet me.'

'Come to me tomorrow morning, jijaji. What will Narayan Dasji think if someone tells him I turned his son-in-law away?'

The next day, Janardhan conducted Hari to the imposing buildings on Canning Street and Clive Row, where they walked into a white mansion.

'Shouldn't we find a door in the back?' Hari asked anxiously.

When they began to cross the lobby, three sahibs passed them. Hari had never seen three together. He held his breath but they passed without incident. He wished Janardhan would walk softly—the sound of his footsteps seemed to reverberate all over the building, announcing their presence. Was that prudent in a place like this?

Janardhan strode confidently to a door of frosted glass and ran his hands over the golden letters in its centre. 'Senior director,' he whispered, before pushing it open.

A Bengali clerk rose quickly from his desk and came forward to block their path. Janardhan got into an argument with him—in Bengali. Hari understood very little. Eventually, the man pointed to a bench and went back to his desk.

They sat and waited.

'In Ralli Brothers and Hoare Miller, Marwaris have to enter through a door in the back,' said Janardhan. 'In Graham & Company, sahibs complain about the stench. They have their own staircase which no one else may use. But this is Yule Sahib's office. See this sign on the back of the bench. "Europeans Only". Yet you sit comfortably, and no one will say anything.'

Hari was, in fact, not comfortable. It was hot and humid. His kurta, crisp when he left Lalgodam, was now drenched with sweat. 'Where is the sahib?'

Janardhan pointed to a double-door behind the Bengali clerk.

'What are we waiting for then? Is the sahib in the middle of a puja?'

Janardhan smiled. 'Yes. His pujas turn a good profit, because his gods are more generous.'

Remembering the two traders he had met on the train, Hari said, 'I know two men in this company. We came together from Shekhavati. Should I mention them to the sahib?'

'There are thousands of clerks in Andrew Yule & Company. Do you think the senior director knows every one of them?'

'How does he know you, then?'

'Trust me, jijaji.'

Hari fretted. Janardhan had always been smug, even when losing large sums in 67 Cotton Street. If they were to be thrown out of this building, he would say, 'Indra Bhagwan calls, Indra Bhagwan dispatches.' And that would be that. He would make humiliation look like triumph. Why had Hari agreed to come to this office? His dhoti had now withered, and drops of sweat rolled down his legs.

Hours later, when the clerk rose to summon them, Hari thought they were being asked to leave. They passed through swinging double-doors—Janardhan first, followed by Hari, who was almost hit by the return swing—and Hari found himself within six feet of Yule Sahib. The room was pleasantly cool. In one corner, a machine mounted on a post whirred continuously, its blades blowing the sweetest breeze Hari had felt on his cheek. There was no punkah-puller to be seen anywhere.

He had not been prepared for such a small office—it offered no space in which he could hide. Because the sahib did not look up, Hari gradually found the courage to study him. He was darker than expected, with brown hair and a thick moustache. The breeze from the machine did not seem to ruffle his hair, which was well-combed.

They stood patiently. Finally, the sahib put down his pen and looked up. Hari saw strange blue eyes. The sahib spoke. 'Johnny.'

'Good morning, sir,' Janardhan said, and nudged Hari.

Hari repeated the words with difficulty. The sahib shook his head. 'He is too young, almost a child.'

'Brother-in-law,' said Janardhan. 'Family. Trust.'

The sahib's astonishing blue eyes now rested on Hari, who wondered if they would pierce his heart. 'Have you worked with jute?'

Hari turned to Janardhan in panic.

'Teacher, sir,' said Janardhan, pointing to himself.

'What's your name?'

Hari froze—the sahib had addressed him directly.

'Hari,' said Janardhan.

The sahib placed both hands on his desk. *Impossibly pink nails*, thought Hari.

'Harry and Johnny. All right. We'll see.'

'Congratulations, sir,' said Janardhan. The sahib frowned. 'On your wedding, sir. In Bara Bazar we did a puja.'

'Why, thank you, Johnny.'

'We will hear of a son, sir, no?'

Yule Sahib laughed. 'I must tell you, Johnny, that my wife does not think much of Calcutta. I might just have to pack up and go home.'

'Johnny will become orphan, sir.'

'You will do all right.' The sahib pointed to Hari. 'Does he have your nose for jute?'

'Brother-in-law, sir. Same town, same nose.'

As soon as they had left the building, Hari turned on Janardhan. 'Why did you make me go through that? It is clear the sahib does not like me.'

'You will not be marrying his sister. Get him good rates on jute and he will reward you.'

'Why will the sahib deal with me when he has his own banyan, whose task it is to get him good rates?'

'Of course he has his banyan: a rich Marwari who earns thousands of rupees in a month. And he has a Chota Sahib under him. And a hundred under-brokers and clerks to bring him rates from all over Calcutta. But he does not trust them. Did your Masterji not teach you about Raja Bhoj? That king had a thousand spies to tell him what his people thought of him, yet he slipped out of his palace every night to walk the streets disguised as a beggar. Now, a sahib cannot do what Raja Bhoj did—he cannot look like a Bengali or a Marwari, so what does he do? He finds himself a boy who can tell sada-jute from tosa-jute merely from the smell, whom he can trust, and who speaks some English.'

'So you are a jasus! A spy for the sahib?'

'The name does not matter, the commissions do.'

'What if Yule Sahib's banyan finds out? Does he not lose commissions on sales arranged by you?'

'Perhaps he already knows. His commissions run into thousands; he cannot afford to throw a sulk over small amounts. Remember: Yule Sahib is neither his jija nor his saalaa, and he did not come from Vilayat to visit the Kalighat temple—if you give him better rates than his own banyan, he will buy from you. Just as you are a bania to Bengalis, a sahib is a bania to you.'

'My father said I was not to speak to sahibs.'

'You need never speak to him again. He has seen you, and he knows you are my brother-in-law. Yes, he does not wash before he eats, nor after; he does not eat with his right hand, nor clean his buttocks with the left. And he has married his own sister: a cousin, he will say, but there is no difference between your sister and your uncle's daughter. But remember, this is no ordinary sahib. For years he lived in the Bengal Cotton Mills compound, talking to Bengalis and Biharis, sometimes working with them as no sahib would. That is where I met him. Now he is married, and his memsahib has forced him to buy a house in Garden Reach, but he still likes to keep his ear to the ground. You would not guess from the way he speaks to you that he is the richest sahib in Calcutta, richer than Lord Curzon. Did you see that electric fan in his office? It runs without a punkah-puller. Do you know how much it costs? Eighteen rupees every month—for the fan and the electricity—until it goes back to the company. I know; I am the one who went to Kilburn & Company to pick it up. The sahib keeps it running day and night, even when he is not in the room, so he need not turn it on when he enters his office. Who would not be a jasus for such a sahib?'

They had reached Cotton Street. Hari remembered the bills he was to pick up in a gaddi. 'I must go now. When do I start work for the sahib?'

'You work for me, not the sahib. On Tuesday, we will go to the Hanuman temple and seal our agreement in front of Hanumanji. You will then speak to Khemchandji. Arrange for a small shipment of jute bales from Daulatram Gulabchand—pakka 400-pound bales, because Andrew Yule will not accept kachcha bales.'

'But Khemchandji already sells to Hoare Miller.'

'Yes, but you will give him higher rates.'

'How?'

'You will tell him that the sahib gives you higher rates.'

'Why will the sahib do that?'

'He won't. Indeed he will expect to pay less than his banyan pays for similar purchases, and he will want good tosa-jute in return. You will collect his money and add to it—not much, just half-an-anna for a rupee—to make the rate look better.'

'So I will give my own money to Khemchandji?'

'Use the commission that Khemchandji will give you.'

'So I will work for nothing. What will I live on?'

'A boy of thirteen can live on very little. Or should.'

'I came to Kalkatta to earn money ...'

'So did Nathuram Saraf, sixty years ago. The Bara Sahib of Kinsell & Ghose found him asleep in his warehouse. "What do you know about cotton?" he asked. "Everything," replied Nathuram, who was merely a cook for Ramdutt Goenka, the head munim at the firm of Sevaram Ramrikhdas. "Find me buyers for that roll of Manchester," said the Bara Sahib. Nathuram looked at the roll—it meant nothing to him—and quoted a price that was far higher than the market could support. Mr Kinsell burst out laughing. "If you can fetch me that rate," he said, "you get to be my banyan." Two days later, Mr Kinsell's whole stock had been sold at the quoted rate, the banyan of Kinsell & Ghose had been removed from his post and Nathuram appointed in his place. Everyone knows the rest—how he became banyan to Hoare Miller, brought his relatives from Mandawa, set up basas for them, built mansions in Shekhavati…'

Hari sighed. 'That will take years. I must eat today, and tomorrow.'

'Have you saved nothing from 67 Cotton Street? Borrow the rest. I will lend you a little at anna-saikada interest. Slowly, you will find ways to increase your take. Tosa-jute does not degrade noticeably if you mix a little sada-jute with it. The sahib will not mind a slight increase in rates after he has bought from you for a few months, and Khemchandji will not begrudge you a slight decrease. Ask any Marwari how he earned his first thousand rupees. He will tell you: a pie here and a pie there.'

Hari laughed. 'What about the next thousand?'

'Once you have a thousand, doubling it takes half the time. But remember, you must not mention in Lalgodam that the sahib gives you a commission, or Khemchand will withhold what he gives you.'

'How much will the sahib give?'

'Not much. A sahib, too, has to sell his jute. I get 50 per cent of what he gives you.'

'Why you?'

'You work for me, not the sahib. You are my jija or the rate would have been higher.'

Suddenly alert, Hari sought to press his case. He knew he need not back down, considering Janardhan represented his wife's family. 'Fifty is too high. My wife will expect gifts when I return to Shekhavati.'

'All right, twenty-five. My sister's happiness depends on you.'

On Tuesday, after they had been to the temple and Hari had sworn an oath before the pandit, Janardhan took him to Chitpur Road, where they walked amidst bales of jute stacked in dark, damp godowns. Janardhan pointed here and there—sada-jute, its cheap fibres weak and dazed and full of knots, tosa-jute with strong and continuous strands, hydraulic presses that tied the strands into 400-pound bales. Hari watched in wonder. 'Where does it go?'

'It used to go to Dundee.' Hari had heard the name before. 'Some still does. Andrew Yule sells at least three lakh bales every year. Most now goes to mills outside Calcutta.'

'I have seen those mills.'

The sun had set when they returned from Chitpur Road and turned into Amherst Row.

When they parted outside Lalgodam, Janardhan said, 'You cannot be a clerk forever. This winter, you will place jute for Daulatram Gulabchand. The next summer, you will double your winter earnings by placing the goods of Indra Bhagwan. To earn anything in this great Kalkatta, you must stay at least another year.'

Hari stayed another four years. His arrangement with Yule Sahib soon expanded into agreements with other sahibs, to whom he began to supply bales from firms other than Daulatram Gulabchand. Every winter, he rose early to go to Chitpur Road and inspect bales that had arrived from the east and were being unloaded from bullock carts. He ran the fibres between his fingers, smelled them, gauged their dampness and strength. Then, with an account of available stock inside his head, he walked the lanes of Bara Bazar, promising a hundred bales here and a hundred there, giving discounts, making verbal agreements, watching his credit accumulate. A small profit here and there—he relied on volume, not margin—built itself into a respectable account with Daulatram Gulabchand, where he collected a 12 per cent per annum interest on his deposits.

By February, jute shipments would dry up as new planting began in the east. With nothing to do, he would loiter about gaddis in Armenian Street or look for a chance to meet a sahib in Clive Row. He would learn Bengali by arguing with shopkeepers. As soon as the rains began, he would be ready with his capital. The morning trips to Chitpur Road would be replaced by hours spent on rooftops, watching the sky, and afternoons spent in the courtyard of 67 Cotton Street, placing Indra's goods, trying to double the money he had set aside during winter.

Even as he laid bets on the rain, he was aware that far in the east, in Mymensingh and Faridpur and Tippera, the new jute crop was ready. Now it was being cut, now being retted, now being thrashed in the water to shake its fibres loose. Now the fibres had been tied together and loaded on a boat, now the boat had found its way, through the Jamuna and the Padma and the hundreds of rivers that drew water from them, to a bania somewhere in Jessore, who was now pressing it into 300-pound bales using an old manual press. And now the bales were on their way to Calcutta in a train, where they would be offloaded in a damp warehouse in Chitpur Road. Then it would be time, again, to turn away from Indra and toward the golden fibre.

He never mentioned 67 Cotton Street to anyone in Lalgodam, and found other haunts where they took bets on rain. He won and lost large amounts. On some days, Hari was a rangbaaj and Janardhan the lagayival. On others, their roles were reversed. He rarely bought anything, getting by on the kurtas and dhotis he had brought from Shekhavati.

He was now seventeen—fluent in Bengali, comfortable in Bara Bazar, on intimate terms with shopkeepers in Cotton Street, known to other jute under-brokers, and on good terms with jute traders who had memberships in the Jute Balers' Association.

In early 1904, Khemchandji summoned him to his gaddi. Hari rarely saw the old man these days—he returned to Lalgodam late every evening, just in time to eat at the basa and go to sleep in his corner of the mattress. He had barely spoken to Hemraj in the last two years.

'You have grown taller,' Khemchandji remarked.

'It is the Shekhavati grain.'

'Do not be flippant with me,' Khemchandji said sharply.

Hari was taken aback.

'I have decided to increase your rates in the basa by 50 per cent. And you will be asked to pay rent every month—the munim will deduct it from your account in Lalgodam. You will be charged what we charge clerks in other firms who choose to live in Lalgodam.'

'But I work for you, Khemchandji.'

'And for others.'

Hari was embarrassed. Khemchandji perhaps knew all about his jute sales for other firms. Did he also know about 67 Cotton Street?

'Your father sent you in my care. Do not do anything that will bring shame on my head.' Hari did not know what to say. Fortunately, Khemchandji had other pressing matters at hand. 'Before you leave Lalgodam today, speak to the munim about your basa rates.'

As he walked out, Khemchandji called again. 'There is news from Rampura. Your mother is ill.'

Hari clutched the iron railing and looked down into the courtyard. He had completely forgotten home in the last few years. Neither he nor his father had written until he had begun to believe, almost superstitiously, that he must not be the first to break the silence. As the years passed, the number of events to be recounted had multiplied until it had become impossible to imagine a postcard—Master Bholaram would not countenance a letter in an envelope—that could convey all he had to say. And now there was this. Khemchandji did not say what type of illness, and he was too afraid to ask.

He tried to imagine what the last five years had meant in Shekhavati. Rukmini was almost 20. She would certainly have had children by now. Why had no one told him? Jasoda would be 16, old enough to go to her husband's home, and would have lost some of her swagger. Muniya would be thirteen, certainly married and awaiting her father-in-law's summons in a couple of years... That was the matter with going east, as they always said in Shekhavati. It was so far that a boy who left for Disavar orphaned himself. He rushed out of Lalgodam, bought a postcard, and wrote:

'... Unless Raamji decides otherwise, I will arrive in Rampura before Holi. If you so wish, send a message to Narayan Dasji Nangaliya that Parmeshwari's muklava can be arranged before the chaumasa begins...'

Here he paused, embarrassed that he had named his bride, and that, too, in a letter to his father. The image of Master Bholaram reading this aloud disturbed him. His father sat on his cot in the double-ceiling, one foot resting on moist sand, while Master Bholaram squatted at the door, peering at the postcard through his spectacles. On reading the offending name, his voice would falter. He would cover his embarrassment by summoning a fit of coughing. His father would look away in consternation. In the inner room, listening from behind the curtain, her shawl pulled low over her head, his mother would gasp ... He should not have been so bold. Why mention the muklava? Would his mother not arrange for it in any case? The eighteenth was upon him and his bride was past sixteen. Was this not the obvious time to send for her? But now it was not proper to destroy a one-paisa postcard. Very well, he would post it and hope for the best. They would pass it around in Rampura, and no doubt speak of it in Chirawa. Hopefully, they would make some allowance for his stay in Disavar.

In the space that remained—here he rued his woefully large hand—he wrote:

'... If I have made mistakes, please forgive me as you would an immature son, on this Falgun sudi panchmi in the Vikram Samvat year of nineteen hundred and sixty one.'

Then he addressed the postcard to Master Bholaram and posted it.

The very next day, he spent 92 rupees and 4 annas to pack a steel trunk with gifts, and deposited 250 rupees, his whole capital, with Janardhan, to be invested in 67 Cotton Street, should the betting season begin before his return. His train was to leave Howrah Station late in the evening. He waited until Khemchandji had finished with his munims, then approached him with the news.

'Do you have any accounts to settle?'

'I had borrowed 9 rupees, 8 annas, 2 paise and 2 pies six years ago, for my train fare from Delhi to Kalkatta.'

The munims having dispersed, it was Khemchandji himself who opened the red binder with Hari's account. 'Are you ready to return it?'

Hari nodded.

'Your present account with the firm will cover that sum, at ten-anna-saikada interest.'

'I had also borrowed 3 rupees for my first Diwali in Kalkatta.'

'I see no entry for it,' said Khemchandji. 'Perhaps it was entered in your father's account in Rampura.'

'I would like it to be debited from my account in Lalgodam. You could ensure that it is credited in Rampura.'

'All right. That will leave no more than three paisa and a pie in your account.'

'That is fine,' said Hari, thinking of the 250 rupees in Janardhan's hands. It was just as well that he had not banked all his money in Lalgodam.

'Tell Hemraj to give you some letters for Master Bholaram,' said Khemchandji, before going back to his accounts.

That evening, Hari left Calcutta. He sat on the bench in the middle, as he had five years ago. Under his feet was a steel trunk, and in his lap a bundle of cloth, inside which were wrapped six wheat rotis, mango pickle and some fried flour balls from the basa in Lalgodam.

3

Arriving in Delhi, he found himself unequal to a long camel ride across the Shekhavati desert and hired a camel cart instead. They rode for a day and two nights, passing Loharu, crossing the river that took them into Shekhavati and making their way to Chirawa. Hari struggled to keep thoughts of Parmeshwari from his mind. The sixteenth was upon her. Would she have changed much? He hoped not, but he himself was not the boy who had married her. He was seeing the tibbas after a long time, and in those years Shekhavati had become quaint. He was amused when the cartman responded smugly, on being asked to speed up as they approached Chirawa, 'A camel can be rushed no more than the sun.'

The sahibs in Calcutta would have accepted the claim about the sun, he thought, but they knew that camels could be rushed. Indeed, they would have dispensed with camels and taken trains. Before his very eyes, he had seen horse-drawn trams give way to electric ones on Harrison Road. Of course he had never taken one, preferring to walk instead of wasting money on a ticket.

They passed Chirawa early in the morning. Hari slept through the day. The sun was setting when the cart descended into the riverbed between Nawalgarh and Rampura. He saw shadows dance on Daulatramji's haveli. Five years ago, the haveli had been a lesson in hubris. Now that he worked at Daulatramji's firm, he felt sympathetic toward the haveli, and disappointed that Daulatram had not lived to enjoy his triumph. It had decayed further, in accordance with its name—Daulatram's Grave.

As soon as the cart climbed up the opposite bank to enter Rampura, a group of children began to trail it. Hari did not recognize them—they would have been infants five years ago. Their clamour worried him—they would announce his arrival before he reached home, and before he had had time to ascertain if Parmeshwari had indeed come to live in Rampura. She could not, of course, be sent to her father-in-law's house in Hari's absence, but it was possible, even likely, that her father would have dispatched her for a day or two.

'Harilalji!' shouted a boy.

'Hari Bhaiya!' said another.

So they knew who he was. He replied irritably. 'Go away.'

'What have you brought us from Disavar?'

It was dark when the cart stopped outside his house. He climbed down, careful not to get his dhoti caught in the undercarriage, and approached the door. How should he enter? He could not very well run inside—he was no longer twelve. He was a trader from Disavar, a man who placed jute for Daulatram Gulabchand, an under-broker who collected commissions from David Yule, the richest sahib in Calcutta. In any case, his mother would frown on an unchecked rush into the house. Excessive enthusiasm was inappropriate no matter how joyous the occasion. He who flaunted his joy was inviting the gods—there were so many of them, and they were always jealous—to do him harm.

The door was open, as always. This he found to be another quaint custom in Rampura. The lowest fruit-seller in Cotton Street double-locked his box before going to sleep. He went down on his knees, placed a finger on the doorsill, ran it through his hair, and called, 'Babuji Raam Raam! Harilal from Kalkatta wishes to enter the house.'

He heard his father stir in the double-ceiling. Woken from his late-afternoon nap, Duli Chand appeared at the edge of his hideout, bare-headed and dishevelled. 'Chiranjeev Harilal. May you live long.'

After Hari had touched his father's feet, Duli Chand said in wonder, 'You grow taller by the day, Hariya. What kind of bajra do they eat in Disavar?'

'They give bajra to their cows.'

Duli Chand's gaze fell on the camel cart. 'Where did you hire him?'

'Delhi.'

'Couldn't you find someone to split the fare with you?'

'I came alone,' said Hari, adding quickly, 'but the fare was reasonable. I bargained with great diligence.'

As if to prove him wrong, the cartman refused to accept his money. They had agreed on the fare in Delhi, but he had not anticipated the length or difficulty of the journey, nor that Rampura was such a small village, which meant he would have to go to Sikar—out of his way—to have any hope of getting a return fare to Delhi. After the matter was settled—to no one's satisfaction—he helped bring Hari's trunk and bundle inside and rode away, grumbling. The children at the door were shooed away and Hari's mother led him to the hand-pump behind the house, where he washed his hands and feet, taking care not to waste water lest he earn a rebuke about his Disavar ways. He noted that she did not look ill, but was afraid to ask an inauspicious question immediately on arrival.

He was asked to face east. A piece of camphor was lit on a brass plate; a short aarti was sung. When his mother reached to paint a tilak on his forehead, she said, 'You are too tall and too thin, Hariya. The bajra they feed you in Disavar has gone to your legs. Good Shekhavati bajra goes into the belly.'

'Have you brought her to Rampura yet?' he asked, in a whisper so his father would not overhear.

His mother scattered grains of rice over his head. 'Whom?'

'Parmeshwari, of course.'

She frowned. 'It is not proper to name your bride, especially in your father's presence.'

'I asked you, not him.'

'Drink this,' she said, giving him a brass tumbler.

He took a sip and made a face. 'What is this?'

'Panchagavya.'

'What's in that?'

'Drink it, Hariya. You have been in Disavar with Musalmans and sahibs. I do not know who cooked your rotis and who touched your water. I have heard they buy milk in shops and drink water out of taps. This will cleanse you.'

'You have not answered. About the one I may not name.'

'Ask your father. You have become impertinent in Disavar.' Her puja finished, she said, 'You have not asked after your sisters.'

Ashamed, he first asked about Jasoda, who had sworn to turn her husband away when he came for her.

'She is safe, in her father-in-law's house in Sikar.'

'You sent her to her father-in-law without telling me?'

'Last year. She was past fifteen, Hariya. The sixteenth was upon her. Her in-laws were insistent.'

'Khemchandji said you were ill.'

'Must someone be ill for you to return? You are home. That is what matters.'

Ah, that had been a ruse to bring him home. He was annoyed. 'And how is Rukmini Bai in her father-in-law's house?'

'She has just given birth to a boy.'

'Why did no one send me a postcard? Would a quarter-anna have been a waste to let me know I am an uncle?'

'We knew you would be home before the postcard reached you.'

'What of Muniya?' he asked, his anger rising. 'No doubt you have married her off without consulting me.'

'The thirteenth is upon her. The Shastra says that a girl must be married off when she turns eight.'

'Well, you could not have sent her off to her husband. Where is she?'

'Behind you.'

He turned around. Muniya stood in the kitchen door. His anger melted away. He advanced toward her, meaning to lift her off her feet, then remembered that she was a married woman. 'You are still a little girl. What will your husband say when he first sees you?'

She giggled. She is not like Jasoda, he thought, who would have responded with a taunt of her own. It was true: marriage did not change a girl in the slightest degree. It was when she went to her father-in-law's house, years later, that she turned into a woman. No doubt Parmeshwari was the same girl he had seen in the silver glint of moonlight. This was reassuring—he felt warmly towards the girl but would not know what to do with the woman.

'Tell me,' he asked, 'what do they put into panchagavya?'

'I see you do not remember the date. Ma will not say it, fearing ill omens. Today is Falgun sudi dwaadashi.'

'So?'

'Holi is three days away.'

'Ah,' he said. He had been born three days before Holi. He had turned seventeen.

'That is why Ma gave you panchagavya.'

'And what goes into it?'

'Milk, curd, ghee, cowdung and cow urine.' She saw the disgust on his face. 'You have been in Disavar too long.'

He smiled. 'But I thought of you daily.'

'You thought of *her*, not me.'

Horrified, he put a finger to his lips. 'Do not say that aloud!' Indeed, he had not thought of her amidst his dealings with Johnny and Indra Bhagwan. She had barged into his mind only on the way back.

'What have you brought for her?'

'That is not a matter for children,' he said sternly, and walked toward his father's double-ceiling.

'I am not a child,' she said, following him.

He climbed the ladder into the double-ceiling. He had been allowed inside only once before: when his father had told him he was to go to Disavar. Now, on reaching the top rung, he realized he had not asked for permission, and that no one ever climbed in but his father and the servant, who laid a bed of cool sand every morning. Duli Chand sat on his cot, fanning himself with a corner of his dhoti, and seemed surprised. Muniya giggled. Duli Chand peered over the edge and scolded her. 'Bring him lemonade.'

She receded, still giggling. Duli Chand sighed. 'The girl does not behave like a married one. And I must send her away in a year or two.'

'She will come around when the time approaches,' Hari said.

'When she departs, all my daughters will be off my hands.'

Hari liked the conversation already. Here he was, speaking to his father about his sister's going-away to her husband, man to man. Yet he did not know how to broach the matter that occupied him. Knowing that a direct question was inappropriate, he asked, 'Should we send a message to Narayan Dasji?'

'What for?'

He was embarrassed and ashamed. No one brings up the subject of his own wife, he knew, least of all a son who has returned after five years. He must let time pass, during which he must express concern for his mother and sisters.

It was Duli Chand who spoke. 'For a few weeks, the daughter-in-law will worship Gangaur in Chirawa, as your sisters will in Rampura. Then, we will send a message at the end of Chaitra.'

Eager to expiate, Hari asked, 'Why has Rukmini Bai not come to Rampura for Gangaur?'

'Jasoda will arrive tomorrow. Rukmini's father-in-law was against the idea of travel at such a time. She has just given birth.'

'I know. Have you seen the boy?'

'No, but we will go soon,' said Duli Chand.

At night, Hari brought out the gifts he had brought from Calcutta: an embroidered shawl for his mother, a gold nose-ring for Rukmini—to be presented when Duli Chand visited her—shellac bangles encrusted with pearls for Jasoda and Muniya, and a silk dhoti for Duli Chand.

'What have you brought for *her*?' asked Muniya.

'Call her bhabhi,' her mother said sternly.

In his mind, Hari saw the face of his young bride, radiant in moonlight. 'Something that will look good on her.'

Muniya giggled. Hari's mother gave him a look of disapproval; he did not elaborate.

He spent the next eighteen days watching his sisters worship Gangaur with other Rampura girls. The patch of dirt in front of the house was swept clean; idols of ash and cowdung were installed. Every morning, he walked to the dam to gather fresh duub grass for the puja. While the girls sang, he watched from inside the house. An unmarried girl worships Gangaur to get a good husband, his mother told him, and a married one prays for her husband's well-being. He imagined Parmeshwari sitting before the same idols in Chirawa, singing the same songs, sprinkling water with the same duub grass, asking Rowa Bai—the patron goddess of Gangaur—for the gift of his health.

Every day, Gangaur ceremonies would end by noon. After a nap, Hari would join his father in the shop, sit behind a pair of scales and weigh bajra grains, barley, pulses, turmeric, cucumber and melon for his customers. He did this out of a sense of duty, knowing that a son, even if employed elsewhere, was expected to sit with his father in the shop and learn the trade. The sums his father handled were small. In this year of plenty, bajra was barely above two rupees to a munn. When pouring two sers into a corner of someone's dhoti—spread out to receive the grain and then tied into a knot—he would think irreverently of the fifty rupees to be gained or lost in 67 Cotton Street, then accept two annas from the buyer and return a paisa. Inside the cash box, he would see piles of copper coins with barely a silver rupee among them, and sense the futility of the whole enterprise.

In late April, after Gangaur had ended, Duli Chand rented a chariot—the same that had been used for Hari's wedding—to bring his daughter-in-law home. Hari was dressed in a silk kurta, silk dhoti and red turban. A ceremonial sword was tied at his waist. This time, he went alone.

Narayan Dasji had decorated his house for the occasion. Hari's mother-in-law welcomed him with jaggery, lemonade and an aarti, and placed eleven silver rupees on a brass plate. Parmeshwari was brought out in a red skirt, her face and shoulders covered in a sequined shawl, as women sang and Hari stood by. It felt like a second wedding, with fewer guests, but now he found the ceremony tiresome. When Parmeshwari placed her foot on the steps of the chariot, the usual wails began—indeed he heard the same women. The same nevgan accompanied them to Rampura.

Their departure had been delayed by a few hours, so the sun came up well before they reached home. An occasional neem tree was in bloom, and the meenjar flowers of khejra bushes flooded the desert with a sweet smell. Parmeshwari was immobile, shawl drawn over her face, her body resting against the nevgan. Hari sat with his back to them, legs dangling listlessly over the side. He dreaded the elaborate ceremony that awaited them in Rampura.

Jasoda and Muniya stood at the door, brass plates in hand, carrying clay lamps lit with ghee. A sheet of silver coins had been laid at the door. There was laughter as Hari's sisters negotiated the price of admission. They settled on twenty rupees for each sister, and Parmeshwari was allowed to place her foot on the silver to enter the house. She had brought two steel trunks from Chirawa—one contained her trousseau, the other gifts for everyone. These were opened in the inner room. Men received silk kurtas, women earrings, anklets and arm-bands. Neighbours were presented silver necklaces. There was much nudging and winking between Jasoda and Muniya. They had seen the bride's face in the inner room, and gave Hari mixed signals about their discovery. Now they would suggest she was pock-marked; now, for a rupee, they were willing to admit she was flawless. Hari played along—they did not know that he had already seen her face on a quiet, moonlit night.

Late in the evening, his sisters pushed him into the room, giggling. The nevgan was sitting on the bed with Parmeshwari in her arms. Hari regarded the scene with disapproval—the sixteenth is upon her, yet she needs a chaperone! He signalled to the nevgan. She giggled, pulled her shawl over her face and ran out of the room. When she opened the door, he heard the sniggers of his sisters outside. Annoyed, he slammed the door and latched it, aware that they could still see through cracks in the wood.

He stood far from the bed, his back to the door, hoping to hide his bride from his sisters. Parmeshwari had a shawl pulled over her face. He had heard countless stories of bridegrooms who had won their brides over through talk, gifts and supplication, yet none mentioned the state he found himself in. He was in despair. In his years of walking the lanes of Bara Bazar, placing jute bales for Yule Sahib or trailing Janardhan in Cotton Street, he had not thought much about his bride. On the way to Rampura, he had thought of nothing else, but his mind had been set on the face he had seen under the moon. Five years had passed. She was not the girl he had seen then. He had never heard her speak, and barely remembered the face. He did not know where to start—she was forbidding in a skirt and shawl, uncommunicative, and covered from head to toe. To be standing in 67 Cotton Street at that moment, looking at the sky with Johnny grinning beside him!

He took a step back and leaned against the door, and felt a sharp pain in his side. His sisters had pushed through a pin. Springing away in irritation, he heard a sound from the bed. A chuckle, perhaps. Gaining confidence, he pulled a velvet purse from his kurta pocket, walked towards her and placed it on the bed. She waited a full minute—he found the delay appropriate—before her hands emerged from the shawl to pick it up. He saw henna on her palms and fingers, extending all the way up her forearm, and gold bangles that were too large. She opened the purse. It contained twenty-one silver rupees. Her fingers closed around a coin.

'That is the Queen of England,' he said.

Her hand froze. He sensed a frown through the shawl and realized he had made a mistake. What would she know of a dead queen? Then the immensity of his own experiences filled him—he had come from Kalkatta, placed jute in Bara Bazar and spoken to Yule Sahib. He was a man of the world. Looking directly at her, he said, 'And you are the Queen of Shekhavati.'

She laughed. Her eyes glistened under the shawl. Resolutely, he went to the lantern and turned down the wick until it was extinguished, then tiptoed to the door and held his breath, knowing his sisters stood on the other side, eyes pressed to holes. Well, he could do nothing about them. He threw open the window. The desert lay shimmering under a moon that was nearly full—it was the second day of the month of Baisakh.

Quietly, he opened his trunk, pulled out a package, unwrapped it and held it out to her. 'It has collapsed during travel,' he said, 'but I will have a dhobi press it back into shape.'

'What is it? A turban?'

'Every memsahib in Kalkatta wears one,' he said. 'Once you put this on, you need not cover your head with a shawl.' Gingerly, he pressed the hat on her head. She did not protest. 'It is too large for you,' he said with disappointment, 'but you will grow into it in a few years.'

On the sixth night, Parmeshwari went to the window to watch the waning moon. She had taken to wearing the hat when in the room. It came down over her forehead and nearly to her eyes, so she had to keep pushing it up. The mountain of flowers on its crest had looked more imposing in Chowringhee. Now, in the moonlight, the flowers formed a curious pattern—not colourful, because everything was silver, but a mass of curls and corners that framed her small face. He was reminded of the face in the bullock cart. Gently, he let a finger touch her cheek. She turned away shyly.

He trembled, struggling to hold back emotions he had never sensed before. For years he had known of sinful ways—through stories, jokes and rumour—yet never allowed them to intrude into his mind. The clerks in Lalgodam were almost all married. Their wives were in Shekhavati, and jokes about separation were common. Hari knew that some of them went to loose women in Bowbazar. Being younger, he had been excluded from such excursions. With Janardhan, there had never been any talk that his father would have disapproved of—aside from the matter of gambling, of course. Yet he now noticed that the shawl had slipped off her shoulders, that her skirt stopped short at the ankles, and that her bodice did not come all the way down to her hips, leaving the waist exposed. But he must not look! Would he dare to touch? Was he no better than the men in Lalgodam?

Filled with shame, he turned away. What had Master Bholaram said about the stage of Grihasthya, which he had entered upon marriage? He must beget children, enjoy material comforts in moderation ... ah, moderation again! How was moderation to be defined?

Hari seized his bride and buried his face in her bosom, ignoring her cries for help.

Summer came quickly, as it always did. At dawn, he would

ride a camel far into tibbas dotted with meenjar flowers, and return with armfuls of gundi fruit for Parmeshwari, hiding it in the folds of his turban so his mother—the only one up so early—would not comment on it. Then he went to the fields to wash, returned to eat bajra rotis laced with ghee and sangar pickle, and drank water sweetened with cumin. Parmeshwari would be up too, helping his mother in the kitchen, pretending not to notice him, as was proper, and never letting Duli Chand catch a glimpse of her face. In the afternoon, he would feast on dhaalu fruits—at this father's insistence, to aid his digestion—and take a lazy nap under a neem tree. In the evenings, he sat desultorily in his father's shop, doing what was asked, with his mind on the approaching night of revelry. When there were no customers, he squatted in the back and chewed on lesu seeds—bitter but 'good for you', said his mother—and dwelt on the face of his bride.

At night, they lay in passionate embrace near the open window. They would not have spoken a word all day, out of propriety, yet there was nothing to say in the evening. In the train on his way back, he had prepared the stories he would tell her—about Yule Sahib, Chitpur Road, Lalgodam, Khemchandji, and above all her cousin Janardhan—but now he found no time to mention any of them. They had become specks in a vast dust storm, as indeed had his time in Disavar. On some nights, unable to sleep because of the heat, they sneaked out through the window—he jumped out first and helped her out, feeling the delight of manhood when he carried her a short distance before setting her down—and ran across the desert, climbing dunes, avoiding khejra bushes for the thorns, and for the spirits and djinns who lived inside them, collecting meenjar flowers that had fallen to the ground. Once, he hitched the camel to the cart and took her for a ride among the tibbas, laughing when the camel reached far out to nibble on khejra leaves and the cart overturned, throwing them in the sand.

Three weeks after Gangaur, Jasoda returned to her father-in-law's house. Before she climbed into the cart, her mother had her remove the pearl-encrusted bangles that Hari had brought from

Calcutta. These were stowed safely in her trunk. Hari watched the cart roll away, relieved. He now had to contend with only one sister—Muniya—in his desire to spend as much time as possible with Parmeshwari.

The first rain of the year was seen at the end of June. Hari walked the fields to see the planting of bajra, speaking to men who had bought their seed from his father. Duli Chand owned no land, but the success or failure of the crop directly affected his stocks, so he spent much time overseeing the planting, inspecting bullocks and camels, and scouring the sky for rain. For sport, Hari walked the furrows behind camels pulling ploughs, seeding the space between bajra rows with watermelon and cucumber. Because he had recently returned from Disavar, there were jokes about his awkwardness in the field. Duli Chand beamed when such comments were made, and Hari submitted, not displeased himself.

The crop began to show in a few days. In the month of Saavan, dark clouds massed over Rampura and the riverbed ran with a trickle of water. The dust of tibbas settled down, wells were full of water and duub grass blanketed fields that had not been planted, becoming thicker near the dam, where children went daily to measure the water level, which was reported and commented on. It rose steadily—seven fingers, eight, eleven…

'A few such days,' said Duli Chand, 'and the bajra will grow to eleven feet.'

Muniya ran all over Rampura, from the dam to the fields to the riverbed, defying her mother—who kept reminding her that she was now a married woman—contending that her mother-in-law, in distant Jhunjhunu, held no power over her until she formally went to her father-in-law's house. Under the peepul tree at the door, women ground bajra from the previous year, cleaned sangar beans, kneaded grams and flour with oil into a paste, rolled the paste into papad and laid them out to dry, rushing to bring them in whenever the sky threatened rain. Parmeshwari sat among the women, pickling sangar beans. Hari's mother would not have allowed her to run about like Muniya, or take her turn on swings that had been hung from peepul trees—that sport was for daughters, not daughters-in-law.

Hari watched them, lying under a tree far enough that they would not notice him. Sitting in crimson skirts, with shawls covering their faces—because a man might pass by—they turned their grindstones in rhythm and sang the Peepli all afternoon.

The peepul you planted before you went east
Is now a great, dense tree
I was only a child but am now a beautiful woman
Come back, son of my mother-in-law...

Mounds of bajra were gradually depleted, to reappear as flour hills. Most of the women were daughters-in-law who had been married into Rampura and had husbands in Disavar. Some had left recently, some had been gone a long time; some were said to be on their way back, some had not been heard from for years; some were believed to have died, some had been ambushed by robbers on their way to Delhi and left to wander among the blistering tibbas.

Your father wants great wealth
Your mother craves fine jewellery
But I thirst to sit with you in our bed
Come back, son of my father-in-law

There was a woman with a gold nose-ring whose husband had opened a shop in Jorhat in Assam, and had recently sent two hundred rupees through a gumashta. There was a girl whose sixteen-year-old husband had left the day she arrived in his house with her trousseau. He was to return in three years; she had waited six. She still wore her mangal sutra round her neck, along with silver arm-bands, a nose-ring, a large red bindi between the brows and a line of vermilion in the parting of her hair—all signifying that her husband was alive, when everyone knew he had been lost to robbers or sand storms, or any of the other tragedies that may befall a man who goes east. Who knew what lay beyond the desert, and who could trust the messages that arrived? Postcards got lost, letters were written by impersonators, packages arrived months later, even a telegram could be a lie, aside from being so expensive that it was used only to announce births and deaths.

Barren tibbas may sprout bajra
The poor may become rich some day
But my youth, once gone, will never return
Come back, brother of my sister-in-law

Two things never come to an end, they said in Rampura—the making of papad and the singing of the Peepli.

The month of Saavan passed, followed by Bhadwa and Ashwin. It was to be a winter of plenty. In Kartik, golden cobs of bajra weighed down the swaying stalks everywhere. Men were awed at its great height, as they were every Kartik—Hari noted it was no taller than it had been in previous years. He watched the harvesting. Mountains of cobs lay outside every house. Duli Chand's stores filled up. Bullocks were turned loose to separate the grain from the cobs, rotis of freshly ground grain were baked. The rains had ended, but pools and puddles lay all around, reminding everyone of Indra Bhagwan's bounty. There were many pujas and yagyas; much money was earned by pandits.

Late in the month of Pous, when the fields were grey and mornings cold, Duli Chand summoned Hari into the double-ceiling and asked, 'When do you plan to set out?'

'For Chirawa? But your daughter-in-law has just arrived in her father-in-law's house…'

'East.'

Hari had not thought of Calcutta for months.

'In Falgun, you will have been in Rampura for a full year,' Duli Chand said. 'A man returns from Disavar but rarely, and then only for a month, to bring gifts and taste the joys of home. His customers in Kalkatta exert a greater pull on him. He tires of women's talk, their songs and their pickles and their papad.

It is in his nature to rush back, as it is in his mother's nature to implore him to stay.'

Hari thought of Parmeshwari's arms, and the camel-cart bumping along the tibbas. 'I will leave two weeks before Holi.'

'Holi is only a month away,' said Parmeshwari in dismay that night. There was no accusation in her voice, not even entreaty. He knew, and she knew, that a man must go to Disavar, just as a woman must make papad and pickle sangar beans. A bania could not plant bajra; he could not join the armies of Maharaja Madho Singh of Jaipur; he could not wander with travelling musicians—he had to do what banias did, and he had to live where his customers lived. It was inconvenient—this great distance between Shekhavati and Disavar—yet this was what Raamji had decreed for Shekhavati.

He did not leave two weeks before Holi, or even after Holi, but stayed another three months. It was only in July, when his presence in Rampura had become an embarrassment, that he finally announced his departure. His father agreed readily, even though he would be travelling in the inauspicious chaumasa months.

Parmeshwari cried all night, softly lest her mother-in-law hear her outside the room. Hari pretended not to notice. He had not told his father that she was pregnant. It would have been highly improper for a man to tarry by his wife merely because she was with child.

In the morning, preparations were made. To his consternation, leave-taking was more elaborate now that he was a married man. He was to travel by camel-cart in spite of the expense. His bundle contained rotis, chillies, crushed gram flour, fried flour balls soaked in ghee, sangar pickle and a lump of boiled rice. No bajra. The bundle and a copper pot of water were placed on the cart. The hour approached. His mother asked anxiously, 'What keeps Lakshmi's Ma?'

Lakshmi's Ma did odd jobs around the house—washing utensils, sweeping floors, bringing water from the well. Her daughter Lakshmi had died a year ago, but the name had stuck.

'Gauri is here,' Parmeshwari said.

His mother shook her head, and Parmeshwari understood. Gauri was a widow. It would not be right for her to watch Hari leave. Lakshmi's Ma, on the other hand, was a suhagin—her husband was living—so her presence at Hari's departure would be auspicious. Indeed, Gauri was sent into the kitchen on some pretext.

Duli Chand grew impatient by the minute. 'Panditji said not to leave in the third prahar, and it is almost nine in the morning.'

As soon as Lakshmi's Ma arrived, Hari's mother thrust a brass pot into her hands and positioned her to the left of the door. 'Stand still, Lakshmi's Ma, and let the water drip.'

Summoned by Hari's mother, a few Brahmin women had gathered at the door. When Lakshmi's Ma had taken her station, they pulled their shawls over their heads and, with right hands placed on cheeks, began to sing. Hari's mother painted a tilak on his forehead, placed jaggery and curd on his tongue, scattered rice, and said, 'Remember not to look back.'

Hari had been watching the ceremonies in dismay. He knew that Parmeshwari stood behind a door, and that she could not come out to see him in Duli Chand's presence. He was seized with a sudden fear of Disavar. The journey seemed impossibly long. And what awaited him there but hostile Bengalis and indifferent Marwaris? But it was too late. The cart stood ready. The women were singing. And Parmeshwari had already been hidden away.

He climbed into the cart. As it rolled away, his mother emerged from the house. With tears streaming down her face, she seized the brass pot from Lakshmi's Ma and turned it over, spilling water in the wake of the cart, watching the puddle in the dirt with satisfaction. Then she went inside without looking back, so as not to create an ill omen at the start of her son's journey.

4

Arriving at Howrah Station three days later, he threw his trunk on to a tonga and directed it toward Bara Bazar. The tongawala wanted to cross Howrah Bridge at low tide, because once the tide came in, bullock carts had a difficult time negotiating the hinged span of the bridge, causing traffic jams and ensnaring tongas. They approached the bridge quickly, but were held up by a procession of young men holding banners in Bengali and English and chanting a song in Sanskrit. The tongawala turned impatiently to Hari. 'What do these men want?'

Hari shrugged. 'I have returned to Kalkatta after a year.'

'If they had work,' the tongawala said, 'they would have no time to protest.'

An hour later, when the tonga finally deposited him at Lalgodam—the tongawala wanted Hari to pay for the delay; he refused—Hari sensed an unnatural calm in the building. The flour mill was deserted; its canvas belt was looped idly around the flywheel. The usual cloud that hung at the entrance had cleared. Worried, he went upstairs, noting the absence of the usual bustle. In his office on the third floor, Khemchandji was by the cash box, conversing with another man whom Hari recognized as the head munim of a firm in Cotton Street. Hari crawled over the mattress to touch Khemchandji's feet, and received a limp pat on the head. The usual question about the current rates of bajra in Shekhavati was not asked.

'I do not understand this "swadeshi",' Khemchandji was saying. 'They say Manchester cotton is foreign. Why, then, do you sit in English trains? Or cross the Howrah Bridge?'

'It is an excuse to disrupt business,' said the other munim.

'We do not ask "Is it Indian cotton or Manchester cotton?" We buy what Andrew Yule & Company sells, and we sell what people buy. If Curzon wants two Bengals, let him have two. We will open shops in both.'

'The less we say about it, the better,' the munim said. 'In *Sanjibani*, Krishna Kumar Mitra says ...'

'Newspapers!' Khemchandji said contemptuously.

Hari waited patiently until the other munim had left, then asked Khemchandji what the matter was. Khemchandji thrust an old copy of *Sanjibani* into his hands and left the room. Although Hari could speak Bengali, he could not read it. There were no gumashtas about. He knew the one person who would have all the answers. Folding the newspaper, he walked briskly to Cotton Street looking for his saalaa.

He found him sitting at a tea stall. They had not seen each other for a year. Janardhan sprang up to embrace him, then remembered and bent over as if to touch Hari's feet. 'Raam Raam, jijaji. When did you return?'

'An hour ago.'

'How is Parmeshwari Bai?'

Hari let out an audible sigh. Janardhan winked knowingly. 'You will get used to it. Perhaps you should think of bringing her here.'

'And will she live in Lalgodam?'

'You will have to rent rooms. In a few years, after you have opened your hosiery shop…'

'I have brought you laddus and churma from Rampura. Come to Lalgodam in the evening.'

'How are the rates in Shekhavati?'

'Low, as they have been for years—bajra is two rupees.' Holding up the newspaper, he asked, 'How are the rates in Kalkatta?'

Janardhan's face fell. 'It is this partition business. Curzon has said there will be two Bengals, East and West.'

'Curzon is not the King.'

'He is the King's man, the Lat Sahib. He can give himself as many Bengals as he wants.'

'What is wrong with two Bengals?'

'The bhadralok do not like it.'

'I see no loss in this. People in both Bengals will buy cotton.'

'The bhadralok do not buy or sell. Those in the east do not

mind partition but those in the west do, and those in Calcutta hate it.'

Hari pointed to the copy of *Sanjibani* again. 'What does this say?'

'This was what started all the swadeshi trouble.'

'Swadeshi?'

'Indian cotton ...'

'But it is Marwaris who sell Manchester cotton. That makes Manchester cotton Indian.'

'Don't say that to anyone else. These are swadeshi times. Bengalis make daily bonfires. Sometimes they burn Manchester cotton, Lancashire cloth or gunny from Dundee; sometimes it is merely dhotis and saris that they think are foreign-made. Who can tell? At first, it did not matter. If people burn their clothes they will buy new ones to replace them, and the bania will benefit. But now they are threatening a total boycott. This is not a good time to be dealing in cotton.'

'What about Yule Sahib?'

Janardhan shook his head. 'Yule Sahib's banyan has seen the opportunity to strike back. He had been losing commissions to me for years. Now Yule Sahib thinks people like me, and not Bengali bhadralok, are responsible for this swadeshi business.'

Hari hesitated to ask the next question. It was inappropriate to bring up the subject immediately upon arrival, but his whole capital was at stake. 'What about... our business?'

'With no one buying Manchester cotton, there is no money to go around. What will people bet with?'

Hari looked around. The sky had cleared, but Cotton Street had not recovered from a morning drizzle. There still was a patter of raindrops on the pavement—drips from dozens of pipes that emerged from upper floors.

'So much rain, all wasted,' Janardhan said. 'No one will make a paisa out of it.'

'Has all work in number 67 stopped, then?'

'It opens, but business is slow. The police are hostile. Everyone is afraid.' He looked at the sky, as if pleading for patience with Indra. 'Once this swadeshi matter has died down...'

Hari could hold back no longer. 'Our money? Is it safe?'

He used the usual Marwari habit of saying 'our money' when referring to money that was his, and hoped Janardhan would not think him too impatient.

'Invested in the market,' said Janardhan, 'with a lagayival and a rangbaaj. But everything is closed today. There is a general strike. They took out a procession on Howrah Bridge.'

'I saw it.'

Hari walked back to Lalgodam with a heavy heart. It had begun to rain again, and every drop stung him. The shuttered shops on Harrison Road had altered the appearance of Bara Bazar. Why had Curzon not let things be when sales were brisk?

He had little work for the next month, watching in consternation as cries of swadeshi swallowed all business. There was no cotton to be placed, no jute for which buyers had to be found. Early in August, the two of them went to a meeting outside Town Hall, where a thousand boys had gathered, wearing black badges and singing. Hari had heard the song before, on Howrah Bridge the day he returned from Shekhavati.

Bande Mataram!
Rich with thy hurrying streams,
bright with orchard gleams,
cool with thy winds of delight,
green fields waving Mother of might...

Speaker after speaker railed against Curzon and partition. Pledges were made to boycott foreign goods. A man with well-combed hair and a lush beard recited a poem in a thin voice. Janardhan nudged Hari. 'That is Tagore Babu. Zamindar.'

Hari watched in horror. What did the speakers mean when they said they would awaken the sleeping soul of Bengal? Once awakened, would this soul not buy Manchester cotton? Where would he get his commissions? 'The bhadralok are losing customers every moment they spend away from their shops, wasting their time in song and poetry.'

'They do not have shops, jijaji.'

The troubles ebbed after partition in October. Yule Sahib began to find customers again, and Hari lounged around Chitpur Road as he had before. Much money had been lost. The monsoon had ended, but 67 Cotton Street opened for a week of betting before shutting for the year. Hari rushed there, hoping to put the last showers of the year to good use. That morning, he had climbed to the rooftop basa in Lalgodam and studied the sky. It was going to be a muggy day—humid but not wet. He saw dark clouds, but sensed that they would float across the sky all afternoon, foreshadowing rain but never yielding a drop. He would be a khayival that day.

He ran into Janardhan as soon as he entered number 67. A fruit-seller approached them. 'Khaya? Khaya?'

'Two hundred and fifty,' whispered Hari.

Janardhan's eyes widened in fear. 'You are a bania, jijaji, not a gambler. Never bet more than half of...'

'This is our last chance. And I know it will not rain.'

'Leave your money in the market, then. No one will remember swadeshi in a year. The odds will be better too.'

'But it will not rain today,' Hari said firmly.

'Let's at least find out what odds he is offering.'

'Khaya!' Hari said firmly to the fruit-seller, then walked to a cubicle in the corner and laid his bet. The man's jaw dropped at the amount pledged. Janardhan turned away in resignation.

It did not rain that afternoon. Hari and Janardhan sat at a stall in Cotton Street and drank endless cups of tea, looking up every few minutes and bracing for the first drop of rain. As six o'clock approached—the time when bets would be settled and number 67 would close—Hari's excitement grew. The odds had not been too good, so he would no more than double his money, yet it was a large amount. In one afternoon, he would have earned what his father did in three good months in his shop in Rampura.

Janardhan was subdued. Hari had decided to be magnanimous in triumph and not taunt him about his extreme caution.

A few minutes before closing, a dozen policemen came marching down Cotton Street and charged into number 67, rounding up fruit-sellers and questioning the traders whose cubicles lined the court. The door to the left—inside which sat the rain-gauges—was broken open. Hari heard rain-gauges being smashed and pipes being wrenched open. Panicking, he got up to look but withdrew on seeing an English sergeant enter the court.

'We must not be seen here, jijaji,' Janardhan said urgently. They mingled with the crowd and walked to Harrison Road, breathless with fear and excitement.

He had never been in such danger before. To have policemen breaking and smashing things next to you! 'What do they want?'

Janardhan sighed. 'They want to shut down number 67.'

'But why?'

'They say it is illegal.'

This was a revelation to Hari. He knew there was something disreputable about this business, which was why it was not to be discussed with Khemchandji or mentioned to his father. Yet everyone laid bets, big or small, in a court somewhere in Bara Bazar. Why would a bania pass up a chance to speculate? Was there a man in Bara Bazar, even among the bhadralok, who would not want to earn a little on the side? And if two men wished to lay a wager, with the loser willing to pay up, what was wrong with that? Did not Yudhishthir gamble away a whole kingdom in the Mahabharat?

'The bhadralok speculate on jute and opium at the exchange,' he said, 'and you have told me the sahibs bet on horses at Kidderpore.'

'This is how the sahibs pay us back for swadeshi, which was not even our doing.'

'You never told me it was illegal,' Hari grumbled.

Janardhan laughed and slapped Hari on the back. 'You are a clever one, jijaji! Why did you think everyone at number 67 spoke in whispers? Why were the gauges placed inside a double-ceiling?'

'What happens now?'

Janardhan shrugged. 'There may be protests. Nothing will come of them. Sahibs do not back down.'

'And our money?' Hari asked, shivering in the suddenly chilly October afternoon.

Janardhan stopped; Hari became aware of the sounds of Harrison Road—the clucking of tongawalas and the screeching of electric tram cars. 'A bania sees both profit and loss in his lifetime.'

Hari spent the next few weeks loitering about Harrison Road, distraught. The relationship with Yule Sahib had frayed—the sahib was away in England, he was told whenever he went to see him. Janardhan had been kind after the loss of his money, but there was no mistaking his disapproval at Hari's rashness in betting his entire capital. And Janardhan's own business had suffered too. They sat at tea stalls, gumashtas with no bills to collect, no bets to make and no jute to sell, blowing into tea cups and ruminating on this run of ill-luck.

In Lalgodam, Khemchand Biyani was usually in a foul mood. Through Hemraj, Hari discovered that the Marwaris of Bara Bazar had sent telegrams to the Manchester Chamber of Commerce, asking it to intercede with the government to prevent partition. Having failed, Marwaris were now paying the price. Traders all over Bara Bazar were sullen because they had lost Durga Puja sales, the best time of year, to the swadeshi trouble. Along with cotton, the opium, jute, insurance and banking businesses of Daulatram Gulabchand had suffered. Khemchandji postponed his trip to upcountry branches of the firm.

Janardhan took Hari to a protest meeting organized by the Marwari Association. A gentleman Marwari, dressed like a sahib, read a speech in English, pausing occasionally to allow a man to translate into Hindi. Janardhan said, 'That is Babu Johrimal, from the firm of Johrimal Sagarmal.'

Babu Johrimal spoke in an even tone, but the translator imbued his words with fiery passion. 'Everyone knew that sahibs win and lose large sums at the Calcutta Turf Club,' he said. 'How is betting on horses different from betting on rain? Marwaris are being victimized for the swadeshi trouble,' he said, 'when they were already victims of it.'

'They say Cotton Street is congested and Bara Bazar is dirty,' Babu Johrimal continued. 'But how does betting on the rain make it dirtier? Does more rain fall in Cotton Street because two poor men from Shekhavati have bet a rupee on it?'

The reason for the crackdown, Babu Johrimal said, was simple: when Marwaris speculated on jute or opium, they caused an increase in prices that brought more revenue to the government. Every time a Marwari sent a telegram to Jaipur quoting cotton rates, the government collected a rupee. But betting on rain brought the government nothing.

Proposals were passed, reposing faith in the Bengal government and dissociating the Marwari Association from swadeshi. A suggestion was made that Marwaris in Calcutta stop all speculation on opium sales, causing the price to crash. Someone pointed out that opium steamers were due to sail for Hong Kong, so, as a matter of caution, it was agreed that speculation would be halted for only one day. 'We have suffered much because of swadeshi. We do not want to add to the losses suffered by honest traders.'

They left the meeting. Janardhan said, 'I heard Babu Johrimal say the same things eight years ago, when the government first banned number 67. Nothing came of it.'

All resistance among traders vanished as the end of the English year approached. There were feeble attempts to wring some sales out of the festive season for sahibs. At Christmas, Hari went with Janardhan to Dalhousie Square to see the crowds. On the last day of the English year, sahibs and bhadralok lined Chowringhee to watch the Lat Sahib and his memsahib go by on elephants.

'The Lat Sahib is going to the races,' Hari said bitterly. 'There he will bet on horses.'

'This Kalkatta is no longer profitable, jijaji,' said Janardhan. 'I am going back to Shekhavati.'

Hari was astounded. Of all the men he knew in Bara Bazar, none had seemed more at home than Janardhan. 'When?'

'Tonight. The Delhi train leaves Howrah Station at nine.'

'But why?'

Janardhan sighed. 'You know what they say about Marwaris, jijaji—we come to Bengal with a pot and a blanket, and steal the land away from its people. This is not our home.'

'What will I do once you are gone?'

'You are a gumashta at Daulatram Gulabchand. You still get twelve rupees every month, whether or not you place jute for anyone. I trust you will not do anything rash. My sister's happiness depends on you.'

'Could I at least go with you to Howrah Station?'

'Meet me at the junction of Harrison Road and Chitpur Road at eight o'clock.'

Hari walked through Harrison Road with a heavy heart. Electric lights glittered on either side. Marwari shopkeepers had taken to celebrating the English New Year, he noted. Shops were still open, selling tea and English cakes, and displaying signs that Janardhan would have been able to read.

When he arrived at Lalgodam, there was no trace of the festive spirit in Harrison Road. The building was dark. Khemchand Biyani sat at the cash box, his face lit up by a lantern. Unusually for the time of day, Khemchandji was alone. He looked displeased to see Hari. 'Sit down, Harilal.'

He has bad news from Rampura, Hari thought.

'An English sergeant came to Lalgodam today.'

Hari wondered how this related to him.

'No sahib has entered the building in twenty-five years,' Khemchandji said.

Hari held his breath.

'He was looking for you. I took care not to mention 67 Cotton Street.'

Hari gasped. Khemchandji had known all along! He had been a fool. If only he had mentioned this years ago, Khemchandji would have forbidden it and he would not be in this situation today.

'Are you eighteen yet?'

'The nineteenth is on me; the eighteenth was completed on Falgun sudi dwaadashi.'

'They do not send an English sergeant to seek a mere pickpocket.'

Hari looked down shamefacedly. 'I will return to Shekhavati immediately,' he said. He would go with Janardhan—at least they could comfort each other.

Khemchandji shook his head. 'Your father sent you in my care. A boy does not return to Shekhavati in this manner. I have heard of your work for Yule Sahib.'

Did Khemchandji know *everything* about him?

'You made but one mistake: never bet more than half of what you can.'

I will do whatever he asks, Hari thought.

'My old munim Chaman Lal lives in Bogra, a village 200 miles to the east. Now in East Bengal, after partition. Take a train at Sealdah Station and get off at Santahar. From there, you can find your way to Bogra, 25 miles away.'

'What will I do in Bogra?'

'Chaman Lal will think of something. I will give you a letter. A bania always finds something to sell wherever people live.'

'I will need at least a few thousand,' said Hari, surprised at his own audacity.

'Chaman Lal will lend you the money. Go and pack your trunk. I will settle your basa account later. The train to Santahar leaves in an hour from Sealdah Station.'

Hari was overwhelmed by Khemchandji's generosity, but knew it would be inappropriate to make a display of gratitude. He rose to his feet calmly. As he turned to go, Khemchandji opened the cash box and pulled out a slip of paper. 'I almost forgot. There was an urgent telegram for you.'

'I cannot read English,' Hari said.

'You have been in Kalkatta for six years,' Khemchandji admonished. He ran his eyes over the telegram and struggled over the words. 'It is from Master Bholaram Shastri. A son has been born,' he said, before filing the telegram away.

'They should not have wasted a full rupee on a telegram,' Hari said softly.

'The telegram boy was tipped an anna,' said Khemchandji.

'Add it to my account, along with the rupee,' said Harilal mournfully. 'They should have dropped a postcard.'

'Hemraj is going back to Rampura for a few weeks. Do you want me to send a message with him?' Khemchandji asked.

'Tell my father that rates are low, but could go lower.'

Thirty minutes later, Hari left Lalgodam. His trunk was light—he had bought no dhotis or kurtas in Calcutta, and the only turban he owned was on his head. A few rupees were tucked at his waist. He carried the trunk on his head all the way to Harrison Road to meet Janardhan, who shook his head on seeing the trunk. 'I told you not to do anything rash, jijaji. Do not forget that you are still employed by Daulatram Gulabchand. A gumashta cannot run away without notice.'

'I am no longer with the firm,' said Hari.

Janardhan was distraught to learn about the sergeant, but relieved to find that Hari would not go back to Shekhavati.

'If you ever return to Disavar,' said Hari, 'come to my shop in Bogra.'

'You will place ten thousand bales of jute, jijaji. When you come to Shekhavati as a great seth, do not forget me.'

Hari laughed wanly. 'I do not have your nose for jute, Johnny.'

'Same town, Harry, same nose.'

Janardhan bent over to touch Hari's feet. Hari stepped back and folded his hands. Janardhan climbed a tonga that took him to Howrah. Hari watched him go, then threw his trunk on a tonga going in the opposite direction to Sealdah Station. In a few hours, a new English year would begin. A strange town beckoned in the east. Far to the west, in Shekhavati, Parmeshwari lay on a cot with his son.

5

The train to Santahar was empty—a few men lay here and there, snoring. No one leaves Kalkatta to go to a place like Bogra, Hari thought mournfully. He lay down on the middle bench, using his bundle for a pillow, keeping one foot planted on his trunk to ward off thieves. At seven, the train groaned and crawled out of Sealdah Station, but did not pick up speed. At each stop there was a crush of passengers bearing pots and bundles, and Hari was obliged to first sit up, then put the bundle in his lap, transfer the trunk to the rack above, and finally squat on the bench, squeezed against an old Bengali man who regarded him with curiosity but did not push him away. He dozed off, and was woken hours later by the man. It was dark. The train was emptying out.

'Dada, are we in Santahar?'

The man studied Hari's face in the dark. 'Marwari?' Hari nodded. 'This is Damookdeah Ghat. We must cross the Padma here.'

Hari rushed to the window to see the river, and folded his hands. The man watched him indifferently. 'Hurry up.'

Hari followed him out. They walked briskly for a quarter-mile to a ghat, where they were herded up a wooden plank into a launch ferry. The upper deck being full, the Bengali pointed downward; they descended to the lower deck. Hari found himself pressed against the walls of the vessel, sitting near a porthole barely two feet above the water, with men huddled all around. The ceiling was low, so anyone trying to move would have to crawl to the ladder that went to the upper deck. The launch sputtered, and the riverbank pulled away. The Padma slept, spread like a dark sheet all the way to the horizon. Hari put a hand through the porthole, scooped up some water and let it trickle down his throat, marvelling at how fortunate these Bengalis were to drift daily on the Ganga. In Shekhavati, men stored water from the Ganga in bottles. They brought it from Benares and Haridwar, and traders returning from Bengal would be asked for a bottle.

Those who forgot to bring any would be admonished, because then it would have to be bought in Sikar. Every home had a bottle of gangajal stowed away in the upper shelves, to be used sparingly in pujas—a few drops on Raamji idols, a trickle at Lakshmi's feet, a wet hand over a son's head. Here it flowed freely, all of it, to be drunk at will, sprinkled on a thousand heads, spilled, spat out and waded in. And the Bengalis did not even notice, sitting indifferently in a launch ferry as it churned through sacred water.

The Bengali regarded Hari with amusement. 'This is not the Ganga.'

'The name does not matter,' Hari said. 'The Padma comes from the Ganga, does it not?'

'The Ganga goes into the Hooghly,' said the man, casting a look of contempt at the dark sheet outside. 'The Padma is the water that is left over.'

The ferry approached the left bank of the river near Sara Ghat. Because the bank moved almost by the week, fishing boats marked the path on either side, lighting it with yellow and amber lamps. The launch shuddered; its engines shut off and it glided into position on the bank. Coolies could be heard on the shore. There was a scramble to get off. A plank was laid from the upper deck to the muddy flat to which the ferry was moored. Hari followed the other passengers to a tin shed and sought out the Bengali man. Railway carriages stood waiting. These appeared to be smaller than the ones that had brought him from Calcutta. Metre-gauge coaches, said the man. Then followed another scramble to board the new train, and more screeching and hissing as the train started.

'How long is it to Santahar?' he asked, afraid the train would pass the town while he slept.

'Four hours,' said the man.

Santahar station was larger than he had imagined—a dozen sheds and a tea stall that was closed. Drowsy coolies eyed the train, which disgorged half its load: almost everyone was changing at Santahar. It was six in the morning. Most passengers unfolded bed-sheets and blankets on the platform and went to sleep, some under the shed and some outside it. Hari watched the train creep away in dismay. He had been told that the connection to Bogra would not be available until the next day. What was he to do for one full day in this forgotten Bengali town?

He left the station. Outside, he engaged a bullock cart to take him the 25 miles to Bogra. The driver was a Musalman who squatted in the front and fell asleep as the cart found its way among shops that surrounded the station. Sitting in the back, balanced between two strips of bamboo and watching his trunk and bundle anxiously, Hari wondered if the rope thrown over them was secure enough. The Musalman's own possessions were piled similarly on the cart and he did not seem to care. After a while, Hari lay down on the bamboo strips and fell asleep.

He was woken by the first rays shooting over a mangrove clump. The cart laboured up a dirt track winding its way through golden fields. Palm trees lined ponds along the track. Paddy heaps lay strewn across the plain, drying. Women were busy around them, beating stalks against barrels, logs, stones and meshes. Men stamped on paddy stalk with their feet. Bullocks walked in circles, crushing stalk to dislodge the grain. The Musalman turned around and, on noting Hari's unknowing gaze, said, 'Aman. It has been good this year.'

Hari stared. The Musalman asked, 'Where are you from, babu?'

'Kalkatta,' said Hari, thinking that made him sound more local than Shekhavati.

The Musalman nodded—Hari's ignorance was explained. 'Rice,' he said.

The cart plunged into a low-lying area and the bullocks were suddenly knee-deep in a sheet of water.

'We will drown!' Hari cried.

The Musalman was indifferent. 'Merely a shallow beel.' The bullocks gained dry land. 'There were no beels in this area twenty years ago,' he said. 'Do you see that railway line?'

Hari noticed, for the first time, the track that ran along his left. That was the train he would have taken if he had waited a day in Santahar.

'The railway raised an embankment for the track,' the man said. 'And now we have a lake where there was dry land—the water cannot get out.'

'I do not see a lake,' said Hari.

'Come during the monsoon. This whole region becomes a beel.'

'What happens after the Aman harvest?'

'We sow Aush,' said the Musalman.

'What is Aush?'

'Rice,' said the Musalman.

Hari sighed—Raamji loved this Bengal, where they fed bajra to cattle and had so many names for rice. He let his legs dangle from the cart and surveyed the endless expanse of yellow, dotted with men and women—now far away—threshing, beating and singing. What would a man from Shekhavati give to look over such fields of gold! Had bajra ever looked so full? Were these mango trees? Were those crows and parrots? And which bird was that, the brown one that looked like a crow but was smaller?

'Myna,' said the Musalman.

'I have never seen a myna,' Hari whispered to himself. Then he was embarrassed at his own sentimentality. What would Khemchand Biyani say? 'Send a boy of eighteen to do business in Bogra, and he speaks of birds.' Composing himself, he studied the Aman harvest with new eyes. Much rice, much wealth. Would not these men want to sell this rice and buy clothes? Toys for their children? Trinkets for their wives? A bania could prosper in a place like this. And after his customers had spent their earnings, he could loan them more to keep buying. He need never fear for his money, because there would be a second harvest, and a third. No one wasted time looking at the sky here; no one stood amidst grey furrows to declare, 'If it does not rain by the second day of the second fortnight in the month of Aashaadh, break your plough and use it for fuel ...' because it would rain. It would always rain.

The sun had cut its arc across the sky when Hari saw the first sheds of Bogra. This was a much larger town than Santahar. Shops with tin roofs lined the street; there was a confusion of bullock carts at every intersection; bales of jute lay in the dust; mountains of bananas were on display. Stopping at a few stalls to ask, he found his way to Bara Gola, which was a large shed divided into many rooms under a roof of corrugated iron, and where he had been told Chaman Lal kept a shop.

As expected, the cart-driver quibbled about the fare. After this had been resolved, Hari walked to the cubicle that had been pointed out to him and laid down his trunk and bundle in the dust. Chaman Lal was sitting cross-legged, picking his teeth with his little finger. Hari folded his hands. 'Babu Chaman Lalji?'

Chaman Lal responded with the merest nod. Hari touched his feet. Another nod. Hari unwrapped a corner of his dhoti and thrust the note from Khemchand Biyani into his hands. Chaman Lal glanced at it—not really reading it but somehow divining the contents—and pointed to a corner of the cubicle. Hari sat down, cross-legged, on the mattress.

'Is there much celebration in Kalkatta?' Chaman Lal asked.

'Yes. For the new English year.'

'Good for business.'

Hari nodded uncertainly. He had heard Khemchand Biyani express disapproval of Christmas celebrations, and did not want to commit himself either way. As he had in countless offices in Calcutta, he sat for a long time while Chaman Lal remained busy with his books or simply stared at the road. He knew he was being tested for patience. He did not even request water, or ask where the urinal was. At dusk, when the line of bullock carts had begun to thin out, Chaman Lal closed his books, locked away the cash box and looked at Hari, who betrayed no reaction, as he knew he should not.

'I have known Khemchand Babu a long time,' said Chaman Lal.

Hari nodded in appreciation.

'They say Daulatram Gulabchand rests on his shoulders. He is as much owner as munim.'

Hari indicated assent.

'You look young to be starting out by yourself in Disavar.'

Hari shrugged. 'Daulatramji began when he was eleven. The nineteenth is upon me.'

Chaman Lal frowned. Hari knew he had made a mistake—presumption was another name for hubris.

'Do you speak Bengali?'

After five years in Calcutta, Hari thought he had become comfortable in Bengali, but he had found himself straining to understand the cart-driver from Santahar. The Bengali they spoke here was different from the one in Calcutta. So he said, 'A little. One can get by with Marwari in Bara Bazar.'

'This is not Bara Bazar, where a man may go days without speaking to a Bengali. Bogra is a town of Musalmans.'

'At least there are no English sahibs here,' Hari pointed out, hoping that a favourable comment about Bogra would sit well with Chaman Lal.

'English sahibs are easy to please; it is Musalmans you have to careful about. This is a mofussil area, unlike Kalkatta.'

'Are all customers Musalmans?'

'Some are Hindus. But a Marwari sees all Bengalis—Hindu or Musalman—equally. A customer has no religion because he has money. Musalmans will pawn their gold earrings with you; they will buy your… What do you deal in?'

Hari was unprepared for the question. In his years in Calcutta, he had been a jute broker, speculator, rangbaaj and lagayival, but never a shopkeeper.

'Grain,' he said uncertainly. Then, feeling he should be specific, he added, 'Rice. Aman rice. I am told the harvest has been good.'

'Yes. Now they will sow Aush, to be harvested in Saavan. Some will then sow Boro, some will go back to Aman… The land never tires in Bengal—three crops a year, and much more in between.' Seeing the look of awe on Hari's face, Chaman Lal quickly added, 'But you must not think rates will always go up. A bania must turn a profit in good times and bad.'

'What do you deal in?' Hari asked. Aside from a mattress and a cash box, the cubicle was bare. There was no stock, no sign of anything available for sale.

'This and that,' Chaman Lal replied vaguely. His arm swept over the road. 'This area is called Marwari Para. The houses are all owned by Marwaris, and the shops—in Raja Bazar, Fateh Ali Bazar and Sat Matha—also belong to Marwaris. It is best if you live in Marwari Para. To the south, beyond Sat Matha, live Hindu Bengalis. Musalman Para is on the other side of the river, around the mosque.'

'I did not see a river when I came.'

'The Karatoya. It lies to the east of Marwari Para; you came from Santahar in the west. But you will never need to cross the river. The ghat is on the west bank—that is where the jute boats come.' Chaman Lal turned up the corner of his mouth in disgust. 'The smells from the fish market sometimes come across the river, all the way to Marwari Para. And you know what else they slaughter there...'

Hari shrugged, wishing to show he was not as green as Chaman Lal thought. 'There is a fish market in Kalkatta too. I passed it daily on my way from Amherst Row to Cotton Street...'

Chaman Lal was annoyed. 'Our fish market is not like the one in Kalkatta, where sahibs buy their meat. You will know when you see it, though I see no reason why you should. Most Musalmans understand us—when you drink water, they will leave your shop; should you ask for water in their shops, they will call a Brahmin cook—but some do not. Usually, they will not trouble you unless provoked, and a wise bania will never give provocation. You may have heard the saying: why anger a Musalman for a salaam? Heed that advice—if he asks for a salaam, give it to him. It costs nothing.'

Six years ago, Hari had been intimidated by Bengalis in

Calcutta. Gradually, he had learned to understand them. He was no longer unnerved when they called him 'Mero', nor embarrassed to bargain aggressively at a stall run by a Bengali. It had helped, of course, that the Bengalis in Calcutta were Hindus, that they celebrated Durga Puja and sang bhajans to Krishna. Now, he was confronted with Bengalis who were Musalmans. How was he to deal with those who lived east of the Karatoya? He had already been disappointed when he first saw Bara Gola. Chaman Lal seemed to think it was the centre of town, but it was just a tin shed. In Shekhavati, houses had proper roofs—even if made of thatch and grass—the air was clean and there was no slush on the street. For all the lushness of its countryside, Bogra was ragged and dirty.

'Should I start in Santahar?' he asked. 'It is on the main railway line from Kalkatta to Siliguri.'

'In Santahar, you will have to speak Bengali. There aren't many Marwaris there. You could start in Rangpur or Rajshahi, but Khemchand Babu sent you in my care, here in Bogra.'

Hari sensed that this was a command, not a suggestion.

'You have not yet seen the Karatoya,' said Chaman Lal soothingly. 'Everything comes down the river—coconuts, bananas, jute—and goes to Santahar. The Karatoya joins with the Jamuna, so we get good jute from Mymensingh, Tippera and Faridpur—not the knotted fibre that grows in Rangpur—and some make good money out of it. What is Santahar? A village with a few huts.'

'But the Musalmans...'

'The Musalmans in Santahar are more aggressive, while the Nawab of Bogra is Hindu-minded.'

'There is a nawab?'

'Nawab Sobhan. His family once owned all of Bogra but he has sold much of the estate. It was Marwaris who bought it—giving him good rates—and it is Marwaris who loan him money to spend his time in Kalkatta.'

'Does he have a shop there?'

Chaman Lal chuckled. Hari noticed the missing teeth. 'A nawab has no work. He lives off the tenants on his land; he goes to the races; he chases memsahibs. There was one who had him in her powers—a Yehudi woman by the name of Mozelle. They say he has many children by her, but they will not inherit the estate—that will go to Altaf Ali, his grandson. He is Hindu-minded like his grandfather. And he likes memsahibs too!'

In Calcutta, Hari had believed that memsahibs were to be found only in the company of sahibs. No doubt these were women of poor character, as were these nawabs, but it was comforting to know that the nawab liked Hindus. 'How much is the rent for a small room in Bara Gola?'

'Bara Gola is not a good location,' said Chaman Lal, offering no explanation for why he himself rented there. 'I will find you a shop near Sat Matha. They call it that because seven roads meet there—anyone coming from Santahar must pass through it.'

Hari wondered if Khemchandji's letter had also mentioned money.

'I have Khemchand Babu's permission to loan you three thousand,' said Chaman Lal, reading his mind, 'at bayis-anna-saikada interest.'

Hari calculated. More than 16 per cent annually, even higher when monthly compounding was considered. Khemchandji had not been especially generous.

'The rate is not unreasonable,' said Chaman Lal, 'considering you are only… how old are you?'

'Eighteen. The nineteenth is on me, to be completed on Falgun sudi dwaadashi.'

'You are tall for your age.'

Hari suppressed the desire to say something about Shekhavati grain—he knew it would not be appreciated. 'Where do I buy stock?'

'I will take you to a dealer. You will also need sacks and scales.'

'And weights.'

'Use stones,' said Chaman Lal stiffly. 'It isn't as if you are weighing silver. When can you start?'

'Tomorrow,' said Hari eagerly.

'I will watch you day and night. I pass Sat Matha twice a day—in the morning and the evening—and I expect to see you seated behind the cash box whenever I pass. A boy has no other business in Disavar. Why else has he come here? Do not waste time with friends—I hope you will not make any—and do not fall into the habit of laughing and joking when seated on the gaddi, as is common among young boys who come here from Shekhavati.'

'Where do I get a cash box?'

'Use the pockets of your kurta. They are large enough for now.'

'I do not know much about rice,' Hari said uncertainly.

Chaman Lal made a dismissive sound. 'You will learn.' He stood up, indicating that the interview was over. 'You may put your trunk in a corner here until you have a shop. There is a basa in Bara Gola where you may eat. Ask the servant for a lota of water when you need to use the latrine.'

'Where is the latrine?' Hari asked, suddenly conscious of the pain in his bowels.

'Behind Bara Gola. Be careful in the slush there. There are scorpions.'

'Where will I sleep?'

'Right here, on the mattress. Did you bring a mosquito net?'

Hari shook his head. 'I have never used one before.'

'This is not Kalkatta. Mosquitoes will suck you dry at night. Ask the servant to buy you one on credit. Six annas. You may repay the shopkeeper at aath-anna-saikada interest.'

Chaman Lal stepped out of his cubicle, preparing to walk home. 'I will send the munim to register your shop tomorrow. He will need a name for the registry. Whose son are you?'

'Shri Duli Chand Tibrewal.'

'And your grandfather?'

'Shri Laduram Tibrewal.'

'I will register it as Laduram Duli Chand,' said Chaman Lal as he turned to go.

Hari thought for a moment. 'No. Register it as Harilal & Sons.'

Chaman Lal regarded him curiously. 'How old did you say you were?'

'Eighteen. The nineteenth is on me, to be completed on Falgun sudi dwaadashi.'

'How many sons do you have?'

'One, but there will be many more.'

'How old is he?'

'Gopi Chand Tibrewal. Born in Rampura, Shekhavati, Pausha sudi shashtami.'

Chaman Lal frowned. 'That is yesterday.'

'Yes.'

'You cannot name a boy merely a day after his birth, much less name a shop after him. It is inauspicious. Has Duli Chandji consulted a pandit?'

'I will pay the pandit to say that the name is appropriate.' Before Chaman Lal could raise another objection, Hari said quickly, 'All my sons will come to Bogra. They will learn Bengali, sell rice and jute, and speak to Musalman customers with many salaams. One day, they will take over Harilal & Sons.'

Chaman Lal sighed. 'Khemchand Babu has sent you to me, so I will take care of you. But I have seen countless boys come and go, and only the modest ones are still sitting in shops today, bantering with customers and filling their cash boxes. The flashy ones have gone back to Shekhavati, empty-handed.'

With a last disapproving nod, Chaman Lal threw a shawl over his shoulder and walked out in the haze cast by the setting sun. Hari shuddered, thinking of Janardhan—the flashy one on his way back to Shekhavati—as he unwrapped his bundle on the mattress while Chaman Lal's servant prepared to draw the shutters.

3

BOGRA

1

Harilal & Sons began business in a small cubicle at Sat Matha, where the seven thoroughfares of the city intersected. Chaman Lal took Hari to the registry office, where a Bengali clerk noted, '*Harilal & Sons, Pushsha 8, 1312*'.

Hari turned to Chaman Lal. 'The date is wrong.'

'Bengali date,' Chaman Lal explained. 'You have spent too many years in Kalkatta.'

The clerk said, 'I could put down the English date too.'

Hari had merely wanted to record the Vikram Samvat day of 'Pausha sudi ashtami, 1962', but was loath to admit that he still did not understand the English calendar, so he gave assent. The clerk added, 'January 2, 1906.'

'I do not understand a word of English,' Chaman Lal declared with pride, 'and I have been in Disavar for fifty years.'

'I myself picked up no more than a dozen words in five years,' Hari said ingratiatingly.

After they had both signed—Chaman Lal in Bengali and Hari in Modhiya—they returned to Bara Gola. A loan of three thousand from the firm of Daulatram Gulabchand was formalized, with Chaman Lal and a munim as witnesses; Hari's signature was recorded in the books. Chaman Lal opened his red binder to a new page and folded it twice on itself, vertically, to create four columns—outflow, receipts, amounts receivable and liabilities. Daubing his ring finger in a paste of roli, he drew a red swastika on the page. After the roli had dried, he sprinkled a few grains of rice on it and entered the sum of three thousand against Harilal Tibrewal in the outflow column. Hari was disappointed to see the entry. He had hoped the loan would be kachcha—not recorded on the books. Did Chaman Lalji not trust him that he was subjecting him to this legal rigmarole?

Divining his thoughts, the old man said, 'This is still a kachcha loan: a piece of paper means nothing. It becomes pakka only if a government officer witnesses the signature and stamp duty is paid.'

In the afternoon, Chaman Lal took him to Fateh Ali Bajar, where an agreement was signed for the purchase of sacks of rice and daal on credit. Hari transferred his trunk and bundle to his cubicle at Sat Matha. In the evening, a pandit was engaged for one rupee—or taka, as they called it in Bogra—to do a puja. The first entry in Hari's ledger showed an outflow of that rupee, followed by the liabilities recorded for the sacks of rice and daal. He slept in his cubicle that night—a mattress had been installed and a white sheet draped over it. The next morning, he rose early and walked to Bara Gola, where he bathed under a hand-pump and was scolded by Chaman Lal for being careless with water. Returning to Sat Matha, he dusted the gaddi with a bamboo broom, opened his doors and sat down next to his new cash box.

He waited all day. At first he sat cross-legged, as a bania should on his gaddi. Tiring, he raised a knee. By afternoon, he was leaning against the cash box. In a thriving shop, Duli Chand used to say, the shopkeeper is never visible because he is always unsealing sacks in the back; you will never catch him scanning the street for customers; it is they who must vie for his attention... That day, Hari watched bullock carts loaded with paddy husk, Marwaris with jholas in their hands, beggars shivering even in the heat, cows returning from pasture and goats being led to abattoirs. It was only at dusk that someone approached him. It was only a boy. Even so, he held his breath.

The boy wanted salt.

Hari considered. In Fateh Ali Bajar, a one-munn bag of salt had cost him three rupees and two annas, which worked out to slightly more than an anna for a ser. His father's quotes usually began at twice the wholesale rate to allow for some bargaining by the customer, so he should perhaps start at two annas to a ser.

But the boy looked too poor to buy more than one or two tolas. Hari summoned Master Bholaram's tables. 'Three tolas for a pie.'

The boy looked uncertain. Musalman, thought Hari wistfully, just a poor boy in a torn kurta and dirty lungi with no money.

'Six tolas,' the boy suggested.

'Four.'

The boy shook his head and turned away. Heart pounding, Hari rose to stop him. The first customer of the day must never be turned away. How often had he seen his father bow to unreasonable demands made by the first arrival in his shop! It was only a Musalman boy, but he must not go empty-handed. He called, 'Five tolas for a pie.'

The boy relented. Hari picked up the scales, aware that his weights were approximate—mere stones—and hoping he had erred in his own favour rather than the boy's. The boy fished copper coins from his lungi and held them out. Hari was not certain he should touch the boy's hand, and was grateful when he placed the coins next to the gaddi. As his first customer walked away with a packet of salt, Hari sighed. To be standing in 67 Cotton Street and betting five rupees as a lagayival! Why had he come to this mofussil town? Who in Shekhavati had heard of Bogra?

The next day, he decided to post his prices. Able to write only in Modhiya, he paid a paisa to a Musalman to put up a board in Bengali, and an anna to another for prices in English.

Harilal & Sons
General merchants
Aman 1 cwt, 3 8 5
Wheat 1 munn, 4 14 8
Sugar, 1 khandi, 28 8 0
Kerosene oil, 1 tin, 15.8 ser, 4 0 0
Salt, 1 munn, 6 4 0

A week later, Chaman Lal came to the shop unannounced, saying Khemchandji had dispatched him to check on Hari. This seemed unlikely—Hari could not believe that Khemchandji, sitting on his gaddi in Lalgodam and worrying about the lakhs of rupees owed to Daulatram Gulabchand, had sent Chaman Lal a postcard about him. But he was solicitous, as one must be with a creditor. Chaman Lal was displeased to see the price list.

'Why do you need a list, where every customer may see what you charged the previous one?' Tapping his temple, he said, 'This is where a bania stores his price list.'

Hari nodded sheepishly.

'And why are your prices stated in munn and khandi? This is a retail store. No one will buy more than a ser of anything. I see you have never sat on the gaddi with your father. What does he deal in?'

Hari was forced to tell Chaman Lal that his father had the same store in Rampura. Chaman Lal's face showed contempt, which multiplied when he saw the second price list in English. 'The young ones try to make a display of their English, but those are not the ones who get customers.'

As soon as Chaman Lal left, Hari took down the English list, ruing the one anna wasted on it.

Over the next few months, he adjusted to the pace of life in Bogra. Business was slow. Money came in annas, paise and pies; silver rupees were rarely seen. Credit was hard to come by, and the interest charged on his loan from Chaman Lal was high, so he earned very little. He ate meals in Bara Gola, slept in his cubicle at Sat Matha and sat behind the cash box all day. This was what his father had done all his life in Rampura, and his grandfather before him. He knew he must not complain, that a boy who sat on his gaddi day after day was wiser than the flashy ones who hoped to earn thousands in a day. Wealth was to be accumulated slowly through small, steady profits, not through occasional windfalls. Such wealth was more stable, more durable, indeed more *moral.* Even the gods wanted a bania to acquire his riches gradually—that was why sudden ascent was usually followed by a quick fall.

Before he left Rampura with Hemraj, Hari had spent two

years in his father's shop. He had sat on the gaddi listlessly, showing no interest in measuring out scoops of bajra or jowar, drawing frequent rebukes. But he had not failed to learn the tools of a bania's trade. Along with the list of prices he was supposed to store in his mind was another that he had learned in Rampura—sugar could be increased with chalk dust, salt with powdered stone, black pepper with papaya seeds, crushed chillies with brick powder, asafoetida with soapstone, ghee with oil and mashed potato, saffron with tendrils of maize cobs... He began cautiously and hesitantly, uncertain that the ways of Shekhavati applied in Disavar. As the weeks passed he became bolder. He had noted that the stock he bought in Fateh Ali Bajar was of dubious quality—the stones in the daal were plainly visible. He could not, of course, confront his suppliers, who were Chaman Lal's acquaintances—that would have been like mentioning 67 Cotton Street in Lalgodam: everyone knew about it, no one mentioned it. So he carefully modulated his own concoctions depending on the quality of his stock, and consoled himself that he was losing no money on the stones in his daal. As long as he did not overplay his hand, his customers would not complain. That is what his father would have done, and that was perhaps what Chaman Lalji would have counselled. Was not Daulatram's empire founded on a lie? Had eleven-year-old Daulatiya been fussy about the purity of that gold sample, he would still be in Rampura, rubbing pieces of gold on slabs of kasauti.

The first boy he befriended in Bogra was Mangiram Kabra, whose father was his largest supplier. Mangiram was a year older than Hari. His family had come from Shekhavati more than a hundred years ago. Unlike other Marwaris, they had stopped their annual visits to Shekhavati—they had few remaining relatives there, and no haveli. They lived in Fateh Ali Bajar in an old house above the shop. Fifty years ago, Mangiram's grandfather had bought the property from Nawab Sobhan—who was gradually selling off the estate to pay for his extravagances—on terms favourable to the nawab. In the following years, the nawab and his son-in-law had borrowed much more, and were now heavily indebted to Mangiram's family. Whenever an outbreak of ill-will with Musalmans had threatened their security, Mangiram's grandfather, and then his father, had sought the support of the nawab, which had been readily offered. As a consequence, they felt quite secure in Bogra and were not prey to the anxieties that plagued other Marwaris.

Mangiram was a frequent visitor at the Nawabbari—the nawab's estate in Fateh Ali Bajar—which was within walking distance from his house. He went to collect on old loans, to lend more money, or simply to remind the nawab's retainers that the creditor still lurked, but was rarely admitted to the nawab's presence—Nawab Sobhan was now an old man, and Nawabzada Altaf Ali, his grandson and heir, spent much of his time in Calcutta.

On most evenings, after Hari had taken the inventory and closed his books, he would walk to Bara Gola for dinner—rice, daal, roti and mango pickle—and then find his way to Fateh Ali Bazar, where Mangiram would have closed shop and gone upstairs to his wife. Hari would send word and Mangi would come down. They would sit in Mangiram's gaddi and talk about market rates, suppliers and, often, the nawab. A servant would be sent downstairs with cups of tea—Hari had now learned to drink endless cups, in the manner of Bengalis—and they would talk late into the night, until it was time to return to his cubicle at Sat Matha.

It was Mangiram who took Hari to the Nawabbari. The estate sat on the west bank of the Karatoya. On three sides, it was surrounded by a wall and guarded by an imposing gate of cast iron, which was attended by a keeper; the fourth faced the river. At eleven every morning, the nawab's tenants and creditors were admitted into the Nawabbari to make their cases—the one to plead leniency in cess and the other to plead payment of arrears. Both contended with the nawab's retainer and clerks and, on the rare occasion, with Nawabzada Altaf Ali.

Because Mangiram was a regular caller, the keeper knew him well. Hari followed him through the gates. Two leashed Alsatians growled in a corner. They walked through a garden, and then an orchard—guava, blackberry, pineapple, jackfruit and tamarind—with a view of the riverbank. Steps led down to the water; boats lay moored. Mangi said, 'Nawab Sobhan had a steamer of his own. When he went to Calcutta, he sailed down the Karatoya—which flows into the Jamuna and then the Padma—got off at Damookdeah Ghat and took the train to Sealdah Station. All this to avoid crossing the Padma by ferry from Sara Ghat to Damookdeah Ghat, because it was too crowded.'

They approached the nawab's mansion, hidden behind a grove of mango trees, and entered the audience hall. Hari stared at the ornate ceiling, and portraits of sahibs and memsahibs on the walls.

'Mistresses,' Mangiram said. 'Some are English. And that one is Mozelle Cohen, the Yehudi woman who gave the nawab a son.'

'What about the sahibs? Are they husbands to those memsahibs?'

Mangiram shrugged, uninterested. 'Lat Sahibs, perhaps.'

The hall was deserted. They were headed to the retainer's office, but Mangiram made detours, making a great show of his familiarity with the Nawabbari. 'Billiards room, music room, smoking room, powder room for memsahibs...'

They crossed the hall and sat on a bench outside the office, waiting to be called in. A porcelain water jug stood in the corner. Hari bent over to shut its leaking tap.

'Do not touch that,' Mangiram whispered.

Hari withdrew. 'It is leaking.'

'That is the nawab's filter,' Mangiram said. 'Improved carbon block, from London.'

Why does the nawab filter his water? Hari wondered. Was it not sufficient that he drank from the Karatoya, which was almost as sacred as the Ganga? But a Musalman would not know that.

When they were ushered into the office an hour later, Hari was shocked to see Mangiram fold his hands obsequiously before the retainer. Was not Mangi on good terms with Nawabzada Altaf Ali? And did that not make the retainer—a mere factotum—inferior to Mangi? There was no evidence of that in the meeting, which ended in three minutes with a command that Mangi present himself again in one month to receive a tenth of the interest owed. Mangi withdrew—there was not a wrinkle on his forehead.

'That went well,' he said as they walked back through the audience hall. 'The Nawabzada is Hindu-minded like his grandfather.'

'That is because he owes two lakhs to Hindus like you.'

Mangiram was offended. 'Do not say that! As long as the nawab is our friend, we will come to no harm in Bogra. What is money? The dirt on one's palm. Altaf Ali has fallen on hard times since the division in his family. He no longer gets the full revenue from his lands—seven-sixteenth goes to a cousin, Satani Miya, and the Nawabzada must live off the remaining nine-sixteenth.'

Suddenly, Hari yearned for Shekhavati, where a bania was not surrounded by Musalmans, and did not have to present himself before the underlings of nawabs who strained water in porcelain cylinders.

He had now been in Bogra for almost two years. Winters were colder than in Calcutta. He lay shivering under a blanket in his cubicle and dreamed of Parmeshwari. Khemchandji had certainly informed his father that he was in Bogra, yet there had been no postcard from Rampura. Perhaps his shame had travelled home—everyone knew of his activities at 67 Cotton Street, and that an English sergeant had come to Lalgodam to inquire about him. He was too embarrassed to write, fearing the rebuke any response would contain. His son was almost two now. What had they named him? He must go to Rampura. As soon as his cart crossed the riverbed near Daulatram's haveli, he would seek a pandit and give him a rupee to change the boy's name to Gopi. Gopi Chand Tibrewal... That was what he told himself as he fell asleep every night. But, of course, he would go nowhere—a bania lives where his shop is, his father had said, or he will lose both his home and his customers. Even if he were to disobey his father, there was the loan from Chaman Lalji at the extortionate rate of 16 per cent. He must add more brick dust to his chillies, more chalk to his sugar…

In the winter of 1907, he received a visit from Chaman Lal, whom he had not seen for months. The old man walked into the cubicle with a proprietary air and sat down on the gaddi, next to Hari, close enough to see the coins in the cash box itself. Hari cringed. Only a creditor would dare behave thus, and he did so when collecting on debts.

'Khemchandji asked about you,' said Chaman Lal.

He is asking about the loan, Hari thought, not about me. 'The market has been slow… They say rates will rise when the sahibs undo partition.'

Hari had no reason to believe either—that the two halves of Bengal would be re-joined, or that rates would rise as a result—but he had to offer some response, any response, for having fallen behind in payments. At 16 per cent, any delay was going to sap his ability to repay the loan at all.

Chaman Lalji scooped up some sugar from an open sack, frowned and threw it back. 'When Daulatram was offered three rupees by his supplier, he asked for only one. Do you know why?'

Hari knew very well, but thought it wise to let Chaman Lal complete the lesson. The story was perhaps apocryphal anyway.

'One rupee was all he needed to walk to Mirzapur,' said Chaman Lal.

Hari knew what would follow.

'Not everyone can be a Dharmaraj Yudhishthir, who never strayed from the righteous path. Raamji knows this—He looks the other way when a bania puts something in his sugar. But when a man needs one rupee he must not ask for three.'

Hari decided not to raise the obvious point: Yudhishthir gambled his wife and kingdom away when it suited him. Chaman Lal continued. 'I will tell Khemchandji that you work hard, and that I have yet seen no signs of laziness.'

This sounds like a warning, Hari thought.

Before he left, Chaman Lal withdrew a crumpled postcard from his pocket. 'Khemchandji had given your father my address in Bara Gola. This came for you.'

Hari gasped. The card had been folded in half. He recognized Master Bholaram's hand right away—a single line, squeezed in the top left corner as if the writer had anticipated a much longer letter.

'If Raamji so wishes, Duli Chand Tibrewal will see the auspicious town of Bogra with Harilal's son (may he live long) on Pous badi 1.'

He stared at the postcard for a long time. It was uncharacteristic of his father to waste so much space—why had he not filled up the card with details? But, of course, it would not be proper for him to mention Parmeshwari. What mattered was that she was coming, and bringing his son, in six days! His joy gave way to panic: where would she live? They could not all sleep in his shop. Where would he get the money to pay for their upkeep? And his son would need toys… He could not ask Chaman Lalji for another loan. There was only one person in Bogra who could help. He ran to Mangiram's shop in Fateh Ali Bazar, pulled his friend into a quiet corner and asked him for a hundred taka.

Mangiram was generous. 'I have lent to a Musalman nawab for half-anna-saikada,' he said. 'Why not give the same rate to a bania from Shekhavati?'

Hari found rooms in the building across the road from his cubicle—two rooms and a verandah on the first floor—at a rate he could not really afford. He had a servant clean the rooms and lay cots inside. He transferred small bags of his stock—rice, daal, flour, sugar—into a corner of the verandah so Parmeshwari would have something to cook, making a mental note that he must set aside some sugar before mixing chalk in it. For five days, he sat dreamily on the gaddi, thinking of Parmeshwari and wondering what his son looked like. The day before their arrival, he was seized with another matter—where would his son go for his first tonsure? In Shekhavati, a family would let its sons' hair grow until at least two or three boys had reached the age of three. They would then be taken together to the temple of Shyam Baba in the town of Khatu—a few hours away by camel cart—where a barber would shave their heads. It was improper for a boy to have his first tonsure anywhere else. But what could a Marwari in Bengal do?

Mangiram laughed it off. His family had lived in Bogra for three generations. Their tonsure ceremonies were held on the banks of the Karatoya, which, he assured Hari, was just as proper. 'Do not worry about his hair,' Mangiram said, 'but get your son a toy. He will see his father for the first time—he will never forget what you give him tomorrow.'

Hari knew exactly what he wanted for his son.

They came in a bullock cart. He saw them right away as the cart approached Sat Matha. They must have gone to Bara Gola, where Chaman Lalji would have directed them to Sat Matha. Hari was with a customer. He pretended not to notice, aware that his father was looking this way and that to locate his cubicle. Nanuram sat in the front with Duli Chand. Why had he come? Who was minding the shop in Rampura? Parmeshwari was in the back with his mother, their heads covered in shawls. He could not make out who was who, and did not want to look. His son was probably in one of their laps... but now the cart had come to a stop and his father had climbed down—he could pretend no longer.

He rushed out, checked himself—he must not appear too excited—and touched his father's feet, thinking of Parmeshwari seated a few yards from him. But he must go through the motions. He was being judged.

'May you live long, Harilal,' Duli Chand said.

Hari stood up. There was pain on his father's face. He looked like he had been crying. Hari put it down to the rigours of the long journey from Shekhavati. Calcutta would have been a shock to them. How had they managed their way through the Howrah and Sealdah stations?

Nanuram began to unload. Hari saw the flailing of a little arm in the cart. Nanuram lifted the boy off his feet and set him on the ground.

Hari examined his son. He stood wide-eyed, in a silver kurta and shervani that had crumpled in travel. A velvet cap lay askew on his head. Hari spread his arms. 'Come.'

Gopi did not respond. Nanuram laughed and commanded the boy. 'Go on! Touch your father's feet.'

Gopi continued to stare.

'The boy does not know you,' said Duli Chand, and his voice seemed to come from the depths of exhaustion.

Hari went into the shop, brought out a cage and held it up. 'This is yours.' It was a brown myna. A smile broke over Gopi's face, and he allowed his father to pick him up in his arms.

'He is thin,' said Hari. 'Does he not eat well?'

'You should not have wasted money on a bird,' said Duli Chand. 'He is only two.'

Nanuram transferred their trunks and bundles to the rooms Hari had rented. The women went upstairs, still swaddled in their shawls. Hari watched Parmeshwari through the corner of his eye, hoping the intensity of his feeling would somehow convey a message to her. Gopi was taken away in Nanuram's arms, the myna cage dangling from his hands. Duli Chand sat down on the gaddi with Hari and fell silent. Suddenly, there was nothing to do or say. His father was here in Disavar, and was sitting on his gaddi as if he had been there all along. He was unaccountably sad. And there was a customer asking for mustard seeds. Hari noted with concern that his father paid no attention to the rate or the customer's bargaining, and did not so much as glance at him, when he weighed out the seeds, to ensure he was not giving away too much.

Duli Chand spoke his first words an hour later. 'I did not like Kalkatta—Bara Bazar was too dirty. And I do not like this Bogra.'

'It is cold today,' said Hari. 'Tomorrow will be milder.'

'There are too many Musalmans here,' Duli Chand said. 'Everywhere I look, I see a man who eats beef.'

Hari was startled. Most of his customers were Musalmans. That they ate what was unspeakably horrible did not come in the way. It was neither spoken nor heard. When Mangiram and Chaman Lal spoke of Musalmans, they did so indirectly and delicately, never using words that would clearly identify the subject as a Musalman. Now he was suddenly filled with dread at the possible sins he may have committed in his father's absence. What had Master Bholaram said? *She is mother to the eleven rudras*... What had he done to protect her in Bengal, Masterji would ask, where she was slaughtered daily?

'Even in Rampura, our women do not show their faces outside the house,' Duli Chand said. 'What will they do here, where every eye belongs to a Musalman?'

'There *are* Hindus in Bogra.'

'But they are Bengalis who do not possess the morals of Shekhavati men. And the grain in Bengal...'

'How is Ma?' Hari asked. He was being bold, but he felt he had earned the right after being on his own for so many years.

Duli Chand sighed. 'Raamji loved her, so he called her to his lap.'

This is a mistake, Hari thought. He must not say anything inappropriate. He had seen his mother walk upstairs to the verandah. Indeed, he could see two women right now through the metal grille on the verandah—across the road—as they prepared a meal. Exhaustion had no doubt embittered his father. Or a quarrel in the train. Or a collapse of his business in Rampura.

'It was I who sent them to Khatu—your mother, my daughter-in-law and your son—for the boy's tonsure. "It is too early," she had said, "he is not yet two." "Better now than later," I replied. "Who knows when the boy will have to join his father in Disavar? Once he goes, it will be years before he returns, and the first tonsure may be done nowhere but in Khatu, so it is best to do it right away." Nanuram went with them. On the way back, the cart overturned. Nanuram says the camel climbed a tibba to nibble a khejra bush. Who knows? Shyam Baba has his ways.

He could have turned the cart over before they reached Khatu, but he allowed them into His town. He accepted the child's hair. And He chose to take her away on the way back. There was not a scratch on the boy or the daughter-in-law, or even on Nanuram. But your mother...'

Hari turned away, overwhelmed. He was not supposed to make a display of grief. There were customers outside—his father would disapprove. What bitter fruit this tonsure had given! He had been fretting over this with Mangiram. If only his father had been negligent, they could have done the ceremony near the Karatoya, and the boy would now be playing in his grandmother's lap.

'I saw two women in the cart,' he said, still hoping.

'Lakshmi's Ma. She lost her husband to the pox. "I will take care of your grandson in Disavar," she told me, "and the grandsons who will come after this one." She has no children and no husband. Such a woman will go where she is taken. At least she will not go hungry in my home.'

Hari asked why Nanuram had come along.

'You need a munim in Bogra,' Duli Chand said.

And then it dawned on him: his father was here for good. The shop in Rampura had been shut down. They *lived* in Bogra now, and his cubicle at Sat Matha was their only shop, their only means of earning anything! How would he feed so many mouths? And where would they live? The rooms had been rented for a month at an absurdly high rate. For years he had felt lonely and abandoned, and the thought of his family in Rampura—with a home and a shop—had comforted him. He was merely trying to earn some money in an outpost in Bengal. His stay was an expedition, a foray, a phase in his life that would end with enormous wealth—as had almost happened in Calcutta. But now Bogra was where he lived, and this cubicle was where he earned his living. And his father was too exhausted to do much but sit on the gaddi.

'Muniya has already gone to her father-in-law's house. I said to Nanuram: my three daughters are now off my hands. What will

I do in Rampura? Harilal could use hands in his shop in Bogra. Let us go help him.'

Hari said nothing about the poor state of his finances—the debts to Chaman Lal and Mangiram—or the state of his shop, where he sold just enough to continue his payments to Chaman Lal.

That night, after Parmeshwari and Lakshmi's Ma had cooked dinner—plain rotis without ghee and dry spiced potato—Hari was alone with Parmeshwari for the first time in three years. Nanuram had gone to sleep in the shop, taking Hari's place there. Lakshmi's Ma snored in a corner of the verandah; Duli Chand had taken one room, Hari and Parmeshwari the second one. She spread a sheet on the bare floor and sat on its edge. Gopi was sprawled in the centre, his bald head exposed. Hari came into the room. Instinctively, she pulled a corner of her shawl over the head. For a while he stood uncertainly, wondering where to pick up the thread. He looked at Gopi's face—startlingly innocent in sleep—and began. 'The boy looks like me.'

She shook her head playfully. The shawl slid off her head, and then her shoulders. He noted approvingly that she was fuller, as befitted a mother. And he was also conscious of an intense desire to seize her as in Rampura. But she was no longer the girl who had submitted. No, he would have to control himself. In desperation, he murmured a few lines from Hanuman Chalisa. A deity who warded off ghosts and spirits could certainly protect him from his lust... Then he stopped short, because Parmeshwari had giggled. She had heard his words—he thought he had whispered under his breath—and was taunting him. Laughing, he put his arms around her and pulled her close. Raamji has been generous, he told himself as he undressed her guiltily. Let me not rejoice lest he find my pleasure excessive and take it away.

The next day, a pandit was called. On the payment of eight annas, he pronounced the name Gopi Chand auspicious for the boy.

Hari learned the details of his mother's death over the next few days, through Parmeshwari's sobs and Nanuram's monosyllabic responses. They had had no trouble getting to Khatu. On the way back, they had been warned about dacoits and sandstorms, and Nanuram scanned the tibbas anxiously. They passed a shallow gorge formed by two dunes. The camel became disoriented by a loud report—the sound of a musket, Nanuram said, though he had never heard one before—and began to climb the sides to chew on a khejra bush that grew from the walls. The cart lurched sideways. The cartman yelled and used his whip freely, but the camel would not let go and the cart tipped over. Parmeshwari fell with Gopi Chand in her arms. Nanuram managed to land on his feet. Hari's mother fell head first. They brought her to Rampura and cremated her near Daulatram's haveli, where the riverbed still showed a trickle after the rains.

'I lay in the sand with Gopi Chand in my arms,' recounted Parmeshwari, sobbing. 'He was silent. Why will he not cry? I wondered. I shook him, held him up. His eyes were open but he would not make a sound. I took an oath—to offer one and a quarter munn of churma in the Hanuman Temple at Salasar—and slapped him. He began to wail. Hanumanji saved his life. We must remember the oath the next time we go to Shekhavati.'

Later, Lakshmi's Ma told Hari that the oath taken by Parmeshwari had played no role in reviving Gopi Chand. 'He did not have a scratch on him. Raamji had already protected him. He did not cry only because he never cries, even when he is hungry.'

'An oath cannot be broken,' Parmeshwari said. 'We will offer churma at Salasar.'

'A boy who never cries was surely a saint in his previous life. Gopi Chand is a fakir, a mahatma. I have seen few such children. I have heard he did not wail even during tonsure. Which boy of two does not cry on seeing a barber with a blade?'

Parmeshwari was forced to concur—she was the one who had told Lakshmi's Ma this. And thus they went on. Hari found such talk meaningless. A far more disturbing notion occupied his mind—that he was the instrument of his mother's death. Had they not sent him a telegram saying his mother was ill? It was meant to be a joke, a trick played on him so he would return in a hurry, as he had. But Raamji had taken note, and perhaps seen in this a wish to die.

A man has two mothers, Master Bholaram had said—the first gives him milk for the first year, the second for the remaining years of his life. The first had been called by Raamji and the second was being slaughtered every day before his eyes. All around him, Musalmans were feasting on her flesh… Why had he come to Bengal to see this? He brought out a slate and chalk from the back of the shop and wrote clearly in Modhiya, forming his words slowly, using small letters that Masterji would have approved of.

'A man does not sit and watch the slaying of his mother. Fifty years ago, a Brahmin soldier named Mangal Pandey rebelled against the English sahibs in Barrackpore. Whom was he defending? His mother, the cow. Kill me if you must, he said, but I will not bite into cartridges that contain the grease of the cow. The sahibs hanged him. Then they had to kill the thousands who rose in response—in Delhi, Lucknow, Meerut and Kanpur. People now call this a war against the English government. No, it was a battle to defend the cow.'

The essay pleased him. He noted his steady hand and hoped he had spelled everything correctly. No doubt this had also helped him practise his Modhiya. Masterji would have liked that. And no one need see the essay. He would erase this to write the next one. Why waste paper when a slate was available? As for his mother, a pandit would help him expiate for the sin. All that was needed was a puja and some expense.

2

On his third day in Bogra, Duli Chand came to sit beside Hari in the shop, thrust a hand into each sack, examined the grain as Chaman Lal had done, and threw it back with a knowing nod.

'Everyone in Bogra does it,' Hari said guiltily. 'We have five mouths to feed. The old times are gone, when one could find desi ghee in a shop.'

Duli Chand removed his turban and fanned himself, though it was quite cold. 'Raamji watches everything. Who am I to say anything?'

Hari took that to be acquiescence. He knew that his father slipped stones into his daal in Rampura—which shopkeeper would not, given the times?—but thought it best not to bring it up.

Duli Chand took to rising early and going to the Karatoya for a bath, even on very cold mornings. Returning, he would sit near the cash box, count money, hand out change, take the inventory and tally accounts every evening. He taught Hari how to stack silver rupees so a tall pillar would not fall to its side, how to quickly separate copper coins from bronze, and how to estimate the number of one-anna coins in a heap—skills that Hari increasingly found to be no more than a nuisance.

In the rooms across the road, Parmeshwari spent her days cooking in the verandah. She was with child again. When she stood up, Hari could see her from his seat in the shop, but Lakshmi's Ma soon installed curtains and blocked his view. She had proven to be unequal to Bogra or Bengali—disdaining both the town and the language—and was, therefore, confined to the rooms, where she cared for Gopi Chand, and helped Parmeshwari cook and clean. It was she who dispatched Nanuram to buy vegetables every morning and then harried him about the rates, though she was illiterate and barely understood how much he had spent. Nanuram would smile, pretend to give an account of his expenditures, then go downstairs to Hari.

Duli Chand was always in terror of being violated by a Bengali—Hindu or Muslim—by having one eat or drink in his presence. Fearing prying Bengali eyes, he frowned whenever Parmeshwari pushed the curtains aside to look down into Sat Matha. His spirits rose with the coming of summer, when the dry heat reminded him of Rampura, but by the end of June, the sun was obscured by dark clouds and Bogra was a swamp of slush and mosquitoes. Drains overflowed; one had to navigate carefully through muddy lanes filled with excreta. Duli Chand daily extolled the virtues of clear sand and open skies. He has completely forgotten the Chhappaniya, Hari thought in wonder.

Every morning, when Hari opened the shop, his father planted himself on a chair in the street, to stare down evil in the world around him. He railed against the slush at Sat Matha, admonished shopkeepers who used too much water when washing, and watched hawk-like as Muslim butchers led cows to abattoirs, afraid to challenge them but hoping to shame them by force of will.

'They take these cows to the Nawabbari in Fateh Ali Bajar,' Hari told his father, adding quickly, 'but the Nawabzada is Hindu-minded.'

'Why does he eat beef, then?' Duli Chand demanded.

'A Musalman cannot give up his ways. He keeps the cows in a shed in the Nawabbari, so he need not buy his beef when he craves it.'

For two years, Hari had ignored the butchers who passed by, remembering what Chaman Lal had told him on his arrival in Bogra: why anger the Musalman for a salaam? A bania was not a Rajput—it was not in his blood to pick fights with Musalmans or anyone else. He did not ride a horse, shoot a musket or throw a spear. In Daulatramji's times, Marwari banias travelling through Shekhavati went in caravans and hid their coins in pouches sewn into camel harnesses. When attacked by robbers, they handed over the jewellery they had bought for their wives rather than put up a fight. A bania saw no profit in grandstanding—the necklace he gave to the bandit could be earned back, the life he might lose through bravado would end his earning power forever. And the honour… What was honour? Life was granted by Raamji, honour by men. Indeed, why anger the Musalman for a salaam? It was not as if he killed the cow in front of the bania's eyes; it wasn't as if he insisted that the bania eat beef. Why must the bania seek him out, pry into his affairs and invite retribution in a Bengal full of Musalmans? There was rice to be weighed and tobacco to be sold, children to be raised and weddings to be arranged. If the Musalman killed the cow, the sin would accrue to him. A bania must not sin and a bania must not abet sin, but when had Raamji asked him to prevent others from sinning?

Soon, Duli Chand discovered the Calcutta Pinjrapole Society for the protection of cows, which had branches all over Bengal. A Pinjrapole box was placed in the shop, with a slot in its lid wide enough to accept one-rupee coins. Its key was given to the Pinjrapole man, a Marwari trader from Raja Bajar. Every evening, depending on how many customers had come for the day, Duli Chand dropped a coin into the box—a paisa, two paisa, sometimes an anna. Once a week, the Pinjrapole man brought his key, took the money and wrote out a receipt. Duli Chand speared these receipts on a wire, pushing them down until they met previous ones. The pillar of receipts was now three inches thick; he regarded it with great satisfaction.

He also prevailed on Hari to buy a share in a goshala outside town, where old cows were kept safe from Muslim butchers and buried discreetly on death. Two cows were adopted. A monthly expense was fixed for their upkeep. On most mornings, after his bath in the Karatoya, Duli Chand walked to the goshala to look at his cows.

Chafing under the burden of these expenses, Hari realized he would have to find another shop to occupy Nanuram, who was quick with his Bengali—he was already able to banter with customers—but had little to do. Hesitantly, he asked his father if he had brought any money from Shekhavati. Surely he would have sold his stock before shutting down the shop in Rampura? Duli Chand's response was vague, and Hari was too embarrassed to ask again. Being in Mangiram's debt, he could hardly ask him. And he would not dare approach Chaman Lal, whose loan of three thousand weighed heavily on him.

At Mangiram's suggestion, he began to travel to the weekly market in Gobindganj, 25 miles to the north, leaving Nanuram to mind the shop at Sat Matha. Mangiram supplied the stock—rolls of handspun cloth—and took a per centage of his profits. At dawn, Hari would be in a bullock cart passing through beels, listening to the cartman's song. His stock would be in baskets behind him. The sun would rise to his right and set the paddy aglow. The cartman would speak of the Aush harvest. Hari would nod drowsily. In Gobindganj, he would sit surrounded by his baskets, eat the rotis Parmeshwari had packed for him, chew on mango pickle and bargain hard with customers, who would start at a third of his quoted price. In the evening, he would return by the same bullock cart, baskets light and pockets heavy. Sometimes he had a good day; there were weeks when he earned barely enough to pay for the cart. As the cart approached Bogra in the dark, he would think of Parmeshwari's embrace. On arriving, he would note that Nanuram had shut the shop and climb upstairs to the verandah, where Duli Chand would be sitting on a cot. Parmeshwari would squat next to the oven—shawl drawn over her face on account of Duli Chand—and Gopi Chand would clamour to be picked up in his arms. He would sit on the cot and describe rates to Duli Chand, but his mind would be on Parmeshwari's back, watching every move and trying to interpret in it a taunt, an invitation or rejection. He had arrived at a curious understanding of her that would not have been possible in Rampura, where his mother was mistress of the house. They spoke little, even when they were alone at night with Gopi Chand sprawled between them. She never asked about Gobindganj or the shop downstairs, and he did not mention the kitchen. Doing so would have disturbed the balance they had achieved, where each was dependent on the other without saying so. He undressed her silently; their embrace was unhurried. They lay entwined for hours in the dark, naked, their contentment making all talk superfluous. She was getting heavier. Lakshmi's Ma, whose knowledge on these matters had been legendary in Rampura, had assured him that the child was a boy.

In winter, eleven months after she had arrived in Bogra,

Parmeshwari gave birth to a son. Lakshmi's Ma parted the curtains in the verandah, pushed a brass plate through the grille and beat it with a pair of tongs. In Rampura, everyone would have understood the signal: it is a boy, it is a boy... In Sat Matha, no one seemed to notice. Three men pushed a cart laden with rice sacks, a Musalman was followed by his wife in a burqa, and a bania sat cross-legged outside his store.

'The less they hear about your good fortune, the safer your son will be,' said Duli Chand. He called a pandit, who suggested that the name begin with the Sanskrit 'da', so the boy was named Durga Prasad.

In spite of his grandiose name, Durga was a weak child. Three days after birth his skin acquired a yellow tint. The vaidya summoned by Duli Chand prescribed a herbal paste to be rubbed into the boy's skin twice a day. The yellowness did not go away. Mangiram knew of a Bengali doctor who had a clinic near Bara Gola. Chaman Lal vouched for the doctor too. Hari sent for him.

'I cannot allow a Bengali to touch the child,' said Duli Chand.

'He is a Hindu.'

'But he eats fish and touches Musalmans.'

'He has an LMF degree from Dhaka,' said Hari.

'No degree can wash the dirt off his hands.'

Durga Prasad's condition deteriorated. The whites of his eyes began to darken. Duli Chand relented, on condition that the boy be given a bath after the doctor had touched him, but Dr Saha did not touch the child at all. As soon as Lakshmi's Ma held him up for inspection—Duli Chand had forbidden Parmeshwari to come out of the room—he pronounced his judgement. 'Jaundice.'

Hari turned to his father with a look of vindication. The doctor prescribed a powder—he prepared it right there using a mortar and pestle—took a rupee and left.

'There is no need to wash the boy,' Duli Chand said grudgingly to Lakshmi's Ma.

That evening, Parmeshwari sent Lakshmi's Ma to Hari to get daal and jaggery for the kitchen. While waiting, she washed a brass plate with clay and ash, drew a vermilion swastika on it—remembering to use the ring finger of her right hand—and arranged four copper coins under the four arms of the swastika. After rice had been sprinkled on the coins, she made two heaps of daal and jaggery on the plate, folded her hands, shut her eyes and recited the Mahamrityunjaya mantra, which was known to deliver the greatest sinner from the clutches of death.

Lakshmi's Ma took the plate down to the road. Dusk had fallen. Carts lay here and there; men stood around stalls. She surveyed the seven roads that intersected at Sat Matha and selected a quiet corner, where she laid out three mango leaves. On these, she emptied the plate, taking care not to mix daal with jaggery. Retreating, she found a spot from which she could observe the corner unseen and waited, holding a corner of her shawl over her nose to block the stench of drains. A beggar approached the mango leaves. Bending over, he picked up the coins and popped the jaggery into his mouth, then poured the daal into a fold in his lungi and quickly walked away. Lakshmi's Ma came back, satisfied.

'Did you see his face?' Parmeshwari asked anxiously.

'Of course. I will never forget him,' Lakshmi's Ma said, with some guilt because she had not really marked the man's face as well as she should have.

For three days, Lakshmi's Ma stood at Sat Matha and looked for the beggar. At the end of the third day, Durga Prasad's jaundice faded away. Lakshmi's Ma returned from her vigil to tell Parmeshwari, 'I cannot find the beggar. He is dead, and he took the boy's yellowness with him.'

'He was an old man,' said Parmeshwari, although she had not seen the beggar and Lakshmi's Ma had given no indication of his age. 'He has been saved from hunger and horrible illnesses that were sure to come. And he will be reborn a brahmin in his next life, having given up this one for a little boy.'

Durga Prasad's recovery sent a wave of joy through the house. As he would have in Rampura, Duli Chand asked Hari to arrange for songs. This proved difficult. In Rampura, it was easy to find widows who would sing for a pie or two. Here, the few Marwari widows who could be located were not as willing, or as familiar with Shekhavati songs. Only three were found. They were installed in the verandah. The curtains were pulled aside so the songs could cross the road and reach the shop, where Mangiram joined Hari. As soon as the singing began, Duli Chand frowned.

'In Rampura, a woman whose husband is named Krishna falls silent when his name occurs in a song—she is too modest to utter it. I see no such etiquette here. They sing loudly, all together, showing no inhibition when saying "Krishna" or "Raam" or "Hanuman", as if they do not have husbands at all.'

'Their husbands are dead, babuji,' said Hari.

'A dead husband's name may be uttered no more than a living one's.'

Mangiram said, 'But how will a woman ever sing a song, then? If her husband is named Krishna, her father-in-law Raam, and her brother-in-law Hanuman, which god will she call upon in her songs?'

'You have been in Bengal for too many years,' Duli Chand said. 'A woman whose husband is named Krishna could substitute that name with "Gopal"; the wife of Hanuman Prasad may choose to say "Bajrang" instead. Why do you think Vishnu Bhagwan has a thousand names? So a devout woman may know them all and thus avoid naming the men in her family.'

'But who keeps an account of such things?'

'Harilal's mother did...'

And here Duli Chand stopped. Hari was astonished: his father rarely mentioned his mother. When she was living, they had spoken only when necessary, and then through their children. When he did address her directly—usually in a fit of pique—there would be hours of silence to follow the transgression. He had betrayed no grief at her passing. It was Parmeshwari who sobbed when describing how she lay dead among the tibbas, and Nanuram who had wiped away tears when recounting the accident. His father had said little. No one seeing him now—sitting erect on the gaddi wearing his Shekhavati turban—would know that he was grieving, if indeed he was. Now, having mentioned his wife once, he said no more.

Durga Prasad recovered fully, but Parmeshwari did not. The joy with which she had borne her pregnancy was replaced with constant pain and anxiety. She walked about the rooms with a gaunt expression, a tired old woman at the age of twenty, unable to pick her son up in her arms. Even Duli Chand, in whose presence she was always veiled, commented on her condition. Hari put it down to the cares of motherhood. 'Shekhavati girls are strong,' he said confidently. 'The foul air of Bengal cannot sap her strength.'

'Send her to Chirawa with both boys. I will write to Narayan Dasji. Nanuram could go with her in the train.'

'She cannot go in her condition.'

It was embarrassing enough to Hari that he was discussing his wife with his father, but to speak of her pregnancy with him! He knew he had been hasty. Durga Prasad was no more than three months old. But what was he to do? Was it not Raamji who sent him to Parmeshwari each evening, desiring her even as Durga Prasad clung to her breast? If he was to abstain, why had Raamji not given him the strength to do so? Why was his heart so full of lust, of sinful thoughts that chased him all day and found expression at night? And why did she not push him away, pleading for the infant who was being denied his mother? Every day, while seated in the shop, he made resolutions that he could not keep at night. And now Raamji had sent this third child as punishment for his lust.

Duli Chand had not known that Parmeshwari was pregnant yet again. He wondered if she was strong enough, but the prospect of a third grandchild did not displease him. 'No one can read Raamji's mind,' he said weakly.

Parmeshwari found this third pregnancy burdensome. Lakshmi's Ma had taken Durga Prasad under her wing, but Gopi

Chand would not submit to anyone but his mother, and he was not yet four. Aside from the cares of running her household, she had to contend with severe exhaustion. Lakshmi's Ma began to wear an expression of concern. She had been midwife to countless women in Shekhavati, and had delivered both Gopi Chand and Durga Prasad. One evening, immediately after Hari had closed the shop and come up to the verandah, she whispered to him, 'I have never seen such a belly. The baby rides too high.'

'Doesn't a high belly indicate a son?' Hari asked.

'Yes, but it is also pointed. That tells me the boy is standing up in the womb.'

She suggested that Hari call the doctor who had treated Durga Prasad. Duli Chand ruled that out immediately. How could he allow a Bengali man to touch and prod his daughter-in-law?

Early in October, Parmeshwari's water broke while she was squatting in the kitchen to knead dough. It was hot and humid, and the stench of drains in Sat Matha had climbed all the way to the verandah. Lakshmi's Ma called out across the road. Hari shut the shop and went upstairs. Parmeshwari was in her room, which Lakshmi's Ma had locked from the inside. Two hours later, she opened the door. 'The boy is standing in the womb.'

'Could you not turn him around?'

'I do not need to,' said Lakshmi's Ma with wounded dignity. 'I could bring him into the world standing up. There is nothing I have not seen.'

'Then do it! Why have you come to me?'

Lakshmi's Ma hesitated. 'It is dangerous.'

Hari waved her away, indicating she should proceed. Three hours later, he heard the cry of his third son, Tribhuvan Lal, along with a wail from Lakshmi's Ma, which confirmed his fears. He rushed toward the door but was stopped short by Duli Chand.

'You cannot go in yet, Harilal.'

Ignoring his father, Hari pushed the door open. Gopi Chand followed him into the room, crying, conscious of great misfortune. Lakshmi's Ma sat on the floor by the bed, the infant in her arms.

Parmeshwari lay still, looking at her son. There was much blood. Hari indicated to Lakshmi's Ma that she should leave. She fled the room, the unwashed baby in her arms. He heard Duli Chand scold her outside. Shutting the door, he sat down on the bed, took a limp hand in his, saw the blood soak into his dhoti and said, 'Parmeshwari.'

She chuckled, though it caused her pain. He had never called her by name before. She knew what was expected. 'Harilal.'

The word stood still between them. No woman in Rampura had ever let the name of her husband pass her lips. He would carry this image in his mind with the first one—the face of a girl asleep under the moon, in a bullock cart bumping over the tibbas. He felt tears in his eyes.

'Where is Durga?' she asked when she saw Gopi Chand standing beside him.

'Asleep.'

'Durga is the weak one,' she said. 'It is he who will need your care.'

He sobbed, knowing his father could hear him outside the room. What use had he for restraint now that she was gone? Yes, he said, he would take care of Durga, and also Tribhuvan Lal, who had taken his mother's life, and Gopi Chand, whose tonsure in Khatu had taken away his grandmother.

An hour later, Duli Chand entered the room with Nanuram and Lakshmi's Ma. Hari lay sprawled on the bed, covering Parmeshwari, and Gopi Chand stood sobbing.

'Get up, Harilal. Raamji asks you to.'

Hari slid off the bed and lay on the floor, eyes shut. *I am a corpse like her*, he thought, *yet it is she they will take away*. On seeing his father's blood-drenched clothes, Gopi Chand let out a scream. Duli Chand turned to Lakshmi's Ma. 'Wash the body. I will call the pandit.'

Hari watched the ceremonies without comment, asking himself again and again what part he had played in this. Had he been remiss in the shop? Had he been too free with stones in his daal, too sloppy with his weights? But Raamji would forgive a bania his trade, as he forgave the brahmin his greed, the kshatriya his vanity and the English sahib his swagger. Why blame a man for his nature? Who but Raamji had sown that nature in him? And it was He who had planted lust, in bania as well as sahib, which had driven Hari to embrace her every night. Ah, why had he been cursed with this murderous affliction? They said that chanting the Hanuman Chalisa warded off the most dreadful ghouls and spirits. If only there had been a Chalisa to keep lust at bay!

The pandit chanted beside her body. *Nainam chhindanti shastraani, nainam dahati paavakaha, nachainam kledayantiyaapo na shoshhayati maarutaha.* Weapons cannot cut it, fire cannot burn it, water cannot soil it, wind cannot dry it...

But, of course, fire shall burn it, Hari thought. He knew the pandit spoke not of her body but the essence, but how was he, Harilal Tibrewal, to see that soul that nothing could destroy? What use did a bania have for a soul at all? Buy cheap and sell dear, Master Bholaram had said. What else was there to existence, aside from stock that could be touched and felt and smelt and bought and sold, and what remained when it had been taken away? No doubt the pandit knew this too. He chanted as if this was merely another ceremony—a puja at Diwali, the inauguration of a new shop, the birth of a baby, or the purification of a man who had touched a Musalman. They were all the same to him. After each he was fed, given gifts and a silver rupee. In each he chanted the same lines. And soon they would take the body away, lay it on a pyre and set it ablaze, giving the lie to everything the pandit had said.

'A man does not grieve like a child, Harilal. Raamji breathed no more than twenty-one years into her, but she spent those years well. She has given you three sons.'

It was Duli Chand, peering into the room. Hari sensed disapproval in his eyes. He got up and went out into the verandah, where the pandit handed him a bottle of itra to be sprinkled on her. They had washed the body and laid it on a wooden bier, which Gopi was circumambulating as the pandit chanted. A woman led Durga—barely a year old and walking unsteadily—and Lakshmi's Ma carried Tribhuvan Lal in her arms. All three have circled their mother, Hari thought, without understanding what has happened. Even Gopi had only the faintest idea. On the pandit's instructions, he placed two little pearls on the pupils of her eyes and threaded her ears with gold. Down in the road, a cow stood stomping, awaiting its part in the ceremony. The noise had disturbed her. She lifted her tail and produced a gob of dung that plopped down in the dirt. No one noticed.

In the afternoon, Duli Chand conferred with Hari and others regarding cremation arrangements. Hari wanted to take the body to the Padma near Sara Ghat station.

Mangiram said, 'The train to Santahar is full. Nawabzada Altaf Ali's begum has given birth to a boy today. The nawab's tenants are going to Kalkatta to celebrate.'

Duli Chand sighed. 'My grandson labours under great misfortune. He took his mother's life, and he has been born on the same day as a nawab's son.'

'Let us take a bullock cart to Santahar,' said Hari, 'and then the train to Kalkatta from there. We can get off at Sara Ghat.'

'Sara Ghat is on the Padma, not the Ganga,' Mangiram pointed out.

'The Padma is the same as the Ganga.'

'The Ganga empties into the Hooghly and goes to Kalkatta,' said Mangiram. 'The Padma is merely what is left over.'

Hari had heard this argument countless times—that only the right branch of the Ganga, the Hooghly, inherited her sacred essence—but he had crossed the Padma on his way to Santahar three years ago. He had seen her at night, remembered the yellow and amber boats lighting the ferry's path, and felt the pull of her waters. Who was Mangiram—a man who had lived with Musalmans all his life—to say she was not sacred?

'When my grandfather died, we took him to the banks of the Karatoya,' said Mangiram. 'The ghat is in Raja Bazar.'

'I want her ashes to flow in the Padma.'

'The Karatoya is sacred too,' said Mangiram. 'When the Goddess Parvati died...'

Hari had heard this story too: on Parvati's death, Shiv had performed the Rudra Tandav dance, threatening to destroy the universe. To forestall him, Vishnu cut Parvati's body into fifty-one pieces. One of these pieces had fallen into the Karatoya, making her waters sacred. When first told the tale, Hari had concluded that the Marwaris of Bogra had concocted it to justify their cremations.

'The Padma,' he repeated.

'It is hot,' said Duli Chand. 'We cannot reach Sara Ghat until noon tomorrow. The body will not keep.'

At dawn, they took her to the Karatoya, past the Nawabbari in Fateh Ali Bajar, to the riverbank in Raja Bajar. Three other pyres burnt silently, each with a group of men around it. Not yet four, Gopi Chand stood next to Hari, head shaven, watching the ceremony with a blank expression. He had been dressed in a cotton dhoti; his chest was bare. Hari led him round the pyre and had him pour ghee into his mother's mouth, clapping a hand over his eyes to prevent his seeing the face. As the flames crackled, Hari glanced at the river, swollen after the rains. The sun rose on the opposite bank. Boats piled with jute were pulling ashore; men were scrambling on board to organize the unloading. There was much shouting, pulling and pushing. Bullock carts waited, ready to take the bundles to Santahar, where they would be loaded into trains bound for Calcutta. There, the jute would be taken to warehouses in Chitpur Road, where it would be dried, sorted and pressed into bales, each weighing 400 pounds. It was among these bales that Hari and Janardhan had spent their best years in Calcutta. Even now, boys like him perhaps lounged about the warehouses, making deals, placing the jute with Andrew Yule & Company, or buying some for Daulatram Gulabchand to be sold to Rallis Brothers... It would be so much cheaper, he thought, if the jute could be dried, sorted and pressed in Bogra before being sent the 200 miles to Calcutta. But who in Bogra knew anything about jute baling? And who could afford a baling machine?

'Nothing is permanent,' he heard his father say. 'Raamji places one on this earth, and Raamji takes one away. A man must go about his business.'

The flames were dying down. The boats in the distance had now fallen silent, their jute unloaded. Men lay sprawled on decks. Smoke drifted lazily from cooking fires. A song lilted across—Bengali or Bhojpuri: Hari could not tell at this distance.

He looked at the embers. Her ashes would flow down the Karatoya, mix with the Jamuna and Padma and then join the sea. He turned to his father. 'I will set up a jute press.'

3

Two weeks after Parmeshwari's death, Hari approached Chaman Lal for money to buy a jute baling machine.

'You have not returned the three thousand owed to the firm,' scoffed Chaman Lal. 'On what grounds do you ask for a new loan?' Having spent his life working for Daulatram Gulabchand in its Calcutta and Dhaka offices, he usually referred to the firm simply as 'the firm'.

Knowing that Chaman Lal sometimes dispatched jute from Bogra to Santahar—for each munn transferred, he received a commission from Daulatram Gulabchand—Hari said, 'I am not asking for a loan but proposing a partnership. The capital will be yours, the labour mine. You would be a sleeping partner. We would each take half the profits.'

Chaman Lal thought long and hard. Hari could guess what passed through his mind—he was old, on his way to decrepitude. He had no sons; his wife had died long ago; his daughters had been married off. By now, Hari also knew why Chaman Lal's cubicle in Bara Gola betrayed no signs of activity—he had nothing to sell. Aside from his meagre jute commissions, the little he earned was as a pawn-broker. Musalmans brought him their trinkets—rings, arm-bands and necklaces—against which he lent small sums after weighing each item carefully with his scales. Not being a goldsmith, his assessment was approximate, so he was conservative in his valuations and his rates were as high as 35 per cent. He lent only to customers he knew, asking each one to imprint his thumb, as a sort of signature, in a ledger. The recesses of his cubicle were stacked with little paper packets, each containing a bauble with the name of the borrower, the amount lent and the date mortgaged written in Modhiya. Some of the Musalmans returned to claim their trinkets, some did not, so Chaman Lal was a regular supplier of old jewellery to the goldsmiths in Fateh Ali Bajar, where he could often be found haggling over a cummerbund.

He offered one last objection. 'No one has seen a jute press in Bogra. Few Marwaris outside Kalkatta own one.'

'We will be the first.'

'A press costs much.'

'We will buy an old one in Kalkatta.'

'I will take a two-thirds share in return for my capital,' Chaman Lal said.

The next day, Hari learned that Chaman Lal's vaunted capital—for which he wanted a two-thirds share in the profits—was no more than 250 rupees. He was aghast. Here was a Marwari who had served Daulatram Gulabchand for decades and had connections and interests all over Bengal, yet all his wealth could be accommodated in the upper compartment of a small cash box! Where had it gone? Did not the firm pay its munims at least sixty rupees a month? And did not Chaman Lal, as did everyone else, set aside a fair amount every month for his dotage, knowing he had no sons? Perhaps his daughters' weddings, or his wife's long illness, had been ruinous.

In any case, Hari would have to look for capital elsewhere. Only one person could make thousands available—the one who had financed his first shop. He would turn again to Khemchand Biyani, head munim of Daulatram Gulabchand. He would go to Calcutta.

Leaving his three sons with Lakshmi's Ma and the shop in Duli Chand's care, he left for Santahar, taking Nanuram with him. From there, they took the train to Sara Ghat, crossed the Padma on the ferry, and continued to Calcutta on the broad-gauge line.

Nanuram had passed through Calcutta briefly on his way to Bogra two years ago. He watched the crowds wide-eyed while Hari sat placidly in the tonga they took from Sealdah Station. Bara Bazar was much the same—piles of garbage, fruit stalls in Machua, metal works and tram cars on Harrison Road. Nanuram was dazzled, and still more impressed when Hari scolded the tongawala. They turned into Amherst Row and stopped before Lalgodam. The flour mill was silent. Hari paid the tongawala, making sure he haggled over the fare, to Nanuram's great admiration. They went up to the third floor. Most of the gumashtas were out in Bara Bazar. The munims greeted him warily, offered him a glass of water and made discreet inquiries about his affairs in Bogra. Apparently, his exploits in 67 Cotton Street were well known. The English sergeant may have forgotten him, but in Amherst Row he was treated almost like a man on the run. He was told that Khemchand Biyani was on a tour to the Kanpur branch, and was expected to return in three days. 'Khemchandji is not looking for a gumashta,' said a munim.

'I have not come to become a gumashta,' Hari replied. 'I want a loan.'

'You have already received one.'

Everyone knows, thought Hari. He had imagined that the loan of three thousand was a personal favour, an exception made by Khemchandji, not a routine business matter recorded on the books. 'I need a second loan to buy a jute baling machine.'

The munim was sceptical. 'A tall boy must be careful not to miss the puddles on the road.'

For three days, Hari and Nanuram stayed at Lalgodam, paying for room and board. They walked about Bara Bazar, buying nothing, staying clear of Cotton Street, and waiting for darkness, when they would be able to return to Lalgodam and sleep. Hari was afraid to visit old contacts—traders from whom he had collected payments, lagayivals he had dealt with, rangbaaj men who knew him well—because he did not know how far word had travelled of his near-arrest. Without Janardhan, he felt defenceless in Bara Bazar. He went to Clive Row to see David Yule sahib, hoping he had the power to call off English sergeants, but the sahib was in England.

On the third morning, Khemchandji returned from his trip and was immediately surrounded by munims. That evening, Hari waited until Khemchandji had closed his books and put away his spectacles, then stepped forward and touched his feet. Khemchandji seemed not to recognize him.

'Harilal,' said Hari, 'son of Shri Duli Chandji of Rampura.'

'Ah.' There was disapproval in Khemchandji's voice.

'I have repaid, with interest, a third of the loan you extended through Chaman Lal Babu.'

'Chaman Lal,' repeated Khemchandji, perhaps not remembering the man or the loan. Then, suddenly lucid, he said sharply, 'The English sergeant came thrice after you left.'

'I knew you would protect me,' said Hari, hesitantly.

'Bengali constables kept looking for you for a year. Unlike the English sergeant, they can be turned away for a consideration.' Khemchandji carefully positioned his spectacles on his nose again, opened a binder, ran his finger down the page and looked up. 'The total expense was sixteen rupees. Entered into your account at an interest of chaubis-anna-saikada.'

Instinctively, Hari grumbled about the interest. 'That is 18 per cent. The three thousand in Bogra was given at 16 per cent, and rates are certainly lower in Kalkatta...'

Khemchand Biyani fixed him with a cold look. 'That was a business loan; this is a police matter.'

He sighed. 'I will settle the account with Chaman Lalji.'

'Very good,' said Khemchandji, and his tone implied that all business was settled. He seemed to assume that Hari had come all the way to Calcutta merely to settle charges incurred in buying off Bengali constables.

Hari waited until Khemchandji had locked the cash box and, as expected, asked conversationally, 'How much is wheat in Bogra?'

'Low. A munn can be had for four rupees on a bad day.' This was lower than the rate Hari quoted his customers, but he knew that a downward adjustment would prolong the conversation.

Khemchandji shook his head. 'I live with robbers in Bara Bazar! We just bought five munn for the basa upstairs, at five rupees, nine annas and three paisa to a munn. This from a man who regularly buys jute from the firm and claims to give me a preferential rate.'

Hari expressed his horror of unscrupulous Bara Bazar grocers.

'Chaman Lal says jute procurement is becoming difficult, too,' said Khemchandji. 'Rates keep going up even as the quality drops. It is these European firms. They want to buy directly from mofussil areas instead of going through us. What will we do then—export to Dundee?'

Hari seized the opportunity. 'That is why I have come to Kalkatta. I want to buy a jute baling machine.'

Khemchandji was taken aback. 'What do you know about jute baling?'

'Do you not remember that I supplied your jute to Andrew Yule & Company? I can tell sada jute from tosa jute, Mymensingh fibre from Faridpur stock, knotted strands from smooth ones. I can sniff out dampness from a mile, I can…'

'Baling is not the same as selling bales to European firms. Have you ever seen a machine?'

'Yes, on Chitpur Road.'

'Those are hydraulic presses. Only sahibs can afford them.'

'I know. I was hoping to buy a kachcha press and take it to Bogra.'

'It is not easy to set up a baling machine. You need engineers; you need kyals.'

'Kyals?'

'Coolies who operate the baling machine. Musalmans, usually.'

'Bogra has more Musalmans than Kalkatta.'

'You will have to take some kyals from here. Wait for a year. The sahibs do not let us speak in the Jute Balers' Association, but once we have our own Baled Jute Association...'

'Why do I need an association? I need your help to buy a machine.'

Annoyed, Khemchandji asked, 'You need the Association to raise capital. Where did you think you would get that?'

'Chaman Lalji procures jute for you in Bogra. Why send it by train to presses in Kalkatta? Why not have them dried, sorted, pressed and baled right there in Bogra? The bales can then be shipped to Chitpur Road.'

Khemchandji regarded Hari with renewed interest. 'So you want to do this in partnership with the firm?'

'Daulatram Gulabchand could be a sleeping partner. The capital would be yours, the labour mine.'

'And what will Chaman Lal do?' Khemchandji asked sharply.

Hari's silence provided the answer.

'Chaman Lal has reached the age when a man retires to Benares,' admitted Khemchandji. 'But I do not turn my back on old munims.'

'He will be the head munim in the jute press,' Hari said quickly. 'We could give him 5 per cent of the profits. Fifty for Daulatram Gulabchand.'

'The capital is all mine,' said Khemchandji. 'Seventy-five for the firm, 20 per cent for you.'

'Seventy for the firm, 25 per cent for me,' said Hari.

'I will require Chaman Lal to send me a report every month.'

'Where do I buy a kachcha press?'

'I will send you to Surajmal Jalan tomorrow. If he asks about your capital, tell him it is from your shop in Bogra. Do not mention Daulatram Gulabchand. And tell him he has my vote on the Baled Jute Association.'

Hari was amused. Khemchandji was using him to get into competition with Surajmal Jalan even while seeking Surajmal's assistance. He rose to leave.

'Do not take Chaman Lal lightly,' said Khemchandji. 'A man who has spent forty years in jute knows how to turn a profit.'

Two days later, Hari and Nanuram returned to Bogra. Chaman Lal did not take kindly to the idea of becoming Hari's munim. 'You are like a son to me,' he said stiffly.

'You could continue to procure jute for Daulatram Gulabchand,' said Hari, 'and collect your commission on it. In addition, you can supervise the kyals and collect 5 per cent.'

The partnership was formalized. Land was rented in Raja Bazar near the ghat on the Karatoya—an old tin shed not unlike Bara Gola, surrounded by a yard.

The next month, Hari and Nanuram went to Santahar to supervise the unloading of their jute baling machine from the train and the loading of its parts on bullock carts. Two kyals had come with the machine. Six hours later the first cart, loaded with giant pulleys, screws, hammers and ropes, arrived at Sat Matha. Boys gathered around it and shopkeepers watched curiously. Lakshmi's Ma was allowed to descend to the road to sprinkle rice, paint a swastika on the first pulley, and sing a song in praise of Vishwakarma, lord of all machinery. The carts continued through Fateh Ali Bajar—where they generated considerable interest in the wholesale grain market—to Raja Bazar. Two days later, an engineer arrived from Calcutta to put the machine together and install it under the tin shed. It was a kachcha press, operated by hand screws from an upper floor like the capstan of a ship by gangs of kyals. In Chitpur Road in Calcutta, Hari had seen hydraulic machines that could press five munns of jute into a single bale, but those were all owned by European firms. Even in Calcutta, few Marwaris owned a hydraulic press.

The first day of operation was auspicious—Pausha sudi shashtami, the day Gopi Chand turned four. The two kyals from Calcutta had trained an army of seven. Three men stood on the upper floor and lowered the capstan. Loose strands of jute had been loaded into a rail car positioned beneath the press. A hammer descended, compressing the strands against the plate.

Thick needles stabbed the bale. Loops were run around it and tightened, and a pulley system deposited a clean brick of jute—two feet by two-and-a-half—on to a giant scale, which registered the weight: four munn. 320 pounds. A pandit daubed roli paste on this first brick, poured ghee, lit a joss stick and distributed prasad.

A small office had been constructed in a corner of the yard. Hari placed Gopi Chand on the mattress. The boy immediately tried to open the cash box. Everyone laughed, even Chaman Lal. Duli Chand said, 'He will be a great bania some day—the biggest jute baler in Bengal!'

Nanuram and Duli Chand were now transferred to the jute press, to sit with Chaman Lal in the office and supervise the kyals. The jute came down the Karatoya from Mymensingh and Faridpur, after having travelled down the Jamuna and the Padma. The boats were unloaded, and jute fibre—tied loosely into bunches—was brought in bullock carts to Raja Bajar, where Chaman Lal walked down the line of carts, pushing a hand deep into piles and pressing the fibre between thumb and forefinger, wiping his fingers gingerly with a handkerchief, displaying great contempt for the coils, muttering 'sada', 'tosa' or 'mesta', shaking his head to say 'too damp' or 'not properly retted'. There was much haggling and quarrelling. Sellers demonstrated the strength of their crop by stretching single strands while Chaman Lal exposed knotted and blackened fibre to make the opposite point. After a price was agreed upon, the jute was transferred to the yard, where it was sorted by quality and spread out to dry in the dirt, and on the roof of the tin shed. Finally, the kyals collected it and pressed it into bales that were taken to Santahar, from where they went by train to Calcutta.

The jute press solved many of Hari's problems. It was profitable from the start, and it removed his father from the shop, where he had been in the habit of offering unsolicited advice. Hari was left alone to weigh grain at leisure and to enjoy the antics of his three sons, who played daily among the sacks. Sometimes the children went with Duli Chand to the press, where they ran wild in jute strands drying all over the yard. Meanwhile, the store was expanding. It now sold cigarettes—cheap McDowell & Company ones of which fifty could be had for a rupee, as well as the imported Pall Mall brand that few in Bogra could afford—matches, soap, kerosene and mustard oil in addition to ghee, trinkets, umbrellas and clay toys for children. Hari sat there all day, counting his cash and aware of his growing wealth. Lakshmi's Ma took care of his sons, leaving him free to concentrate on the shop. A man without a wife, he thought wistfully, has no business other than business. For the two years that Parmeshwari had been in Bogra, she heard Hari fret over loans and interest payments. Now, within a year of her death, he was able to pay off the full three thousand he had borrowed from the firm.

When he made his last payment—630 rupees at once—Chaman Lal had been indignant, knowing that a portion of the money had come from the jute press. 'You are using my labours to pay off your loan.'

Hair had shrugged. Since the discovery that Chaman Lal had almost no capital, he had had little respect for him, thinking him a man meant to be exactly what he now was: a munim. Determined to obstruct the payment, Chaman Lal had fingered the notes. 'I want silver, Harilal. I do not trust paper.'

Hari pointed out that the amount was large. How was Chaman Lal to send 630 coins to Calcutta?

'That is on my head,' Chaman Lal said.

Hari stuffed the notes back into his dhoti. 'I will get you coins. But make an entry in your books—interest stops accruing today. Harilal & Sons is no longer indebted.'

In late 1911, when the press had been in operation for two years, shops in Bogra were closed to mark the English king's arrival in Calcutta. Hari rose early that morning. Having nothing to do, he walked through the fog to Raja Bajar, unlocked the gates to the jute press and walked in. The office was open. He knew Chaman Lal had a second key. Peering in, he saw the old man on the gaddi, head in his hands. When he looked up at Hari's arrival, his eyes were full of tears. Hari had never seen a grown man cry, much less Chaman Lal, whose fifty years in Disavar had replaced all joy and sorrow with a constant sullenness.

He soon learned the cause—Khemchand Biyani was dead, having drawn his last breath much like his master, Seth Daulatram, seated at the cash box in Lalgodam. Two years ago, when in Calcutta to buy the baling machine, Hari had thought that Khemchandji looked rather robust. He was certainly in full control of the firm, and there had been no whispers about his health at all.

'He was younger then me, almost a son,' said Chaman Lal. 'Raamji takes the good ones away.'

'What will happen to the firm?' Hari asked.

'Jainarain—Daulatramji's youngest son—has arrived from Haridwar, but he knows nothing about running the business. He would have squandered his father's wealth if Khemchandji had not preserved it for him. He will perhaps find a new head munim.'

'Whom he will select?'

'It does not matter. The new one will not be the trader Khemchandji was.'

'Do you think our arrangement with Khemchandji is on the books? If it was kachcha, the new head munim will not know of it...'

Chaman Lal regarded Hari contemptuously. 'You are young, Harilal, but even the young possess compassion. Khemchand Biyani has been called away by Raamji. Will you not stop to think of him for a moment?'

Ashamed, Hari walked back to Sat Matha to give the news to his father and Nanuram.

Three days later, Chaman Lal came to Sat Matha. After spending a few minutes sampling the grain and commenting on its quality, he suggested that all the sạda jute—the cheapest quality—bought in the press be shown in a new book, separately from the higher quality stock. Hari wondered why that was necessary.

Chaman Lal said, 'We buy too much sada, more than the Kalkatta office likes. If we show half the sada in a different book, the proportion of sada in the main book will be just right.'

'But the Kalkatta office will add up the sada from the second book,' said Hari.

Even as he said this, he realized that Chaman Lal did not mean to show the second book to the Calcutta office, and instantly regretted the remark. Master Bholaram had said again and again that a bania must never display ignorance in matters of accounting. But what of Khemchand Biyani, dead only three days? Would this not dishonour his memory?

'Of course, this would not have been right in Khemchand Babu's time,' Chaman Lal said quickly.

Three days of mourning have brought great happiness to the old man, thought Hari.

'I thought of Khemchand Babu as my father,' said Chaman Lal, forgetting that, on learning of his death, he had described Khemchandji as a son. 'I would not dream of reneging on a promise made to him. Were he to shut his eyes and say—Chaman Lal, you are free to do what you like—I would still send him both books. But this new munim: who is he? A young boy who has not earned his position, who does not understand the firm. It will take him a year merely to visit all branches. Who owes him anything? What right does he have to enforce arrangements made by Khemchand Babu? Does he not know that I was a munim to Khemchand Babu himself for twelve years?'

Hari sensed that Chaman Lal would go on and on until absolved of guilt. 'It is to your credit, Chaman Lalji, that you have never bought any jute off the books. A less honourable man would have tried, but not you.'

Overwhelmed, Chaman Lal replied, 'And I tell you this, Harilal, only because I have become fond of you. People tell me it was my loan that started you off in Disavar. "You were kind enough to give that poor boy a start," they say. I reply, "No, it was his thrift and industry. Granted, I greased the wheels, but it was he who turned them."'

Over the next few months, the sada jute bought by Harilal & Sons gradually declined on the books, until a similar decline was shown by mesta, followed by tosa. Within two years of Khemchand Biyani's death, two registers were fully operational in Raja Bazar—the official one shown to the Calcutta office, and the unofficial one seen only by Chaman Lal and Hari. Their arrangement with Daulatram Gulabchand had not changed, so they continued to share profits in the same proportions as before, based on the amounts shown in the official register. By an unspoken agreement, returns in the second register were split equally.

The second register proved to be very profitable. Hari was able to buy the rooms he rented at Sat Matha, and eventually, the whole building. He moved his shop across the road to a cubicle in his own building, and became landlord to the shopkeepers next to him. On the upper floors, his family expanded into two new rooms.

In the summer of 1913, Duli Chand expressed a desire to visit his daughters in Shekhavati. 'I want you to come with me,' he said. 'You have not seen your sisters for years.'

But Hari could not leave his shop, now more than ever when business was brisk. Also, it would be unwise to leave the jute press in the restless hands of Chaman Lal, whose greed seemed to increase with age. There was yet another reason, a vague one that could not be articulated, for not going to Shekhavati. Hari had come to believe that Raamji did not want him to return. His departure from Shekhavati with Hemraj had been a final break. The camel had crossed the dry riverbed and entered Loharu, and he was not to return. He had gone back once, and returned to find Bengal in turmoil and English sergeants at his heels. Like Daulatramji, he was destined to spend his life in Disavar. Had not the ojha mentioned pools of water full of lilies? No, he would not go, and he would not say why because his father would not understand.

'If you do not go, let me take your sons for their tonsure. Gopi has had his, but Durga and Tribhuvan may never again get the opportunity to visit Khatu. Indeed they have never seen Shekhavati. They think of Bengal as their home.'

Durga was four and Tribhuvan three. Because Hari could not have their hair trimmed before their first tonsure in Khatu, they had never seen a barber. Every morning, Lakshmi's Ma tied their hair in braids, which had now become so long that they had to be looped and tied together again. They suffered taunts from other children, and particularly from seven-year-old Gopi Chand.

'I have spoken to Mangiram,' Hari said. 'He says their tonsure can be done on the banks of the Karatoya, right here in Bogra. He did that for his son.'

'Mangiram is a fool. He was born in Bogra. He has never eaten the bajra from Shekhavati. Did you not say his son looks weak? That is what happens to those who are careless with tonsure. And we know not of the misfortunes yet to strike him.'

'But Durga and Tribhuvan are too young to go with you. It is a long journey.'

The next day, a disappointed Duli Chand left for Shekhavati accompanied by Nanuram. Lakshmi's Ma packed three baskets of mangoes for Hari's three sisters—they would be a delicacy in Shekhavati—and it was decided that Duli Chand would buy gold nose-rings for them in Calcutta before he took the train to Delhi.

Left alone in Bogra, Hari saw an opportunity to complete his boys' tonsure. A barber was engaged—Bengali, because Hari could not find a Marwari one. On a morning deemed auspicious by the pandit, Lakshmi's Ma dressed the boys in cotton dhotis and kurtas and marched them to the ghat in Raja Bajar, just beyond the jute press, where Hari waited with the barber and pandit. A puja was done before an idol of Shyam Baba, and the pandit declared the bank of the Karatoya to be a representation of Khatu in Shekhavati. Four-year-old Durga went first. His kurta was removed and he squatted on the riverbank, looking east at the rising sun while the barber shaved his head, leaving a tuft of hair in the back. He began to cry.

'Be quick,' Hari said to the barber. 'The child is only four.'

Within minutes, both boys were shaven. The pandit collected the hair, tied it up and threw it in the river. Hari watched the locks float down the Karatoya, imagining that they would mix with the Padma downstream. Laughing, Gopi led his brothers to the water, where they could see their reflections. Now it was Tribhuvan's turn to cry.

'It will grow back soon,' Gopi said, 'and you will no longer have to contend with braids.'

The next day was Bakr-id, when Muslim kyals in the jute press would not work. The press was closed. Because there were no Muslim employees in the shop, it was open. A man stood in the road, asking for a Pall Mall cigarette. Hari pulled out a pack from the wall to his left but the man shook his head. He wanted only one. Disappointed, Hari opened the pack, handed out a cigarette, and saw the man put it between his lips. Five months ago, when Hari had moved the shop to his own building across the road, Nanuram had hung a length of coir in front of the shop and lit its end. It burned slowly all day. 'This is our cigarette lighter,' Nanuram had said brightly, having borrowed the idea from a paan stall.

Hari had protested. He wanted customers to buy packs and cartons, not single cigarettes as they would at a paan stall, but Nanuram said people were encouraged to buy if they could light up right away.

'You must remember to put it out every evening,' Hari had said, 'or it will burn down the shop.'

He eyed the rope disdainfully as the man lit up. Now that the shop had expanded, the whole wall to his left was lined with cigarette cartons. Duli Chand often grumbled about the smell, and tolerated it only because of the high margins on cigarette packs. Even so, he never touched the cartons himself and advised Hari to hire a clerk so he would not have to either.

Upstairs, Lakshmi's Ma had finished bathing the boys. She sent them down to the shop to play. Hari watched them indulgently as they opened bags, upset cartons and played with the scales. Then he remembered the closed press—it was carpeted with drying jute in which the boys loved to roll around. There would be no kyals, but Chaman Lal was certainly sitting in the office, doing accounts.

'Take your brothers to Raja Bajar,' he told Gopi Chand.

They left, Gopi Chand holding Durga by the hand, who in turn pulled along three-year-old Tribhuvan. Hari watched them go. Gopi was short for his seven years, so the three heads—two of them bald—bobbed up and down together, until they turned the corner.

Chaman Lal saw the boys come into the yard and paid little attention. He had no particular interest in them. More and more of his time was spent in the press, even when there was nothing to do. The second jute register had given him a regular income and rendered his pawn-broking business superfluous, so his cubicle in Bara Gola was usually closed, and he was thinking of giving it up. His health having deteriorated in the last year, he had begun to contemplate the possibility of death. This had created a strange vacancy in his mind. News that would otherwise bring him joy—such as the steadily increasing profits in the press—left him unmoved. Confused by this new development, he found it safer to remain busy with accounts and registers, where arithmetic shielded him from the blankness within. He heard the boys scream in joy as they tore through the jute in the yard, knew that the sound should have pleased him, and went back to staring at nothing.

Because it would not rain for at least another month, a corner of the yard was being used to store bales of pressed jute, stacked five high. Gopi Chand climbed this tower, followed by Durga Prasad and Tribhuvan Lal. At three, Tribhuvan was already stronger than four-year-old Durga, who had never fully recovered from the illnesses that attended his birth. His four years had been spent battling afflictions: measles, for which Hari had to pay seven brahmins to appease the goddess Sheetla; the pox, which had miraculously vanished without leaving scars; and recurring fevers. Being the weakest at every game they played, Durga found himself under constant threat from Gopi and Tribhuvan.

Standing on top of the jute tower, Gopi called, 'Durga is an ass. See how slowly he climbs. Beware, Tribhuvan, for he will kick you with his hind legs.'

Tribhuvan laughed dutifully and Durga struggled up the bales, panting. From the top, Gopi saw a rail car sitting idly near the press. Had the kyals been present, they would be loading the car with sorted jute in preparation for sliding it under the piston. This gave Gopi an idea. He descended the bales swiftly and cut through the grounds, scattering ropes of jute here and there. Jumping into the car, he proclaimed, 'I am George, King-Emperor, and this is my train.'

His brothers joined him. Tribhuvan stood on the rail tracks, pushed the car with all his strength but failed to move it. Durga was invited to join. Their combined might was unable to budge the car. With a contemptuous snort, Gopi jumped off and pointed to Durga. 'You are the weakest. You can be George.'

They lifted Durga into the car, positioned themselves at either corner and pushed hard. The car groaned and yielded, inching along, its passage resisted by strands of jute lying across the tracks.

'Babuji said we were not to go near the machine,' said Tribhuvan.

'You cannot stop the King-Emperor's train!' yelled Gopi.

The pulleys in the press were held in place by a chain and hook mechanism, but the kyals had neglected to thread the hook into the chain, there being no need for caution because they were the only ones who ever operated the machine. As the rail car gathered speed, its vibrations caused the chain to slide. The piston began its descent as the car, with Durga inside, approached it. Tribhuvan saw the piston, grabbed the moving car and pulled back as hard as he could. There was a strange moment when Gopi was pushing the car while Tribhuvan was trying to stop it, just as the piston completed its descent and struck the front of the car, jamming against it. Seated in the front but facing backward to look at Gopi's laughing face, Durga received a blow to the back of his head and was thrown to the floor of the car. He lay unconscious.

Still pushing, Gopi received the force of the piston through the car and was hurled backward on the tracks. Tribhuvan, who had let go and stepped aside, watched them in horror. It was he who screamed.

Hari had dozed off in the shop when he heard the commotion. The day had been slow because of Bakr-id. A crowd was advancing from the direction of Raja Bazar, led by an old man. When they came closer, he saw that the man was Chaman Lal, walking unsteadily, trailed by excited children and holding in his arms a boy with a bald head.

'Gangajal!' Chaman Lal screamed. 'Get me some gangajal!'

Upstairs, Lakshmi's Ma had heard the call. She ran into the road with a bottle full of water from the Ganga. Durga was laid in the shop and gangajal sprinkled on his face. He did not stir.

'Use more, Harilal,' Chaman Lal said. 'Empty the whole bottle on his head.'

Hari did so. Durga Prasad opened his eyes. A cry went up, 'Jai Ganga Maiya!'

Hari folded his hands, promised a gift of churma in Khatu the next time he went to Shekhavati, and looked gratefully at Lakshmi's Ma, who had known exactly where to find the bottle in the kitchen. Durga sat up and began to sob.

'He will recover,' said Lakshmi's Ma. 'I will prepare a plate of daal and jaggery.'

But Hari noticed something strange in his son's manner. 'I will take him to Dr Saha.'

'Do not let a Bengali touch him,' said Chaman Lal, forgetting that he had vouched for Dr Saha at Durga's birth. 'Ganga Maiya has already revived him.'

Hari lifted his son in his arms and took him to Dr Saha's clinic near Bara Gola. The crowd followed him all the way, with Gopi describing the accident in great detail. Dr Saha spent a long time examining Durga, turning his face from side to side, shining a light into his eyes and snapping his fingers to study his reactions.

'There is no vision in the left eye,' he said.

'Of course there is,' Hari said. 'Can you not see me, Durga?'

Durga nodded.

'He can see with the right eye,' said Dr Saha, and then demonstrated this by putting a hand over the boy's good eye.

'I see no blood in the eye,' said Hari. ' He was hit in the back of the head, not the eye.'

'There is trauma to the right occipital lobe,' said Dr Saha.

'You just said it was the *left* eye that was damaged!'

Dr Saha sighed. 'Bring him to me in three days.'

Chaman Lal said, 'Do not take the boy back to the doctor. He just wants his fee again.'

That evening, Hari punished Gopi Chand. The boy was made to stand in the shop with two sacks of daal, each weighing eight kilograms, in his hands. Every time he dropped a sack he was ordered to pick it up again, until his hands were calloused and his face bathed in tears. Being younger, Tribhuvan received no punishment.

After Lakshmi's Ma had put the boys to sleep, Hari went into their room—they slept together on a mattress—and watched them. Gopi was sprawled in the middle, face caked with tear drops. Tribhuvan lay on his side, and Durga had gone to sleep on his stomach. The two looked strangely naked because of their baldness. Hari examined the back of Durga's head in the glow of a lantern. There was a bump just below the tuft of hair that the barber had spared when shaving the boy. The doctor had given an English name to this, but Hari knew better—the first tonsure of a boy must happen in Khatu, in the temple of Shyam Baba. It was not sufficient that the Karatoya flowed into the Padma, which was a branch of the Ganga. Poor Durga had borne the brunt of his father's carelessness. And he was the one whom Parmeshwari had mentioned in her last breath. She had known, even then, that he was the one who needed care. Hari sat for hours, watching his sons, shuddering at the thought of accidents still to happen, until the lantern had drunk its oil and the wick burned through.

When Duli Chand returned from Shekhavati, he heard the

tale of Durga Prasad's accident as one who had anticipated it, and his annoyance at the boys' improper tonsure was replaced with concern for Durga's well-being. He said, 'It was this Dr Saha who cured Durga's yellowness. A boy whose life has been granted by a doctor can never grow up healthy. He will always be weak.'

'Gopi will not get into mischief if I send him to a guru. He is seven. You sent me to Master Bholaram at that age.'

'Let him sit in the shop—there he will learn all he needs to know.'

'What of the other two? They are too young for the shop.'

'A boy is never too young for arithmetic.'

'Lakshmi's Ma can prepare them for Guruji's school every morning.'

'Lakshmi's Ma is a dai, a servant. Not a mother,' said Duli Chand.

Hari knew what his father meant. He continued to weigh grain, staring at the scales with ferocity, using the method Master Bholaram had taught him to keep his mind from wandering, to avoid losing count as he moved heaps of rice from the left to the right. 'Raamoji Raam, Duyeji do, Tineji tin, Chaubeyji chaar...'

But Duli Chand would not be silenced. 'When a man needs a mother for his sons, he marries.'

Hari thought of Parmeshwari. She had uttered the word 'Harilal' before dying, and mentioned Durga as the weak one. And she had said nothing else.

'I will have Chaman Lal Babu ask around for a suitable girl,' said Duli Chand as he rose to go upstairs. 'You are already twenty-six—too old even for Disavar, where men marry late. It will not be easy.'

Left alone, Hari wearily eyed the cigarette cartons stacked to his left. What did Bengalis see in this poison? He fingered a cigarette, then pulled the snake of burning coir closer and lit it. The smoke flowed smoothly into his lungs. He was surprised. There was no coughing, no wheezing, none of the nauseous sensation he had been told to expect. He took another puff, then another, turning his back to the road so no one would see.

4

There was a Marwari school in Bogra, run by a teacher who had come from Shekhavati. Guruji enjoyed a reputation for strictness, thrashing his boys with a bamboo switch at the slightest provocation and inflicting harsh punishment on those who got their multiplication tables wrong. He held forth in a classroom behind a jute warehouse near the Karatoya. The building was owned by a wealthy trader in Fateh Ali Bazar, and the school was consequently named in his honour—Seth Jhunjhunwala Marwari Pathshala. It was the general opinion among Marwaris that Guruji could set right the most stubborn of boys, so that was where Hari sent Gopi, whom Duli Chand believed to be already on the road to ruin. The school charged two rupees for a month's tuition. Each brother would add only a rupee to the fee, so Durga and Tribhuvan were sent too.

'They will watch and learn,' Hari explained to Duli Chand. 'When Guruji thrashes Gopi, they will take the lesson to heart. And Gopi Chand's school costs less because of them.'

Lakshmi's Ma dressed the boys in clean kurtas and dhotis—the short three-yard dhotis meant for children—and Gopi was given a slate and chalk. As they approached the warehouse in Fateh Ali Bajar, Guruji could be heard scolding a boy. Gopi wrapped his arms around his father's legs, pleading. Hari was in a bind—he had begun to treat Gopi harshly because, as his eldest son, he expected the boy to set an example to his brothers. Gopi's sullen nature made such treatment easier. Now, however, he was reminded of the two-year-old who had stood at Sat Matha on his arrival in Bogra, cap askew on bald head, staring wide-eyed at a myna bird. Yet a boy had to learn arithmetic—from a teacher if not his father—or he would be unsuitable for the shop. Why, Hari himself had resisted going to Master Bholaram in Rampura when he was seven, and he was glad his father had ignored his pleas.

Resolutely, he pulled Gopi into the room. Durga and Tribhuvan followed. Twenty boys were seated cross-legged on the floor, slates in their laps. Guruji stopped mid-sentence at Hari's entrance. Although it was humid after the rains, he had a shawl draped over his shoulder. Judging Gopi to be the eldest, he asked, 'Whose son are you?'

Following instructions given by Lakshmi's Ma, Gopi announced formally, 'Shri Harilal Tibrewal of Sat Matha, son of Duli Chandji Tibrewal.'

Hari beamed. The boy had passed his first test.

'Recite the multiplication table for one-and-a-half,' said Guruji.

Gopi stared. Guruji's face wore contempt. 'All right, the table for two.'

Gopi did not know that either.

'Which costs more, Aman or Aush?'

Gopi remained silent.

'What does your father deal in?' Guruji asked gruffly.

'Daal, rice, salt…' began Gopi.

'Ass!' bellowed Guruji. 'Do you not sit on the gaddi with him? How old are you?'

'Seven. The eighth is upon me.'

'Almost eight, and he has never sat at the cash box with his father. He has never weighed a ser of daal!' Guruji regarded Hari with sympathy and turned away, murmuring, 'Why do I get all the asses?'

Hari was satisfied. This was a Guru all right. 'I have brought the younger ones too,' he said, 'so they may learn along with their brother.'

Guruji nodded absently. Hari withdrew, retracing his path quickly to Sat Matha before any of his sons thought of following him back home.

The boys went to Guruji's school for three years. Hari heard their tales every evening while he ate his dinner. Gopi soon learned that there were 80 tolas in a ser, 40 sers in a munn and 8 munns in a khandi. He learned how to weigh 10 sers of daal with three-ser weights, how to keep count when weighing small amounts again and again, and how to quote prices to a sahib: in English pounds, each of which was half a ser. Hari was amused to hear this last one—in his eight years in Bogra he had not seen a single sahib.

It was not clear what Durga and Tribhuvan gained in school. Once, on being scolded by Guruji, Durga wet his dhoti and burst into tears. Everyone laughed and Durga returned home in shame. Gopi often complained of Guruji's beatings, to which Duli Chand would respond, 'A guru's beating is the lesson of life.'

When Gopi had been in school for a year, he was taught some Modhiya. With a reed pen, Guruji wrote in large Modhiya letters on a piece of cardboard:

Babuji has gone to Ajmer. Send the big ledger.

Gopi brought the board home, placed a sheet of translucent paper on it, and traced Guruji's letters with a pencil, forming his own Modhiya words. Hari was horrified. 'Will you waste a whole sheet for one line?'

Then he demonstrated his own prowess with a pencil, by writing over and over again on a postcard: *Babuji has gone to Ajmer. Send the big ledger. Babuji has gone…* Gopi studied the result. 'Twenty-three lines.'

Master Bholaram would have been disappointed, but Hari felt this was not the time to discuss his own failings. 'Twenty-three with a pencil. With a reed pen, I could have written the whole Mahabharat on this postcard.' Some exaggeration was appropriate, he told himself, considering the importance of the lesson. 'The government will charge you a paisa for a postcard, whether you write one word or a hundred.'

'What if the letter is short?'

'Then you have no reason to write it. Do not forget: Raamji gives generously to the man who does not waste.'

'You wasted a paisa on that postcard,' Gopi said.

Hari was annoyed but impressed. 'It was well-spent because there was a lesson in it for you.'

The postcard was passed around. Durga saw it, Tribhuvan looked at it, and it was folded away in Gopi's kurta pocket, to be shown at school. Hari felt smug. Indeed, there was much more he could tell his sons if he put his mind to it. Consider that line:

Babuji has gone to Ajmer. Send the big ledger.

It was the first line written by every boy in Shekhavati, and everyone knew what was special about it. When written in Modhiya, the same words could also be read as,

Babuji died today. Send the elder daughter-in-law.

And that was the lesson Master Bholaram had taught: words meant different things to different people while numbers were truthful. The one bowed to context, the other only to the truth. But, of course Gopi, would not understand, although he was as old as Hari had been when Master Bholaram said this.

In the wet month of Bhadwa in 1915, Hari was troubled by news that Guruji had put together a skit with the boys, to be performed during the festival of Ganesh Chaturthi on the fourth of the month. Because Seth Jhunjhunwala owned the school building, his grandsons were given the lead roles of Raam and his three brothers. A fifth grandson played the role of Sita. Gopi was Hanuman, Durga a monkey in Hanuman's entourage, and Tribhuvan was allowed to follow the group to Sat Matha. The troupe stood outside Hari's shop and addressed itself to the verandah upstairs. Guruji called,

Listen! Gopi's mother!
Your son goes to school
Teach your boy a lesson
Give his friends some sweets
And hand the Guru his fee

'Master Bholaram did not ask his students to play frivolous games,' Duli Chand said wryly. 'He taught them multiplication tables.'

'This is Disavar,' said Hari, who was enjoying the scene. 'Allowances must be made.'

Duli Chand looked at the boy playing Sita, wrapped in a sari. 'Why is there a girl in the road? Is that proper?'

'That is Jhunjhunwala's grandson.'

Lakshmi's Ma brought down a plate of jalebis. Hari handed Guruji a silver rupee. Because the boys were dressed as gods, goddesses and monkeys, they had trouble swallowing the jalebis, losing talons and wings, and adjusting quivers, arrows, arm-bands and cummerbunds. Someone stepped on Hanuman's tail and tore it clean off his buttocks. The boys laughed. Guruji turned to Gopi. 'You may tell your mother that her jalebis are delicious.'

Hari was taken aback. Lakshmi's Ma was past fifty, and her manner, dress and appearance gave away her position as a servant, but Guruji had not noticed.

'She is a dai,' he said softly to Guruji. 'The boy's mother was called away by Raamji.'

Embarrassed, Guruji tried to make amends. 'She must have come with you from Shekhavati. Servants from Shekhavati have more dignity than those in Disavar—one mistakes them for family members.'

A sudden wail interrupted him. Gopi had thrown his jalebi to the ground and planted his feet firmly in the dirt. His face was streaked with tears. The piece of foam glued beneath his nose—to create Hanuman's simian upper-lip—was covered with snot. The other boys watched uncomfortably. Hari felt tears in his own eyes. He and Gopi were the only ones who had seen Parmeshwari die. No one else knew that she had called him by name, or that he had held her hand before it went cold. And here was the boy, rude and sullen and impudent, suddenly reminded of his mother. It was he who suffered her absence, not Durga or Tribhuvan, who indeed thought of Lakshmi's Ma as their mother.

'Be quiet, Gopi Chand,' Duli Chand scolded. 'The tenth is upon you.'

'We must go to the next house,' Guruji said uncomfortably.

Hanuman's body parts and accessories—tail, upper lip, crown, mace, red loincloth, bows and arrows—were removed from Gopi's body and fastened on to Durga's, who was delighted to be promoted. Jalebis finished, they trooped off to the next house, where Guruji repeated his call.

Listen! Badri's mother,
Your son goes to school...

'You may come inside now,' Hari said to his son, who was still in the road, watching the other boys blankly.

Gopi sat down in the back among sacks of daal. Hari stifled the urge to cry, aware that his father was watching. In the evening, while he tallied the inventory and prepared to go upstairs, Duli Chand said, 'A man finds a wife so his sons may have a mother.'

Hari walked up to the verandah silently. The moment would pass, he told himself. He would forget, as would Gopi. A man came to Disavar to earn what he could. There was the shop at Sat Matha. There was the jute press. There was the hosiery store he was thinking of buying so Gopi could have a shop of his own. And there were the shops to be bought for Durga and Tribhuvan when they grew up. His sons did not need a mother—they needed a shop each.

5

Toward the end of 1915, Lakshmi's Ma expressed a desire to retire to Benares. This was conveyed to Hari by Duli Chand, who had returned from the jute press for a nap and found himself in conversation with her.

'She wants to end her life on the banks of the Ganga.'

'She is not old enough to die,' said Hari. 'And who will take care of the boys?'

'The lump at her throat...'

'It is not growing. It will not kill her.' Hari was surprised to find his father advocating for her. He had shown no previous interest in Lakshmi's Ma. It was odd, too, that she had chosen Duli Chand to advertise her intentions. 'She knows no one in Benares. What will she do there? Who will feed her?'

'She will find work. A woman like that—who can deliver a baby, clothe him and cook for him—could find work anywhere.'

Hari regarded his father suspiciously. 'She cooks for you, too, yet you seem reconciled to her departure.'

Duli Chand sighed. 'It is written in the Shastras: death near the Ganga is auspicious. Who am I to dispute that?'

Hari procrastinated for weeks, but Lakshmi's Ma was insistent—she wanted to leave before the month of Pous, so she would not have to travel in the biting cold—so he yielded. A steel trunk was presented to her. Into it she threw everything she owned—three saris, a few silver bangles and an image of Raamji, together with a bundle containing rotis and an onion. Duli Chand handed her twenty rupees. She bent over to touch his feet, caressed each of the three boys—Durga began to cry—folded her hands before Hari, and went downstairs. Nanuram accompanied her to the railway station near Bara Gola, where she would take the slow train to Santahar, followed by the mail train to Calcutta.

By evening, there was no trace of Lakshmi's Ma in the house. She had left behind nothing—trinkets, pictures, clothing—because she had collected nothing. It was as if she had never lived there.

A widow was hired to cook and clean, and to prepare the boys for Guruji's school every morning. She did not know that Duli Chand liked his rotis slightly uncooked while Hari preferred them burnt to a crisp. The boys were uncomfortable around her. There was gloom in the house. Hari spent longer hours in the shop, going upstairs only when hunger overpowered him, to eat a dinner he no longer enjoyed.

It was then that Guruji decided to test his students. An exam was announced without warning, and the whole class—boys as old as ten and as young as three—was given the same problems in arithmetic. Answers were written on slates and passed to Guruji, who pressed a stick of chalk against each slate to draw ticks or crosses. The three boys brought their slates to the jute press, where Hari was sitting with Chaman Lal. Gopi and Durga had failed the exam; Tribhuvan had passed. Durga's failure could be explained by the decreased vision in his left eye from the accident in the press, but Gopi's discomfort with arithmetic was galling to Hari. 'I spend four rupees on your fee every month, yet it is clear you learn nothing.'

'Have him sit in the shop,' Chaman Lal suggested. 'There is nothing a guru can teach that he cannot learn in the shop for free.'

'What about Durga?'

'Send him to the press every morning. I will teach him everything about jute baling.'

Hari regarded Chaman Lal gratefully. It had been more than two years since the boys' accident in the press, when Chaman Lal had rushed out to find Durga lying next to the baling machine, bleeding. He had run from Raja Bajar to Sat Matha with Durga in his arms. Since then, Hari had noticed a softness in Chaman Lal's manner, especially toward Durga. Perhaps this was the result of advancing age, and the fact that Chaman Lal had little contact with his daughters in Shekhavati, whose children he had never seen. He had now transferred his grandfatherly manner to the boys, and Durga seemed to have received much of the benefit.

'Very well,' Hari said, 'I will keep Gopi in the shop with me, and Durga will come to you. Make what you will of him. If he disobeys you, punish him as you would your own grandson.'

'What of Tribhuvan?' Chaman Lal asked.

'The master in the government school is a 'BA Fail' Bengali who teaches some English. I will send Tribhuvan to him.'

So, Gopi began to sit in the shop and Durga in the press, and Tribhuvan went every morning to the government school, where he was given a slim book titled *Telegraph Teacher*. Within a few days he knew English words such as 'come', 'go', 'buy', 'sell' and 'good morning'. Hari proudly arranged a demonstration for Duli Chand, who was unimpressed. 'Master Bholaram knew those words too, yet he was unable to find a bride.'

'The boy is only six,' said Hari. 'By the time he is of age, he will speak English like a sahib, or at least a Bengali. Every Marwari in Bengal who has a marriageable daughter will be at my door.'

'You speak of Tribhuvan's wedding,' said Duli Chand, 'but it is your own wedding you should think of. The boy needs a mother.'

Duli Chand had not raised the matter for a few weeks. They

had learned to live without Lakshmi's Ma, but her absence showed: the house was unswept, the beds unmade and the boys unwashed. The assurance with which Hari had climbed up to the verandah every evening—knowing his home was managed by someone he understood—had vanished. Every day he wished he had stood firm and denied her wish. Perhaps money would have helped? But such a woman had little use for money. Now that she was gone, the illusion of stability she had sustained following Parmeshwari's death was gone too. Yet he could not accede to his father's wishes. It was too soon. And soon it would be too late. He was destined to enjoy his sons, and Raamji had granted no more. 'I am too old,' he said softly, looking away, casting about for a reason.

'In Disavar, men older than you think nothing of marrying at their age.'

Tribhuvan stood within earshot, preparing to demonstrate more English mastery and collect accolades. Perhaps the boy should be sent away, thought Hari.

'Chaman Lal has found a girl,' Duli Chand said.

Hari was shocked by the presumption. It was one thing for Chaman Lal to show affection to his sons, another to find him a bride.

'She is the granddaughter of Dungarmalji of Sikar. The family came to Bogra thirty years ago and now lives in Gobindganj.'

Since he stopped selling Mangiram's cloth in the weekly market there, Hari had not been to Gobindganj. It was not a large town—huts, tin sheds and a few buildings of brick, as in Santahar. Perhaps one of those brick buildings belonged to the family his father now spoke of.

Duli Chand continued. 'The family is respectable—no bankruptcies, no known losses, no unpaid debts. And Gobindganj is only 25 miles away. Our guests will not have to travel far.'

He is already thinking of the wedding, Hari thought in panic. Something had to be said to stem the torrent of words. 'A nice girl, perhaps. One who will not be hard on my sons.'

'Of course,' said Duli Chand. 'They are my grandsons, too. Why would I want a sharp-tongued daughter-in-law? Chaman Lal has seen the girl. Silent as a cow. Well-behaved. He had her recite three whole chapters of the Bhagavad Gita, and was shown a notebook in which she had filled half the pages with the word 'Raam'. All by herself, and in Hindi, not Modhiya.'

Hari tried to imagine the girl's face and recoiled. It was sinful to form an image that would replace Parmeshwari. But he knew he must respond, because his father would take silence to be assent. 'What does her father deal in?'

'Cloth. He used to have a shop in Bogra, near Fateh Ali Bazar, but then built a house in Gobindganj and moved there. His cloth goes to Rangpur, Rajshahi, even Goalpara and Jorhat in Assam. Who knows, you may have seen him on your trips to Gobindganj.'

And he is probably not much older than me, Hari thought sourly.

'The girl has five brothers,' said Duli Chand. 'Imagine that! Five brothers, all older, and only one sister for the five. They will spend generously for the wedding. Your sons will have five uncles—five bearers of gifts.'

'My sons will have a new mother,' said Hari, hoping by this to console himself.

'And you will have a wife.'

Hari turned away. The thought was glib and offensive. No, he would not have a wife; he would have a mother for his sons. 'How old is the girl?'

'Fifteen. The sixteenth is upon her,' Duli Chand said, adding quickly, 'That is not considered an advanced age in Disavar, where a Marwari often has trouble finding a match for his daughter.'

'It must be difficult for the fathers of girls in Bengal.'

'I am told a girl in Disavar may go seventeen years without being married off,' said Duli Chand. 'But this also means we could bring her to Bogra in a year or two. Had she been younger, your sons would have had to wait longer for their mother.'

Over the next four weeks, Hari sat in the shop and tried not to think of the wedding, even as Duli Chand made it a point to mention it to every customer. Nanuram was entrusted with arrangements. Mangiram offered to arrange for bullock carts for the wedding party, which was to go the 25 miles to Gobindganj. Chaman Lal drew up a list of Marwaris to be invited.

'There are no Marwari barbers in Bogra,' Nanuram informed Duli Chand. 'Should I ask a Bengali or Bihari to deliver invitations?'

Duli Chand was horrified. 'A Bengali barber for my Hariya! No one will come to such a wedding.'

'That is what other Marwaris in Disavar do.'

'Ask around in Rangpur. It is a large city. There are five hundred Marwari families there.'

'I know no one in Rangpur.'

'Ask Hariya. He has customers. Look as far as Dhaka. We must have a Marwari barber. Even if he has not seen Shekhavati, his father would have.'

Three days later, a man named Chotiya presented himself at the jute press, having been sent by Hari's business contacts in Rangpur. Duli Chand scrutinized him suspiciously. 'He is too fair-skinned,' he said to Nanuram. 'Are you sure he is a barber?'

Nanuram pointed to the wooden box in Chotiya's hand. Duli Chand shook his head.

'Anyone can carry clippers and a razor, but is he a barber by caste? And how do we know he is from Shekhavati?' Turning to the man, he asked sternly, 'Name your country.'

'Bikaner,' said Chotiya.

'All right,' said Duli Chand begrudgingly. Bikaner lay to the west of Shekhavati, but it would have to do.

After Chotiya had shaved Duli Chand and partly allayed his suspicions, he sat down with Nanuram to memorize the invitation, and to learn where the houses of Marwaris stood in Marwari Para—Raja Bajar, Fateh Ali Bajar and Sat Matha. Over two days, he delivered the invitation to 160 homes: *Duli Chandji of Rampura in Shekhavati has called you to the wedding baraat of his son, Chiranjeev Harilal, which will go from the jute press in Raja Bajar to Gobindganj on Pausha sudi 13.*

After Chotiya had brought back responses, Nanuram did a headcount. Duli Chand protested. 'We have invited too many. Why spend two annas on a task that could be completed in one? Besides, 125 men will not fit in the three carts Mangiram has promised.'

'Hari Babu's first wedding took place during the Chhappaniya famine,' said Nanuram. 'We bathed every second day and counted every bucket of water. Now, Hari Babu is the proprietor of Harilal & Sons. His jute bales go all the way to Kalkatta.'

'But he is twenty-nine, not a young boy.'

'There are Bengali men in Kalkatta who get married for the first time at thirty,' said Nanuram, who knew very little about Calcutta. Indeed, he had been there only once, when Hari had gone to buy the jute press six years ago, not counting the time he had passed through Calcutta on his arrival from Shekhavati.

'That is all right for Bengalis, not for us,' said Duli Chand. 'The Shastras say a boy should be married off when he turns twelve, and a girl when she turns eight.'

Nanuram persisted. 'The Shastras also say that a bania is not tight-fisted on three occasions: births, weddings and deaths.' He had never read any of the Shastras, but was consoled by the certainty that Duli Chand had not read them either.

Duli Chand sighed. 'I suppose we must take these 125 to Gobindganj now that they have accepted our invitation. I will ask Mangiram for more carts.'

'And we will skip no ceremony, make no allowances for being in Disavar,' said Nanuram enthusiastically. 'Even during the Chhappaniya, we sang the proper songs, gave the proper gifts and did not rush the pandit.'

At dawn on Pausha sudi 13, the guests gathered in the jute press compound. It was cold and foggy. Jute strands had been swept away, the baling machine had been polished, and the office mattress had received a new sheet. Everyone was given tea while awaiting the auspicious hour. Hari sat in the office, surrounded by men who, he thought, were at least slightly dismissive of the occasion, this being a second wedding. My first wedding was darkened by the Chhappaniya, he thought, and the second because it is the second. He did not participate in the general banter. Outside, Nanuram brought the mare around. Hari clearly remembered the horrors of his last ride. Somewhat irreverently, he wondered why men in Shekhavati did not set out to claim their brides on camels. A camel was a beast meant to be ridden—Hari could fall asleep on one, or spend a whole night comforted by the gentle roll of its hump, but a mare… The auspicious hour arrived. He was led out. He saw the flicking tail, the impatient legs, and the red saddlecloth decorated with sequins. He was hoisted into the saddle. There was some laughter—were they laughing with him or at him? He paid no attention to the pujas, songs or aartis, or the plates of jaggery, rice, vermilion and burning camphor. Someone had pressed a turban on his head; someone else attached a diamond brooch to its crest.

Irritably, he asked, 'What is the pandit waiting for? The mare is getting restless.'

Duli Chand said, 'A man going to fetch his bride does not show impatience.' Turning to Nanuram, his father whispered in a voice loud enough for Hari to hear, 'A wedding does not have the same charm when the bridegroom is not young. I remember how good he looked in a red tunic when he was twelve.'

Hari remembered only the discomfort and the coconut digging into his side, and the long journey over blistering sand. But he also remembered the bullock cart flying under the moon, and he remembered her face. He was filled with guilt. Look at him! Almost thirty, father of three, setting out like a greedy boy who must have another rocking horse. And why had so many assembled to witness his shame?

He heard Nanuram answer his father. 'The bride looks no more than twelve.'

He was suddenly reminded of the other party to this farce.

There was a girl in Gobindganj—fifteen, but twelve to look at—awaiting his arrival. There were her brothers, her mother and her father. This wedding was not his to stage—it was theirs too. Very well, he would steel his heart against the sin and play the role of bridegroom. Pulling Nanuram closer, he asked, 'Have you seen the girl?'

'Which girl?'

Hari was exasperated. Nanuram knew exactly what he meant. Must he play the part all the time? 'Dungarmalji's granddaughter,' he said impatiently.

Nanuram's face dissolved into a smile. 'You will see her soon enough!'

Hari persisted. 'But Chaman Lalji has seen her?'

'Be patient, Hariya,' said Duli Chand, though his eyes twinkled and he nudged a few guests to draw their attention to his son's impatience. 'Dungarmalji is a respectable man. Do you think his granddaughter would expose her face in Chaman Lal's presence? Especially Chaman Lal.'

This caused general laughter. Chaman Lal joined in. He did not enjoy a reputation for lasciviousness. Indeed, he did not enjoy a reputation at all—most Marwaris in Bogra noticed him no more than the slush or the mosquitoes—but it tickled his vanity to be singled out.

The pandit announced that the auspicious moment was at hand. A scramble ensued as Nanuram and Duli Chand sought to clear a path for the mare.

'Grab the reins,' Nanuram said.

Hari remembered no such requirement on his last ride. Then, everyone had been content to let Master Bholaram control the mare. 'Hold the reins for me,' he told Nanuram. 'I will rest a hand on your shoulder.'

'The bridegroom has mounted,' Duli Chand announced, as if Hari had not been seated in the saddle for a full ten minutes, and asked, 'Where is the bindavar?'

'Durga!' Nanuram called.

Urgent hands pushed a shy and resisting Durga Prasad into the centre. He had been dressed in a white shervani and red turban similar to Hari's, and looked like a little bridegroom himself. He was lifted by Nanuram and deposited in the saddle in front of Hari, who had been told that this was the custom in Disavar: a young boy dressed as the bridegroom accompanied the bridegroom to the bride's house, especially if the groom was advanced in age, as Hari was. Having never sat on a horse before, Durga flailed his arms and grabbed Hari's left thigh. Hari kept one hand on Nanuram's shoulder and brought the other around Durga, pressing him tightly against his body. This calmed the boy. *When I lose my balance*, Hari thought nervously, *we will fall together*.

'It is improper to use your own son as the bindavar,' Duli Chand said.

'I could find no one else,' said Nanuram. 'Hari Babu has no nephews in Disavar.'

'What about Mangiram's son?'

'He has the pox.'

The mare was led to Sat Matha, with the guests following. Hari and Durga were taken off the mare and the mare discharged. Gopi and Tribhuvan—dressed in silk kurtas and dhotis but not as bridegrooms—demanded to know why Durga had been granted the privilege of playing the bindavar.

'You are too old,' Hari said to Gopi. 'You will soon be a bridegroom yourself, why must you play a bindavar?'

This calmed Gopi, and Tribhuvan was bought off by the purchase of a green coconut. On further thought, Duli Chand had all the guests treated to green coconuts. There was much slashing of coconut shells that were dashed to the ground, one after another, after the guests had drunk the water. Duli Chand demanded and received a discount from the coconut seller.

Nanuram looked about him. Sat Matha was a mass of red, pink and yellow turbans, silk kurtas and dhotis, and foreheads smeared with red tilaks. He turned to Chaman Lal. 'We could almost be in Shekhavati.'

Chaman Lal nodded vaguely. He had left Shekhavati more than fifty years ago, and never gone back. He had only a sketchy recollection of his childhood there—it had long dissolved into a haze that defined his past in Shekhavati, Calcutta, Dhaka, far-flung branches of the firm, and finally in Bogra. He had no memories, merely an acute sense of numbers, weights and jute bales that peopled his present.

Mangiram arrived with a dozen bullock carts, and Nanuram supervised the loading of trunks and bedding. Groups were formed, a headcount was completed. Men were helped on to the carts. It was late in the afternoon when their carts passed the first shops in Gobindganj, where Dungarmalji had arranged to welcome his guests. Seven men wearing red turbans awaited them with tumblers of tea.

A grain shop had been converted into a rest stop for the occasion. The owner, an acquaintance of Dungarmal's, was part of the welcome party. Hari was led to the back of the shop, where he was given a glass of milk flavoured with almonds. He noted the bits of saffron floating in it.

'Drink well, Kunwarji,' the shop owner said, assuming the role of the bride's party. 'Your days of irresponsible behaviour are over!'

Hari thought the joke in bad taste. Could the man not see that he was a full-grown man, and did he not know this was not his first wedding, and that he had three sons? Perhaps the whole idea was doomed. What if this girl did not take to his sons? The eleventh was already upon Gopi. Would he accept this girl, who looked twelve at fifteen, as his mother? If only Lakshmi's Ma has chosen to stay in Bogra for a few more years…

'The elephant is here,' Nanuram announced.

Hari frowned. 'Does Gobindganj not have a mare for hire?'

Nanuram's eyes twinkled. 'A mare was fine for Bogra, but Gobindganj is your father-in-law's town. He must see you ride an elephant. Besides, it is very auspicious if the groom is seated on an elephant when he strikes the toran.'

'In Chirawa I struck the toran from a mare, and no one thought it improper.'

'That wedding was laid low by the Chhappaniya, and you were known as Hariya. Now I call you Hari Babu. It is not the same.'

'You take pleasure in marrying me off a second time,' Hari said wistfully. 'You, who have never married.'

Nanuram smoothened his kurta over his frail frame with an air of dignity. 'I am married to Harilal & Sons.'

Hari could not resist a chuckle. 'Have you taken a vow, Nanuramji? A bride will fatten you.'

'I am too old,' said Nanuram, who was thirty-nine. Indeed, in his white kurta and dhoti—both cotton, both impeccably pressed—Nanuram looked impossibly old. Always thin, he had wasted away over the years. His cheeks were sunken, his chest had collapsed around his ribs, and his back, once erect, was beginning to acquire a gentle stoop. Hari fancied that he even saw a missing tooth. Could a man reach dotage at thirty-nine merely by willing it?

The shopkeeper had gone out on hearing of the elephant. He returned in a state of wonder and asked Nanuram, 'Where did you get the elephant?' he asked. 'In Shekhavati there are many rajas, but here in Bengal…'

'The Nawab of Bogra,' Nanuram said.

'A Musalman,' the shopkeeper pointed out.

'He is Hindu-minded,' Nanuram said. 'We will paint a tilak on the elephant's forehead and sprinkle gangajal on it, and the pandit will do a puja before the bridegroom touches the beast.'

'In Shekhavati, a bridegroom may not mount an elephant until he has fed the whole town,' said the shopkeeper.

'Bogra is ten times larger than Rampura,' Hari said eagerly, hoping this would defeat the elephant plan. 'How will you feed everyone? Send the beast back.'

'I gave the nawab a good rate,' Nanuram said. 'He will not return the money. And it took the elephant two days to walk to Gobindganj.'

'Perhaps you could feed only those who live in Marwari Para, not the whole town,' the shopkeeper suggested. 'Why waste money on Bengalis?'

Nanuram nodded, committing himself to nothing. He found the shopkeeper meddlesome and was eager to leave the shop, but had to wait for half an hour while a puja was conducted. As soon as the elephant had been purified, Hari was brought out of the shop amidst much excitement. A group of naked boys had surrounded the elephant, gaping, pointing and laughing. After they had been shooed away, a ladder was unrolled from above and Hari climbed to the howdah—a sturdy wooden crate reinforced with cross-bars, padded with leather seats and strapped to the elephant's back—that was surprisingly spacious. Gopi, Durga and Tribhuvan climbed up, one by one, until there were no more seats. The mahout sat outside the howdah, on the elephant's neck and within reach of its flapping ears. When the beast moved, the howdah rolled terrifyingly, and Durga began to cry.

'Look at the mahout. He is not afraid,' Hari said to reassure him, but he himself was on the verge of panic. With every roll it seemed the howdah would be wrenched from its fastenings. That would be a nice spectacle, he thought—the groom and his sons flying down like the messengers of Yamaraj, Lord of Death.

The procession marched ponderously through the lanes of Gobindganj, following the elephant, which was preceded by three men playing a song on clarinets. When passing through narrow lanes, the elephant's head grazed the eaves of houses, and Gopi reached out to touch the thatch, inviting rebuke from Nanuram, who walked next to the elephant. Hari himself had no stomach for sight-seeing. Should the elephant pass under an arch, it was quite possible for a man to be knocked off his seat. He sank low in the howdah, peering over the side in wonder even as fear gripped him.

Dungarmalji's house was a two-storeyed brick building in the centre of the market, testifying to his position as the leading cloth merchant of Gobindganj. The ground floor housed the shop and a storeroom; the family lived upstairs. The shop had been decorated. Banana trees had been transported whole and strapped to pillars. An arch of mango leaves framed the main door. Now representing the bride's party—because of the scarcity of Marwari barbers—Chotiya stood at the door and held up the toran, inviting Hari to strike it. A branch of the neem tree was sent up the elephant. Hari raised it, preparing to strike, but Chotiya's hands would not reach high enough, and the branch was too limp to be directed downward.

It is either too high or too low, Hari thought irritably. Raamji does not want me to strike a toran.

'Bring a thicker branch,' Duli Chand said nervously.

'I knew an elephant was a foolish idea,' Hari muttered.

The toran ceremony was in danger of being ruined. 'Could we get a mare?' Duli Chand asked, worried.

'Not right away,' Nanuram replied. Then he had an idea. 'Send the barber upstairs.'

Someone objected. 'He cannot enter the house until the toran has been struck.'

'But he represents the bride's family now,' Nanuram said.

This was accepted, and Chotiya went into the house. Upstairs, a string was threaded through the hole at the top of the toran. Chotiya emerged on the balcony, leaned over and dealt out the string until the toran was suspended just above the elephant's head.

'Strike it now!' Duli Chand called.

Hari raised the branch again. As he brought it down on the plate, Chotiya turned away to answer someone behind him, causing the toran to bob up. Hari missed. A laugh went up among the guests. 'Let Kunwarji work hard for his bride!' shouted someone from the bride's family. Warming to his new role, Chotiya bobbed the toran up and down in the air like a puppeteer, daring Hari to strike it. After three missed attempts, he realized he had overplayed his hand when a frown appeared on Hari's brow, and let the plate swing gently. The branch struck it so hard that it nearly flew off.

'The toran has been struck,' Duli Chand announced.

Women began to sing the Kaaman. A tired Hari was brought down from the elephant. His sons followed. Dungarmalji's wife appeared at the door to put a tilak on Hari's forehead. There was giggling when her hand failed to reach Hari—already tall, he had been made to stand on a stool, while she was a short, squat woman.

'The boy is tall!'

'He is not a boy.'

'You must bend your knee, Kunwarji, or your mother-in-law will have to climb into your arms to reach your forehead.'

The ceremony was completed, and the curtain of women parted to reveal the bride herself, dressed in a red skirt and a sequined shawl that covered her head and most of her face. She was short and slight. He bent over again, eagerly peering through the shawl but afraid he would seem too eager. She placed a ball of fried dough on his head. He stood up straight. The dough plopped to the ground and was crushed under someone's foot. The women laughed. 'She will lord it over him!'

Ah, Hari thought, I should have balanced it on my head. But women will say anything. Who was this little girl to intimidate him?

After they had garlanded each other—Hari having to bend over again—and all the songs had been sung, he stepped off the stool and was led into a room inside the house, where they waited for the auspicious hour. Meanwhile, Chotiya tied the toran above the front door.

Gopi had told his brothers that, being of the groom's party, they would be made much of during the wedding. So when a few women—in red skirts and shawls like the bride—pulled them into a room to ask about their father, they went gladly.

'Is your father short-tempered?'

'Very,' Gopi replied smoothly, 'especially if the turmeric is not right in his daal-bati.'

'Ah, he likes daal-bati?'

'And sangar pickle, mango pickle, raw mangoes, moong papad...' Gopi unfurled a long list, watching with pleasure the confusion on the women's faces. 'I hope the girl can cook.'

'Speak respectfully! She is going to be your mother.'

Gopi snorted. 'I completed the tenth on Pausha sudi shashtami. The eleventh is upon me. How old is she?'

'This boy will be a handful for Manki,' a woman murmured.

'Is that her name? I do not like it,' Gopi declared. The women giggled.

Hari sat through the wedding ceremonies in a state of despair, conscious that he had finally broken the cord that tied him to Parmeshwari. The next evening, with one ceremony remaining before their return to Bogra, he told his father, 'I will not sit for the pahrani.'

'It is your wedding,' Duli Chand said. 'You must see what gifts your father-in-law has to give you.'

'Gopi could sit in my place.'

'Your previous wedding was darkened by the Chhappaniya. Here, this girl has five brothers to provide for her, and Dungarmalji is not a tight-fisted man.'

But it was Gopi who sat next to Duli Chand on the bed, which had been covered with a silk shawl. Hari remained in the next room, but could hear the lists of utensils—silver, brass and steel—and jewellery that were read aloud, along with rings, shawls, silk dhotis, gold chains, and a silver bowl filled to the brim with one-rupee coins. Everything was loaded into the cart that was to take him and his bride back home.

They returned to Bogra the next day. Following his instructions, his room had not been decorated. The bed had a simple white sheet, on which Manki sat cross-legged, her skirt fanned out around her, and her shawl pulled over her face, while women from Sat Matha came to see her. When Hari entered the room in the evening, the nevgan—who had come with Manki from Gobindganj—rose to go, but Hari stopped her. He sat down on the bed, far from Manki. Her shawl was thin: he could see her face in the glow of the lantern. *Perhaps she is beautiful*, he thought. A clay parrot lay next to her on the bed. He turned to the nevgan. 'I will sleep in the verandah. Give her a second blanket if she is cold.'

Late in the night, he went down to the shop, opened the cartons in the back and took out three Pall Mall cigarettes. He had not smoked for a year, and thought he had given up the vile habit. He was shocked when the smoke lifted his spirits.

The next morning, there was a quarrel between Gopi and Manki. He had entered her room, seen the clay parrot she had brought from Gobindganj, and wanted it for himself. Manki refused. The nevgan tried to intervene. Gopi screamed. Hari rushed into the room to find Manki in the arms of the nevgan, crying, and Gopi triumphantly holding the parrot aloft.

'Give it back,' he commanded.

'It is mine,' Gopi said. 'My new mother has given it to me.'

A shake of the nevgan's head told Hari this was not true. Angrily, he wrenched the parrot from Gopi's hands and returned it to the nevgan. Gopi sought to reclaim it, upon which Hari seized him, turned him around and slapped him hard. Manki stopped whimpering, and Gopi watched his father in stunned silence.

'The cart will be here in an hour to take you back to Gobindganj,' Hari said to the nevgan. Before leaving the room, he said to no one in particular, meaning to address himself to his wife. 'I hope you found Bogra to your liking. You will see more of it in a year.'

Then he stalked out of the room and went downstairs to open the shop. Bringing out his slate, he wrote, 'She gives milk for ten years between the ages of three and fourteen, and may calve eight times in that period. In return for this bounty, she asks for little—fodder, a warm blanket on winter nights, and protection from the butcher when her milk dries up. Why would anyone, especially a devout Musalman, wish to harm her? Mir Musarraf Hussein wrote years ago: it says nowhere in the Quran that a Musalman must make a meal of the cow.'

6

Three weeks after the wedding, Hari found Lakshmi's Ma sitting in the verandah with Durga in her lap. The goitre at her throat had grown into a grotesque ball that hung loosely, threatening to detach and roll away at any moment. On seeing Hari, she grinned shyly.

'They told me you had gone to Benares to die.'

'I found no peace in Ganga Maiya's lap,' she said. 'And your sons need me.'

'They needed you three months ago.'

'I will take good care of them.'

'They are used to living without you,' Hari said drily. 'Why have you come back?'

'But it was your father who sent for me.'

Then it dawned on Hari: Duli Chand had brought her back because it was he who had sent her to Benares. She had not gone of her own will, and certainly not to die there. Whoever heard of such a thing? Widows went to Benares and Brindavan when they had no one to look after them, not when they had a comfortable position in a bania's house. He had been tricked: she had been sent to Benares so his father could coerce him into marrying. His irritation found as its object the woman before him.

'Go back to Benares right away. The boys have a mother now.'

'But she will not come home for another year,' Lakshmi's Ma said smugly.

Hari was exasperated, but there was nothing to be done now. Very well. His sons needed a mother, even if he did not need a wife. He sat down to his dinner, and the fragrance of fresh rotis on red-hot coals softened him somewhat. Then Durga began to wail and Lakshmi's Ma clutched him to her bosom. The eighth is upon him, Hari thought contemptuously, and he still needs a mother's breast. Then he wondered if Manki—spare, slight and waif-like—would be able to give the boys what Lakshmi's Ma did.

Tribhuvan had now been in the government school for

six months. He had memorized the 150 English words in the *Telegraph Teacher* and had been asked to buy a dictionary. Hari grumbled—if the boy was to learn from books, why was the teacher being paid two rupees every month? And if books were needed, should not the expense come out of the teacher's salary? The request was denied.

Meanwhile, Gopi sat at the scales every day with Hari, who noted that he was aggressive with customers—to the point of being brusque—and quick to recognize grain and spices, even as he was slow with accounts. Indeed, he still needed his slate to add or subtract sums that Hari could juggle inside his head, and he had a horror of multiplication tables. Master Bholaram would have been disappointed, but Duli Chand found his grandson's performance quite satisfactory. 'It will take a year or two—he will be able to run the shop by himself. You will no longer need an old man like me to assist you.'

During the rains, the Karatoya swelled and rose to a mark never breached before. The ghat in Raja Bajar was submerged. Waves lapped just outside the jute press, which was located on a high embankment. It became impossible to dry jute in the yard because of incessant rain. A tin shed was hastily erected and the strands spread under it. The press remained closed for weeks. Meanwhile, Sat Matha had become a sea of slush, and Hari had prevailed on his father to give up his chair in the road and climb back into the shop, which was on higher ground.

On the last day of Bhadwa, Duli Chand went to the Karatoya for his morning bath. Instead of going directly to the ghat, he went to the jute press, crossed the yard, and opened a door in the wall that faced the river. Chaman Lal was in the office, waiting for the kyals. He saw Duli Chand go through the door, wade into the river until it was waist-high and raise his folded hands to the sun. He was naked above the waist. After his Surya Namaskar, he bent over to dip his head into the water.

Chaman Lal did not think much of it when the head did not re-appear. It was possible for Duli Chand to return home without going through the jute press—a dirt path led to Raja Bazar. That path would be slippery and muddy now, but men used it every day, and Duli Chand often took it when the press was locked. It was only an hour later, when Gopi came to the press to ask about his grandfather, that Chaman Lal first dwelled on the matter. 'Yes, I saw him. He returned to Sat Matha without going through the yard.'

'But he is not in the shop.'

'He may have gone upstairs to his room.'

'Lakshmi's Ma has not seen him.'

'He could be anywhere,' said Chaman Lal, suddenly aware of disaster.

Hari spent the whole day looking for his father. After scouring the riverbank all along Raja Bajar and asking everyone they saw there, Gopi, Durga and Tribhuvan visited every shop in Sat Matha, Fateh Ali Bajar and Raja Bajar. They went to the goshala and spoke to the Pinjrapole man. They combed the railway station and the warehouses in Bara Gola. No one except Chaman Lal had seen Duli Chand that morning.

'He may have taken a boat across the river,' Hari said to his sons.

But no boatman would agree to cross the swollen Karatoya, and there was no conceivable reason why Duli Chand would go to Musalman Para on the eastern bank. In his eight years in Bogra he had never stepped outside Marwari Para, except during the one trip he had made to Shekhavati.

A week passed. Gloom settled on the verandah in Sat Matha. In this state of uncertainty, Hari could neither engage pandits—how could he perform the last rites for a father who may be living?—nor turn his attention from the disappearance. He still opened the shop every morning and sat through the day, weighing grain, filling his cash box, accepting the occasional expression of sympathy, and running in his mind—yet again—all the possible ways in which his father could be safe yet unable to return home. The servant still placed Duli Chand's chair in the road every day. Hari did not ask him to stop—it was easier to perpetuate the illusion. Every day, he wondered if he should make some sort of a declaration that would settle the matter. Should he contact his sisters in Shekhavati? What would he tell them? How long must he wait before accepting what he feared? It was written in the Shastras that while everyone had to go, the trick was to go properly—without haste, without being surprised, and commemorated by the proper rites performed by a son. Would the spirit of a man taken away in this manner ever find peace?

Four weeks after Duli Chand had disappeared, a pandit arrived in Sat Matha, saying he had been instructed by a spirit to make his way to Hari's shop.

'But my father has not released his body,' Hari said irritably. 'He may be in Santahar or Gobindganj, or even in Rangpur. I have business associates there, who will send word as soon as they have located him.'

The pandit sighed tolerantly. 'Raamji gives and Raamji takes, my son. Your father has asked that you accept this.'

'Where did you see him?' Hari demanded.

The pandit appeared surprised. 'In my mind, of course. He is a *pret*, a disembodied spirit unable to go to the court of Yamaraj. He will remain a *pret* until you complete the last rites—all thirteen days—as well as the gift of a cow. He will hound his loved ones, circle them, stalk them, talk to them in their dreams.'

Raamji has taught different wiles to different men, Hari said to himself. A bania mixes brick dust in chilli powder, a brahmin speaks to *pret*s in his mind.

'All right. Make arrangements for the puja.'

After thirteen days and the expenditure of two hundred rupees, the pandit declared that the *pret* of Duli Chand Tibrewal had been released by his son's labours, had crossed the Vaitarani river with the help of the cow gifted to him, and was safely on his way to the court of Yamaraj, where he would hear the verdict on his future lives after a careful examination of his sins in this one.

When Hari opened the shop the next morning, he told the servant, 'Remove that chair from the road.'

Surely the *pret* had flown away, because he felt a lightness in his heart. He could sense, too, that Gopi was relieved, from the manner in which he was sprawled carelessly in the back of the shop.

That afternoon, Hari walked to Raja Bajar. For six weeks he had avoided the press, afraid to look at the door his father had passed through on his way to Raamji. The yard had suffered from neglect. Rains had brought down a portion of the wall and soaked the jute, even that lying under the tin shed. In the office, Chaman Lal laboured next to a lantern—because it was overcast, the office was dark even in the afternoon. Durga sat cross-legged to his right, dutifully checking the inventory as part of his apprenticeship.

Chaman Lal had aged by years in six weeks. His eyes dwelt vacantly on his binders, and it was obvious he was doing nothing even when he appeared to be busy. He started at Hari's entry. His lips trembled and he looked as if he might cry.

'Do not stop on my account,' Hari said kindly, perpetuating the pretence that Chaman Lal was busy. 'The whole press now rests on your shoulders.'

This reference to Duli Chand's death washed away whatever restraint Chaman Lal possessed. He began to sputter. 'Duli Chand Babu was younger than me. I keep telling myself—what if I had tried to stop him from…'

Hari did not let him finish—to his mind, such talk was reckless—and pointed to Durga. 'The boy needs you. Without your guidance, who will teach him about sada, tosa and mesta jute?'

Chaman Lal fell silent. When he spoke, it was clear his mind was made up. 'I have been in Disavar all my life, Hari Babu. I wish to return to Shekhavati.'

Hari was stunned. Chaman Lal had never expressed the slightest interest in Shekhavati.

'I will leave for Kalkatta next week.'

This caused Hari to exclaim, 'But you cannot go away! At least not so quickly.'

'But I can,' Chaman Lal said wistfully. 'Your munim Nanuram can look after the press as well as I can. And your son,' he indicated Durga, 'will soon be old enough.'

'He is not yet eight.'

'A bania's son learns quickly. Besides, he is your son.'

This bit of flattery left Hari cold. He knew Durga was not particularly sharp, and Chaman Lal had given no previous indication that he held Hari in high esteem. At best, he had softened toward Durga after the accident in the press.

'I would like to sell my 5-per cent share in the press to you. You and the firm will then become joint owners.'

Hari had no idea that Chaman Lal thought himself a shareholder in the jute press. Daulatram Gulabchand was the sleeping partner—having put up the capital—and he the working partner, with Chaman Lal merely a munim, entitled to 5 per cent of the profits on account of his relationship with Khemchandji. Of course, this had not been formally recorded, and both Chaman Lal and Hari earned far more than their share through the second book, which had never been shown to the firm. But now the old man seemed quite certain of his 5-per cent ownership, and there was little Hari could do to dissuade him in his present state.

The next week was busy. Books were transferred from Chaman Lal to Hari; papers were signed; kyals were told of the new arrangement; a telegram was sent to the Daulatram Gulabchand office in Lalgodam. The cubicle in Bara Gola—which Chaman Lal still rented, though he did no pawn-broking there—was disposed of. Clothes were given to beggars, utensils donated. After much negotiation, Chaman Lal agreed that his 5-per cent entitled him to no more than two hundred rupees—this valued the press at four thousand. On the day he left, Lakshmi's Ma cooked him a dozen rotis and wrapped them in slices of raw mango. Hari and Nanuram went to the station to see him off. As the train crept away, Hari wondered how much the old man had stowed away during his seven years in the press. If he could maintain a second register that they hid from the firm, he could very well have operated a third seen only by him. Who knew how much jute had been bought and pressed over the years? In the last week, Hari had searched the office surreptitiously but found no other books. Of course, Chaman Lal was too wily to leave records lying around. Very likely, everything he had earned lay hidden in the bottom of his small trunk, which now sat under his bench on the train.

Hari decided to go to Calcutta. He had freed up some money by selling his share in the goshala, which had been bought only to please his father. Combining this with the money earned through the second register, he could buy out the firm's share of the press if the head munim in Lalgodam could be convinced that the press was not doing well, and therefore, worth little.

He took Tribhuvan with him, partly because he hoped to show off the boy's English in Lalgodam. In his absence, Gopi would mind the shop and Durga would sit in the jute press under Nanuram's supervision.

This was Tribhuvan's first trip, anywhere, in a train. He sat in wonder all the way to Santahar, and was even more astonished when the mail train to Calcutta picked up speed. At Sealdah Station in Calcutta, Hari was dismayed to find that the usual swarm of tongas had vanished. Instead, strange men with pale skin and narrow slits for eyes converged on him, each pulling a two-wheeled ricksha and offering to take him anywhere for an anna. No wonder the tongas had vanished—who would take one if a ricksha could be engaged for an anna?

Out of habit, he said, 'Half-anna.'

To his astonishment, the man agreed. He threw his bundle in the back of the ricksha, hoisted Tribhuvan on to the seat and climbed in after him, and was horrified when the man placed himself between the handlebars like a horse. For a moment they were balanced precariously on two wheels, about to tip backwards and have their heads smashed on the pavement, but the man was strong. Standing on tiptoe, he pushed down hard on the handlebars, righted the ricksha and began to pull it.

'What kind of a tonga is this?' Tribhuvan asked, frightened. 'Why is there a man instead of a horse pulling it?'

Hari himself was utterly confused but replied smugly, 'This is a Kalkatta tonga.'

Tribhuvan leaned closer and whispered. 'This man does not look like a Marwari or a Bengali. Is he a sahib?'

Hari laughed. 'Sahibs don't pull rickshas.'

The ricksha clattered over the cobblestones in Bara Bazar, always in danger of tipping over but somehow managing to stay balanced. They turned into Amherst Row. As soon as the handlebars had been laid down in the street outside Lalgodam, Hari jumped off in relief, telling himself he would never take such a ricksha again.

The flour mill was in operation, but Lalgodam looked different. While the building was unchanged—decaying walls, balconies with iron railings, drying dhotis and kurtas, the hand-pump in the corner—the third floor was quieter, gloomier and less busy. He saw a few gumashtas he used to know—they seemed not to recognize him—and sought out the head munim, who sat in Khemchandji's place behind the cash box. Instinctively, he bent over to touch the munim's feet, then realized that this was not Khemchand Biyani. To cover his embarrassment, he slapped Tribhuvan on the back, asking, 'Where are your manners?'

So it was Tribhuvan who bent over and received a blessing from the old man. Hari had imagined that he would have some trouble identifying himself and explaining the arrangement Khemchandji had made regarding the press, but Chaman Lal had passed through Lalgodam two weeks ago—on his way to Shekhavati—so the new munim already knew of the matter. He asked, 'What are the jute rates in Bogra?'

Hari was immediately suspicious. The munim knew the rates all over Bengal very well, indeed better than Hari himself: the firm paid for jute bales as far east as Mymensingh. No doubt he also knew, through Chaman Lal, that Hari had come to buy the firm's share. Until Hari could determine why the question had been asked, it was best not to answer and commit himself. He painted an expression of discontent on his face. 'The rates rise and fall, mostly fall. Who can control them?'

'In Kalkatta, a bale can go for eighty rupees these days because of the war in England.'

'Wars,' said Hari, struggling to summon an advantageous response. He knew of the recent rise in rates because of the war, but did not know if the higher rates had been shown in the official book by Chaman Lal.

'Rates have doubled since the war started,' continued the munim. 'Balers have seen good profits.'

Ah, it was clear. The munim was talking up the business in Bogra so he could extract a good price for the firm's share. He knew he must resist. 'The Kalkatta rates are for pakka bales of five munn. We do not have a hydraulic press in Bogra. Our kachcha bales are four munn.'

'Each would still fetch sixty-four rupees,' said the munim.

'Not quite. No one pays the full rate. And margins have not budged because everyone in Bengal knows of the Kalkatta rates—they have raised the price of jute to match it. Even sada has doubled. The baler gets very little, no matter what the bales go for.'

'I saw the books,' the munim said suddenly, abandoning the discussion on rates. 'You deal mostly in sada jute.'

Hari studied his face for signs of irony but found none. Was it possible that Chaman Lal had revealed more than he should have? But there could be no possible advantage for him in doing so. Here, a word about Khemchand Biyani would be appropriate. 'Khemchandji was like a father to me. I started in Kalkatta in his care.'

The munim sighed and looked skyward. 'Who can replace Khemchandji?'

Hari sighed in concert.

'But the times are different. The firm is not what it used to be. Much has changed in Kalkatta since the war started.'

'Yes, no more tongas and no more haggling with tongawalas,'

Hari replied, hoping to steer the conversation to safer subjects. 'I found a new ricksha that brought me to Lalgodam from Sealdah for half an anna.'

'Half an anna?' The munim asked, surprised. 'You were cheated. The usual rate is a paisa. Perhaps a pie more if it is raining.'

'Ah.' Hari was deflated. 'But what kind of a man was that? He did not look like a Bengali or Bihari.'

'Chinaman. There are hundreds like him. Their rickshas have driven tongas out of Bara Bazar. The tongawala must feed both his horse and himself; the Chinaman is his own horse.'

'A bania could learn from a Chinaman,' said Hari.

'What do you propose to offer for our 70 per cent in Harilal & Sons?' the munim asked.

Hari was not yet prepared to be so specific. And hopefully the munim meant only the jute press, not the shop in Sat Matha on which the firm could not lay any reasonable claim. The question clarified one matter: what Khemchandji had negotiated to be the profit split was now being considered a share of ownership. That was not unfavourable from Hari's point of view: the capital had all been the firm's, after all.

'The last few years have not been good for baling,' he said, reprising his previous argument. 'The machine breaks down too often, the kyals are restive...'

'What did you pay Chaman Lalji for his 5 per cent?'

'A hundred...' Hari began and, on seeing the munim frown, quickly added, 'and fifty.'

'Chaman Lalji passed through Kalkatta two weeks ago, on his way to Shekhavati.'

So it was true. What a shameless old man Chaman Lal was, to strike one deal with him and another with the munim! But he knew he must not submit meekly. Tribhuvan sat next to him, watching. The boy must not see his father get bullied by a mere munim. Who was this munim anyway, when Hari had known Khemchandji well, perhaps better than this munim himself? If he had enjoyed half the stature that Khemchandji did, Chaman Lal would not have dared to start that second book in Bogra.

'Chaman Lalji was with the firm for fifty years,' Hari said. 'A man wants to retire at his age.'

'Yes. And a business that deals only in sada jute was not to his liking. Now, if you also pressed some tosa…'

Now Hari was alert. Did the munim know of the other register? Would Chaman Lal be foolish enough to incriminate himself merely to spite Hari?

'Khemchandji spoke well of you,' the munim continued, 'so we will settle for a fair price. He would not have wanted to bargain with you.'

Hari was relieved. And he knew this was his chance to quote a price for the firm's share. He had come to Kalkatta with a sum in mind. Now, he thought it wise to raise it by 15 per cent before making the offer. Given the circumstances, he could not offer less. The munim accepted readily.

As they walked out of Lalgodam, Tribhuvan asked, 'What were you talking about?'

Hari lifted his son on to his shoulders. 'Harilal & Sons now belongs to Harilal and his sons.'

The next day, he took Tribhuvan to Harrison Road, where they bought a cricket bat—no one in Bogra had one—and a bottle of strawberry jam from a shop that sold to sahibs. Tribhuvan reminded Hari of his desire to own books in English.

'I will buy you the Ramayan and the Bhagavad Gita,' Hari said. 'There is more wisdom in one shlok of the Gita than in all your English books put together.'

'But I must learn English if I am to pass my tests in the government school.'

So Hari took him to College Street where, from hundreds of stalls, they selected one. The shopkeeper showed them a booklet. '*First Book of Reading*, Pyarecharan Sarkar.'

'If the boy is to learn English,' said Hari, 'he should buy something written by a sahib, not a Bengali.'

The man slapped a well-thumbed book on the counter. 'Everyone buys this. Blackie's *Self-Culture*.'

'This looks old.'

'Second-hand,' said the shopkeeper. 'Why pay twice as much for a new one? Would the words be different?'

'The pictures will have faded.'

'It has no pictures,' said the man.

'How is the boy to understand so many words?'

'Use this,' said the man, bringing out the fattest book Hari had ever seen, thicker even than the *Mahabharat*. '*Oxford English Dictionary*.'

What an astute bania this man is, Hari told himself.

'I also need those,' Tribhuvan said, pointing to an array of fountain pens.

'What is wrong with your slate and chalk?' Hari asked irritably.

'One cannot write English with chalk.'

'I will ask Nanuram to lend you his pen.'

'He has a reed pen. And I need two of those,' Tribhuvan said, pointing to the book written by the Bengali.

'Why?' Hari asked.

'One for myself, one for Mohammad Ali.'

His son was buying books for a Musalman! 'Who on earth is this Mohammad Ali?'

'The Nawabzada's son. We are the same age, exactly. He goes to the government school with me, and he has promised to let me see the Nawabbari.'

That was one of the perils of sending Tribhuvan to the government school—the boy spoke to Musalmans there. For three generations, Mangiram's family had funded the nawab's profligacy to be able to enter the Nawabbari. Now, his son had paid six annas as the price of admission.

They took the train to Santahar. Tribhuvan was perched triumphantly on a large bundle—his books had been packed by the shopkeeper—and swung his cricket bat so wildly that Hari thought he might hit the other passengers.

The more he thought of the price he had paid for the jute press, the worse he felt about it. No doubt the munim had fooled him by pretending to possess inside knowledge of the goings-on in Bogra—Chaman Lal would not be so rash, even if he felt no affection for Hari. He should have stuck to the original price. Indeed, the purchase could have been delayed for a year or two. Who knew how long this war would last? Its end would send jute crashing, together with the value of the jute press. Only a fool bought in the middle of a war... He could not sleep. Late in the night, when the train was on the Hardinge Bridge, he touched his kurta pocket and was gratified to find a lone cigarette and a box of matches. Although he smoked infrequently, he had taken to carrying cigarettes in ones or twos, almost as talismans.

He looked down at the dark Padma, remembering the days before the bridge when he took the ferry across the river, and lit a cigarette. The smoke gave him instant relief, which turned to horror when he found his son watching him. The cigarette slipped from his hand, tumbled over the window bars and vanished into the darkness below. Absently, he wondered if it was irreverent to throw a cigarette into the Padma. But Tribhuvan was watching, and an explanation was necessary.

'For my illness,' he said, knowing his son would not believe him. Everyone knew that Hari had never been sick, that the Shekhavati bajra he had eaten as a child had given him a constitution no Marwari in Bengal—with its rice and its mangoes—could ever dream of. Hari never tired of boasting about this, and a boy who had memorized 150 words in the *Telegraph Teacher* would certainly remember.

Tribhuvan did not ask, 'What illness?' He merely stared in a manner Hari found impudent. He leaned toward his son. 'Do you like your cricket bat?'

Tribhuvan nodded eagerly.

'And the dictionary? And the book for the Musalman boy? Well, do not tell anyone,' he said, too ashamed to elaborate but hoping his son would understand.

They did not speak until the train reached Santahar early in the morning. When taking the slow train to Bogra, Tribhuvan refused Hari's offer to carry his package and lugged it into the carriage by himself.

In Bogra, Hari went straight to the jute press and Tribhuvan ran upstairs to the arms of Lakshmi's Ma. In the press, Durga was sitting in the office, looking bored. Nanuram was supervising the kyals. Hari pulled him aside and said, 'I have bought the press.'

Not one to make a display of his emotions, Nanuram nodded indifferently.

'Have you been going to Sat Matha?' Hari asked.

'There is no need to,' said Nanuram. 'Gopi has done very well, all by himself. The boy has suddenly grown up, sitting at the cash box day and night, and showing not a trace of childhood impulsiveness. Only eleven, and you should see how he bargains with customers!'

His heart swelling with pride, Hari replied. 'He was born in Shekhavati; what else would you expect? Look at poor Durga—born in Bogra, always ill. And Tribhuvan's head is full of English words no one has any use for.'

'When a boy can keep a shop, it is time to find him a bride,' Nanuram said.

I have been negligent, thought Hari. Gopi was already eleven. But now who would find him a bride? Hari's wedding had been arranged by Chaman Lal, who knew everyone in the Rangpur-Bogra area. The other person who could make a match was Mangiram, but Hari was loath to ask him. Mangiram's son had died of the pox. There had been much grieving. For a day or two, Hari entertained the idea of offering one of his three sons to his friend as restitution for his loss, but abandoned the plan as too fanciful. He had since seen little of Mangiram, except in the pujas that followed the disappearance of his father. It was too early to seek his help with Gopi's match—this would only serve to remind him that his own son was gone. There remained only one man who could take on the task. He said to Nanuram, 'It was you who noticed that the boy has grown up, so I count on you to find me a daughter-in-law.'

Nanuram was overwhelmed. 'It is a great responsibility, Hari Babu. Your first son...'

The cricket bat was a sensation among the Marwari boys of Bogra. Gopi laid claims on it—being older than Tribhuvan—and put it on display in the shop at Sat Matha, propped up between sacks of rice. Few had seen or touched an actual bat; they used sticks and branches in their games. Boys came to watch and touch, commented on its wrinkle-free skin, solidity and polish. Some were allowed to hold it, others given the privilege of flourishing it, imagining themselves to be the cricketer Ranjit Singhji. They turned it over and studied the logo, ran their hands over the letters, then handed it back to Gopi, who returned it to its place, where it sat like a trophy.

'Why do you keep it on display like a bag of salt?' Hari asked his son. 'Tribhuvan bought it so he could hit balls with it.'

'That will destroy its polish,' Gopi said.

'Every time one of these boy touches it,' said Hari, 'some of the polish comes off.'

That was what gave Gopi Chand the idea. Within weeks, he had a flourishing rental business. He lent the bat for four annas, for two weeks at a time. Before being handed over, it was carefully inspected. Scratches were noted by both parties, with Nanuram as witness. Money was deposited in an account maintained by Gopi. Regular renters were given discounts. There was a waiting list. Gopi played favourites, raised rates when he could and brought them down on a whim. In a few months, with its polish gone, the bat ceased to attract renters, so the business was closed, the money from Gopi's account transferred to Hari's cash box, and the bat returned to Tribhuvan.

Meanwhile, Nanuram had found a match for Gopi: a family in Santahar with an oil depot of their own.

'The girl is somewhat advanced in age,' Nanuram said, 'but Gopi too has passed eleven. The family is well-off.'

'I will not question your judgement,' Hari said. 'Send for Chotiya.'

The barber was called, instructed and sent off to Santahar, where he verified that the family did not belong to the Bindal Gotra—being in the same gotra as Hari's family would have made a match impossible. He returned to advise that the girl be brought to Bogra for an engagement ceremony.

Hari objected. 'She cannot come to the boy's house. Surely you know that, having arranged so many matches?'

'That is how we do it in Bengal,' Chotiya said.

Three days later, the girl arrived in Sat Matha, wrapped carefully in a red shawl, with her father, uncles and an aunt, and was immediately sent into a room while Hari sat with her father and uncles in the verandah. Lakshmi's Ma had cooked daal-bati.

'What do we deal in?' Hari asked, though he knew the answer. He had resorted to the Marwari practice of politely saying 'we' when he meant 'you'.

'Oil,' said the girl's father. 'And what do *we* deal in?'

'General store,' Hari said. 'Flour, pulses, kerosene, cigarettes.'

'Cigarettes?'

Hari chuckled. 'Only to be sold! And there is a jute baling press. We get bales from the east—Mymensingh, Faridpur, Narayanganj—over the Karatoya, press them and send them to Kalkatta. You may have seen my bales at your railway station—they pass through Santahar, where they change to the broad-gauge line to Kalkatta.'

'There is much jute at Santahar railway station,' said an uncle, noncommittally.

'May I ask how old the child is?' Hari asked, though he knew this too.

'Nine,' the father said. 'The tenth is upon her.'

Hari frowned, as he knew he should. He was also aware that Gopi, hidden behind the door, was listening.

'We are told the boy himself is eleven,' the girl's father said quickly.

Hari shrugged. 'This is not Shekhavati... Should we complete the ceremonies?'

The girl was brought into the verandah dressed in a pink skirt, with her shawl drawn like a veil across her face. Gopi was pulled out of hiding. The boy was shy, Hari noted, almost unnaturally so. 'Stand still! This is your engagement.'

The guests laughed. Hari positioned his son next to the girl, and a problem became apparent to everyone at the same instant. The girl was a few inches taller than the boy.

'He is only eleven,' Hari muttered in confusion. 'Girls grow fast, but boys catch up...'

'A child should never stand next to her husband,' the girl's aunt said soothingly. 'These are new-fangled customs here in Disavar.'

Hari's glance fell on Durga—standing outside the immediate circle—and Tribhuvan behind him. A solution presented itself. 'Where is that thick book you brought from Kalkatta? The one with meanings of words?'

The *Oxford English Dictionary* was produced. 'An English book,' the girl's aunt remarked disapprovingly. In response, Lakshmi's Ma painted a swastika on the first page using a paste of vermilion. The book was placed next to the girl and Gopi stepped on it. Turning to the pandit, Hari commanded, 'You may begin.'

The pandit lit a joss-stick and began to chant. After the ceremony was complete, the gifts had been presented—five silver coins for Hari, a silk kurta-pyjama for Gopi and embroidered caps for Durga and Tribhuvan—and the guests had left, Gopi drew Nanuram aside. 'Nanuramji! What is her name?'

'Whose name?'

'The girl's.'

Nanuram was nonplussed. 'How does that concern you?'

'Please.'

Nanuram shook his head. 'I do not understand the way things are these days. All right: Sharda. But you must not tell your father you heard from me.'

'Sharda. I like the name.'

'Do not repeat it!' Nanuram said before he stalked away, even as he recalled that the same question had been asked by Hari, many years ago in another world.

7

Late in 1918, Nanuram suggested that it was time for Hari to bring his wife home from Gobindganj. He had been married for two-and-a-half years, and the girl had crossed the age of seventeen.

'I know,' Hari said irritably. 'My sons have Lakshmi's Ma to look after them. Let the war in England end.'

'They say it has already ended. Jute rates are falling.'

Hari had been postponing the trip to Gobindganj on one pretext or another. Mangiram had asked, twice, when he planned to bring his bride home. Durga had wondered aloud when he would see his mother. Finally, on receiving a postcard from his father-in-law, he could put it off no more. The message was not specific—it merely inquired about jute rates and his health—but he took the hint. Reluctantly, he took a bullock cart to Gobindganj, feeling lonely in his bridegroom's shervani as the cart passed paddy fields, and suffered silently through the ceremonies accompanying Manki's leave-taking.

They sat next to each other in the back of the cart. She carried two things in her hands—a notebook half-filled with the word 'Raam' written six thousand times, and the clay parrot that had aroused Gopi's envy two years ago. Not a word was spoken. They reached Bogra. She pulled her shawl tightly about herself as they passed Raja Bajar and Fateh Ali Bajar on their way to Sat Matha. Her red skirt attracted attention. Shopkeepers looked up. Hari knew them all, and tried to bury his face in his shervani, hoping they would not make eye contact with him. How ridiculous he must look in his shervani! A groom at thirty-one…

At Sat Matha, Lakshmi's Ma had arranged elaborate ceremonies for the bride's entry to the house. Hari waited until

Manki was safely in the stairwell that led up to the verandah, then strode into the street. Women began to sing, and he could hear the bustle upstairs, where Durga and Tribhuvan were clamouring to sit in their mother's lap. All afternoon he walked aimlessly, going to Bara Gola past Chaman Lal's shuttered cubicle, then cutting across Fateh Ali Bajar to the riverbank, then walking up the bank until he arrived at the jute press. As the sun sank, he went into the yard to watch the kyals at work. From time to time, he stole into the tin shed where, behind bales of jute stacked 12 feet high, he smoked Berkeley cigarettes, aware of his recklessness—a spark from his cigarette could set the jute aflame and turn his whole stock into ash.

He went home late in the evening, after the markets had closed. The ceremonies were complete; the women had left. Lakshmi's Ma had washed the boys. He noted with satisfaction that Manki hovered over the oven in the verandah, face still hidden behind a corner of her shawl: that was unnecessary, considering there was no one—a father-in-law or an elder brother of her husband's—who could outrage her modesty. At least she gives herself no airs, he told himself. Her first day in her father-in-law's house, and she is already busy in the kitchen.

'You need not cover your face,' he said gently, 'except when looking down into the road.'

She did not respond, and he took it to be the shyness of a bride. What had Chaman Lalji said about her? Silent as a cow...

Gopi, Durga and Tribhuvan sat cross-legged near her, eating. Manki flipped rotis on the coals and Lakshmi's Ma slapped them on the boys' plates. Hari studied his sons' faces, trying to discern their feelings. No doubt they had heard countless stories of second mothers, of love withheld or given sparingly, and they were wary. It was possible that Gopi still had vague memories of Parmeshwari. The other two had received a mother's love, such as it was, from Lakshmi's Ma. It would not be easy. He started with the one he knew was most compliant.

'Durga, this is your mother.'

Manki's hands stopped their dance over the coals. She had just thrown a roti on the embers. Hari watched it inflate. A vapour trail escaped from it. He sensed that she was studying Durga from behind the veil, while Durga's eyes were fixed on his father. Slowly, the boy bit into a roti and nodded, not looking at his mother.

'Will you not touch your mother's feet?' Hari asked.

Durga rose and sought out Manki's feet. This was difficult, because she was squatting on a low stool and her skirt had billowed around her. With an embarrassed chuckle, she pushed a foot out. Durga touched it hastily and returned to his place.

'Wash your hands!' Lakshmi's Ma scolded, before he could touch anything on his plate again.

Next, it was Tribhuvan's turn to touch his mother's feet, wash his hands, and go back to his dinner. Finally, Hari turned to his oldest son. 'Gopi?'

Gopi shook his head vigorously, stood up and ran off, dinner unfinished. Hari chuckled uneasily. 'He will come around,' he said to no one in particular. Manki's hands began to move again. The roti on the coals had been burnt black.

When he entered his room that night, Manki was already in bed, dangerously close to its edge, with her back to him. The clay parrot hung from a bedpost. She stirred when he climbed into bed. Sitting as far from her as he could, he tried to think of something to say, and remembered that there was no room in the house where a woman might bathe. The boys used the hand-pump in the verandah, as did he, in full view of everyone. Lakshmi's Ma bathed there too, fully clothed, rising early in the morning so no one would see her. Often, he woke up to the sounds of her bath and remained in bed until he was sure she had finished and gone into a room. Perhaps he should warn Manki about this, but it was a minor matter, almost too trivial to inform his first words to his wife.

'I have given you three boys,' he said, 'Take good care of them.'

Then he lay down with his back to her and fell asleep, grieving silently. In the middle of the night, he was startled by her crying. Why has Raamji blessed this marriage? he asked himself. Can he not see it will bring joy to no one?

The next morning, he watched Manki bathe the boys with the help of Lakshmi's Ma. Tribhuvan set off to school with pen, paper and *Self-Culture*, Durga went to the jute press and Gopi took his seat in the shop downstairs. Manki appeared to have bathed—Lakshmi's Ma must have told her about the pump the previous day.

There was much joking in the shop that day. Customers could not resist commenting on Hari's restlessness. Hari Babu's mind is no longer in the shop, they said. He sits at the scales and appears to weigh grain, but he thinks of the one upstairs. Today is a good day to buy from him—quote ridiculously low prices and he will yield, because he wants to get it over with so he can return to his thoughts. He will give you a munn when you pay for a ser, a khandi when you pay for a munn... Finally, Hari could stand it no longer. Leaving Gopi in-charge, he went to Raja Bajar. The kyals in the press were too poor to dare make such comments, but the twinkle in Nanuram's eyes was exasperating. Hari went through the door to the bank of the Karatoya—now reduced to a stream in the winter—and watched boats laden with coconuts trying to find the ghat. Every few minutes one would get stuck in the mud, and the mallahs would disengage it by planting bamboos in the water and pushing against the riverbed. A cry of 'Jai Ganga Maiya' would go up, as if any river could call itself the Ganga.

He sat on the bank all day, returning to Sat Matha late in the evening when he knew his sons would be asleep. Lakshmi's Ma was waiting in the verandah. 'Bhabhiji has not eaten all day,' she said.

It annoyed him that she had already begun to call his wife Bhabhiji, as if Manki had lived in Sat Matha for years. Should she not have waited a few days before accepting the arrangement? And then there was Manki herself: seventeen years old yet intractable. Silent as a cow, Chaman Lal had said... Her silence was the pout of a child, not the equanimity of a mother.

'Does she not like your cooking?' he asked angrily. 'If so, she can make her own rotis.'

'She grieves for her mother,' said Lakshmi's Ma.

Sighing, he went into the room. She was sitting in bed, knees raised to her chest, shawl covering her shivering shoulders. She had been crying. The parrot lay next to her. Like her, Hari had not eaten all day and was already in a foul mood. The sight of the parrot set his heart aflame. Why was this girl still a child at seventeen? Parmeshwari was a mother at that age and had never seen it fit to complain, nor given herself the luxury of grieving for her mother. Why, Gobindganj was only 25 miles away!

'Lakshmi's Ma will bring you dinner,' he said coldly.

She shook her head. 'My mother will soon send for me. I do not want to live here.'

He was enraged. Who was this twit of a girl? Had she borne children? Had she seen a loved one die? Had she been to Shekhavati? Did she know of a world where one had to dig 120 feet to strike water? Had she ever heard of the Chhappaniya?

He strode toward her, hand raised, ready to strike.

He saw her tremble as she prepared for the blow, and sensed how slight she was, and that she was a woman, not a child. For a moment, he forgot Parmeshwari, the doctor with his LMF degree, and little Gopi standing beside him while Parmeshwari asked him to take care of Durga. He knew only that this quivering woman was his wife, and that he had been alone for almost nine years. *What am I to do, Masterji?* he asked. There was no one to stop him, no Master Bholaram to counsel restraint, no one to warn of sin. Her own mother would have egged him on, her father would not have listened to her pleas. Raamji himself had commanded him. Why did no one burst through the door to pin him down?

He seized her. Alarmed, she tried to gather her shawl but he snatched it and flung it away. She covered her face with her hands and cried aloud, waiting for his blows. He gently pulled her arms aside and smothered her with kisses. She started to cry again. He was about to cry too, but held back his tears. She was not Parmeshwari, he kept telling himself as he folded her into his arms, but she was his. And Master Bholaram would have said he had not sinned.

Late in the night, he watched while she lay asleep. If lust kills, he thought, why has Raamji not given me the strength to resist it? Quietly, he mouthed the words of Hanuman Chalisa, ending with a plea. 'I have taken one life; do not let me take another. I will find no joy in her embrace; you must in turn protect her from me.'

The boys never found in Manki the mother he had hoped they would. She took care of the kitchen, the washing and the cleaning. Her silence, much touted by Chaman Lal, proved to be of the indifferent kind. Every morning, he had a bucket of water for his bath, and a clean kurta and dhoti. Every night there was joyless pleasure. She took care of pujas and ceremonies and settled into an uneasy relationship with Lakshmi's Ma, who remained mother to the boys. Durga and Tribhuvan largely ignored her, but Gopi displayed a hostility that Hari could not fathom. He spent more and more time in the shop, climbing upstairs to the verandah only late in the evening, anticipating without eagerness their night together.

With the end of the war, jute prices collapsed. He decided to open a hosiery store in Bara Gola, partly because he wanted to remove Gopi from the shop in Sat Matha, where he used every opportunity to run upstairs and quarrel with Manki. It would help in any case to have the boy run his own shop now that he was thirteen. Chaman Lal's cubicle had been shuttered for two years. Hari rented it, had shelves inserted into the walls and opened the store with stock from Rangpur. Once a month, Nanuram began to travel to Calcutta to buy dhotis and bed-sheets for the store, bringing back rolls of cloth wrapped in burlap. Margins were small for Indian cotton, and few in Bogra could afford Manchester dhotis. There was little money to be made from the cloth itself, and Gopi did not know when to stop bargaining and accept the price offered, but the store was still profitable, because the burlap sacks in which the cloth came from Calcutta were reinforced with steel cables and strips of wood, for which Hari found a ready market in Bogra.

There was less and less work in the jute press. The lines of bullock carts waiting to unload their jute had vanished. Fearing that Durga would become idle, Hari decided to send him to the weekly market in Gobindganj, where he himself had gone years ago. On a Sunday morning, Durga rose early and bathed, allowed Manki to do a puja and set off in a bullock cart. Aside from rolls of cloth, he was carrying a basket of mangoes—a gift for Manki's brothers, whom he would visit when in Gobindganj.

He returned late in the evening. Hari had waited for a full hour, growing increasingly anxious. When Durga climbed up to the verandah and set an empty basket on the floor—he had delivered the mangoes to Manki's family—Hari knew he had sold nothing. The day had been a waste, and much expense had been incurred for the cart. Lakshmi's Ma gave him dinner. Hari watched his son eat—guiltily, he thought. Whenever Lakshmi's Ma blew into the coals, Durga's face lit up, exposing the slight squint he had developed in his left eye, which now saw less and less. Hari was overcome with worry. What would happen to Durga in a few years, after Gopi and Tribhuvan had been married off? Who would give his daughter to a boy like Durga? He looked thin and spindly like a coolie from Bihar. Such a boy could hardly travel to Gobindganj by himself, let alone sell anything in the crowds there, having to jostle with other Marwaris for space. Manki was partial to him—the only one of the three towards whom she displayed some warmth—perhaps because of his damaged eye, but even she would be consumed with her own child in a few months.

Every afternoon, after the bales had been unloaded in the press, Durga now walked to the hosiery store in Bara Gola, where he folded dhotis and put them away after they had been shown to customers. Although he did not complain, Hari knew he suffered under Gopi's harsh gaze. It was odd that such a docile boy should be named after the goddess Durga, who rode a tiger and slew demons. Hari knew of only two ways in which a boy could be turned into a man—send him to sit in a shop, or find him a wife who will burden him with the responsibilities of children. The first had failed, the second would have to be tried as soon as he was of age.

Meanwhile, he waited for the birth of his son with some trepidation. Everyone had heard stories of the dreaded second mother, who tolerated sons from a previous marriage until her own child came along. But he knew of no other way a bania spent his life—he married and his wife bore him children. Hopefully, the difference in age between the brothers would come to their rescue: Tribhuvan was the youngest, and he was already ten. Perhaps they could see the new child as a ward, almost as a son, rather than a brother?

The child arrived. Lakshmi's Ma came down to the shop to tell him Manki was in labour. He sent for Dr Saha, disregarding what his father might have thought, and remained in the shop instead of going upstairs. His sons sat with him.

It was Dr Saha, not Lakshmi's Ma, who came into the shop to give him the news: the child had not lived.

Hari displayed little emotion and allowed Gopi to supervise the ceremonies that followed. A pandit was consulted. He ruled that a full cremation was not necessary because the child had never been born. A bundle of cloth—that was all Hari saw—was taken to the Karatoya by Gopi, Nanuram and a servant. They returned an hour later. Hari never asked where it had been buried, nor whether it had been a boy or a girl.

The pandit recommended a puja to placate the evil eye that, he said, had resulted in the still-birth, but Hari knew he alone was to blame. He had not yet paid the full price for that tonsure near the Karatoya. Mangiram's son, whose tonsure had been done similarly in Bogra, not in Khatu, had died of the pox three years ago, and now Raamji had made his will known regarding Hari's child.

He did agree to the puja, however, largely for Manki's benefit. Whether or not it soothed Raamji's ire, it would give her reason to hope. And it would give her something to do to swamp her grief. The puja that resulted was far grander, and much more expensive, than he had envisaged. Twenty-one brahmins were called all the way from Calcutta, housed and fed. For three days Sat Matha wore a festive look, and crowds collected to see the pandits light the great fire and chant from the Rigved. Hari watched with a mixture of awe and disgust, and irritation that many of the men had come only to eat the consecrated halva that was distributed to everyone, even to beggars.

A calm settled on the verandah after the puja. Manki returned to her kitchen—though Lakshmi's Ma still did most of the cooking—and Hari busied himself in the shop. The day after the last brahmin had returned to Calcutta, Hari brought out the Pinjrapole box that had been put away after his father's death and pushed a one-rupee coin through its slot. A message was sent to the office in Raja Bajar that donations could be collected once a week, as they had been before. Receipts piled up. Hari speared them on a wire as his father had done. He sent a message to the goshala, saying he would resume payments for the upkeep of his three cows. Once a week, he began to walk to the goshala grounds to see his cows—ageing beasts that no longer gave milk. Through the cold weather, he insisted that his cows be covered in burlap sheets on cold nights. Like his father had before him, he began to eye Muslim butchers anxiously, as they walked by his shop leading cows to the slaughterhouse. At night, he would wonder if the cows in the goshala were shivering in the cold, and would throw away his blanket as a test, then pull it back over his head guiltily.

As winter eased, so did his anxieties. In spring, he was drawing the shutters in Sat Matha when a figure emerged from the dark and stood before him. It was Chaman Lal, much the worse from wear and tear but apparently healthy, and with nowhere to live. Hari did not ask for an explanation. It was often said that a Marwari who came to Bengal never went back, however much he might wax nostalgic about Shekhavati. He stayed, although Bengal was crowded and dirty, and full of Bengalis who did not like him. This had something to do with the Karatoya, the Jamuna, the Padma and the thousands of streams between Bogra and Jessore, and the beels and ponds and slush and mosquitoes, and the crops of Aman, Aush and Boro that sprouted from an endlessly generous earth. Where would a bania live but near his customers, and where would *they* live if not in Bengal? Lakshmi's Ma had gone to Benares but was back in Bogra. Daulatramji never strayed outside Calcutta. Janardhan had left Bengal only because of the English sergeant at his heels. And now Chaman Lal was back, sitting on Hari's gaddi, shivering under a thick blanket and speaking in the mournful voice of the vanquished.

'Whom did I go back to? My daughters are settled. They have children who do not know me. They think I speak Marwari with too many Bengali words that they find jarring. They say I waste water, that I am spoiled by the hand-pumps in Disavar. They wonder why I crave rice—who am I, they ask, Seth Daulatram?'

'I know, I know,' said Hari. He knew.

'It is dry in Shekhavati, Harilalji. Drier than you remember. I had forgotten the dust, the bare skies and the sandstorms. I had forgotten how to eat bajra or ride a camel. No one needs an old man, and they need him even less when he returns from Bengal.'

Hari noted that Chaman Lal had called him 'Harilalji'. What would have pleased him three years ago now nearly brought tears to his eyes. 'You are young yet, Chaman Lalji,' he said, not believing it.

'My home...'

'Your home is in Bara Gola. I have opened a hosiery shop in your old cubicle. You may sleep there. And you may sit in the press, where Durga still has much to learn from you.'

'Where do you buy your dhotis for the hosiery store?' Chaman Lal asked.

Hari found this sudden return to alertness disquieting. Chaman Lal was an old bania, after all. 'Cotton dhotis in Rangpur, Manchester dhotis in Kalkatta.'

'There is trouble in Kalkatta. I was there yesterday and I met the munim in Lalgodam. Gandhiji wants the firm to stop selling Manchester dhotis.'

'They say all sorts of things in Kalkatta. And Gandhiji will not come all the way to Bogra to see which dhotis people wear.'

He was wrong. The next morning, he found Nanuram and Gopi sitting in the gaddi downstairs, when they should have been in Bara Gola opening the hosiery shop. 'What are you doing here?'

'They did not let us open the shop,' Nanuram said.

It irritated Hari that Nanuram had made no protest. If men from the Congress Party should ask a man to shut his shop, was he to comply like a Congresswala? That was the difference between a bania and his munim, even one as constant as Nanuram—the bania counted lost profits, the munim his free time. 'Go back at once. Customers prefer the morning.'

'Do not be impulsive, Hari Babu,' said Nanuram, and Hari detected a trace of condescension. 'As long as the shop is closed they cannot take away the stock. They want to burn Manchester cotton, as Congresswalas did in Bombay.'

This made no sense to Hari—Gandhiji had asked Congresswalas to wear khadi and boycott Manchester cotton. Very well. If people preferred khadi, he would sell khadi and stop stocking Manchester. But what good would it do to burn Manchester stock?

In the evening a large crowd gathered at Sat Matha, where the Bogra Congress Committee made a bonfire of Manchester dhotis. There was chanting and singing. Bundles of cloth rode on every shoulder, ready to be burnt. A stall did brisk business selling Gandhi caps.

'Who runs that stall?' Hari asked Nanuram.

'A bania from Raja Bajar.'

'That is a good business to get into. Buy a hundred Gandhi caps when you next go to Raja Bajar. Ask for a discount. '

He stood at the edge of the crowd, looking at the sea of Gandhi caps, and noting ruefully that none of the men were banias. He who had nothing to sell had nothing to lose; it was the bania who would pay for this burst of passion.

'Look at these men,' he said to Nanuram. 'Most cannot afford to buy Manchester cotton. They want to burn it so others may not buy it either. If the Congress Party wants to burn good dhotis, why not give them away to these men? Better still, why not sell to them at a discount?'

Speeches were made. Some men in the front tore off their kurtas and hurled them into the flames. A shower followed—vests, shawls, dhotis, saris, lehangas. A man even took off the dhoti round his legs—stripped right in front of the crowd, amidst laughter and hooting and shouts of 'Gandhiji zindabad'—bundled it up and tossed it into the fire. Someone aimed a leather chappal from behind. It flew over the crowd and landed near the rim of the fire, scattering cinders. Then a dam broke—all sorts of shoes, chappals and belts flew into the furnace. Hari watched, fascinated. The fire gradually became Agni Devta, accepting every oblation man might offer—no matter how impure, tainted by arrogance or enmeshed in maya—and turned it into sacred vibhuti, the pure ash that cleansed all. He was suddenly in harmony with the Congresswalas. This was what the bonfire meant! It was not a repudiation of the British Raj, a rejection of foreign goods or a symbol of the non-cooperation that Gandhiji had proclaimed; it was an agent of purification for tonsures done improperly, bodies writhing in lust, and marriages consummated in sin. He must throw something into this inferno!

He pushed through the crowd until the fire sat warmly on his face. He was so close that it seemed Agni Devta would burn his clothes right off his body. He folded his hands. The crowd faded away. He took off his kurta and placed it reverently on the pyre. Then he felt a tug at his dhoti and turned around. Tribhuvan stood behind him, squeezed among the men, cricket bat in one hand and football in the other, looking bewildered. 'Nanuramji needs you in the shop.'

Hari waved the boy away. 'Not now...'

'Nanuramji needs you.'

'Give me that!'

He snatched the cricket bat from his son's hand and raised his voice. 'The sahibs' game has no place in Bengal!'

A cheer went up in the crowd. 'Gandhiji ki jai!'

He raised the bat with difficulty—it was heavier than he had thought—and flung it into the fire. Tribhuvan gasped and began to cry. Someone grabbed the football from him and held it up.

'Throw the football too!'

Hari saw the tears rolling down his son's cheeks and the face of Agni Devta melted away. The crowd became a rabble of Bengalis and Biharis. What was he doing with this riff-raff? He snatched the football from the man and restored it to his son. The man protested. 'Burn the football!'

'Cricket is a sahibs' game,' said Hari, 'but football is Bengali.'

He took Tribhuvan by the hand and turned away, pushing through the crowd. Somewhere in his mind was the thought that the kurta he had thrown into the fire had been of khadi, very likely from the Ahmedabad mills that Gandhiji championed, therefore not expensive.

For the next few days he fretted in his closed shop while bonfires sprouted all over Bogra. The market for Manchester cotton had vanished.

'Gandhiji has dammed up a river,' Nanuram said. 'As soon as the dam breaks, men will rush to buy Manchester cotton. And they will need even more of it because Gandhiji has burned up all the dhotis they had.'

Hari grumbled. 'Meanwhile, I sit in a shuttered shop, waiting for a breach in this dam.'

The next day—the fifth of the boycott—Hari received a postcard from Tribhuvan's master in the government school, saying that the closing of the school was affecting Tribhuvan's studies, and that the boy should be sent to Calcutta because his diligence entitled him to a better school.

Hari agonized over this. Sending a boy to Calcutta opened

the door to much mischief. He himself had nearly come to ruin in 67 Cotton Street. Yet Tribhuvan was not like him, or Durga or Gopi—he was unable to bargain with customers or calculate discounts even as he received high praise from his teacher.

Preparations were made as soon as the boycott ended. A day was fixed for Tribhuvan's departure; a message was sent to arrange for his stay at Lalgodam. Manki was pregnant again, and Hari wanted his son to see the child before he left. He was filled with foreboding while Manki went about her days blithely, showing no sign of emotion. The first child has hardened her, he thought. A girl of eighteen had been transformed into the mother of a still-born, who now confidently awaited her child. She did not know about the tonsures—Hari had not shared his fears with anyone—or of any of the other sins added to her account, but Hari did. There was much that Raamji would not overlook—the brick dust in his red chillies, the mashed potatoes in his ghee, the smoking, accidental contact with Musalmans, a sip of water in a customer's shop... How careful could a man possibly be?

On the last morning in June, Manki went into labour. Hari decided against calling Dr Saha, whose presence had not saved the first child. It was hot and dry. He sat in the shop, showing no sign of concern but trembling whenever he heard someone in the verandah. For hours he strained to hear the baby's cries—he would accept a daughter, he told himself, hoping Raamji would overhear—but women kept peering down into the road from the verandah and whispering among themselves. What could there be to talk about after so many hours?

He sat all day. It was fitting that business was slow. No one wanted grain from a man in disfavour with the gods. When he saw the women slink away—one by one, shawls pulled low over their faces—he knew without asking: this child was still-born too. How many times could Raamji punish one for the same sin? No doubt Manki blamed herself as she lay in her room, inconsolable, watching the stone-cold face of her infant in her arms. What would she say if she knew it was his fault? Had she been a heroine in the Mahabharat, she would have learnt the truth from the gods. A voice from the sky would have addressed her: Why do you grieve for your lost child, woman? Look into your husband's heart and you will see the cause.

He stepped out of the shop and looked up. His sons were in the verandah, all three of them, looking into the road gloomily. Poor Tribhuvan was to leave for Calcutta in the evening. His trunk was packed, his bedding had been rolled, and he had hoped to see his brother before departure.

Nanuram arrived with the pandit and went upstairs. 'We do not need a pandit,' Hari absently told himself, 'we know exactly how to dispose of the body. Such situations are the norm in this family. We have not seen a live birth for almost eleven years, when Tribhuvan Lal was born standing in the womb. And that birth resulted in a death, too.'

He knew what the pandit was saying upstairs—there was no sin in burying a still-born on the banks of the Karatoya without the proper ceremonies, said the Shastras (said the pandit for a small consideration, eyes growing wide at the unexpected windfall). My loss is his gain, Hari thought bitterly. He prays daily for still-born children, so he may save grieving fathers the expense of funeral rites and gift himself three silver rupees.

Nanuram and Gopi descended the staircase. Nanuram carried the bundle in his arms. This has become a familiar sight in Sat Matha, Hari told himself. They looked this way and that, conspiratorially, like thieves making off with loot, and started toward Raja Bajar, where they would go to the riverbank.

'Wait.' He did not know why he had stopped them. He may have meant to say something to mark the occasion, but grief overpowered him. 'Wild animals are known to dig up bodies,' he said brutally. 'Bury it deeply, and cover the area with retted jute so it looks like kyals have been unloading a boat nearby.'

Nanuram did not respond.

At dusk Hari went upstairs, unable to sit alone in the shop. The verandah was dark—Lakshmi's Ma had not lit a lamp. Gopi drifted about aimlessly. Durga sat next to Lakshmi's Ma in the kitchen. Tribhuvan squatted on the trunk he was to have taken to Calcutta. Hari watched the boy with a mixture of pride and pity. Look at him! Not yet eleven, but already able to read in English. But how was he to go to Calcutta? The pandit had said that one may not travel for thirteen days after a death.

'Give the boys their dinner,' he said to Lakshmi's Ma before going into his room. Manki sat in bed, bent over a notebook that lay open in her lap, writing carefully with a pencil stub. He glanced at the page. She had filled it over and over with the one word she had learned to write in Hindi. *Raam*. Because she did not leave spaces between her words, each line became one long word: raamaraamaraamaraa... Hari shuddered. Split differently, that one word could be read as Maraa Maraa Maraa Maraa, *died died died died...*

He lay down next to her and fell asleep.

The next morning brought a postcard from Calcutta—the Lalgodam clerk he had contacted about Tribhuvan's stay had responded. Hari asked Tribhuvan to read it aloud.

'The news is not good.'

'I know,' Hari said, impatiently. 'Nothing good happens these days.'

The letter spoke of riots in Calcutta. Marwari shops had been looted for dhotis and saris. There had been a police raid at Lalgodam. Sergeants had sealed off all eleven offices of Daulatram Gulabchand on the third floor. They had charged the firm with cotton gambling.

Hari interrupted. 'Marwaris do not gamble.'

'The police mean speculation.'

Tribhuvan continued. Cash boxes and books had been seized. Clerks and munims were being interrogated. Fear stalked Lalgodam as men awaited the next raid. Jainarain was on his way to Calcutta from Haridwar... Tribhuvan looked up. 'Who is Jainarain?'

'The owner of the firm,' said Hari, not wishing to describe

the sad tale of Daulatramji's sons. 'What eighty years, sixteen famines, the crash of opium and the coming of synthetic dyes could not do, the sahibs have done in a week—they have torn down Daulatramji's house.'

'Sahibs have forgotten how much money Marwaris gave to the War Loan Fund,' said Tribhuvan.

Hari was disturbed to hear this—it sounded like the talk of Congresswalas. Whom had the boy been speaking with? 'What happens in Kalkatta does not matter in Bogra,' he said carefully. 'A bania sits on his gaddi and sells. He does not notice wars, only prices.'

'I would like to leave for Calcutta today,' Tribhuvan said, suddenly.

By now Hari was resolved not to let the boy drift away. It had been a mistake to indulge a schoolmaster's fantasies. 'Why not sit in the shop like your brothers? You could start in the jute press. Then we will buy a shop for you near Bara Gola...'

But the boy seemed already lost to him. He was too well-mannered to defy his father, but his heart had left home. Were Calcutta ablaze, he would still want to go there. 'The firm has been shut down. I know no one in Kalkatta now,' Hari said desperately.

'I have friends.'

'Whom do *you* know?'

'Mohammad Ali is going there. He will leave tonight.'

Hari was aghast. His son would live with a Musalman! But Tribhuvan had already thought of this. 'I will live in Dahi Hatta, not with Mohammad Ali. The Nawabzada's son will provide help when I need it. His family has a house in Calcutta.'

Hari's mind was in turmoil. His son was in the sway of the Nawab of Bogra, and he had been an accomplice to the plot. Who ever returned from Kalkatta after having seen it? He could postpone the departure for thirteen days but he knew, and Tribhuvan knew, that the pandit would waive the restriction for a small sum, having already overlooked so much else—there had been no cremation, no offer of rice balls to the spirit, no readings from the *Vishnu Puraan*, no puja planned to mark the thirteenth day. A rupee would do the trick—the Shastras had a way of bending to one's will at the glimpse of silver.

Then he stopped short. What was he doing: circumventing the rules of propriety to send his son away with a Musalman boy? He should be working feverishly to achieve the opposite: break the bond between the two and clasp his son tightly to himself. Tribhuvan could open a shop in Bogra and sell whatever he wanted. True, he had shown no great aptitude for weights and scales, but who could doubt his intelligence? It was not lack of skill but interest that had kept him from sitting in the shop, as well as preoccupation with this studies. The first thing he should do is take him out of this government school, where Bengali teachers daily poisoned his mind...

'Do not worry about the expense,' Tribhuvan said. 'I will share the room with three boys, and I will buy nothing without your permission.'

That evening, the two of them walked to the railway station near Bara Gola. Tribhuvan carried his trunk and bedding on his shoulders. Hari had failed to reason with him, and was too shaken by the death of the child to remonstrate further.

The train to Santahar arrived. Tribhuvan pushed his trunk into a carriage, climbed in and stood at the door.

'Go and find a seat,' Hari said. 'Do you know how to change trains in Santahar?'

'Yes. I will take the broad-gauge line there.'

'Do not stand near the door when the train pulls into Sealdah Station. Coolies will want to carry your bedding. Do not be fooled. Beggars in Kalkatta are aggressive. Keep your money tied at your waist and hidden in your dhoti. Go outside the station and take a ricksha to Dahi Hatta—look for a Chinaman, he is cheap.'

'All right,' said Tribhuvan, but it was clear he was not listening.

There was a scramble of coolies as the train inched forward. Hari was seized with panic. The boy was not yet eleven. How would he live alone?

He shouted. 'What kind of a school will you go to? Who is the Guruji there?'

'Kanodia Industrial School. It has masters, not Gurujis, but it is a Marwari school—all the students are Marwaris, so you need not worry. I will learn Hindi, Bengali, perhaps even some English. And furniture making.'

Hari's confusion was complete. Furniture making? Had not Master Bholaram said that all a bania needed was arithmetic? What was his son going to do when he grew up? He began to walk with the train so the boy would remain in sight.

'Do not give the Chinaman the rate he quotes. Start by offering half what he asks for. Four years ago, the rate was a paisa from Sealdah to Bara Bazar, a pie more if it was raining.'

Tribhuvan nodded and turned away. The train picked up speed.

'And do not go to Cotton Street!'

The train slid away. I have lost two sons in two days, Hari thought mournfully.

It was dark when he returned home. In the verandah, Lakshmi's Ma squatted against a wall, snivelling. When she first arrived in Bogra with Parmeshwari, she had been newly widowed, and that had been preceded by the loss of her daughter Lakshmi. This had etched permanent lines of grief in her face, relieving her, perhaps, of the need to express it. Now, the tears on her sunken cheeks sent a shiver through him. Gopi sat sullenly in the kitchen and Durga was nowhere to be seen. *This is a house of gloom*, he thought as he tiptoed around Lakshmi's Ma and entered his room, where Manki lay sprawled on the bed. Something had happened while he was at the railway station. He lit a lantern. In its glow, he saw the clay parrot, the one Manki had brought from Gobindganj, lying on the floor in two pieces, the secret of its rattle—a stone—sitting exposed in one half.

He was filled with pity, reminded that she was only nineteen—a young girl whom he had transformed into the mother of two dead children—while he was thirty-three. 'I will get you another one,' he said softly.

She shook her head and began to cry. He left the room. Outside, Lakshmi's Ma turned to him. 'A boy should not say such things. It has been only a day.'

And then it was explained to him. Gopi had laid claim to the parrot again. Manki had refused. In spite, Gopi had described the burial. It had been a boy, he had said. A beautiful little boy with soft, downy skin and a black sore in its spine. And perhaps it had moved a little when the shovel began to throw dirt. Manki had dashed the parrot to the ground. Gopi had continued.

'Do not say more,' Hari said to Lakshmi's Ma.

He turned viciously on Gopi. What a monster he had reared for fourteen years! Lifelong ingrate, uncouth dullard who had nearly killed Durga in the jute press and was now bent on destroying what peace remained in the house. Tribhuvan had been fortunate to get away but poor Durga would have to live with a damaged eye for the rest of his life. No punishment was too great for such a brute... He slapped and kicked Gopi until Lakshmi's Ma stopped him with her screams, which travelled all over Sat Matha and collected a small crowd in the road below.

Gopi lay on the floor, curled up. His nose was bleeding. 'Take him away,' said Hari.

'The boy will fear you for the rest of his life,' Lakshmi's Ma whispered. There was disapproval in her voice.

'That is just as it should be.'

He left the house and walked through Raja Bazar, heading north toward the goshala in great agitation, smoking a Berkeley. I have lost three sons in two days, he thought. The only one who remains mine is Durga, and he is half blind... How many sons must a man beget before he can have one for himself?

In the goshala he sought out the three cows whose upkeep was his responsibility, and watched the oldest as she chewed. She was weak. Her ribs were plainly visible. Flies swarmed around her. He was filled with tenderness, combined with guilt that he had discontinued payments after his father's death. How foolish he had been to begrudge his cows a slight expense when the very waste they produced was worth so much more! That night, he wrote on his slate:

> 'The Mahabharat says: *Lakshmi gavaam muutre puuriishhe cha basati*, the goddess Lakshmi resides in the urine of the cow. Ask a pandit what this means and he will launch into a discourse, but ask a bania and he will explain quickly—there is wealth in the urine and the dung of the cow, because Raamji has created no better fertilizer. Who does not need this fertilizer? It provides the bania in Bogra rice to sell, the Thakur of Nawalgarh bajra to give away, and Yule Sahib in Calcutta jute to send to Dundee. The cow is mother to all of them.'

He would give more money to the goshala. And he would visit every day to gaze at his cows chewing lazily, flicking off flies with their tails.

8

Nanuram's prediction turned out to be correct. As soon as Gandhiji ended his boycott, sales of Manchester dhotis soared. Durga rose at dawn to rush to the store and returned late in the evening, carrying in his kurta pocket the earnings of the day, because Hari was afraid to leave so much cash in the store overnight. Nanuram was sent to the store to help. Hari's own shop at Sat Matha, the original Harilal & Sons, became less and less profitable as margins on grain and cigarettes declined. Gopi hung listlessly about the hosiery store, doing little. Hari had not spoken to him since the thrashing in summer, and they managed to avoid each other in the evenings.

From time to time, Tribhuvan sent postcards from Calcutta, usually asking for money.

The letters were in Hindi—Tribhuvan knew no Modhiya—so Hari had to seek a munim to read them. Although Tribhuvan's requests were made using the code Hari had taught him, the munim could guess what the letters asked for, and commented that the amounts had gradually increased.

Chaman Lal continued to go to the jute press, grumbling at the kyals' laziness, fingering strands of jute and commenting on its dampness. He had lapsed into a dreamy state of non-existence, devoid of anger, bitterness or even the desire to earn money. He sat in the office as if already dead, or waiting for his breaths to run out so he could lie down and go to sleep. Aside from an affectionate manner towards Durga, whom he rarely saw now that the boy was in the hosiery store, he noticed no one, asked nothing of anyone and offered nothing in return.

Sitting in his shop at Sat Matha, Hari told himself that his arrival in Disavar had not been fruitless, after all. Master Bholaram would have noted the sons running the hosiery store and might have tolerated the one studying in Calcutta. And he would have approved, too, of the three cows in the goshala. But when Hari discovered that Manki was with child again, he was disappointed. Raamji had placed life on an even keel, and it had stayed thus for almost two years. There was no pleasure at home. He said little to Manki, and she did little aside from filling books with 'Raam Raam'. Gopi and Durga no longer needed Lakshmi's Ma, who had been reduced to housekeeper and cook. Every night, Hari climbed into bed without a word and Manki offered herself to him dutifully. Neither he nor she affected enjoyment. What pleasures he sought were found in the shop, in the endless accounting of grain and cigarette packets, discounts and mark-ups, in the occasional sin of smoking, and in the contemplation of his cows in the goshala, for whom he had developed an affection that rivalled what he felt for his sons.

He watched the pregnancy in near panic, waiting for the inevitable end. After the death of the first child, Dr Saha had said something—folic acid deficiency—and written out medicines on a piece of paper that Hari had misplaced. Doctors found a disease to hang on every wrinkle in life. He was an LMF from Dhaka, a

Bengali who could not possibly know about tonsures in Khatu. Raamji had already given him three sons while Mangiram, who spent as much as Hari on pujas and pandits, had seen his one son taken by the pox. That would be considered good fortune by many, and some would call that bounty undeserved. This was Bengal, where spirits roamed freely and the evil eye lurked everywhere. Who knew if someone had not cast a spell on Manki? Whatever it was, no medicine prescribed by a Bengali doctor would cure it.

He made a secret trip to the Hanuman temple on the other bank of the Karatoya, near Musalman Para, and left eleven rupees in the sanctum without announcing himself to the pandit. He increased his weekly donation to the Pinjrapole Society, and took two more cows in the goshala under his wing. What more could a man do? Sometimes, while eating his dinner, he watched Manki out of the corner of his eye. She would be seated cross-legged next to Lakshmi's Ma, turning a rosary in her hand and repeating the word she knew so well. Raam Raam Raam…What did she think of the child who would come? Was she not afraid as he was? Did it not concern her that there would be another burial?

Sometimes, his carefully constructed indifference would crumble and he would be seized with fear. Folding his hands, with tears welling in his eyes—he would have to draw the shutters in the shop—he would beseech Raamji: let it be a girl. A girl, yes, a girl! A daughter will cleanse the house; she will ward off the evil eye cast by those who envy my three boys; she will restore balance; she will bring back equilibrium… Then he would sense the futility of so wishing and wonder if he should have been a more devout man. Had he neglected pujas, forgotten to feed pandits? But he had remembered to observe the death anniversaries of both his father and mother, and Manki omitted no detail in her dealings with God. She sang the full Sundarakand every day, bathed and dressed a brass statuette of Raamji every morning, and counted out 108 beads in her rosary eleven times, marking each bead with the name of Raam. And of course there were the notebooks filled with his name over and over again. What more could Raamji want?

Winter was harsh. When it was time, Hari shut the shop early and stood in the verandah, knowing it was improper for a man to be around. Women went in and out of the room. Chaman Lal sat on the floor, awaiting the birth. 'I will see my grandson before I go to sleep tonight,' he said ingratiatingly.

Hari shuddered. The old man was approaching senility, bringing him ill-luck even when he meant well. What grandson? It would be a girl. He would spare no expense on her wedding, he would spoil her rotten... Lakshmi's Ma peered out. Hari rushed to the door but she stood athwart, blocking his way. He was afraid to ask.

'The child is standing in the womb like Tribhuvan Lal,' she said. 'He wants to come out feet first.'

Hari wasted no time. 'Gopi Chand, Call Dr Saha.'

Lakshmi's Ma frowned.

'He cured Durga three days after birth,' said Hari.

'You have seen how Durga turned out.'

Hari turned to Gopi again. 'Go. Do not return without him.'

Lakshmi's Ma spoke with wounded dignity. 'I have brought your sons into this world. I have seen them born early or late...'

'I did not make this world,' Hari said sharply. 'I merely live in it.'

Lakshmi's Ma pulled her shawl over her head and withdrew.

When he saw the doctor, he almost lost his nerve. There was nothing about him that inspired confidence—a small, dark man with a nervous shuffle and a hand that trembled. But then he saw Gopi carrying the doctor's bag and was reassured. However small the man, the bag was large and solid, and stuffed with things that saved lives and delivered children.

An hour passed. When he finally heard the cry of the infant, he was slumped in a chair, half-asleep. The door was flung open. Hari stood up. Lakshmi's Ma had tears streaming down her face. 'It is a boy.'

He gasped. His legs gave way and he had to grip the metal grille to remain standing. What grand farce had Raamji set in motion? To give him a living child—living, yes, for he could hear it crying inside the room—but a boy, destined to die soon! If three boys had brought such misfortune, what would a fourth do?

He searched his mind frantically for something he could do to ward off impending disaster. A puja, yes, a puja with twenty-one pandits and generous offerings. A day of feeding for the beggars of Bogra. A trip to Benares, another to Haridwar, perhaps one to Ganga Sagar. Did they not say that one trip to Ganga Sagar brought the benefits of a hundred pilgrimages? Then he remembered something his mother had told him: Raamji took pity on boys with pitiable names. It was the arrogant ones with grandiose tags—Rajendra, Indrajit, Yogendra, Suresh—who were taken away first. Very well, he would protect his son with the armour of a humiliating label. 'I will call the boy Garib Das.'

Chaman Lal objected. 'Why? The boy is a prince, born into the wealthiest home in Bogra. He must have a name to match. He will inherit the store in Bara Gola. And the grain shop, the press, the share in the goshala…'

'Do not make a list,' Hari said quickly. Only a fool enumerated his possessions for Raamji to take away. 'I am a poor man. And this is a poor boy with a poor name. A boy destined to be a beggar. No matter how many coins he throws into his cash box, he will always be called Garib Das.' Then he turned to Lakshmi's Ma. 'What of the mother?'

'She lives.'

'Garib Das will live too.'

And Garib Das lived. Four weeks later, Hari sat at the scales with the boy in his lap, watching him wrestle a piece of string tied to his fingers.

Hari's joy knew no bounds. He showed the boy to customers, placed him in the scales and weighed him daily, and was especially generous with beggars. And he decided it was time for Gopi's wedding. The boy had been engaged for more than five years.

The wedding was modest, lest the wrath of Raamji be rekindled. Durga was placed in a comfortable chair near the wedding fire. Tribhuvan arrived from Calcutta, travelling alone for the first time. Everyone commented on how thin he looked. Hari stood with Garib Das in his arms while the pandit directed Gopi and his bride around the fire. There were jokes about how Hari was marrying off a son while another drooled in his arms.

Gopi's father-in-law pointed to Garib Das and said to Hari, 'You will have to live a long life, Hari Babu, to marry off this one.'

Hari chuckled. 'Why this one? I will live to marry off Gopi's children. Indeed, I will live to see the wives of Garib Das's sons!'

As if in response, he felt a warm touch on his arm. Tribhuvan said, 'Gariba has pissed on Babuji.' Everyone laughed.

After his wedding, Gopi expressed a desire to take over the cigarette business in the grain shop but Hari forbade it. He wanted his sons to avoid the cigarette business altogether—he feared they would succumb to the habit as he had. His own weakness now began to trouble him even as cigarettes became the most profitable items he sold at Sat Matha. Eventually, he had a brick wall erected through the middle of the shop, cutting it in two. He sat in the half that sold grain, crossing over into the cigarette half only when a customer came along. Because this required him to step into the road, he had hoped to stop smoking by denying himself cigarettes. Within a few months, however, he discovered a loose brick in the dividing wall. By removing it, he was able to extend his hand into the other half and pull out cigarette cartons. Raamji wants me to smoke, he thought ruefully, even as he tortures me with guilt over the habit.

Two years after Gopi's wedding, Nanuram suggested that his wife be brought to Bogra. Gopi had become increasingly short-tempered. When in the jute press, he offended Chaman Lal by treating him like a munim, while in the hosiery store Durga shrank from him and the clerks found his presence burdensome.

'The boy is already eighteen. The responsibilities of married life will weigh on his insolence,' said Nanuram, who himself knew nothing about married life. 'Once children come along, he will be fully cured.'

So Gopi was sent to Santahar dressed as a groom, and returned with his wife. The trousseau was unexpectedly modest for a man as prosperous as Gopi's father-in-law, who owned oil depots in Rangpur and Rajshahi. But Hari's disappointment was tempered by the modesty displayed by Gopi's bride—she wrapped the shawl round her head so skilfully that Hari was unable to get the slightest glimpse of her face.

The meagre pickings displeased Manki. She had expected a gold nose-ring but received shellac bangles. That night, she grumbled to Hari. 'They know I am not Gopi's mother, so they do not worry about giving offence. I will return these bangles to Sharda.'

'Who is Sharda?'

'Gopi's bride.'

'Ah,' said Hari, pleased. What a beautiful name, and how well it sat with that of his son! Gopi and Sharda. He consoled Manki. 'When we marry off Garib Das, his bride will give you a nose-ring of pure gold. And you will have many more sons. Their brides will give you a nose-ring each. You will wear a new ring each day of the week.'

By now, Hari had bought the entire building above the shop at Sat Matha. A room had been especially decorated for Gopi and Sharda. Seeing her in the kitchen, he was filled with pride—what a gentle-mannered girl this was, and how different from Gopi! No doubt she would mould the boy in her own image.

Tribhuvan came from Calcutta to see his new bhabhi, and Hari saw he was full of awe, so much that he extended his stay by a week and spent all his time in Sharda's room, pretending to read his books but really watching his new bhabhi, listening to her stories of Rangpur, and chewing the walnuts she had brought from Santahar. Little Garib Das could not get enough of her, sitting calmly in her arms and refusing to be parted from her, even in favour of Manki, his own mother. Whenever he looked unhappy, Lakshmi's Ma would say to Manki, 'Give him to his Sharda Bhabhi.'

Everyone was pleased to have Sharda in the house, except Manki, who sat in the verandah next to hot coals, warming herself and radiating her dislike, and Durga, who seemed afflicted with a strange shyness in her presence.

Hari mentioned Durga's odd behaviour to Nanuram, who chuckled. 'The seventeenth is upon him. At that age, a boy does not want a bhabhi. He longs for a wife.'

'So many sons, so many weddings,' Hari said with a sigh, affecting impatience so Nanuram would not notice his joy.

'I know, so much trouble,' Nanuram said, playing along. 'I will look around. Durga's wife will be a gentle cow, like the one I found for Gopi.'

Hari busied himself in the grain shop with the contentment of a man whose sons are settled and happy. There were fewer and fewer customers these days, and the ones who came wanted cigarettes. Neither the jute press, with declining margins, nor the hosiery store, where the margins came from selling the packaging, did more than break even, yet he felt prosperous. Sometimes, when there were no customers, he would leave the shop to clerks and go to the goshala to watch his cows. Returning, he would pick up his slate and scribble in Modhiya.

'The earth gives three crops in Bengal every year, so there is no shortage of dried stalks or husk. Add a little salt in summer or jaggery in winter—that is all an old cow asks for. Every month, the goshala spends less than a rupee on each cow, and most of that on the man who cares for her, not the cow herself. She asks for little but returns much more, as a mother does. A bania who puts his mind to it could make a good profit out of a goshala. A Musalman born into a butcher's family may overcome his misfortune by selling the dung and urine of his cows, not to speak of her milk. He will earn far more through these than through her meat. Why, then, must he slaughter her? Should he not, like the bania, look to his profits?'

Soon, Manki and Sharda were both pregnant. Hari alternated between joy and fear. He had begun to study Garib Das closely, and found traces of a new deformity every day. The boy crawled in an odd manner, he thought, and was it not time for him to be walking on his legs? After having committed to all sorts of pujas before his birth, he had neglected to perform them. Surely a name was not sufficient to protect a child? And now Manki's second child was on the way. There was only so much joy Raamji could spare for one man…

The two women awaited their two children, Sharda with grace and Manki with rising cantankerousness. Sharda is a mere child, Hari thought approvingly, yet she seems to bloom in the flush of pregnancy. She walked softly, spoke gently and never once indicated that she was in pain. When Hari ate his dinner, she squatted next to the oven, pulled a shawl discreetly over her face and baked his rotis. Through the shawl he could tell that her eyes were wide open with the assurance that comes to a woman who is about to become a mother. With Manki the story was different. Always weak, she now played the invalid, staying in bed until late in the morning, avoiding the kitchen and fussing about her room. Whenever she became insufferable, Lakshmi's Ma would remember that something was missing in the kitchen—ginger or cardamom or asafoetida—that could not be had in Hari's shop downstairs, and set off for Raja Bajar on a trip that took much longer than necessary.

On the seventh day of Aashaadh, Sharda collapsed into Lakshmi's Ma's arms. It had been a hot morning; the afternoon was dull. A servant was dispatched downstairs. Hari came immediately, trembling with excitement, and marvelled at Sharda's forbearance. Scarcely a sound emerged from her room, as if her gentle nature had conquered the pain of labour. Gopi came running from the hosiery store and wanted to go into the room, but Lakshmi's Ma would not hear of it, so he paced the verandah while Hari sat in a chair. When their eyes met, Hari smiled at his son as he had not for a year. 'It will be over soon. And I will be a grandfather.'

'I will name him Banwari,' Gopi said.

'Do not pronounce the name! It is inauspicious to do so before the child is born.'

Gopi indicated his impatience for such talk with a toss of his head. Hari wished his son had been more modest. Raamji hears and sees everything, and he especially dislikes arrogance...

Later that evening, with Sharda still confined, shrieks pierced the calm in the house. They came not from Sharda's room but Hari's. Manki had begun to feel contractions. Hari rushed into the room, but Lakshmi's Ma followed him inside and sent him out. She was laughing. 'You will be a father again before you see your grandchild.'

'Raamji's gaze is turned to this house today,' said Hari, but there was a tremor in his voice. He had no worries on account of Sharda; as for Manki... Durga arrived after having closed the hosiery store, and asked if he should call Dr Saha.

'No,' Hari said. 'It is not proper.

'But when Garib Das...'

'I have faith in Raamji now.'

They waited together for three hours—Hari, Gopi, Durga and Nanuram—listening to the alternation of Sharda's groans and Manki's screams. Chaman Lal shuffled in to make himself available. Lakshmi's Ma flitted from one room to the next. Women from Marwari houses in Sat Matha came to help and carried odds and ends into the rooms. There was much confusion. Whenever the women passed from one room to the other, Hari prepared to speak to them, but most drew their saris over their faces on account of him.

At sunset, two cries pierced the verandah. Lakshmi's Ma appeared in Sharda's door. 'A girl.'

'A boy!' said a woman at Manki's door. Hari was thrown in confusion. Perhaps he had heard wrong. Gopi should have had a son and he a daughter. What was he going to do with another boy? And who would now protect Garib Das? Five boys and not a girl to temper the excess of good fortune... He must find a name, a despicable name, a modest name that no one would notice. In a voice quivering with fear, he announced, 'We will call the boy Fakir Chand.'

Yes, that would be the right thing. A fakir, a beggar, a wandering sadhu, not a bania with a home and a family and a shop. Even in her most expansive moods, Fate would not be tempted to take such a child away. Thus reassured, he turned to Gopi, who sat slouched on the floor beside him.

'Stand up, Gopi Chand. This is only your first child. A first daughter is Lakshmi—she brings much wealth into the house.'

And she will protect Fakir Chand even more than his name will, he thought. May Raamji never look upon a home in which two boys have been born. 'Bring Fakir Chand to me.'

Lakshmi's Ma demurred. With eyes downcast—she never covered her face before Hari, but did him the honour of speaking with eyes averted—she said, 'He is at the breast.'

Hari nodded in wonder. Manki had not had much milk during Garib Das's first few days. The vaidya had given her herbs but they had not helped, and he had been too embarrassed to ask Dr Saha. He had put it down to Manki's poor health and mourned that his son had been deprived of a mother's milk. Now he hoped Fakir Chand would awaken in her what Garib Das had not.

Later, after Tribhuvan had beaten a brass plate all over Sat Matha to announce the birth, Lakshmi's Ma brought Fakir Chand and the girl out to the verandah, each wrapped in an old sari. Hari held a child on each arm. He looked first at the girl. 'She looks like Gopi.'

Tribhuvan laughed. Gopi turned away in annoyance. Hari turned to the boy, who was asleep. 'You are already an uncle, Fakir Chand. Wake up: your niece wants to play with you.'

9

Nanuram found it difficult to find a match for Durga on account of his left eye. The girl was from a modest home and her family was small. Her father chose to disregard Durga's diminutive frame—he was shorter than Tribhuvan, who was a year younger, and could have passed for a boy of fifteen—but focused instead on the qualities emphasized by Nanuram: he spoke little and not at all in the presence of elders; everyone liked him, even Manki; his wife was unlikely to face the terrors of a stern husband.

Hari upbraided Nanuram for being free with information about Durga's eye. Unless one looked carefully, it was impossible to notice the deformity. Why had Nanuram made such a display of it? It was not as if the boy was one-eyed...

'The girl's family is poor, not stupid,' Nanuram replied. 'They would have employed their own men and found out well before the engagement. It was best to bring it up right away.'

To reduce wedding expenses, the engagement, wedding and muklava ceremonies were all combined into one. The girl was already sixteen, so she came to live in her father-in-law's house directly after the wedding. This had been Nanuram's idea. Hari was troubled by the plan but was assured by everyone—including the girl's father, who was anxious to send her away—that this was now the custom among Marwaris in Bengal.

Durga settled easily into married life. Hari got into the habit of boasting to people that Gayatri—Durga's bride—was so quiet and respectful that he could never tell whether she was in the house, and she spoke so softly that he still could not distinguish her voice from Sharda's. He had been fortunate in his daughters-in-law, at least so far. In Shekhavati, he had heard countless stories of sharp-tongued girls who had rendered homes unbearable for their fathers-in-law, and one would expect such incidents to be common in Bengal, where Marwaris no longer observed the restraints that were customary in Shekhavati.

The next year, Gayatri gave birth to a boy whom Hari named Gangadhar. He laid the boy amongst sacks of grain in the shop, proudly displaying his first grandson. A few weeks later Gopi's wife gave birth to a second daughter, for whom the pandit selected the name of Ahilya. These two births—a daughter for Gopi and a son for Durga—further aggravated Gopi's temper. He found release in picking quarrels with servants, screaming at them, threatening to turn them out, using words that pained Hari and shocked the women. Aside from Gopi, the only one who used foul language in Hari's presence was Manki, who became shriller by the day—a privilege she enjoyed on account of her seniority, though she was only twenty-five years old.

More children were born. Gopi had a third daughter, Durga a second son and Manki a girl, Hari's first daughter. He named her Shanti, relieved that a daughter had finally broken the spell cast on his sons. Seated in the shop, he could hear the clamour of sons, daughters and grandchildren upstairs, tearing through the small verandah, in and out of rooms, laughing, crying, quarrelling, calling to each other in strange lisps, and occasionally running downstairs to sit in his lap while customers watched in amusement. A contented man builds a large family, Master Bholaram used to say. Indeed, this was why a man came to Disavar—to sit in his shop and hear the laughter of grandchildren.

These were children of Bengal, he noted ruefully, unaware of the ways of Shekhavati. They spoke a Marwari peppered with Bengali and Urdu words, and would never learn to write in Modhiya. They would never see the Chhappaniya, which was why the hand-pump in the verandah squeaked all day as endless buckets of water were wasted in baths, latrines and play. This waste was the one irritant in Hari's contemplation of his good fortune, but children in Bengal could not possibly be taught the thrift that came naturally to those who played among sand dunes. Rotis went uneaten and were thrown to beggars, toys were bought and broken, slippers and sandals and hair clips and belt buckles lay strewn across the verandah in heaps, offending his sensibilities. And there was always the hand-pump, leaking and spilling. Thankfully, this waste did not extend to clothes, which were handed down until torn to shreds.

Gopi's manner had changed for the worse since the birth of his third daughter. Hari sympathized. A first daughter was Lakshmi, they said in Shekhavati. She brought wealth into the house. A second was Saraswati, goddess of learning, tolerable but not desirable. And a third daughter? They said nothing about her in Shekhavati, but she was no doubt the goddess Kali who destroyed everything in her path. Who could blame the man with three daughters for being resentful? And how could such a man fail to notice his brother's two sons?

In the hosiery store, Gopi's harsh reign was tolerated both by Durga and Nanuram. For ten years, Nanuram had made trips to Calcutta to buy stock for the store. Now, with the new Dhakeshwari Mill opening in Dhaka, it was decided that dhotis would be bought from there, not Calcutta, because transportation from Dhaka was cheaper. Somehow, Gopi got it into his head that he, not Nanuram, should travel to Dhaka.

'Nanuram could sit in the jute press with Chaman Lal,' he said to Hari. 'He need not come to the store at all.'

Hari was stung. 'Call him Nanuramji. He came with me from Rampura. He isn't a servant I picked up in Bengal. And speak respectfully of Chaman Lalji—he is old enough to be your grandfather.'

Hari knew that Nanuram earned small amounts by overstating the price at which he bought stock in Calcutta. This reduced the already low margins in the hosiery store, but he had learned to tolerate that. Given some rein, a munim will remain faithful; kept on a tight leash, he will strain to deceive. Besides, Nanuram had been with him for almost thirty years, and was surely entitled to a little something for himself. His wants were not many. At fifty-one, his only luxury was a Manchester dhoti, to be worn at weddings.

Gopi did not pursue the matter, but Hari sensed that he was biding his time. His suspicions increased when he received a postcard from Gopi's father-in-law, inviting him to Santahar for an urgent business discussion.

Gopi's father-in-law was an old man—Sharda was his youngest daughter. His father had come from Shekhavati more than fifty years ago, and he had earned good profits in the oil business in Bengal and Assam, which was what Nanuram had reported when making the match. But Hari remembered that the dowry had not been generous and Manki had been annoyed. So he went to Santahar with many reservations, aware that the man commanded more capital than him, but hoping that his age—he was much older than Hari—would make this disparity acceptable to both.

After Hari had been welcomed and fed—with more affection than usual, he thought—Gopi's father-in-law launched into a speech about his love for Sharda and high regard for Gopi. Hari knew the second declaration to be hypocritical. Who could fail to notice Gopi's nature? Finally, Sharda's father expressed a desire that his daughter live in a house near his own, so she might be able to come to him on his deathbed.

'But Santahar is only 25 miles from Bogra,' Hari said. 'I will send her to you the moment I hear of something.' Then, realizing this was not the right thing to say, he lied, 'Of course, you look as young as you did during Gopi's wedding. Why would Raamji think of calling you at all?'

'Twenty-five miles is too great a distance,' Gopi's father-in-law said. 'Death comes suddenly in Bengal. In Rangpur, Tikam Chandji was sitting at his cash box. He extended a hand to give an adhela to a beggar. His munim saw the hand fall back. He was dead before the coin touched the ground. That is how men die in Bengal. In Shekhavati, my grandfather took three full days to pass away. He sat on his deathbed, blessed his grandchildren, completed seven recitations of Hanuman Chalisa, sipped charnamrit and panchagavya, gave away dhotis to brahmins, then willed himself to death at leisure. But those days are gone, and this is not Shekhavati. When Raamji calls, he is impatient. By the time my daughter comes to see me, I will be on my way to the Padma. As it happens, an agency is available in Santahar with the Burmah Oil Company of Assam. The depot is large. It has its own building and land, and the owner wishes to sell. I learned this on the very day Tikam Chandji's death made me yearn for my daughter.'

Suddenly, Hari understood. The man was offering to buy an oil depot and hand it over to Gopi, provided Gopi and Sharda moved to Santahar. Hari knew this was a good opportunity. The oil business had not been affected by the Congress boycott as much as the market for cotton. With jute prices in decline, he had only the shop in Sat Matha—where margins had been whittled away—and the hosiery store. A new business for Gopi would free up the hosiery store for Durga, who was chafing under his brother's harsh reign. Yet he was loath to see a son snatched away like this. Was it not his duty, as a father, to provide a shop for his son? He stood up. 'Gopi has the hosiery store.'

'But there is no money in Manchester dhotis,' Gopi's father-in-law responded. 'Whatever you earn is by selling the packages in which your stock arrives.'

Hari was startled. The old man had obviously learned this from Gopi, which meant his son was privy to the plan. Was this perhaps his idea? Helplessly, he resorted to the usual platitudes. 'What is money? The dirt on one's palm. Comes off as easily as it collects.'

He walked to the door. Then, worrying that he had been impolite, he turned to say, 'When you wish to see your daughter, you only have to send word and I will dispatch Gopi's wife to Santahar by the very next train.'

A week later, Tribhuvan visited from Calcutta. As always, he brought his books with him, and Hari bade him sit in the shop. 'If you must spend your time buried in books, do so in the shop. You will see how a shop is run, and perhaps learn a little.'

He noted that Tribhuvan spoke Marwari with particular difficulty, mixing it with Bengali and even Hindi, as they did in Calcutta. He had begun to wear a black coat whenever he left the house. It was too large for him and came down to his knees, hiding much of his dhoti. He seemed both amused and bewildered by Bogra, and Hari suspected that he no longer liked coming home. Now and then, Manki pointed out that the nineteenth was upon the boy—he was getting too old for a match. She would comment on how thin he was and demand to know what they fed him in Calcutta, if his cooks were brahmins and whether they put ghee on his rotis. Tribhuvan barely responded. He would make his way down to the shop with his books, where it pleased Hari when customers asked about the boy because he was able to extol Tribhuvan's career in Calcutta. Shopkeepers would bring their English telegrams and Tribhuvan would read them aloud. Hari would beam with pride, but his mind would wander when Tribhuvan spoke of his studies, of books Hari had never heard of, and subjects that he considered scandalous to teach in school.

'I pay your fees so you may learn about great men—Dasharath, Parsuram, Raamji—and you speak of Yehudis and Christians. This Shylock appears to be a sensible man.'

'His interest rates were too high.'

'Khemchandji never loaned money at less than bayis-anna-saikada. In English, that is more than 16 per cent. I have never lent at a lower rate myself.'

'Shylock's rates were even higher.'

'Why should they not be? A man must charge as much as his customers are willing to pay, and he must compensate for the Christians who will default. Did you not say that Antonio failed to repay the loan?'

'His ships sank.'

'Then Shylock is entitled to the pound of flesh. It was a pukka loan, formalized on a piece of paper.'

'But he was a Yehudi.'

'A Yehudi in Venice is much like a Marwari in Bengal. No one wants him there but everyone needs his capital.'

Seeing no customers in the shop, he sent Tribhuvan to Bara Gola to take the inventory—he had recently rented a warehouse near the hosiery store for surplus stock. A few grandchildren played in his lap—he had begun to forget who was who—and he could hear someone crying upstairs—perhaps Gangadhar, Durga's two-year-old son.

An hour later, he saw Tribhuvan running towards Sat Matha, shouting. 'Babuji! Come to Bara Gola right away.'

'Do not run like this. People will assume the worst.'

'Gopiya is in a rage, and Nanuramji says he will never enter the store again.'

Out of habit, Hari scolded his son. 'Call him Gopi Bhaiya!'

'Come to Bara Gola. Nanuramji's leg is broken.'

Hari followed his son to the store, secretly relieved that it was only a broken leg, and only Nanuram, not his sons, but the situation was worse than he had imagined. Two clerks stood outside the store. Inside, Durga sat in a corner, trembling. 'And who called you?' Gopi asked insolently on seeing Hari.

'Where is Nanuram?'

'I have dismissed him. I do not want a thief in my shop.'

'Watch your tongue, Gopiya.'

The clerks were reluctant to speak, Durga was too frightened to open his mouth and Tribhuvan had not seen the whole quarrel, but Hari somehow pieced the story together. There had been an argument over the inventory. Gopi had been rude to Nanuram, Nanuram had said something in turn, and Gopi had kicked Nanuram in the thighs. Hari flew into a rage, saying to Gopi, 'If you have kicked Nanuram today, you will strike me tomorrow.' Turning angrily to the clerks, he asked, 'Where is Nanuram?'

He found him sitting on a bag of rice in the new warehouse in Bara Gola.

'You have seen much in your fifty-one years, Nanuramji,' said Hari, knowing that Nanuram would notice the 'ji'. 'This, too, shall pass. The boy is young and headstrong, and Raamji has already punished him with three daughters. Look at Durga—he has two sons.'

He regretted saying this as soon as he did, and in any case it had no effect on Nanuram, so he continued, 'You will not have to sit in the same shop with Gopi again.'

When Nanuram spoke, it was in the manner of a speech, the longest Hari had heard from him in thirty years. 'I have followed you from Shekhavati, Hari Babu. I have no home in Disavar, and I will never leave your side. But it is you I serve.'

Hari silently accepted the tribute and the implied suggestion that Nanuram would not work for his sons, and walked away, feeling helpless. He was not sure how he could make good on his promise.

That afternoon, he had Tribhuvan write a letter to Gopi's father-in-law. The Santahar train had already left, so he dispatched a man on a bullock cart. The message would be in Santahar before nightfall.

'Gopi Chand holds you in the highest regard, and nothing would please me more than to have him learn the oil trade under your guardianship. He will gain the benefit of your wisdom, and you will see your daughter every day. I will be able to provide some of the money needed...'

It was arranged quickly. Hari paid for the depot building, Gopi's father-in-law for the land around it. Gopi and Sharda were to live on the upper floor of the depot, which had previously served as a warehouse and reeked of mustard oil. The tins were moved out; the rooms were cleaned and aired; a rug was unfolded; an oil stove was placed in the corner. In a few days, a bullock cart loaded with pots—supplied by Manki from the kitchen—a mattress, two stools and a bed left Sat Matha and reached Santahar five hours later. The depot was a short walk from Sharda's father's house. He stood outside, supervising arrangements, quite satisfied with the turn of events.

Sharda and her three daughters left Bogra the next day, followed by Gopi himself, who travelled by train with Hari. The depot was already open for business. Gopi's father-in-law beamed at Hari. 'Santahar is no longer the home of your son's in-laws, Hari Babu. It is now his home, and therefore yours. Come as often as you can.'

Hari smiled drily, his eyes on the new board that announced the oil dealership name—Harilal & Sons. Evidently, Gopi had chosen not to remove his father's name, even as he had taken his patrimony and separated himself.

'If you do not come at least once a week,' Gopi said, 'Pushpa,

Ahilya and Parvati will be deprived of their grandfather's love. Come for your granddaughters if not for me.'

'You cannot avoid Santahar even if you want to,' Gopi's father-in-law added. 'When you go to Calcutta, you must change trains here. And the railway station is so close that can hear the whistle of the train from the depot.'

'I think I just heard a whistle,' said Hari through clenched teeth. 'I must run or I will miss my train back to Bogra.' And he walked away. Everyone knew that the passenger special for Bogra would not start for three hours, but he could not suffer another moment at the depot—better to let them think him eccentric at forty-one than to receive yet another invitation to Santahar.

'I will visit often,' he called as he turned the corner, knowing he would not.

Back in Bogra that evening, he wrote a few words on his slate. 'A boy is rudderless without his mother. Who will teach him the proper sanskar? Who will fill his heart with compassion? She need not pick up slate and chalk to give him a lesson. Her mere presence serves to instruct him, just as a cow tied at the door brings harmony to the household, whether or not she gives any milk.'

The next day he bought a cow and tied it to his door, next to the shop.

10

The next year, word arrived from Santahar that Gopi's wife had given birth to her fourth daughter. It was now clear that Gopi would have only girls. Who would take care of him when he was old? Meanwhile, Manki gave birth to a girl too, and Hari heard that Mangiram's wife had had twin daughters. It is the season for girls, he thought ruefully.

After Mangiram's son died of the pox in the days following Hari's wedding, their friendship had cooled. Hari rarely went to Fateh Ali Bajar these days, and Mangiram somehow managed to avoid Sat Matha. His son would have been nineteen, married and perhaps a father. The birth of his twin girls devastated him. His wife had become pregnant after nineteen years. He had taken every precaution: pujas, gifts to pandits, donations to the goshala. To be absolutely certain, he had also paid Dr Saha in advance to be available for a full week. There had been great joy when the doctor informed Mangiram that he would have twins. A box of sweets had arrived in Sat Matha. Raamji had given twins indeed, but forgotten to turn at least one into a son.

Hari went to Fateh Ali Bajar to see his old friend. Mangiram displayed great fortitude, Hari thought, when he said, 'A first daughter is Lakshmi, Hariya.'

'And a second is Saraswati,' Hari added quickly.

They spoke of grain prices, the Nawabzada's Hindu-mindedness, the debts owed to Mangiram's family by the Nawab's grandfather, and the decline of morals among Marwari children in Bogra. Then Hari walked back to Sat Matha, deeply disturbed, reminded again that a boy from Shekhavati must have his first tonsure in Shekhavati in the temple of his family deity, no matter where in Disavar his father had chosen to live. It was at his own risk that a man dared defy that law.

Entering the verandah at Sat Matha, he immediately saw the consequences of that law. After the tonsures of Durga and Tribhuvan near the Karatoya, not one of his sons or grandsons had received a haircut. He would not have dared. Garib Das was eight and Fakir Chand four. Each had long locks, kept in braids. Durga's sons, three and two, were also in need of haircuts. Other sons would follow. Who would take them all to Khatu for their tonsure? He himself would not dare—had he not sensed, when crossing the river to go east into Loharu, that Shekhavati did not want him back? Durga was too timid to take four boys all by himself, Tribhuvan was in Calcutta, and Gopi, father of four girls, would not agree, even if Hari were to swallow his pride and ask him.

11

After Gopi's wedding, Hari had hoped that his wife Sharda would mould him in her image. Instead, Hari had heard murmurs—snippets of conversation between Lakshmi's Ma and Manki, overheard as he climbed upstairs—that some of Gopi's hostility toward his brothers was instigated by Sharda, that her gentle nature cloaked a devious, scheming woman. He had dismissed this as loose talk. Now, with Gopi in Santahar, peace reigned in the house. Whether it was good fortune or Durga Prasad's influence, his wife Gayatri had proven to be as calm and equable as Manki was shrill and excitable. In the five years since Durga's wedding, she had slowly risen in the estimation of Garib Das and Fakir Chand, until they treated her as their mother, though she was only twelve years older than Garib Das. With Sharda removed to Santahar and Manki retreating into her room to fill Raam Raam books, it was Gayatri, with Lakshmi's Ma, who took over the running of the house. Every morning, when it was time for the four boys to go to school, it was she who bathed them, braided their hair and tied it into loops. The four went together, holding hands on the road as they had been instructed—Garib Das leading, followed by Fakir Chand, Gangadhar and three-year-old Bansidhar, who was too young to go to school but went anyway, because four boys cost the same as three.

She rose at four every morning and ground a bag of wheat, then churned milk in the verandah. The groaning of the churn woke up the children, Hari's as well as her own. They stood in a ring around her, from the oldest to the youngest—Garib Das, Fakir Chand, Gangadhar and Bansidhar, and Hari's daughters Shanti and Kaushalya—while she flicked bits of butter off the lip of the churn, letting it fall directly into their mouths. So skilfully did she snap her fingers that not a drop was wasted, nor did she ever touch their mouths, which would have required her to wash her hands with clay. The churning finished, she gave what remained in the pot—the buttermilk—to Garib Das and Fakir Chand, never letting her own sons touch it. Watching her out of the corner of his eye, Hari would be overwhelmed—that a woman should deprive her own sons in favour of her husband's brothers. Then she would set some buttermilk aside for the women of Sat Matha, who came every evening to take spoonfuls, to make curd from milk. Word had got around: whoever ran short of buttermilk at home knew that some could be had in Harilalji's house, where his daughter-in-law Gayatri never turned anyone away.

After she had stored the butter in a clay pot and placed it under a pot of water—to keep it cool—Gayatri milked the cow at the door. Hari often told his customers, with some pride, that the cow allowed no one but Gayatri to approach her, though he knew this was not true: he had seen Nanuram do the milking.

Manki had recently acquired a new brass statuette of Raamji and placed it in her shrine in the kitchen. Her attention had slowly found its focus in the care of this Raamji—she bathed him, dressed him, knit skirts for him, spun him warm blankets in winter, stuffed perfumed wool behind his ears and tied little bells to his ankles. Late in the night, waiting for her to come to bed, Hari could hear her speaking to him in a soft voice, arguing, remonstrating, pleading and giggling. Raamji had become her father, husband and son. Everyone, including Garib Das and Fakir Chand, was satisfied with the arrangement. When Hari shut the shop and came upstairs in the evening, Gayatri and Lakshmi's Ma would fuss over his dinner while Manki would be seated at her shrine in a trance, fingers moving slowly over the rosary while a drone of 'Raam Raam Raam' filled the air.

Gayatri's devotion to Raamji was expressed in less dramatic ways. She was punctilious about festivals and pujas—Holi, Diwali, Shivaratri—as well as the anniversaries that marked the deaths of Duli Chand and Hari's mother. Rice balls were offered to crows, incense was lit and brahmins were fed. During a lull in the evening, when everyone had eaten dinner and the children gone to sleep, she would bring out her spinning wheel. No one knew what she did with the yarn she spun—it was too coarse to be used for clothing. Perhaps spinning was an end in itself: the more she spun, the more she felt the gaze of Raamji upon her.

Watching her out of the corner of his eye, Hari marvelled at how he had finally found a wife of sorts. Parmeshwari had been taken away before she could enjoy her good fortune. Manki wanted no child other than Raamji. Gopi's wife had gone away to Santahar. Tribhuvan would certainly live in Calcutta after getting married, if he got married at all. Of all his sons, Raamji had chosen Durga—diminutive, weak and indecisive, with a faltering left eye—to provide him with the daughter-in-law who was now mistress of his house.

Neither Manki nor Sharda had been particular about improper contact in the household: the washerwoman was allowed to touch kitchen utensils, the sweeper entered the verandah unannounced, and the boys were allowed to buy sweetened water on the road from a man who was certainly not a brahmin. Gayatri put an end to all this. Raised in a home of modest means, she knew all about purification rituals and ceremonies, chants and spells, coatings of cowdung and cow urine, and the dozens of ways in which improper contact could be resolved: rotis were to be dropped into the sweeper's hands without touching them, the woman who cleaned the latrines was to use a ladder placed against the back wall, the washerwoman was not to touch cooked food even as she was allowed to cut vegetables which would then be purified through cooking. Once, when the sweeper used the stairs out of habit, she shooed him away and had Lakshmi's Ma pour a bucket of water down the stairs, after which gangajal was sprinkled all over the verandah, followed by the chanting of *sone vali kilkitiya* over gold jewellery. She kept panchagavya—the blend of milk, curd, ghee, cowdung and cow urine that had horrified Hari in Rampura—handy in the kitchen, to be used whenever someone needed purification. Not trusting the shops in Bogra, she made it herself, using milk, dung and urine from the cow downstairs, curd she had set, and ghee she had clarified in her own kitchen.

In the hot month of Baisakh, Garib Das fell in with some

Bengali boys at school who convinced him that the best kites were those flown on threads coated with a paste of egg yolk. He took Fakir Chand, Gangadhar and Bansidhar across the Karatoya to Musalman Para, where they bought an egg. In a patch of dirt behind the school, they coated their spools of thread with a paste of egg, crushed glass, fenugreek seeds and cream of wheat. It was not clear how Gayatri found out, but she was waiting for them in the verandah. 'Do not set foot inside this house.'

'We used cream of wheat, as we always do,' Garib Das lied.

'The tenth is upon you,' she said. 'Why, your father will soon be looking for brides!'

Lakshmi's Ma brought out the bottle of panchagavya. With trembling hands, Gayatri removed the cork and sprinkled the potion on their heads. Drops rolled down their faces. Bansidhar pointed to Garib Das. 'Gariba Chacha touched the egg.'

Gayatri put her hands over her years. 'Do not utter that word in my presence!'

'It was Bansidhar who broke the egg,' Garib Das cried.

'But Gariba Chacha touched it.'

Overcome, Gayatri turned the whole bottle over Garib Das's head. He stood drenched in cowdung and urine, shaking with rage.

'You are not fit to come inside,' she said. 'Take off your clothes.'

They removed their kurtas and dhotis—even Garib Das, who was nine—and stood naked at the top of the stairs, while Lakshmi's Ma threw buckets of water on them.

Hari heard the tale that evening. Lakshmi's Ma did the talking while Gayatri kept her face covered in his presence. The boys sat in a row, heads hung in shame. The thought of his sons in Musalman Para market was disturbing. 'Tell me truthfully,' he asked Garib Das, 'Did you touch beef?'

Crying, Garib Das shook his head. The boy showed no signs of growing into his name. Two days ago, he had spent a full rupee on a fancy pen without Hari's permission. Gopi and Durga had used nothing but chalk during the years they went to Guruji's school. Even now, Durga got by with a pencil in the hosiery store. Tribhuvan did use fountain pens—one could not write English with chalk or pencil—but here was Garib Das, a boy with a beggar's name, flaunting a fountain pen in his front-pocket like a magistrate or a sahib. And now, as if it were not enough to be careless with money, he was loose with his morals too.

Garib Das's humiliation was felt by all the children. The next day, they stood around Gayatri's milk churn gloomily as she flicked butter into their mouths. Bansidhar was unable to swallow his butter. It melted and flowed down his chin. The others laughed to see him drool. By then, he had thrown himself on the ground and was shaking convulsively. A strange force had seized his body—his fists were rolled tightly, his mouth was clenched and his eyes had rolled into his head. The boys watched in horror until he calmed down. It was Gayatri who recovered first, picking him up and embracing him. His mouth hung open and was dripping blood—he had bitten his tongue. There were tears in Gayatri's eyes.

That evening, just before Hari went to sleep, Manki laid a hand on his shoulder. 'Bansi was seized by the spirit today.'

Hari brushed her off. 'He is only three. How could he have sinned?'

'Gayatri thinks he may have touched something vile in Musalman Para, when Gariba took him across the river.'

Hari turned over and drifted into sleep, his mind full of cow carcasses and slabs of raw meat that the boys were sure to have seen in Musalman Para.

In late May, Tribhuvan came from Calcutta for a week. As usual, Hari had him sit in the shop. He spoke in Bengali with Bengali customers and in Marwari with Marwaris, and everyone knew that he could speak in English with sahibs. All the boy now needs, thought Hari, is a wife. He is already twenty-one! At his age, I already had two sons and a third was on the way.

When customers failed to notice Tribhuvan, Hari would say,

'I can no longer do sums in my head, Banwari. You know how a man becomes once grandchildren begin to play in his lap. But my son Tribhuvan here, he will add everything up for you. He has just come from Kalkatta...'

Or he would say, as if Tribhuvan were already a lawyer, 'A barrister earns four hundred a month, but I do not care for the money. Is it worth letting my son spend his life away from me?'

'The newspaper? Here it is, *The Statesman*. This is all we have today. For me? Of course not. Who will teach this English language to an old bania? It's for my son Tribhuvan. He has just come from Kalkatta.'

When they were alone, Tribhuvan said, 'Gayatri Bhabhi told me about Bansi's seizures.'

Hari was evasive. 'They will go away. The pandit has told your mother...'

'Did you ask Dr Saha?'

'He says they are harmless.' Hari had not asked the doctor, of course, afraid to compound whatever sin Bansidhar had committed in Musalman Para.

'There are good doctors in Calcutta. People like Bidhan Chandra Roy.'

'Who will pay their exorbitant fees? Has anyone heard of a child going to Kalkatta just to see a doctor?'

'Bansi will soon have a younger brother. What if he has the same problem?'

Hari placed his hands on his ears. Such a horrible thought about a child not yet born! Who would have guessed, on seeing Gayatri churn milk in the morning, that her son would be thus afflicted? True, no one could escape the caprice of fate. Raamji himself, who had never raised his voice in his father's presence, was forced to spend fourteen years wandering the dark forests. We must do the best we can while letting the gods do their worst.

'Ganga and Bansi think highly of you,' he said to his son. 'They wait all year for Tribhuvan Chacha to come from Kalkatta. Tell them they must sit in the shop as often as possible—they waste the whole day in idle chatter. A boy could learn a lot in a shop—show dhotis to customers, pack a munn of wheat, weigh a ser of rice... Punish them when you can, because Durga cannot.'

'But Bansi's seizures...'

'The shop will cure Bansi faster than any doctor could.'

'He is three.'

'I was two when I began to sit with your grandfather. If you must play, he told me, play in the shop. You will learn to tell good grain from bad, watch customers come and go and hear their conversation. That is how a boy prepares for manhood and marriage. I know you will not let me get you a bride, but I must soon find one for Gariba. The tenth is upon him.'

'Do not say that aloud, Babuji.'

'Why? Am I to hide my son away?'

'You cannot marry off a boy before he turns eighteen. Or a girl before fourteen.'

'Who says so?'

'The police in Calcutta.'

'I live in Bogra, not Kalkatta. The Shastras say a girl must be married off when she has reached the age of eight. Should I listen to the Shastras—which have been true for ten thousand years—or an English sergeant in Kalkatta, who was born thirty years ago?'

'Marriage before that age is not legal.'

'I was twelve when I married your mother; she was eleven. Was my marriage illegal? Is that the law you will spout when you become a barrister?'

They argued all afternoon. Hari's joy in his son's education was confounded by terror at his strange ideas. When it was time to draw the shutters, Tribhuvan drew a small packet from his kurta and opened it. 'Salt.'

'I can see that,' said Hari, bewildered. 'Why do you carry it in your pocket?'

'This is no ordinary salt.'

'I can see that too. It is damp and dirty. Take a munn of good salt from me.' He pointed to the back of the shop, where salt bags lay stacked from floor to ceiling.

'You have not heard of Dandi, then.'

'Yes, Nanuram told me: Gandhiji went there and did a puja for the ocean.'

'He did not do a puja. He made salt.'

'*This* was what he made? I see your Gandhiji knows how to turn a profit. How much did you pay for this?'

'This is my own salt, Babuji. I made it myself.'

'Did you go to Dandi?'

'I made this in Maheshvathan, five miles from Calcutta. You should have seen the crowds. The whole Congress committee was there. The police stood in a line, unable to do anything while we broke the law. We will no longer eat English salt.'

'We have been eating it for a hundred years,' Hari said drily. 'The sahibs have been your fathers longer than I have. I thought you were in Kalkatta to become a barrister.'

'I go to Congress meetings with Mohammad Ali Bogra—the Nawabzada's son.'

Hari was incensed. 'If your Mohammad Ali thinks so much of Gandhiji, why does he eat beef? Does not Gandhiji say that the cow is our mother?'

'A Musalman does not think so.'

'If he is a friend of yours, why does he keep cows inside the Nawabbari, to be slaughtered at will? Why not give them to the goshala? I see his butchers pass with their cows, and I ask myself why such a man should be your friend.'

'Gandhiji says we will stop slaughtering cows when Musalmans say so.'

'Write a letter to your friend Mohammad Ali. Or to his father, the Nawabzada. Ask him to stop right away in the name of friendship.'

'You could write it yourself,' said Tribhuvan evasively.

'How will the Nawabzada read my Modhiya? Or do I have to learn English for his sake?'

'All right,' said Tribhuvan. 'But I will write it in your name.'

'Use a fountain pen,' said Hari, 'not a pencil.'

Tribhuvan drew a pen from a pocket in his black coat.

'The Quran does not enjoin a devout Musalman to make a meal of the cow, but perhaps the Nawabzada sees profits in the sale of meat. Permit me to respectfully point out that a cow provides twenty-five ser of cowdung a day and three ser of urine at night, if we disregard the urine passed during the day, when it cannot be collected. Those who know also say that the dung produced by an ageing cow is richer in fertilizer than that of a young cow, to compensate for the milk she will not give, and that it is sufficient to pay for her upkeep. The Nawabzada could earn higher profits through the sale of dung, urine and milk than through slaughter. When neither religion nor profit demand a custom, why not put an end to it?'

'I do not think anything will come of it,' Tribhuvan said.

'What would you have me do?' Hari demanded. 'Make salt?'

12

In the month of Aashaadh the next year, Gayatri gave birth to her third son. Hari named him Murlidhar. Gangadhar and Bansidhar cradled their brother in their arms, while Hari turned him this way and that to inspect his whole body.

'There appears to be nothing wrong with him. The boy is healthy.' But he spoke softly, fearful that his words would fall into jealous ears, and aware that Bansidhar's seizures had arrived only after he turned three.

He kept a close eye on Murlidhar. When the boy was two weeks old and all pujas had been completed, he had him brought down to the shop every morning, where he was laid behind the cash box so Hari could observe his movements. He made a note of every development—Murlidhar unrolled his fists at three weeks, held his head up at three months and sat up at five. Anxiety gave way to reassurance. For a day, the boy burped uncontrollably. For a week, a clear liquid was to be found at the corner of his mouth, trickling slowly on to the mattress. Hari had never watched a child thus, not even his own sons.

The others forgot about Murlidhar as soon as he was born. He found his place in the melee of the verandah, where his brothers, uncles and aunts played together, unable to leave the house because of heavy rains. The boys, from ten-year-old Garib Das to four-year-old Bansidhar, ran about in long braids, indistinguishable from Hari's two daughters, who were four and two. Climbing up to the verandah every evening, he would be accosted by seven children, six in braids. A house full of girls, he would say aloud in jest, even if one disregarded Gopi's four daughters in Santahar. Then he would remember why the boys had long braids, think of Manki's two dead children, and a chill would descend on his heart.

Manki had completely withdrawn into her contemplation of Raamji and the filling of books with his name, while Gayatri and Lakshmi's Ma were busy with housework, so it was Hari who first noticed the oddities in Murlidhar's behaviour. The signs were not obvious. Now almost a year old, the boy did not have seizures like his brother, or a deformity like the ball growing at Lakshmi's Ma's throat. There was a certain shyness to him, an aversion to contact that seemed unnatural. Children could be shy, of course, but Murlidhar seemed almost indifferent, eating what was given, asking for little, complaining rarely, and neither laughing nor crying much. Hari was not sure this was an affliction; he did not mention it to anyone, least of all to Tribhuvan—who would insist on consulting an expensive doctor—but the signs were unmistakable, if subtle.

It was Chaman Lal who first said this aloud. Hari had taken the boy to the jute press. The two of them were going over accounts while the boy played on a carpet of jute strands.

'Your grandson has the spirit of Raamji inside him,' said the old man. 'Look how carefully he turns the jute over in his hands, as if trying to determine its quality. That is not how children behave.'

Chaman Lal's comment was not malicious; indeed it was a compliment, as was everything he said in his state of necrosis, but Hari was deeply disturbed. If an indifferent old man could see the boy's affliction, it certainly existed. A fog of disease lay on his children, and he asked himself again and again which of his many sins had led to this. How was a man to build a family in the foul air of Bengal? Was there a Marwari who died unscathed, having once left Shekhavati? Was there one whose children did not suffer the sins of the land?

As if to remind him of the pernicious pulls on his children, Garib Das announced that he and Fakir Chand had taken roles in a Raamleela, a performance of the Ramayan organized by a Bengali teacher at school. This caused an uproar in the verandah. Manki shook herself out of her stupor and forbade it. There would no doubt be girls in the troupe. What if Garib Das or Fakir Chand should be led astray by these girls who, considering they had received permission to perform on stage, could not possibly be from good families?

'We have friends in the Raamleela,' Garib Das pleaded.

'If you need friends,' Hari said, 'look for them among brothers, cousins, nephews and in-laws.'

His closest friend in Calcutta had been Janardhan, his sala. Who but a family member would have been as faithful as Janardhan had been? And had he not provided a family large enough for all his sons and daughters to find friends?

The teacher at school, Surendra Bagchi, sent a messenger to assure Hari that all roles would be played by boys. He was unmoved. It was one thing to welcome Bengali customers, another to sit and eat with them, as boys in a troupe were sure to do. Would his sons touch eggs, perhaps fish? Would they share plates? And why should Marwari boys, destined to sit in their fathers' shops, participate in such frivolity? Bengalis had an affinity for song and dance and other unprofitable indulgences. Even Tagore Babu, who had received a big prize in England for his poetry, went about with singers and dancers, pleading for money at an age when a man watches his sons take over his shop and thinks of retiring to Benares.

'My boys get nervous on stage,' he said to Surendra Bagchi's messenger. 'And they hardly have the time—after they return from school they must sit in the shop.'

'Bagchi Da will train them not to be nervous,' said the man, ignoring the second objection.

A clerk announced that a telegram had arrived. Hari opened it and, noting it was in English, passed it to Garib Das, who appeared to struggle with the words. Hari turned accusingly to Surendra Bagchi's messenger. 'He has been going to your school for four years, yet he cannot read a telegram in English. Now, instead of teaching him that, you want him to frolic around on stage?'

'He is only eleven...' the man began.

By then, Garib Das had deciphered the note. He tugged at this father's sleeve. Hari turned around impatiently. 'Well, what does it say?'

'Tribhuvan Bhaiya has passed his barrister test. He will come to Bogra six days before the dark night in Kartik, and will leave after Diwali.'

Hari snatched the telegram out of Garib Das's hands and held it before his eyes, watching letters that formed such beautiful words. Doubt assailed him. 'How do I know you have read it correctly? You were never any good in the classroom.' He thrust the note into the hands of Surendra Bagchi's man, who glanced at it and smiled. 'It is time for laddus, Sethji.'

'Yes, yes. And tell Bagchi Da that my sons will participate in his Raamleela. Will the performance take place on school grounds? Who will put up the tent? You will need petromax lanterns, chairs, ropes, bamboos, and some sharbat—evenings will remain warm until after Diwali. Tribhuvan Lal Tibrewal, LLB, will be your chief guest.'

'Bagchi Da did not mention a chief guest.'

'A barrister from Kalkatta! The first Marwari barrister in Bogra, perhaps in Bengal. Ask Bagchi Da if he needs help with the tent. Or if he needs matches, batteries, grain, anything you see in this shop. He only has to send a list and it will be delivered, at a discount.'

Bagchi Da's man was quick to seize the opportunity. 'After Bogra, Bagchi Da plans to take the children to Calcutta. They will perform everywhere: the Corinthian Theatre in Dharamtolla, Alfred Theatre in Harrison Road, Minerva in...'

'Who will pay the train fare?' Hari asked, suddenly suspicious.

'Bagchi Da will ask for donations.'

'Let us watch the Bogra performance first.'

The man got up, his mission accomplished. As he left, Hari called out. 'Do not forget to tell Bagchi Da about the chief guest's speech.'

For the next two weeks, Hari eagerly awaited Tribhuvan while Garib Das and Fakir Chand spent evenings in school, rehearsing. Garib Das was to play the demon Raavan, Fakir Chand the goddess Sita. They pranced around the house, Fakir Chand in a skirt wrapped carelessly around him, and Garib Das with a spring-loaded dagger that he was to sink into Garud, the devotee of Raam.

Manki scoffed at the preparations. 'The Ramayan is the sacred word of Goswami Tulsidas. Before you dare utter a syllable you must bathe, then sit cross-legged and bring the image of Raamji into your heart. You must not have soiled hands or feet, must not have seen a bhangi or a Musalman, or touched half-eaten food. It is not right for unwashed boys to run around reciting the Ramayan as if it were cheap cinema.'

'Ladies may not watch the performance,' Garib Das responded, 'so we will not offend your eyes or ears.'

Tribhuvan arrived the day before the Raamleela. Everyone went to the railway station to receive him. Many of Hari's customers were also present, as was Surendra Bagchi. Hari distributed marigold garlands. Being the boy's mother, Manki came too, the only woman so permitted. Though only thirty-one, she had strands of grey in her hair and there was a suggestion of wrinkles on her cheeks. Combined with her slight stoop and usual frailty, she could indeed have been twenty-three-year-old Tribhuvan's mother. She was in a tightly wrapped sari, a corner of which passed over her head and completely covered her face. Being shorter than the men around her, she stood in a circle of her own, carrying a brass plate with rice, water and a paste of roli.

There was the usual scramble of coolies when the train from Santahar came in. A cry went up when someone spied Tribhuvan Lal, standing in the doorway wearing a black coat and white dhoti, hands folded to acknowledge those on the platform. Hari fretted that the boy did not have a hand free to steady himself, should the train stop abruptly. Tribhuvan Lal descended and was immediately enveloped in the arms of the receiving party. Marigolds began to ring his neck, rising higher. Someone cleared the way for Manki. The garlands were pushed away, one by one, to reveal Tribhuvan's face. He leaned forward. Manki reached up and daubed his forehead with roli paste, stuck grains of rice into it, and sprinkled the rest over his head with drops of water. Then, to Hari's great delight, Tribhuvan Lal bent over to touch both his feet and Manki's. He knew everyone had noticed. Nanuram said to him, 'This is what they call sanskar. In Kalkatta the boy may be a barrister who speaks with sahibs, but in Bogra he does not forget he is merely your son.'

Garib Das and Fakir Chand tugged at Tribhuvan's coat, regarding him with a mixture of awe and shyness, while Durga stood by with one-year-old Murlidhar in his arms. Gangadhar and Bansidhar were next to him. Murlidhar had a fixed smile on his face, as if he understood the importance of the event. Hari sensed a flaw in the picture. Although he knew the answer, he asked Tribhuvan anyway. 'You were in Santahar for three hours. What did you do?'

'I sat on the platform and waited for the train. It was too hot to do anything else.'

He had not gone to see Gopi, though the oil depot was within sight of the station in Santahar.

'Tribhuvan has grown taller,' someone said.

'Hari Babu! Should I look for a suitable girl?'

Everyone laughed, even Tribhuvan Lal, who should properly have ignored this. They went home, the boys carrying Tribhuvan's luggage on foot, and Tribhuvan himself in a ricksha.

Hari spent the next day receiving congratulations from everyone in Sat Matha, Fateh Ali Bajar and Raja Bajar. Men visited the shop just to look at Tribhuvan, who sat shyly next to his father, a little behind him, newspaper in hand.

'Should we inform the district magistrate about Tribhuvan Babu's visit?' asked a customer.

'There are other barristers in Bogra,' Hari pointed out.

'They aren't Marwaris.'

'The district magistrate is Bengali. He will not be interested.'

'Forget the district magistrate. We should take a delegation to the Governor in Kalkatta. A sahib will understand what a Bengali will not.'

Hari glowed with happiness, taking care not to show it lest someone accuse him of vulgar display. In the afternoon, a man from the Bogra Congress Committee came by. 'Tribhuvan Babu should come to the party office.'

To Hari, the Bogra Congress Committee seemed a step down for a barrister from Calcutta. 'He is already in the Congress committee. In Kalkatta.'

The man was impressed. 'Which ward?'

'Ward 7. Bara Bazar,' said Hari. He imagined his son walking down Cotton Street with party functionaries in tow—Tribhuvan Babu, we must call a meeting, we must write a letter to *The Statesman*, we must inform Sarat Babu, we must arrange Gandhiji's prayer meeting...

'I am not really a member...' Tribhuvan began.

Hari interrupted irritably. 'Did you not show me the salt you had made with Gandhiji at Dandi?'

'I made it in Maheshvathan near Calcutta. Everyone made salt in those days, even those who were not Congress members.'

'If you made salt, you are in the Congress.' Turning to the party man, Hari said, 'Tribhuvan Babu will visit the party office in three days.'

'But I leave for Calcutta tomorrow,' Tribhuvan said.

'You did not tell me that! Surendra Bagchi in the boys' school has invited you to be chief guest at his Raamleela tomorrow afternoon. Gariba and Fakira will perform.'

'The Santahar train leaves in the evening.'

'All right. You may go to the railway station after watching the Raamleela.'

The next day, Hari saw or heard very little at the school function. He and Tribhuvan sat in front on chairs draped with white sheets. Surendra Bagchi introduced the chief guest. Tribhuvan made a speech that Hari found too short. It was in Bengali, not English as he had hoped. Much time was wasted on Gandhiji's revolt against London and his meetings with Lord Irwin, the Lat Sahib in Delhi; there was not a single word about the LLB degree. The applause that followed was lukewarm.

The Raamleela began. Fakir Chand ran about the stage dressed as Sita. Hari had always thought the boy effeminate because of his light skin and slender frame. His braids had been undone for the role. Now, with flowing hair—was that why Bagchi Da had wanted Fakira to play Sita?—he looked embarrassingly like a girl. When Garib Das made his appearance as the ten-headed Raavan—nine cardboard heads arranged around his dark face, and braids looped over the head to create the grotesque curls of a demon—Hari felt he had erred in permitting his sons' participation. Here was Garib Das, looking darker than usual, playing a villain condemned in eternity. Surely some sin accrued to the boy who abducted Sita, even in jest, and even when Sita was his own brother? What if Raamji were to cast a casual look downward and spy a dark boy wrestling with his fair wife?

When it was time for Tribhuvan Lal to go to the railway station, the Raamleela was stopped. People rose to bid goodbye. Tribhuvan touched Hari's feet, greeted Surendra Bagchi and left the grounds. Hari sent two servants with him, bearing his steel trunk and bedding, and a bundle that contained pickle and rotis prepared by Gayatri.

The Raamleela resumed, but Hari's interest waned. It was hot under the tent. The sweet sharbat served by Surendra Bagchi—paid for by Hari—had arrived in glass tumblers, forcing Hari to refuse it. In Shekhavati, no one would have thought of serving sharbat in anything but clay pots. After clay, brass was acceptable, and allowances could be made for steel, but not glass. Shafts of sunlight were creeping into the tent as the afternoon advanced. By the time Raavan slew Garud and flew away with Sita in his golden chariot, Hari had shut his eyes.

He woke to the sound of applause. The Raamleela was over, but Surendra Bagchi was announcing a second performance—the story of the emperor Shah Jahan and his queen Mumtaz Mahal. No doubt Fakir Chand will play Mumtaz Mahal, Hari thought irritably. Poor boy, condemned to play a Musalman girl. The performance began. Hari stared open-mouthed. Mumtaz Mahal was a girl. Surendra Bagchi had placed an actual girl amidst his boys, and they were all on stage together! He rose from his seat, approached Bagchi Da near the stage, and demanded to know why he had been misled.

'The boy who was to play Mumtaz Mahal fell sick,' Surendra Bagchi explained.

'Why didn't you take Fakir Chand, then? That boy has already played Sita Maiya. Do you think he cannot play a mere queen?'

'Yes, but Fakir Chand...'

Hari climbed the three steps to the stage, strode across it and addressed Garib Das, who was in the middle of a bow before the emperor. 'Straighten your spine! Let us go. And call Fakira.'

They left the school, followed by Gangadhar and Bansidhar, who had been sitting in the back. 'You have completed your studies,' Hari said to Garib Das and Fakir Chand. 'Tomorrow morning, you will sit in the store in Bara Gola with your brother Durga Prasad.'

13

Durga Prasad showed uncharacteristic resistance to the presence of his brothers in the hosiery store. It dawned on Hari that, being the father of three boys, Durga had begun to think of the store as property he would pass on to his sons. So he brought Garib Das and Fakir Chand to the shop at Sat Matha—Fakir Chand in the half that sold grain and Garib Das in the half that sold cigarettes. It was not a happy arrangement. There had been a decline in grain prices over the years. Business was slow. Hari did not need Fakir Chand, and Garib Das's presence in the cigarette store was even more inappropriate. He complained to Nanuram. 'A man with many sons must find many shops for them.'

As if in response, Manki gave birth to another son while Gayatri gave birth to a daughter, her first after three sons. Unlike Manki's previous pregnancies, this one had caused him no anxiety, because he felt that his two daughters, now six and four, had ended the gloom hanging over his sons. He did not even climb to the verandah when she was in labour. On receiving the news in the shop, he did not cast about for a pitiful name like Garib Das or Fakir Chand.

'Let us call him Ishwar Das.'

'Some might call that arrogance,' Nanuram said.

'What turns of fate do I fear now?'

So the boy was named Ishwar Das, while Durga's daughter was named Savitri. The two were laid together in the shop. Customers marvelled at the size of Hari's family. Heart swelling with pride, he would respond, 'Six sons and two daughters. And more to follow. What else does a man wish but that Raamji should give him many children? Only eight grandchildren, I know, but wait for Gariba and Fakira to find brides. And Tribhuvan Lal, of course, not yet married because he was busy studying in Kalkatta. Now that he is a barrister...'

It took a year to find a match for Tribhuvan Lal. Hari was determined that the girl should be from Calcutta, not from the mofussil area around Bogra, but his contacts in Calcutta had dried up. Lalgodam had shut down when the firm of Daulatram Gulabchand collapsed, and its clerks, including Hemraj, had dispersed, some returning to Shekhavati and others joining rival firms in Bara Bazar. So it was not until the cold weather that his efforts resulted in a visit by the girl's father—a wealthy businessman who had an office in Bara Bazar, and who seemed to think he had given a great deal away by coming to a backwater like Bogra.

He sat uncomfortably on Hari's gaddi—as if Marwaris in Bara Bazar used nothing but chairs—regarded the rickshas in Sat Matha with some disdain, and told Hari about his family and businesses. There were many houses, offices, servants and a Baby Austin motor car. The girl's grandfather had been a Rai Sahib—Hari was unable to probe this because the claim was made vaguely and not repeated—and it was possible that Sir John Anderson, the Governor, might come to the wedding. Was it true that the boy had studied law in Calcutta?

'LLB,' said Hari.

'Where does he practise?'

Hari did not know what his son did now that his studies were complete. He replied vaguely. 'Here and there.'

The man looked around the shop and appraised it with a practised eye. 'I see we deal in grain.'

He had used 'we' when he meant 'you', in the formal Marwari manner. And Hari understood, too, the implication that his shop was modest. He responded quickly. 'This is merely where I sit. It is humble enough—it will not do to make a great display among Bengalis. This is not Kalkatta. The slightest indiscretion can lead to unfortunate events. The shop to the left, where you see cigarettes, is also ours. There is a hosiery store near the railway station, a jute press in Raja Bajar, a mango orchard, a share in the goshala outside town, an oil depot in Santahar… And of course there is Tribhuvan Lal's practice in Kalkatta.'

The man nodded, satisfied. 'How many children do we have?'

'Six sons, by Raamji's grace. And two daughters.' Then, remembering that Manki was with child, he added gently, 'A seventh son will be born soon.'

'And many grandchildren?'

'More than I can count.'

The man betrayed only the slightest degree of amusement. 'We have a large family.'

Hari laughed, slightly perturbed by his own braggadocio. A man who openly boasted of six sons was bound to come to grief. 'We live humbly, taking what Raamji gives us. And how many brothers does our daughter have?' he asked, referring to the prospective bride.

'Two,' said the man. 'And she has no sisters.'

Hari was pleased. A lone girl is the goddess Lakshmi. Her father gives her his treasure with great joy. When he has passed away, the brothers keep giving—to her, her children and grandchildren. 'And what do we deal in?' he asked.

'Stock market.'

This was unfamiliar terrain. Hari had never been to the stock exchange in Lyons Range, and had only a vague understanding of what people did there. The man continued. 'We also have a seat on the jute exchange, and membership in the Jute Balers' Association.'

Now Hari was on ground he recognized, and he was impressed. There seemed little that could come in the way of the match when a disturbing thought crossed his mind. 'What is the girl's gotra?'

'Goyal.'

He was relieved. Had she been of the Bindal gotra, she would be considered Tribhuvan's sister, making a match impossible. 'Have you brought her horoscope?'

The man had. A pandit was called. With some encouragement from Hari, he pronounced the match auspicious and predicted three sons for the couple. A date was fixed for the wedding. Within the hour, they had discussed dowry and wedding arrangements. The train for Santahar was to leave in fifteen minutes.

'Please stay the night,' Hari said. 'You are almost Tribhuvan's father now.'

'The stock market does not wait for weddings, Hari Babu' the man said.

Impressed again, Hari said, 'My servant will carry your luggage to the station.'

'I have brought only a small bag.'

'I insist. Let it not be said that you were not treated well in Bogra.'

The man stood up. 'Could you please repeat the wedding date?'

'Samvat 1990, Magh badi 14. It is a Sunday.'

'And the English date? Forgive me, Hari Babu. My life has been spent in Calcutta. When you deal with sahibs and Bengalis, you forget the Samvat calendar. Sir John Anderson's secretary will need the English date, too.'

Hari looked around. None of his clerks would be of help. To keep the discussion private, Fakir Chand had been sent away. Garib Das was summoned. He had been sitting in the cigarette store on the other side of the wall with his ears cocked. Being dimmer than Fakir Chand, it took him a few minutes to do his calculations on paper.

'January 14, 1934.'

'I hope you have not made a mistake,' Hari said. 'This date will be given to the Governor of Bengal.'

'That is the date,' said Garib Das, looking very nervous.

'January 14, 1934,' Tribhuvan's father-in-law repeated, and rushed out of the shop so he would not miss his train. Hari's servant followed with his bag.

On January 10, two hundred men descended on the railway station and occupied one full car in the Santahar train. Hari had invited a man from every Marwari family in Bogra. All his sons were going to the wedding except Ishwar Das, who was not yet a year old, and Durga Prasad, who would remain in Bogra to mind the shop. He was taking along his two daughters, seven-year-old

Shanti and five-year-old Kaushalya. Also in the party were Durga Prasad's sons—Gangadhar, Bansidhar and Murlidhar—but not his one-year old daughter. Manki had not favoured the inclusion of Shanti and Kaushalya in the party, but Hari had argued that the girls were young enough that they could be considered boys. Besides, Tribhuvan's in-laws were city people—they would think it routine that the groom's sisters had come to his wedding.

At Santahar, they had to wait six hours for the train to Calcutta. Silence fell over the party as evening approached. Everyone had tea and samosas. Most dozed off. Garib Das and Fakir Chand went to sleep, as did Gangadhar and Bansidhar. Two-year-old Murlidhar sat in Hari's lap, his face blank. Darkness enveloped the platform.

With Murlidhar in his arms, Hari quietly left the station and walked to Gopi's oil depot. The building had changed since he saw it six years ago. A room had been added on the upper floor—Gopi was expanding his house to accommodate his growing family. Inside the upper room, a lantern cast a glow on a white ceiling. A curtain hung in the window, partly drawn. Hari stood uncertainly in the lane. How would Gopi react to his sudden appearance? He had sent a barber to Santahar, inviting Gopi to the wedding, but the man had returned without a response.

A hand appeared in the window above. He saw bangles. The curtain was pulled aside. His heart jumped. Was that Pushpa, Gopi's eldest daughter? She would be almost nine now. He remembered how he had held Fakir Chand and Pushpa—newborns, uncle and niece—in his arms. Or was that one of Pushpa's three sisters? He did not remember their names. He was filled with shame. What would Gopi have told his daughters about their grandfather? Had they wondered why he never saw them, cradled them in his lap or found grooms for them? He would heal the wound right away. He would walk into the house and demand to see his son. Sharda would cover her face, touch his feet and offer him tea. Pushpa would giggle, and the three younger girls would jump into his lap.

'You should have told me you were on your way,' Gopi would say. 'I would have sent a servant to the station.'

'Why must a father tell his son he is on his way?' he would respond, and everything would be forgotten. He would demand to know why Gopi had not yet found a match for Pushpa. Gopi would pack a trunk and join the wedding party. The four girls would stomp their feet—they would want to go to Calcutta for Tribhuvan Chacha's wedding. Gopi would fret, Sharda would fume, and Hari would settle the matter by letting Pushpa join him. 'These are the last joyful years of her life,' he would say to Gopi, 'before she goes away to her father-in-law.'

He took a step towards the door. Inside the house, someone was shouting, apparently at a servant, about the water being too cold for a bath. Hari was thrown into confusion. A bath at this time of day? The voice was perhaps Gopi's. Murlidhar had heard it too. He wrapped his arms tightly around Hari's neck and began to whimper. Hari had seen this before—the boy would stiffen at harmless sounds, like the bark of a dog, while showing no emotion when a train screeched to a stop.

'He is your uncle; he means you no harm,' Hari said to him. 'And there are four sisters waiting for you inside the house.'

But Murlidhar's grip tightened, and he began to tremble as Hari approached the door. Tears rolled down his cheeks. Hari stopped, unable to subject the boy to this. 'All right. We will go back to the station.'

Murlidhar seemed to understand—his arms slackened. As Hari walked back, he saw that the boy was asleep in his arms.

They reached Sealdah Station in the morning. Tribhuvan was waiting for them with a dozen members of his bride's family, including the girl's father. The guests were greeted with hot tea and kachauris, coolies were engaged for their luggage and rickshas took them all to Bara Bazar, where they were to stay in a public house. Hari noted that the rickshawalas were all Biharis now. The Chinamen were gone.

He walked to Amherst Row, alone, to see Lalgodam. The flour

mill was still in operation, throwing up its usual cloud of dust. Perhaps Jainarain still owned the building and collected rent from his sanctuary in Benares, but there was no trace of Daulatram Gulabchand, not even an old sign on the wall. A few clerks he spoke to knew nothing about opium or cotton, and had not even heard of the Jute Balers' Association.

Bara Bazar seemed more crowded and frenzied. There were no sahibs about, and all the policemen looked Bengali. The Marwaris here seemed to have no connection to Shekhavati. They did not wear turbans or even the caps that were used by Marwari seths when he was a boy—he became conscious of his own turban as he had not been in Bogra. Some of them did not even wear dhotis but had on achkans or trousers. They spoke in Bengali or Hindi. These were not Shekhavati men, he thought, but their children, born amidst plenty in Bengal—men who had never lived through famine, seen a camel cart or watched the sun sink behind tibbas.

The next day, Tribhuvan and Hari went to Cotton Street to rent a wedding shervani. When finished, they drank tea at a stall outside 67 Cotton Street. Hari could not resist a peek inside. The court was silent. A small group of men stood in a corner, speaking in whispers. Suddenly, he was excited. Were these lagayivals or khayivals? He was afraid to ask. The room with rain gauges had been walled off, but he found a door and peeped in. Traders sat at cash boxes, drinking tea and bantering. It looked like a regular Marwari gaddi dealing in grain or jute or spices.

He stood for a long time, watching the men whispering in the court. One of them, perhaps, was the Johnny K of these times...

'They have cleaned it up,' Tribhuvan said. He had followed his father into the court.

Hari was startled. 'Cleaned what?'

'They used to gamble here. On clouds, rainfall, I don't know. The idea came with the men from Shekhavati. It was terrible—fortunes were destroyed, families devastated. Men committed suicides. There were crowds in Cotton Street. Dirt. Mosquitoes.

All for something shady, illegal and unproductive. It wasn't as if they were selling jute or cotton. It was mere speculation.'

Hari felt lonely in the deserted court. Somewhere, Marwaris were still sitting around, looking anxiously at the sky, wondering if it would rain. A thousand miles away in the west, Janardhan was squatting on a sand dune in Shekhavati, teaching boys how to place bets. Or perhaps he was back in Calcutta as Johnny, sweet-talking a sahib in Andrew Yule or kicking a bale of jute in Chitpur Road. But he would have switched to cotton now that there was no money in jute. Buying, selling, speculating... When Hari first came to Calcutta, Khemchand Biyani used to tell a joke—show a Marwari a urinating dog and he will find a way to earn money from it. There was no end to such taunts by Bengalis and even sahibs—a Marwari goes where a dog does not; wire was invented when two Marwaris spotted a coin at the same time; if a fly should fall into a Marwari's tea, he will suck the tea out of it before draining his cup... Hari wanted to tell his son: we are banias, speculation is in our blood. If that is illegal, then a Marwari is but a thief. But Tribhuvan would not understand. He wore a black coat over his dhoti.

It dawned on him that his son had become a Bengali bhadralok.

Then a thought seized him—he would take Tribhuvan to Clive Row and present him to Yule Sahib. How pleased would the sahib be to see what he had done with his son! And imagine the look on Tribhuvan's face when Yule Sahib asked about Johnny! If the boy was a barrister, his father was a business associate of Sir David Yule, the richest sahib in Calcutta, perhaps all of England.

'I want you to meet an old friend of mine,' he said.

'I thought you knew no one in Calcutta, now that Lalgodam...'

'A sahib.' He savoured Tribhuvan's confusion. 'Come.' They walked to Clive Row. 'When the English King wished to see Yule Sahib's jute mill, the sahib had a river dug all the way to the mill so the King might see it without leaving his yacht. Imagine that, a river dug solely for a king!'

At 8 Clive Row, a guard stopped them. Hari pulled himself up. 'Tell Yule Sahib that Harry has come to invite him to his son's wedding.'

The guard did not know who Yule Sahib was.

'The senior director!' Hari said sharply. 'Call your supervisor.'

His boldness intimidated the guard, who stepped inside and carefully closed the door behind him.

'Why did you call yourself Harry?' Tribhuvan asked.

'When a sahib calls you Harry, you call yourself Harry.'

'I am a barrister,' Tribhuvan said with dignity. 'I work daily with sahibs.'

'Then it is all the more astonishing you did not know that already,' Hari responded, irritated by his son's manner.

The guard returned. There was no one named Yule Sahib in the building, and they would not be admitted.

'I asked you to call your supervisor,' Hari said authoritatively.

The guard shook his head.

'Let us go,' said Tribhuvan, offended. Hari followed him quietly to Cotton Street.

In the evening, the bride's family arrived at the public house for the tilak ceremony. Hari sat down with the bride's father and received a formal invitation to the wedding—a parchment wrapped in red cloth, with four gold ginnis stuffed inside. His sons and grandsons sat around him, the children in long braids that were looped around to settle on their shoulders. Someone said, 'Harilalji has a dozen daughters.'

Hari found the joke in bad taste but felt that an explanation was necessary. 'The boys have not been tonsured. After the wedding we will take them all to Khatu, in Shekhavati.'

He instantly regretted the remark. He did not want to go to Shekhavati, filled as he was with foreboding about his return. Meanwhile, the tilak ceremony was nearly complete. Seated in another room, women began to sing.

Let us go for a walk, my dear,
Let us see Victoria in the cool breeze

How could I come with you? I am embarrassed,
Your father stands in the door, your uncle too.

You need not be shy, my dear,
These are new times, this is the current fashion.

How could I come with you? I am embarrassed,
Your brother stands in the door, your grandfather too.

You need not be shy, my dear,
These are new times, this is the current fashion.

Garib Das sniggered. Hari was amused, too. Such a song would have created a scandal in Bogra, but no one seemed to notice it here.

The next day was chilly and overcast. The wedding was to take place in Grand Hotel on Chowringhee—the only hotel in Calcutta fit to receive the Governor, Hari had been told—and had been planned for the afternoon instead of the evening, as was usual, because Sir John Anderson was unavailable later in the day. Pandits had been prevailed on to declare the second prahar—the three hours following noon—auspicious. Unusually for a wedding, an exact hour was fixed—two in the afternoon—because the English guests had to be provided a precise time on the invitations printed for them.

Hari and the children went to the hotel by tram. Their trip to Chowringhee was marred by sad news. The previous evening, the boys had gone to see Victoria Memorial. Outside the monument, Fakir Chand had showed his hand to an astrologer, who had foretold a death.

'My life is forfeit after Samvat 2004,' he told Hari.

'The English date of 1948,' Garib Das added brightly. 'Or 1947, depending on the month.'

'I do not want a lesson in English dates.' Hari was annoyed to be discussing death at such a time. 'Not all astrologers are competent. Some cannot see beyond a day or two in the future.'

'I will be twenty-two in 1947,' Fakir Chand said mournfully.

'After that, I will live on borrowed time. Raamji will call me any moment.'

The tram was crowded, so they were standing between the aisles. Fakir Chand gripped an armrest and began to sob. Hari turned away irritably and thought of Durga Prasad, who had suffered all his life but never complained. And this one, the most light-skinned of his sons, blessed with good health, would go through life complaining that an astrologer had predicted his death.

In Chowringhee, he was astonished to see wide, open roads and lawns—in his years in Calcutta he had rarely left Bara Bazar, and was used to its narrow, dirty and winding lanes. The hotel was grand beyond imagination. He stood shivering with his children in the lobby, afraid to advance further in his Shekhavati turban. Sahibs and Bengalis in western clothes walked about. Any one of these men could be Governor Sahib. It was best to say nothing and go nowhere, until someone he knew should make an appearance. Meanwhile, Fakir Chand's tears were flowing.

'Stop snivelling,' Hari said, 'There are sahibs about.'

The boys were in silk kurtas, dhotis and warm shawls. They had formed a tight circle around Hari—Garib Das, Fakir Chand, Gangadhar and Bansidhar—while Murlidhar was in his arms. Shanti and Kaushalya, dressed in new skirts, stood a short distance away, holding hands. A large chandelier glittering with electric lights hung above them. Whenever the guards opened the doors, it swayed gently, striking dread into Hari's heart. It was his fate, perhaps, to be crushed under this glass monster. When not staring at the chandelier, he studied Bansidhar, looking for signs of odd behaviour. What if a seizure should strike him in the lobby or, worse, during the wedding ceremony inside the hotel, with Governor Sahib watching? The boy should have been left behind in Bogra. Then there was Murlidhar, who sat in the crook of his arm with a vacant look, staring at every passer-by, looking right through, focused on something far away, beyond the draperies on the walls. What if a sharp sound—the cracking of the whip when Governor Sahib's phaeton drew up beside the hotel—should send him into paroxysms? He had wailed for no apparent reason outside Gopi's house in Santahar. What would prevent him from crying aloud near the wedding fire? Hari felt besieged. His sons and grandsons were not fit to stand in this forbidding hotel. His daughters, gentle as cows, were no doubt trembling at the sight of so many sahibs. Granted, the bride's grandfather had been a Rai Sahib, but could they not have planned the wedding inside their home?

After what seemed like an hour, men from the bride's party spied him. They were escorted up a flight of stairs and into a ballroom, where they were seated on large ornate chairs. Hari noted the chandeliers above, again, and the drapes. Everyone was waiting for Sir John Anderson. There were a few false starts when a hubbub in Chowringhee caused men to rush to the door, expecting Governor Sahib to make his entrance. Finally, two sahibs did come in, but they seemed to have no servants, and Hari saw the look of disappointment on the guests' faces. He mustered courage and asked a waiter, 'Which one is Governor Sahib?'

Neither was. Sir John Anderson had chosen to send his secretary instead.

Hari sat next to the fire pit but did not see the wedding. His mind was focused on Bansidhar and Murlidhar, consumed with the fear that one of them would make a scene. He barely saw the bride and groom circle the fire and take their seats again, now as man and wife, while the pandit continued to chant. The chandeliers were swaying, though there was no draught inside the ballroom. Indeed, they had begun to swing violently. The room itself had shuddered. A strange rattling sound—of a thousand chairs and tables bouncing on floors—rose around them. There were screams among the guests. He stood up with Murlidhar in his arms, took Bansidhar by the hand and joined the rush toward the door. They ran down the stairs, into the lobby and out into the street, where cries of 'Raam Raam' filled the air. Conches were being blown everywhere. The rattling stopped almost as soon as

Hari stepped out. The conches died down. In the crowds drifting out of the hotel, he saw Garib Das, Fakir Chand, Gangadhar and, finally, Tribhuvan himself, with his father-in-law. Apparently, no one had been injured. The bride had been taken home by her aunts in a state of shock.

'Raamji has spared us,' said Tribhuvan's father-in-law.

Trembling, Hari nodded. Why had the earthquake come precisely when it did? Was this an omen?

'Raamji has blessed this wedding,' continued Tribhuvan's father-in-law. 'The seven circles were complete before He shook the earth. He waited for the wedding to finish!'

'Yes, yes,' Hari said, relieved. It was a miracle indeed that the wedding was complete before the earthquake struck, and that neither Bansidhar nor Murlidhar had even noticed the shaking. He sought out Tribhuvan, standing in a circle of men who were congratulating him. Hari admired his son from afar until he was spotted.

'No one has been injured,' said Tribhuvan.

'Raamji watched over your wedding,' Hari said absently.

'I made enquiries about your Yule Sahib. He went back to Scotland fifteen years ago.'

'I knew,' said Hari. 'Had he been in Kalkatta, he would certainly have come to the wedding.'

They returned to Bara Bazar. The earthquake had been felt there, too. A few buildings had developed cracks. Conch shells could still be heard in Harrison Road, as a precaution. Late that evening, word came of terrible devastation in Bihar. Thousands had died; whole villages had been uprooted; rivers had changed course.

Gangadhar asked, 'Will the Karatoya no longer flow near Bogra?'

'There was no damage in Bengal,' Hari assured him, though he was worried too.

In the evening, Tribhuvan's father-in-law came to Bara Bazar to bid farewell. This was to be Hari's last meeting with him, so he was forced to bring up a matter that had been troubling him. When they had met in Bogra, Tribhuvan's father-in-law had agreed to provide a substantial dowry, in keeping with Tribhuvan's position. Hari wanted to know if the four gold coins he had received during the tilak ceremony were merely a token gift. If so, when would the rest be given, considering the pahrani ceremony had been cancelled on account of the earthquake? The subject was delicate, and he had little experience—Gopi's father-in-law had been tight-fisted and had prevailed on account of his age and demeanour; during Durga's wedding, there had been no talk of dowry at all because Gayatri's family was of modest means.

'I would not think of going back on my word, Harilalji,' said Tribhuvan's father-in-law, his mouth full of betel juice. 'Men like me trade on their word. In the stock market, a verbal agreement is as good as one written on paper stamped by the government and witnessed by Sir John Anderson's secretary.'

Hari nodded politely, waiting for his answer.

'I have spoken to Tribhuvan Babu about this,' said Tribhuvan's father-in-law, 'and I will make a donation to the Marwari Relief Society. They have already begun work among earthquake victims.'

Hari was afraid to ask how a donation to the Marwari Relief Society could be considered dowry given to his son, but Tribhuvan's father-in-law was happy to explain. All this trouble had been started by a Bengali, Prafulla Chandra Ray, who had written a book saying that Marwaris were parasites—they gave nothing to Bengal while acquiring their wealth in Calcutta. This donation was a response to that charge.

'We do not read such books in Bogra,' Hari said.

'Ah, but it is the rage here. Sir John Anderson has heard of it. Ray wants Bengalis to imbibe what he calls the entrepreneurial spirit of Marwaris—start businesses and set up factories...'

'And what will Marwaris do?' Hari asked sourly. 'Take up writing and music like Bengalis? Go around with a dance troupe like Tagore Babu?'

Tribhuvan's father-in-law shrugged and rose to go. 'One has to get along where one lives.'

He ingratiates himself with sahibs and Bengalis, thought Hari, and he does so with my money. Clearly he had had no intention of paying the dowry. If Raamji had not handed him an earthquake, he would have conjured up another relief society to bestow his gift on himself. And Tribhuvan was complicit. This was what too many years in school led to, as Hari had been warned repeatedly by his father.

Late in the night, as they prepared to go to sleep—all in one room on a large mattress—a messenger arrived from Tribhuvan's father-in-law, bearing a telegram from Bogra. It had been sent by Durga Prasad. With trembling hands, Hari handed it to Garib Das. While the boy fumbled with the paper, Hari muttered 'Raam Raam' with newfound religious fervour. No one had mentioned Bengal in any of the earthquake reports. Given that the tremor had been mild in Calcutta, Bogra should not even have felt it, being further east, but anything was possible…

'What takes you so long?' he asked irritably. The lost look on Garib Das's face sank his heart. 'Tell me, tell me!'

'It is from Durga Bhaiya.'

'I know!'

'A boy has been born.'

Hari collapsed on the mattress, eyes shut. 'Tomorrow morning, send a servant to the Hanuman Temple in Cotton Street with a rupee for the pandit. You are a fortunate man, Tribhuvan Lal. Raamji withholds his arrow until your wedding is complete, then sends you a brother to celebrate it. '

Fakir Chand tugged at his father's sleeve. 'What name did the pandit recommend for the boy?'

Hari regarded him with sympathy—the most fair-skinned of his sons, always mistaken for a girl both for his manner and his long braids, saddled with an unfortunate name along with Garib Das. No wonder the poor boy had been devastated by a mere astrologer. Who would not be, with a name like Fakir Chand?

Some in Bogra would snigger at the birth of this seventh son. How long will Harilalji have to live, they would whisper, to marry off this one? He was reminded that he was forty-seven. And that his lust had taken a life before. Over the years, the children playing in his lap had dulled his senses to the sin he committed again and again, but a wise man heeded the akashvani—the voice from the sky—that he now felt in his ears. For guidance, he had to look no further than Gandhiji, another bania, who had taken a vow of abstinence after Raamji granted him four sons. Surely a man with seven sons could do the same? This seventh would be the last. And he would live to see this one's bride, perhaps even his children. He should have a beautiful name that sprang from a well of love and beauty... But Hari had forgotten to consult a pandit, being busy with wedding preparations, and did not trust the pandits in Calcutta.

He put an arm around Fakir Chand, who was astonished at the display of affection. 'We will name your brother Mohan Lal. And when we marry him off, we will call his bride Radha Devi.'

14

Two days after returning home from Calcutta, Hari went to the Hanuman Temple across the Karatoya. It was a Tuesday, the day favoured by Hanuman. He paid the pandit a rupee and took a silent vow that he would not have relations with Manki for the rest of his life. That night, his bed was moved out to the verandah. Manki was dumbfounded, but her protests were indirect. 'If you sleep in the verandah, you will embarrass Gayatri. She bathes under the hand-pump every morning.'

'I will not open my eyes.'

'Lakshmi's Ma bathes there too.'

'She is as old as me, and the ball at her throat grows ever larger. What need does she have for modesty?'

'There will be other daughters-in-law: Gariba's wife, Fakir Chand's wife.'

'No one will mind an old bania nearing fifty. I am no more a man than the hermaphrodite Shikhandi in the Mahabharat.'

'And what about me?' Manki finally asked.

'You are my daughter, as Shanti and Kaushalya are.'

She tossed her head, stormed into the room and shut the door. From the screeching of her steel trunk inside, he knew she had pulled it from under the bed, extracted a notebook and was furiously filling it with the name of Raamji.

From his vantage point on the cot, he began to see the minutiae of life in the verandah. Gayatri rose at dawn before everyone else, bathed under the pump, sat at her spinning wheel, bundled up the yarn, lit joss sticks in the kitchen shrine and sang to Raamji in a soft, toneless voice. By then, Lakshmi's Ma would have bathed and fired the coal oven, and the smell of baking rotis filled the verandah. Surreptitiously, Hari watched the goitre at her throat swing this way and that as she blew into the oven, wondering when it would burst open and kill her. The last woman to leave her bed was Manki, her sole task being to go from room to room and wake up the children. Soon the house would be full of activity—latrines, hand-pumps, towels, quarrels, laughter, and the babbling of six-month-old Mohan Lal. Lying on his cot under a thick blanket, Hari kept his eyes shut and his mind half-focused on the world around him, bringing up the image of Raamji in the other half to express gratitude. The boys would go to school and the girls would sit down with a pandit to recite the Bhagavad Gita. Finally, at a signal from Manki, he would wake up and begin his day, feeling very old and very satisfied. The most rewarding phase of life was Vriddhavastha—old age—he told himself, and his was just beginning. If only men could pass into his state without first having to go through the wilfulness of youth!

This pleasant state of affairs was disturbed within a year. A chance remark by Garib Das—that he would one day own the cigarette shop—set Hari thinking about the question of inheritance. Aside from the trouble with Gopi, he was worried about Durga's health and future. After he was gone, would

Durga's brothers be generous to him? And what was Tribhuvan's share in the family business? Now that he was married into a family of Rai Sahibs, there was little chance of his returning to Bogra. Would he then expect a payment against his share of the family wealth? Would the older brothers overwhelm the younger ones? Mohan Lal was barely one. How would he stand up to thirty-year-old Gopi? Having no one else to turn to, he raised the matter with Nanuram.

'You are not yet fifty, Hari Babu. You will live to be a hundred.'

Remembering something Gopi's father-in-law had told him, Hari replied, 'This is Bengal, not Shekhavati. Lives are shorter. Men in their fifties lie down on their gaddis, complaining of headaches and chest pains, and do not sit up again. When it comes, Raamji's call is sudden and unexpected.'

'Gopi has already taken his share,' Nanuram said.

'But he has four daughters to marry off. Will an oil depot be sufficient?'

'His father-in-law will help,' Nanuram said. 'The jute press could go to Tribhuvan, who will probably sell it and invest the money in the stock market in Kalkatta.'

'I will need to sell the mango orchard when I marry off Shanti and Kaushalya. It is not cheap to find husbands for two daughters.'

'Durga will take the hosiery store.'

'One hosiery store for his three sons,' Hari said ruefully. 'Gangadhar is nine. Once he gets married, who will look after Bansi and Murli?'

It was clear that neither Bansidhar nor Murlidhar would find a bride—no one would give daughters to such boys after their afflictions became known. And neither would sit in a shop to sell anything. Their only hope was their brother Gangadhar.

'Gayatri Bhabhi will take care of them,' Nanuram said.

'A mother does not live forever.'

'Garib Das will take the cigarette store, and Fakir Chand the grain shop.' The problem was now obvious. 'What happens when Ishwar Das and Mohan Lal are of age?'

Hari sighed. 'A man with seven sons needs seven shops so they do not quarrel after he is gone. Perhaps I could divide the cigarette store. It earns far more than the grain shop.'

Nanuram chuckled. 'Garib Das will want the whole store, and he will not accept the grain shop. He is a shaukeen—a man with tastes and airs. That boy will give you trouble when you choose his bride.'

Indeed, Garib Das's indulgences had begun to trouble Hari. When in Calcutta for Tribhuvan's wedding, he had hatched a plan to watch the film *Alif Laila* in a cinema with Fakir Chand and Gangadhar. Hari got wind of the scheme and forbade it. He also suspected that Garib Das had begun to smoke, surrounded as he was by cigarettes all day. Whenever Gariba stepped into the grain store, Hari would marvel at his clothes: spotlessly white Manchester dhoti—perhaps finagled from Durga in the hosiery store—neatly pressed kurta and a Marwari cap, of the type worn by great seths in Shekhavati, instead of a turban. None of these did much for his appearance: Gariba was thin, dark and slightly hunched, and looked much older than his fourteen years. Recently, his face had broken out in horrible pimples. Manki had brought him sacred water from the Hanuman Temple, his face had been massaged with gangajal, and finally Hari had agreed to let a homoeopathic doctor examine the boy. That had resulted in a bottle full of little white balls and an expense of one rupee. The pimples had continued to sprout.

Lately, Garib Das had taken to buying *Hunterwali* bags and slippers, named after the film. Hari had seen these flood the market in Bengali Para. He had thought the slippers were meant for women, yet Garib Das flaunted them all the time. He even bought *Hunterwali* bangles for Gayatri, who refused them. And one day, Garib Das announced that he would take Fakira and Gangadhar to see *Hunterwali*.

'It is not proper for boys to watch a film about a woman,' Hari said stiffly, 'especially one who lets men photograph her.'

'But she is a memsahib,' Garib Das said. 'An Englishwoman is born without modesty, so she has none to lose.'

'She fights for the poor and the weak,' Fakir Chand said. 'She is Durga and Shakti. The film has a message, like the Ramayan.'

It was clear that the two had prepared their case. 'All right,' Hari said reluctantly, and took twelve annas out of the cash box.

'We need another twelve.'

'Why? Uttara Cinema charges four annas, does it not? There are three of you.'

'*Hunterwali* is a talkie film, playing in Marina. Eight annas for a ticket.'

'They keep finding new ways to raise prices,' Hari grumbled. 'Go quietly. I do not want anyone in Marwari Para to know. And do not talk about the film afterwards.'

They talked about nothing else for months. Customers, clerks and occasional passers-by were regaled with stories. Because a single wall divided the cigarette store from the grain shop, Hari came to know the film quite well. This Hunterwali was a remarkable woman indeed. She wore a mask, ran atop a moving train, leapt from trees on to horses and floated down waterfalls. And the way she cracked that whip! Villains trembled every time she raised her arm. When she brought it down, it was sure to break skin.

Sitting with feigned indifference, Hari found himself wondering. Although her name sounded Parsee, this Hunterwali was a memsahib. Was it possible that memsahibs—not the ones in Calcutta or Bombay but those who had stayed back in England—were women like Hunterwali? Could a woman really lay a whip on a man? What types of men did such women marry, and who dared marry them? He had always imagined Gayatri to be the ideal of womanhood—a wife, a mother as gentle as a cow, a daughter-in-law whose voice was never heard but whose work was seen in every detail of her household. Now who was this Hunterwali? Then he berated himself—it was merely a film, and he had allowed himself to be taken by it like a fourteen-year-old boy.

Clearly, Garib Das had to be married off. His pimples could be overlooked—they would go away in a few years—but no one got married with long braids. It was bad enough that Bengalis laughed at his sons' braids at school; they now had to contend with the taunts of Marwari boys. In the shop, customers asked if Harilalji considered himself an English sahib, given that he had girls sitting in his shop.

He could delay their tonsures no longer. Even if he were to somehow find Garib Das a bride, there was surely some sin attached to marrying a boy off without first surrendering his hair. Raamji sent down punishment in unknown ways. After the earthquake two years ago, Gandhiji had said that it was retribution for not allowing bhangis into temples. But Gandhiji had not seen the cows led by butchers into the Nawabbari—that was as likely to have caused the earthquake. The world was full of sin, and the wise man took care not to be an accomplice. It was best to get the boys tonsured in Khatu. He would go to Shekhavati. He would take them all: Garib Das, Fakir Chand, Ishwar Das, Mohan Lal, Gangadhar, Bansidhar and Murlidhar—four sons and three grandsons. They would all have their heads shaven in Khatu, and no one would ever laugh at them again. He would take Durga along to help him, as well as Lakshmi's Ma to take care of two-year-old Mohan Lal. Manki and Gayatri would remain in Bogra, as would his two daughters. The shops at Sat Matha—both grain and cigarettes—would remain closed.

Durga did not want to go. 'What of the hosiery store?'

'Nanuram will keep it open,' said Hari, 'and we will return two weeks before Diwali, before dhoti sales pick up. Chaman Lal will mind the press.'

'You could do their tonsures in Bogra as you did for Tribhuvan and me.'

Hari did not want to tell Durga that he had lost two brothers—Manki's first two children—to that mistake. He merely said, 'The first tonsure must be done in Khatu. We have done that for a thousand years.'

The next week, after having passed through Santahar and Calcutta, they were in Delhi. Garib Das and Fakir Chand insisted on visiting Red Fort, which was near the railway station, and Qutub Minar, which was not. This delayed them by a day in Delhi. They finished the rotis packed by Gayatri and were forced to eat in a restaurant, which Hari found both abhorrent and wasteful. Because Durga was reticent and soft-spoken, the task of disciplining the boys, especially Garib Das, fell heavily on Hari. Finally, after threats and inducements and promises of camel rides in the desert, they were on a train to Shekhavati. It was an Addha train, so called because it had only two cars attached to the engine. It would take them west to Ringas, near Jaipur, where they were to get off and take a camel cart to Khatu.

Hari's anxiety grew in proportion as they approached Shekhavati. He remembered the day, thirty-seven years ago, when a boy of twelve had ridden a camel across the dry riverbed near Loharu and left Shekhavati. A voice inside had told him he would never return. Like Daulatram before him, Raamji had sent him away forever. Yet here he was, about to re-enter Shekhavati with his children.

The Addha train was nearly empty. *No one goes to Shekhavati*, he thought wistfully. The returning train from Ringas to Delhi would no doubt be bursting with men, and twelve-year-old boys heading to Disavar. On seeing the train at Delhi station, Durga had asked, 'Which car, the first or the second?'

'The second,' Hari had said. 'The further you are from the engine, the less coal your eyes will see.'

They had pushed their steel trunks under benches and thrown their bedrolls between them. After much pointing and gasping at the scenery and leaning far out of the window to catch coal in the eyes, the boys had dozed off, even Garib Das. Lakshmi's Ma sat on the floor, eyes shut, with Mohan Lal asleep in her arms. Murlidhar was alert in Hari's lap, watching trees swirl as the train passed them. Murli is a saint, Manki had begun to say. He is not perturbed by heat or cold, light or dark, or the deafening sounds of ricksha horns at Sat Matha, because his mind is busy contemplating Raamji. Hari had accepted this, and even helped perpetuate the idea when customers asked why the boy looked so passive in the shop. Now Murli watched the land wither away with the same indifference. There were fewer trees, and those that stood were stunted. Fields were greyer; sky was intruding into land. They were approaching Shekhavati, where Raamji had placed them out of spite to await one anxious crop of bajra every year. Food fit for cattle, they said in Bengal.

On the bench opposite theirs sat three men in dhotis, khadi kurtas and Gandhi caps: the livery of the Congress Party. They watched Hari with interest, then asked where he was from. He hesitated before answering. 'Rampura, in Shekhavati.'

'Is that Jaipur territory?'

Hari said it perhaps was. He did not remember which *Thikana* lay in which State. As a child, he had been told that he owed allegiance to the Thakur of Nawalgarh, who paid tribute to the rulers of Shekhavati, who in turn were vassals to the Maharaja of Jaipur. But he did not know who the current Maharaja was.

'They do not like us in Jaipur,' the men said.

The train passed Loharu and quickly crossed a small bridge over a stream. With a pounding heart, Hari realized that this was the riverbed he had crossed on his camel thirty-seven years ago. He was now in Shekhavati.

It turned out the men belonged to the Jaipur Praja Mandal, which was allied with the Congress Party against the Maharaja of Jaipur. They began to recruit Hari to their cause vigourously. Having said he was from Rampura, he could not now claim indifference, and allowed them their harangue. Water drunk from Gandhiji's hands cured polio and the pox, they said. When Gandhiji was in jail, the doors had opened by themselves and the guards had fallen asleep—as they had for Bhagwan Krishna—and the English judge who sentenced him had seen his wife and child die within the week.

'I have never seen Gandhiji but my son has,' said Hari. 'He is a barrister in Kalkatta.'

This made no impression on the men. They launched into a diatribe against the Maharaja of Jaipur. Hari was uncomfortable with such talk, and he sensed Durga's nervousness. They were in Shekhavati, which meant they were in the State of Jaipur. Was it wise to speak thus? Why did it matter that the Maharaja had spent a lakh on his wife's toilette in Paris? If the Maharaja was extravagant, that meant profits for some fortunate banias. And if the Maharaja did not spend, who would in this poor State of Jaipur? Who in Shekhavati could buy anything? You only had to look out of the window—such land would never yield wealth.

They were approaching Chirawa. Parmeshwari's family still lived there. So did Janardhan, unless he had returned to Calcutta. Hari was not meant to revisit those memories. Why had he come to Shekhavati? He wished the Addha train would somehow turn around and go back to Delhi.

As if in response, the train slowed down and came to a stop in the desert. They were a mile from Chirawa. A Jaipur police guard—in full uniform, with a starched turban twice as large as his head—walked down the car. The Jaipur Praja Mandal men hurriedly removed their caps and fell silent. The boys had all woken up. They stared at the desert in wonder, having never seen a khejra tree. Durga peered out of the window and discovered the problem. Their car—the second in the Addha train—had become detached from the first. The engine and the first car had continued, unaware of the decoupling.

The Praja Mandal men were greatly agitated at the news. They were on their way to a meeting in Sikar and a delay would be very inconvenient.

'I will ask the policeman who just went by,' Durga said.

'I will come too,' said Garib Das.

Hari forbade this. Durga walked down the car, alone, and got off the train—he had to jump off because there was no embankment. Hari heard him speak to the policeman outside. Then he came to the window and said, 'The engine has reversed itself. I see the smoke.'

'Come back inside in the train,' Hari said. 'It is too hot to be standing in the sun.'

He asked Lakshmi's Ma to hand out the rotis they had bought in Delhi. The boys ate. He settled down to wait while the Praja Mandal men fidgeted. Unlike them, he was in no hurry to push further into Shekhavati.

A sudden jolt broke his reverie. The engine had arrived, pushing the first car before it, and the two cars had been rejoined. Someone shouted outside. Hari peered out of the window. The Jaipur policeman was running toward the engine, arms flailing. He stopped short and let out a cry, and a strange silence descended on the train. Men were walking about, talking in whispers.

'Why don't they climb in?' the Praja Mandal men asked in exasperation. 'Are we not ready to go?'

Hari leaned out of the window and looked toward the first car, where a crowd had formed. The engine stood still, belching clouds of smoke. Where the second car met the first, a dozen men stared at something on the ground. It was a mangled corpse.

For years afterwards, Hari would remember this first view of that corpse, and the immediate realization that it was Durga's. And he would ask himself why he had not been more insistent that Durga climb back into the train. The policeman was the only one who saw what happened. He swore that Durga had been fully alert when the first car rammed into the second. He had shouted at the man standing on the tracks, he said, but the man had not budged as if he *wanted* the cars to smash him. They had to disconnect the cars and move them apart to extricate the body.

The boys inside the train had now heard the news. Hari put his hands over his ears to drown the wailing. Amidst the tears, he was to remember, years later, that Murlidhar had gazed at his father's dismembered body as calmly as if he were looking at a khejra bush.

They took the body to Chirawa on a camel cart. Hari sat in the back, his heart deadened by pain. The boys clustered around the shrouded corpse, some crying and some dazed. The Praja Mandal men climbed aboard too, as did the policeman.

'Did you know he was going to do this?' the policeman asked as soon as they started.

Hari turned viciously on him. 'He was lost in thought! He did not see the engine because it came from the left. His left eye...'

'How old was he?'

Hari broke down. 'Not yet twenty-eight, with a wife and three sons and a daughter. And six brothers and two sisters...'

'I do not need details of the family.'

Hari looked up sharply, but the policeman had already jumped off the cart. His task was complete—the details that mattered had been noted on paper. It was the Praja Mandal men who stayed with him, helped unload the body at a stream near Chirawa, wrapped it in a cotton dhoti, found a pandit, a barber and a chandal, negotiated rates with them and arranged the cremation. The barber shaved the heads of all three sons—Gangadhar, Bansidhar and Murlidhar—as well as the four brothers. Hari shaved his head too, though the pandit said he was not required to. The chandal collected firewood, the pandit did a puja. Gangadhar was too distraught to discharge his duties. When the eldest son is infirm or unavailable, said the Shastras, the youngest may perform the last rites. So it was Murlidhar who circled the pyre and lit it. They watched the flames for hours, seven boys with shaven heads. Lakshmi's Ma was curled into a ball on the riverbank.

Hari recalled Master Bholaram's lesson. Why did a man crave a son? Because a son was a *putra*, said the Shastras. And who was a putra? *Puut traayate saha*—he who protects you from the hell of *puut* by performing your last rites. Durga had three sons, but the one who had protected him from *puut* was the one who would never sit in Durga's shop nor beget children, and who had not shed a tear at his father's death.

They had had their tonsures in Shekhavati after all, if not in the manner hoped. Such was Raamji's wish. True, their hair would not be presented to Shyam Baba at the shrine in Khatu. It lay in bunches on the riverbank where the wind would sweep it away, but it would remain in Shekhavati.

The three Praja Mandal men stood respectfully at a distance. Perhaps they are hoping for a contribution to their Praja Mandal, thought Hari sourly.

They spent the night in Chirawa. Hari did not inform Parmeshwari's family, and did not seek out Janardhan. All night he walked about the town like a ghost, seeing Durga's image in every shadow, wondering again and again how a man of twenty-eight could fail to see a slow-moving car approach him. What could possibly have been on his mind? The policeman was lying, of course. True, Durga bore the burden of Bansi and Murli, but was not Gangadhar compensation enough for those two? Had Durga not known that Hari would look after those two as long as he lived? No, it was nothing he *did* but who he *was*. Three days after his birth, the Bengali doctor had saved him from yellowness but not his destiny. Even in the jute press, the hammer had spared Gopi and Tribhuvan and chosen to fall on Durga's head. The right occipital lobe, the doctor had said, had damaged his left eye. It was as if the Addha train had known about the left eye. It had crept up on him surreptitiously after choosing its direction. What yellowness in infancy and the train in the jute press had left undone, the Addha had completed. Maybe he had wanted to die, as the policeman claimed, but only because he knew he had to... By dawn, Hari had convinced himself that it was his fault. He had known he was not to return to Shekhavati, yet he had. Durga had paid the price—the same Durga whom Parmeshwari had remembered with her last breath. He had taken care of Durga indeed.

Returning to the railway station, where his children slept on a white sheet—a morgue of bald corpses, he thought—he lifted Murlidhar in his arms and vowed never to abandon him or his brother Bansidhar. A curious peace descended on him and lasted through the return trip to Bogra. Raamji had already shot his arrow. His quiver was empty, at least for now. A man who had already lost a son was invulnerable.

Arriving at Sat Matha, they looked like a band of travelling sadhus because of their shaven heads. One by one, they climbed up to the verandah. Manki looked at them approvingly and scolded Lakshmi's Ma, who was crying. 'This is not an occasion for lament. The boys have had their tonsure. You will no longer have to braid their hair every morning. I trust you took good care of Mohan Lal?'

Still crying, Lakshmi's Ma handed Mohan Lal to his mother and collapsed on the floor. Kaushalya and Shanti came bounding out of the room and laughed to see so many bald heads. 'Look at Murli's shining dome! Gariba Bhaiya has a birthmark we never saw before.'

Shanti was puzzled to see that Hari had shaved. 'Did Babuji get a tonsure too?'

Only then did Manki ask, 'Where is Durga?'

Hari stood still, tears in his eyes. A corner of Gayatri's sari was visible behind a door—she was too modest to present herself immediately upon his arrival. He saw his sons and grandsons around him, all suddenly silent. Then he sat down and wept like a child.

That evening, he waited for a long time at Gayatri's door. When he sensed that she had noticed, he walked into the room. She stood up hastily, pretending to be caught unawares—even in grief, he noted, she observed the rules of propriety. She had cried silently all afternoon while Manki had beaten her chest, smashed her bangles and pulled at her hair. It was as if Manki had been widowed while Gayatri had merely lost a brother. Now she stood before him, face fully exposed—a widow has no use for false modesty—and her eyes meeting his as if they were equals. The frankness of her gaze embarrassed him, and he was almost unable to say what he had planned. 'You are my daughter, as Durga was my son.'

Her tears flowed freely—she did not turn away or shield her eyes.

'Raamji has blessed you with three sons. Gangadhar is almost… how old is he?'

'The eleventh is upon him.'

'In a few years he will take over the hosiery store. But you must not think your son is the one who will look after you, for you still have a father. I will take care of your sons, and I will marry off your daughter as I will marry off my own.'

Sobbing, she sank to the floor. Hari thought she was trying to touch his feet. He took a step back, shocked. At twenty-seven, she was only eight years younger than Manki. Garib Das, his brothers and his sisters already regarded her as their mother. Now, with her face exposed in a plain white sari that did not cover the head, she had superseded Manki, perhaps even him. He left the room.

That evening, the sight of Gayatri in widow's garb set the children crying. Ishwar Das and Mohan Lal were too young to realize what had happened, and Gayatri's sudden transformation was, to them, the tragedy it was meant to mark.

The next few days brought more pain, as Hari had to contend with the lament of Nanuram and Chaman Lal, who broke down completely, recounting the time he had run from Raja Bazar to Sat Matha with an unconscious Durga in his arms, trailed by Gopi and Tribhuvan. Hari was irritated. Who was Chaman Lal to share a father's grief? How could he possibly understand? It was even more painful when shopkeepers in Sat Matha came by to express regrets—their social obligation complete, they would go back to their shops and haggle with the next customer.

It was only then, a week after he had returned to Bogra, that he noticed the missing cow. Normally, the stairwell that led up to the verandah was blocked by a bed of cowdung, and everyone had to jump over it to climb the stairs. Garib Das often complained of the stains on his dhoti, and Hari would remind him that cowdung was purer than ghee, that a stain formed by it was to be treasured. Now, the cowdung had dried and the cow was nowhere to be seen. Hari asked Nanuram, but he had spent all his time in the hosiery store. Chaman Lal was too distraught to be quizzed. Manki and Gayatri had not stepped out of the house at all, and the man in the goshala charged with feeding the cow said he had not seen her for days.

Sitting in his shop and looking at the stake to which the cow had been tied, a revolting thought rose in his mind—the nawab's butcher had taken her away to the Nawabbari. He had a vision of the Chhappaniya, of a boy running through the tibbas calling for Tara, whom he knew his father had given away to a Musalman butcher. His father had sinned in a time of scarcity, when women sold children for a ser of bajra. He had sinned in Bengal, land of rivers, beels, Aman, Aush and Boro. Yet what was he to do now? A bania is not a Rajput, they said in Shekhavati—he does not ride horses or shoot muskets, he merely buys and sells; he does not forcibly recover his cow, he pays to bring her back. Whose help could he seek? But of course, Mangiram was the nawab's biggest creditor—surely his voice would be heard.

He opened the cash box and withdrew from it the neatly folded petition that Tribhuvan had written for him. With the paper in his pocket and Murlidhar in his arms, he hurried to Fateh Ali Bajar, where Mangiram was seated in his shop exactly as Hari had seen him years ago.

'I heard about Durga,' Mangiram said softly.

'That is not why I have come. I want you to take me to the Nawabbari.'

Mangiram was surprised. 'Have you become a creditor to the Nawabzada?'

Hari thought of the books that Tribhuvan had bought for Mohammad Ali in Calcutta. 'Yes. But I do not wish to collect on my debts. I have a business proposal for him, regarding his cows.'

Mangiram sighed. 'I hear the cows when they are slaughtered—the nawab's cow shed is not far from here. But what a Musalman does inside his house...'

'You are his biggest creditor, are you not?'

'When a man owes you a thousand, he is in your power. When he owes you a lakh, it is he who holds power over you.'

'You said the Nawabzada was Hindu-minded.'

'We are banias, Hariya. We do not ride horses...'

'I know, I know! But I do not want to shoot anyone. I merely want to submit a letter.'

'All right, but nothing will come of it.' Turning to Murlidhar, Mangiram asked 'Is this Durga's son? How old is he?'

'Five.'

'What a well-behaved child! He has not said a word since you came in. My daughters are only eight but they would have run into the road by now.'

They walked to the Nawabbari and were let inside on account of Mangiram. Not much had changed: growling Alsatian dogs, gardens and orchards—pineapple, guava and jackfruit; steps leading to the Karatoya, boats moored along the bank. Inside the mansion, Hari stopped before the picture of Mozelle Cohen, the Yehudi woman with whom Nawab Sobhan had had a son. Recently, that son had been embroiled in a dispute with the Nawabzada over the nawab's estate. Had this Yehudi woman been victimized by the nawab, Hari wondered, as Shylock had been by Antonio?

'We must hurry,' Mangiram said. 'They do not like people to tarry in the audience hall.'

Outside the retainer's office, Hari noted the porcelain water filter he had seen years ago. It was still leaking. During the Chhappaniya, men would have licked that water off the floor.

The retainer had aged. He was annoyed to see Mangiram. A Monday was not appropriate for creditors, he said. Had not Mangiram received instructions to present himself the following Thursday? Hands folded, Mangiram informed him that he had not come to present bills, but a letter.

'For Nawabzada Altaf Ali,' said Hari, handing the letter to the man. 'In English, written by my son Tribhuvan Lal, LLB, a barrister in Kalkatta. He is a good friend of the Nawabzada's son Mohammad Ali.'

The retainer scanned the letter indifferently.

Hari continued, 'What a great example the Nawabzada would set if he were to stop eating beef! And think of the profits!'

'You may go now,' said the retainer.

'You will ask the Nawabzada to respond?' Hari asked eagerly.

'Yes, yes.'

They were ushered out. 'Do not forget to mention my son Tribhuvan Lal, who is a good friend of Mohammad Ali.'

They walked back through the gardens. 'I do not think he read the letter,' said Hari, crestfallen.

'You have done your duty,' Mangiram said soothingly.

'Show me the cow shed,' Hari said.

'Which cow shed?'

'Where the nawab keeps his cows. Where he slaughters them. You said it was along the boundary wall...'

'We cannot go there. There may be butchers about.'

'I want to see if their hands tremble when they bring the knife down on her neck.'

Reluctantly, Mangiram led the way to the shed. *It looks much like a goshala*, Hari thought, *except these cows will all be murdered*. They seemed to look at him with hope, beseeching him. He felt weak. It was as if his whole family was tied there, awaiting the butcher.

There were drops of water on his arm. Murlidhar was crying. Seated in the crook of Hari's arm, he gazed at the cows passively and his eyes ran with tears.

'That boy is a saint,' Mangiram whispered.

Hari trembled: Manki had been right about Murlidhar. Like the sages in the Shastras, he did not use words without cause. When he opened his mouth, it was only to chant 'Raam Raam'. He did not play the games children do, did not waste his time in trivial pursuits such as toys, kites, football or cricket. He had no interest in other children. Often, he pushed his brothers away when they approached him. He sat still and stared for hours like a sadhu, rocking himself back and forth in the contemplation of Raamji. Once, Hari found him banging his head against the wall, as if overwhelmed by human suffering.

'Let us leave this Nawabbari,' Hari said to Mangiram, 'or the pain will take the boy's life.'

Over the next few days, Gopi and Tribhuvan were sent

messages about Durga's death. Gopi did not respond; Tribhuvan came from Calcutta. Father and son sat in the shop. The doors were barred. Hari asked Tribhuvan a few perfunctory questions about his law practice before lapsing into gloom. Tribhuvan said, 'At least he died in Shekhavati, and his sons were there to perform the last rites.'

Hari nodded, having consoled himself with that thought many times.

'There is a Marwari Association in Calcutta,' said Tribhuvan.

'What of it?'

'They say that a Marwari woman who loses her husband in her youth should be allowed to find another.'

It took Hari a moment to grasp what Tribhuvan meant. He was baffled rather than annoyed. 'Who would say such a thing? I love Gayatri as I love my daughters, and she will never know the difference.'

'A father is not a substitute for a husband.'

'I do not know what thoughts swirl inside your head, Tribhuvan Lal, but do not be spilling them in Bogra. And do not associate with such men in Kalkatta.'

'She is only twenty-seven.'

'Sati Savitri was not much older in the *Puraan*, and she did not abandon her husband on his death.' First the boy gives away his dowry for earthquake relief, thought Hari, now he comes to Bogra with absurd ideas in his head. 'What would you have me do? Ask Nanuram to look for suitable boys? What will he say to their fathers? "Here is Harilalji's daughter-in-law, who has three sons and a daughter. Would you consider her as a bride for your son?" And how many sons is the bridegroom allowed to have? Will all the sons and daughters live together in my house? How old must the bridegroom be for a middle-aged bride of twenty-seven?'

'You were nearly thirty when you married again.'

Hari gasped in disbelief. Raamji had given him many sons but taken the pleasure of fatherhood away. Gopi was a scoundrel; this Tribhuvan, his head turned by his law degree, scorned his father for re-marrying when all Hari had done was obey his father's wishes; only Durga... Ah, Durga! Why did Raamji have to take him away?

'I see you have become a full man now that you are a barrister,' he said coldly. 'Leave me alone to mourn my son.'

That afternoon, Tribhuvan left for Calcutta.

15

It took little time for Gangadhar to replace Durga in the hosiery store. Only ten, he had already been sitting in the store with his father. He knew how to identify fabric, extol its virtues, quote a price and haggle with customers. What he could not do—take inventory or keep accounts, or travel to Dhaka to buy stock—fell to Nanuram.

Fakir Chand began to divide his time between the hosiery store and the jute press, where Chaman Lal still sat all day, growing ever older, doing little, watching jute rates and quantities decline.

Meanwhile, Hari was increasingly worried about Garib Das. Whenever he peeked into the cigarette shop he smelled tobacco, which Garib Das explained as being the usual smell of a cigarette store as if Hari knew nothing about the business. Although he himself smoked infrequently, he had a horror of cigarettes, placing them in the same category as meat or alcohol. He was also concerned about the expense. What kind of a bania smoked his own stock?

Nanuram assured him that this was a passing phase. 'He is only eighteen.'

'Daulatramji walked from Jaipur to Mirzapur when he was eleven. Even I left Rampura at the age of twelve.'

'Boys take longer to mature nowadays. This is Bengal.'

Then there was the problem of Garib Das's obsession with English cotton. He would present himself in the hosiery store whenever Nanuram returned from Dhaka and select a couple of Manchester dhotis. Hari had never allowed his sons to try on their stock—they had to make do with desi dhotis. When Garib Das complained that they were coarse, Hari had said, 'Measure both dhotis. Each is 180 inches by 44 inches; each covers the legs; each lasts the same number of years; one is as comfortable as the other; one costs a rupee, the other half as much. Which fool would buy Manchester cotton?'

But buy they did; the store had become very profitable. Hari put it down to Gangadhar's presence. This was proof, if any were needed, that a responsible, obedient boy who spoke little, rose early and sat quietly in the shop would be blessed by the goddess Lakshmi.

After the rains in 1939, Tribhuvan made an unexpected visit to Bogra. He came in a black coat and dhoti, as always, and was alone—his wife Kusum did not accompany him.

Following the disagreement with his father over Gayatri, they had barely spoken for three years.

Gayatri made much of him. They were the same age; she had never covered her face before him. Being younger than Durga, he was free to banter with her. He thought nothing of entering her room without warning. While he brought simple toys—plastic cricket bats—for Bansidhar and Murlidhar, and nothing at all for his brothers, Gayatri received a beautiful silk sari. She was too sensible to wear it, and Hari berated him for the impropriety.

'It is white,' Tribhuvan pointed out, and even in that assertion Hari saw effrontery.

'It is silk. Even if it were khadi spun by Gandhiji himself, it would be improper for her to accept gifts in her state.'

He saw that his son was about to retort but had restrained himself. At least he keeps up appearances, Hari thought, and we must be grateful for what we get. Then Tribhuvan began to speak of the war in Europe, as if that were the most pressing matter at hand. Surely he had not come all the way from Calcutta to talk about the sahibs' war?

'The grain market in Bogra is stable but there is no money in jute any more—everyone wants plastic sacks,' Hari said. '*That* is what troubles me. It does not matter that Hitler is in England.'

'Poland, Babuji, not England.'

Hari steered the conversation in a more suitable direction. 'You have been married for five years. Why have I received no news of a grandson?'

A smile broke over Tribhuvan's face. 'That is why I have come to Bogra. Last week, Raamji blessed us with a boy.'

'And you talk of Hitler and England!'

That evening, a pandit was called. A brass plate was beaten. Laddus were sent all over Marwari Para. In every house it was announced, 'Barrister Babu has had a son in Kalkatta.'

Tribhuvan's presence in Bogra made Hari anxious. He spoke more freely than he should have and thought nothing of getting into arguments with customers. His talk of the Congress Party and its campaigns was uninteresting and his opinions often scandalous. He spent too much time upstairs in the verandah, bantering with Gayatri in a voice loud enough to be heard all over Sat Matha, when he should have been sitting in the shop with Hari. True, it was usual for a man to be playful with his elder brother's wife, but surely the brother's death had changed what was appropriate? Gayatri was probably too proper to offer him encouragement, but too timid to point out the impropriety.

When Tribhuvan chose to come down to the shop, he was immediately surrounded by the children, who could not get enough of his stories. He had brought along a radio. Garib Das was asked to explain what was being announced. Having never done well in school, Garib Das stuttered and stammered until Tribhuvan interpreted the announcement. This was Berlin Radio; the sahibs had been defeated in Poland; they would soon run away from Bengal.

'Where will they go?' Gangadhar asked.

'To England, of course.'

'But Bengal is their home.'

Tribhuvan laughed. Everyone taunted Gangadhar, who fell silent.

'I will leave the radio here, but do not keep it tuned to Berlin Radio by day. The police do not like that.'

Shortly after Tribhuvan returned to Calcutta—to Hari's great relief—a barber arrived unexpectedly from Santahar, and delivered his message with a formality that amused Hari, reminding him of the invitation he had sent for Gopi's wedding.

'Gopi Chand Tibrewal, son of Harilal Tibrewal, touches your feet and invites you to his house for the wedding of his daughter Pushpa…'

'How old is Pushpa?' Hari asked.

The barber was irritated, both at the interruption and the impropriety. 'How should I know? What kind of a man do you think I am?'

'All right. Give me the date.'

Gangadhar was fetched from the hosiery store. He knew Pushpa's age—fourteen—because she was a year older than him. Hari was deeply troubled. He remembered Pushpa as a child of three when Gopi's bed was being loaded on to the bullock cart bound for Santahar. How had the years passed? Who else had grown up while he was looking away? Pushpa's sisters, three of them, were all on the cusp of womanhood, all awaiting marriage. Gangadhar had turned thirteen before his very eyes and he had not noticed, not to speak of Gariba, who was eighteen, and Fakir Chand, who was the same age as Pushpa.

He would go to the wedding. It was well understood in Shekhavati that disputes were suspended during births, deaths and weddings. Had not Gopi sent an invitation?

He spent the day in giddy anticipation, turning over in his head the scene that awaited him in Santahar. Gopi would ask for forgiveness; he would readily grant it. Sharda would offer cool water spiced with cumin—her sari pulled over her face, of course—and Pushpa would look shyly at him. Her sister Ahilya would bring him a plate of sweets, and the two younger girls would jump into his lap… But they were too old to be doing that, and perhaps they would not be so familiar, having never seen him.

By evening, his spirits had sunk. Climbing to the verandah, he was besieged by doubt. Gopi had chosen to send this invitation—the first communication from him in eleven years—for one obvious reason: when a man married his daughter off, he expected and received support from his father, unless the father was dead or insolvent. By all accounts, the oil depot had fared well. Santahar was on the main train route that cut across Bengal, north to south, making it easy to supply oil up and down the line, all the way to Calcutta. That, combined with the resources of Gopi's father-in-law, meant that Gopi could not be in need, but as Hari himself had taught his son, an opportunity was not to be wasted. Hari's first grandchild was being married off, and Gopi knew that his father would contribute to the dowry if invited.

He decided to send his children in his place. On the last day of Kartik, as Garib Das, Fakir Chand and Gangadhar prepared to leave for Santahar, he pulled Garib Das aside. 'Tell your brother that I am not well.'

'He will not believe me,' Garib Das said, and Hari sensed mockery. 'Everyone knows you were raised on Shekhavati grain…'

'Hold your tongue.' Barely eighteen, Hari thought irritably, and what cheek the boy has! This one would have to be watched… He pressed a small velvet bag into his son's hand. 'There are four gold ginnis in this. Tell Gopi Chand that this is the dowry I give to my first granddaughter.'

Garib Das turned away, and Hari's eyes narrowed in condemnation. The boy was wearing a Manchester dhoti. He had tried to conceal the fact—it was rumpled, and he no doubt meant to have it pressed in Santahar—but a man who owned a hosiery store would not be fooled. Very well, let him indulge himself. He was going to his niece's wedding, after all.

Until his sons returned three days later, Hari was in agony, torn between anger at Gopi's manipulative invitation and fear that his indifference would cast an evil eye on the wedding. It was with relief that he received news that the wedding was over. Pushpa had gone to her in-laws' house. She would return in a couple of days, and would live in Santahar for the next two years. Her father-in-law lived in a town named Watsonganj in Bihar. The English name confused Gangadhar. He said to Hari, 'Pushpa Bai's father-in-law lives in England. When can we visit her there?' Garib Das laughed, and Gangadhar was crushed when Watsonganj was brought back across the seas to neighbouring Bihar.

The three boys were full of praise for Gopi and Sharda—they had been made much of and given a servant of their own. Considering they represented the bride, not the groom, during the wedding, this was high honour indeed. Gopi is trying to make a point, Hari thought indignantly.

He discovered what the point was soon enough. After the guests had departed, Gopi had called Garib Das into his room. Apparently, he wanted to expand his oil business to Rangpur, seventy miles to the north. Garib Das narrated the conversation to Hari.

'He said, 'Raamji gave me daughters, not sons, and such a man cannot expand his shop. Who will lend a hand, and who will mind the shop after me? My father-in-law is eager to place a relative of his own in Rangpur. But why should I look to my in-laws when I have six brothers?' '

The proposal was simple and direct: Garib Das would get a third share in the Rangpur oil depot as a working partner. Gopi and his father-in-law would put up the money and become sleeping partners with a two-thirds share. The idea was distasteful to Hari.

'You have a home in Bogra. I do not want you to live in Rangpur.'

'But I will not live there. On most evenings, I could shut the depot and take the train to Santahar, then make the connection to Bogra.'

'You have your own cigarette store. Why must you work for Gopi?'

'I will be his partner, not his employee.'

'A *working* partner, without any capital in the business. He will control two-thirds. And you will gain little as the business grows. That is the difference between the Bengali and the Marwari: the Bengali prefers working for someone so he need not worry about jute prices; the Marwari wants to worry about jute prices so he may benefit when they rise.'

'The oil depot will be far more profitable than the cigarette store,' said Garib Das.

Hari knew this, of course, but had not expected Garib Das to say this. Did he not understand that one's own shop, however modest, was preferable to employment in another's? 'Tell Gopi you will go to Rangpur only if you become a full partner, with capital in the business.'

'Where will you get the money?'

'I will sell the mango orchard near the goshala.'

Garib Das began to travel to Rangpur every two days. When in Bogra, he now had little to do. He loitered about Sat Matha, went to the hosiery store, visited the jute press and found his way back to Sat Matha. Gradually, Hari began to notice changes in his son—hair slicked down with pomade, moustache trimmed neatly, cap tilted rakishly on the forehead, gold chain round the neck, kurta sleeves puffed up by a dhobi's steam iron, Manchester dhoti pleated in the front, and pointed Nagra shoes that were polished every day. To Hari's mind, well-oiled, neatly combed hair spoke of good breeding; it discouraged loose talk and reckless behaviour. On the other hand, pomade was a clear signal that the wearer was attempting to improve his appearance. What reason could a marriageable boy have to pay such attention to his looks, and how would that look to the fathers of prospective brides? After watching in dismay for months, Hari confronted his son. 'Why have you bought new shoes? Have your *Hunterwali* slippers been stolen?'

'*Hunterwali* isn't in fashion any more,' said Garib Das. 'People would laugh at me.'

Hari wondered who those people were. All around him, the staid shopkeepers of Sat Matha sat cross-legged in their shops, spent as little as possible on their clothes, and would not know what was in fashion if asked. Did Garib Das have friends in Rangpur who wasted time in frivolous pursuits? Had he fallen in with corrupting company? The boy had a natural proclivity to vulgar display. Hari only had to look away and Gariba would help himself to a Manchester dhoti from the hosiery store, while Gangadhar, and Durga before him, had displayed thousands of such dhotis to customers while wearing nothing but desi cotton themselves. For years, Gariba had been kept in check at Sat Matha. Now, released from his father's care, he had run amok.

When he had been going to Rangpur for a year, Garib Das presented Hari with a strange proposal. The Nawabzada's son, Mohammad Ali Bogra, wished to dispose of his German Opel car, and was willing to sell on favourable terms on account of his friendship with Tribhuvan Lal. 'He says that his friend's brother is like his own brother.'

'He is a Musalman and you are a Marwari,' Hari said sourly.

'He will accept two thousand and two hundred.'

'Do not say "thousand" carelessly. Use the proper term.'

Gariba shrugged. 'All right—twenty-two hundred.'

'Quoting the price correctly does not reduce it.'

'You will be the only Marwari in Bogra to own a car,' said Gariba. 'Even Tribhuvan Bhaiya does not have one in Calcutta.'

'Why would I need a car in Bogra? It is a small town. Fateh Ali Bajar is a five-minute walk from Sat Matha, Raja Bajar another five. All of Marwari Para can be crossed in fifteen minutes, and you have no reason to go outside it.'

'The railway station is further away, and there is luggage to be carried.'

'Take a ricksha. Why waste money on a car that needs petrol?'

But Garib Das would not be denied, and Hari was distraught. The name that had saved the boy's life ill-suited him. His obsession with the steel monster would wipe out the annual profit from the cigarette and grain shops. No doubt Mohammad Ali had found himself a willing victim in Garib Das, and was using his so-called friendship with Tribhuvan—what friendship could exist between a Musalman nawab and a Marwari bania?—to make a sale favourable to himself. 'Tell him we will pay fifteen-hundred.'

'He will not accept. He told me, 'I love this car, Gariba, and would not part with it for the world. But one cannot turn down an offer from a good friend. Had it been anyone else, I would have laughed in his face.'

Hari sighed. 'Let us wait for a week. We must not be rash when the amount is so large.'

In a few days, word had spread that Harilalji was buying the nawab's car. Fakir Chand and Gangadhar looked at him expectantly; Bansidhar asked about the car every evening; Shanti and Kaushalya jumped up and down as if they were already riding it. Manki muttered that Hari must be feeling very rich if he had agreed to buy a useless horse for two thousand rupees. Even Murlidhar interrupted his reverie to ask his grandfather, 'Do you think it could drive through a rice paddy?'

The car was already part of the family.

Mohammad Ali Bogra's driver brought the car to Sat Matha and parked it in front of the shop. The boys descended on it. Gangadhar came running from the hosiery store. Chaman Lal dragged himself from the jute press—he now walked with difficulty and used a stick—to gaze at it. Lakshmi's Ma stood in the verandah, the ball at her throat hanging through the metal grilles. Garib Das installed himself in the driver's seat and blew the horn so many times that Hari had to scold him for wasting the battery.

That morning, Garib Das had spent an hour with Mohammad Ali Bogra learning about the virtues of the new horse. As its master, he now held forth. '1935 Opel Olympia. All-steel body. Two-door convertible, 1.3 litre, 4-cylinder 24-horsepower engine. Can go 125 miles in an hour.' He made up the last claim because he could not remember what Mohammad Ali had said about speed. 'Imagine, we could drive to Calcutta in two hours!'

'Let us start it,' said Fakir Chand.

Garib Das brandished a large key in a leather-bound chain. Before he could insert it into the ignition, however, there was an interruption. Manki and Gayatri had come down to the road. Because they rarely left the verandah, there was sudden silence at their appearance. Gayatri carried a brass plate piled with puja paraphernalia: roli paste, grains of rice, water, marigolds. Manki jabbed her finger at Garib Das. 'Get out of this machine.'

Startled, Garib Das complied.

'A Musalman owned this before you. Why did you jump in?'

She and Gayatri decorated the car with marigolds, stuck joss sticks in its crevices, sprinkled rice and ran fingers daubed in roli paste along its sides. A tilak was painted on the fender and a swastika in the lower left corner of the windshield. Finally, while the children stood with folded hands, an aarti was sung: a song in praise of Vishwakarma, Lord of Machines.

'You may touch the beast now,' said Manki.

'The seat looks soft,' said Gayatri.

Manki turned sharply to her daughter-in-law. 'Come away!'

Reluctantly, Gayatri followed her back up the stairs and into the verandah.

A new problem now became apparent. Garib Das did not know how to drive. The boys spent the afternoon sitting in the parked car, blowing its horn and acknowledging the stares of passers-by. The next day, Mohammad Ali Bogra lent them his driver, and they went riding through rice fields, skirting mango groves and splashing through beels created by the Karatoya downstream of Bogra. It had just rained. The dust had settled and the air was cool. Garib Das sat in the front, next to the driver. As the car navigated pools near the west bank of the river, he stood up unsteadily and declared, 'We will go for a ride every day—to Santahar, Rangpur, perhaps Dhaka, and, one day, Calcutta.'

In three days, the car was out of petrol. It was discovered that, because of the war in Europe, petrol could be bought only through coupons, which were difficult to obtain.

'Mohammad Ali Bogra will get us coupons,' Garib Das told

his brothers. 'Until he does, we will leave the car parked outside the house. Let people see it and know we have one.'

And that was where the car remained, an eyesore for Hari but a matter of pride for his sons, who spent hours gazing at it and never failed to point it out to customers.

He turned his attention to a more pressing matter: a match for his daughter Shanti, who was past thirteen. He did not want to be caught off-guard as he had been with Pushpa. A man with many children had to be ever vigilant: every time his attention wandered, someone came of age. Unfortunately, he had no experience finding husbands for daughters. He learned from Mangiram—himself the father of two daughters who would soon be marriageable—that a first daughter had to be married off in pomp to make the proper impression. Moreover, a man with seven sons and only two daughters would be expected to spend much on his daughter's wedding. What else would he do with the dowry he collected through seven sons?

A match was found. The family lived in Kushtia, a town on the river Gorai 120 miles away. The family was wealthy and the groom, Nagar Mal, was an only child. He had been adopted by his father who, it turned out, was also an adopted child. This troubled Hari a little, but his contacts assured him there was nothing inauspicious about this. Besides, the family enjoyed a status in Kushtia that Hari could only dream of in Bogra: a zamindari of a hundred acres of rice and jute, dozens of mango orchards and a grand mansion on the Gorai. In addition, many of the shops in Kushtia had been rented from the family, which also owned grain stores in Dhaka that brought good rent. Their haveli in Kushtia had been constructed in the Shekhavati style: it had forty rooms with mosaic floors in each, and a cow shed in the back. Hari did not bother asking his contact 'What do they deal in?' because a family with such resources had no need to operate a shop—the rent from their properties was sufficient.

After the wedding had been finalized, he received a message from Shanti's father-in-law, saying he had heard of Hari's interest in cows and wished to share his own efforts in that regard. 'In the shed behind my haveli,' he wrote, 'I keep the best bulls imported from Germany and England. In time, they will produce cows that will yield more than ten ser of milk every day. After the wedding, I will send you a bull for the goshala in Bogra...'

Troubled by this, Hari wrote on his slate—'There is no shortage of bulls in Bengal. In Shekhavati, Nagauri bullocks can pull a cart from Rampura to Chirawa—almost 50 miles—overnight. Why must we bring bulls from England? Why engage in wilful *varnasankar*? Granted, cows born of this miscegenation will yield more milk, but they will calve only thrice in their lifetimes, not the eight times our cows do. Their offspring will provide neither good bulls nor bullocks. Everyone knows that foreign bulls cannot withstand the heat of Bengal. Their necks and shoulders are smooth—the plough will slip off their shoulders. Without good bullocks, how will the Bengali plough his land? If Raamji wished for foreign bulls to mate with our cows, he would have arranged for their birth in Bengal.'

Propriety demanded that he not raise the matter before the wedding, so he decided to bring this up with Shanti's father-in-law after her first child.

Two weeks before the wedding, another message was received: a request that the wedding not be ostentatious, given the 'agitation in Bengal'. Being the secretary of the local Congress committee, Shanti's father-in-law kept himself busy in Party affairs, and it behooved him, he said, not to make a great display of wealth at such a time.

Hari acquiesced, and even managed to summon admiration for this restraint. Here was a man who owned a hundred acres of land marrying off his only son, and he deferred to the state of Bengal and a war in faraway England.

The decorations at Sat Matha were modest: marigold garlands hung from the verandah and a newly painted shop-front. Sweets prepared for the wedding contained no almonds. The wedding party consisted of only fifty guests from Kushtia who came by boat and train. Nagar Mal was perhaps a year younger than Shanti—the thirteenth was upon him—but Hari had not inquired closely.

Tribhuvan Lal arrived from Calcutta with his wife Kusum and six-month-old son, Arjun. Kusum had spent all her life in Calcutta and this was her first trip to a mofussil area in East Bengal. The children made much of her. Gayatri was deferential. The only one unimpressed was Manki, who took one look at her and turned away, whispering, 'Balanjogi, Balanjogi...'

Tribhuvan was shocked. Fortunately, Kusum did not understand the word; it was old Shekhavati usage for a woman 'worth burning', and few in Bengal now remembered it. Even Tribhuvan knew its meaning only because Manki used it frequently.

The wedding fire was lit in the middle of the road, blocking all of Sat Matha. Tribhuvan had brought three sacks of green coconuts from Calcutta. Hari hired a man to stand outside Harilal & Sons, next to the Opel car, and serve them. The Opel had been decorated for the wedding but no one knew how to drive it, so it stayed where it was and the coconuts were piled up in the rear seat. Picking the coconuts up, one by one, the man chopped off their heads and handed them around. Everyone commented on the sweetness of the water. Seated behind Shanti at the wedding fire, Hari realized that his Kushtia relative may have had more than the state of Bengal in mind: there was much ill-will about, and a Marwari making a display of his wealth might attract unwanted attention. There was the book by Prafulla Chandra Ray that Tribhuvan's father-in-law had mentioned in Calcutta. There had been some violence in Calcutta. And he had not forgotten what Janardhan said about the Bengali attitude to Marwaris—we come to Bengal with a pot and a blanket and steal the land away from its people... The days when a man from Shekhavati hired an elephant to take a groom to his bride's house were gone. He had been wise to heed the counsel of Shanti's father-in-law. On seeing him in a khadi kurta and dhoti beside the wedding fire, no one would guess that this man entered a haveli of forty rooms every night, or that he owned bulls imported from Germany. Also, it had been a good idea to invite Mohammad Ali Bogra, who had come at Tribhuvan's urging and now sat in a chair a hundred feet from the wedding fire, where Hari had placed him to avoid any unpleasantness that may arise because of contact with a Musalman. Everyone said that Nawab Sobhan, Mohammad Ali's great-grandfather, had been Hindu-minded, as was Nawabzada Altaf Ali, his father. Surely Mohammad Ali would continue the tradition.

Shanti's husband Nagar Mal was a short, gentle boy—just the type to keep Shanti happy for the rest of her life. He spoke little, and then only to answer questions asked of him. Hari had always been suspicious of the flashy types who dazzled everyone with their style but came to no good, unable to run stable shops or keep their families solvent.

The wedding passed off peacefully. Bansidhar had a seizure just before the bride and groom sat down at the fire, but the groom's side had already been warned of the possibility, so no one was embarrassed. Murlidhar sat with Hari, staring calmly at the marriage fire. People commented approvingly on his manners, and Hari silently accepted the praise, not wishing to elaborate.

The guests left immediately after the wedding to take advantage of low tide on the Gorai, which would have to be crossed in the last leg of their return journey. As they said farewell, Shanti's father-in-law pointed to the Opel. 'Does this motor car run?'

'We do not have petrol coupons,' said Hari, not wishing to mention the other obstacle—that no one knew how to drive it.

'Coupons can be had, war or no war,' said Shanti's father-in-law, 'but the car should be hidden away or evil eyes will pursue you.'

Hari was apologetic. 'It is an indulgence, I know. I do not like it one bit, but my son Gariba will not yield. You know how young men are these days.'

'How old is Garib Das?'

'The twentieth is upon him.'

Shanti's father-in-law chuckled. 'Find him a bride. He will forget about the car.'

Hari laughed aloud. Being the bride's father, he had expressed amusement at every wisecrack emanating from his Kushtia guests that evening, and was rather satisfied with his performance.

The guests departed, taking Shanti with them. Although he had prepared for the occasion, he found himself overwhelmed when Shanti entered the train and disappeared from view. She would be back in a couple of days, to live in Bogra for at least two more years, but he felt he had lost his daughter. This was all the more odd because he had stopped noticing his daughters as soon as they were born. Aside from finding pandits to teach them the Bhagavad Gita and ensuring that Gayatri trained them in the kitchen, he hardly spoke to them. When they turned ten, Shanti and Kaushalya had both become inhibited in his presence and he accepted this as a sign of good manners. Now, with his daughter seated in a train amidst other women, he was shocked to find tears in his eyes. It was dark; no one noticed.

Night fell on Sat Matha. Exhausted, the boys fell asleep. Lakshmi's Ma lay curled up in a corner of the verandah, snoring. From Gayatri's room, he heard the clicking of her spinning wheel and was filled with admiration. Here was a woman who had just supervised a wedding. Now, instead of going to bed, she had resumed her daily routine. She knew nothing about the Congress Party or its spinning programme. Yet, was Gandhiji himself as regular with his spinning?

He peered into Manki's room: in spite of the heat she had covered herself from head to toe with a white sheet. She looked like a corpse. Her Raam Raam books lay open on the bed. Back in the verandah, he looked down at Sat Matha. The Opel stood alone, attended by weary dogs. I should move that car, he reminded himself. Every day that it stands here it breeds ill-will... What great folly, and what shame was his to have yielded to Gariba's fetish!

He was woken by the sound of splashing water. It was dawn. Sat Matha was silent. The dogs had disappeared. He had slept for four hours, no more. He rarely rose so early—the hour was reserved for the women's ablutions. Indeed, the hand-pump in the verandah was being used—Gayatri was bathing. He shut his eyes immediately, ashamed. She was fully clothed, but imagine her embarrassment if she were to discover he was awake! He lay on his back and looked up, marvelling that, in six years of sleeping in the verandah, he had never before been woken by the women in the morning.

His thoughts settled on Gayatri. She had been spinning when he went to sleep. Now, as soon as she finished her bath, she would light lamps in the kitchen shrine, sing bhajans, shake Lakshmi's Ma awake. How much could a woman do by herself? Did she not need a moment to reflect on the tragedy of her life? She was thirty, perhaps thirty-one. Her husband had been taken from her and two of her three sons had been cursed by Raamji. What moved such a woman to rise early and sing bhajans to Him? What had He given her in return? A cow is a mother, Master Bholaram had said, because she gives and does not ask—milk, dung, urine and, on death, her very bones. Here was a mother in his own house, watching his children, giving and not asking.

Silently, he turned again to watch her. She was squatting next to the pump with a bucket and a pot, with which she poured water repeatedly over her head. It flowed down smoothly, plastering her sari to her skin. Her blouse had fused with her bosom, tracing its outline. He was suddenly filled with an intense desire to touch, grasp, grab, pull, squeeze. How had he never noticed it? He had never thought of her as attractive, but widowhood had been kind to her. She had flowered in abstinence—becoming fuller, more contented and more desirable. He could trace the softness of her whole body in the dim light. It was as if she sat naked before him, inviting. How could she not know he was watching? Ah, she had bathed every morning for six years, patiently awaiting the one dawn when his eyes should be open! She understood him as no one did. We have both been celibate, he told her silently, I for six years and you for four. We have both suffered!

Wild thoughts raced through this head. Manki was certainly in her morning trance.

The boys would not be awake for another hour. No one would see, no one would know... He looked at Lakshmi's Ma. The lump at her throat rose and fell with her breathing. Revolted, he turned away quickly.

He sensed that Gayatri had frozen next to the bucket. His cot had creaked when he turned away from Lakshmi's Ma. There was complete silence in the verandah. *She knows*, he thought in horror, *she knows*! Slowly, very slowly, he turned around with a pounding heart until he was facing the hand-pump. His eyes scanned the darkness. The pump lay still. The last trickle of water from its spout had stopped. She was gone.

He shut his eyes in panic. She had seen him, of course, or heard him. Shame overwhelmed him. In his fifty-three years, he had done nothing as execrable. Durga had been dead no more than four years, and here was his father... What demon had urged him to destroy himself? What had Tribhuvan said? A widow needs a husband, not a father. He began to cry silently. You have tested me, he said to Raamji, and I have failed. I will give eleven rupees to the Hanuman Temple, I will build temples in every town in Bengal, I will visit Ganga Sagar, Benares and Haridwar, I will feed a hundred and one pandits, I will give everything away to beggars and bhangis. What should I do to wipe the stain from my heart? Take good care of Durga, Parmeshwari had said. I have taken good care indeed... He curled himself up on the cot, wishing Yamaraj would send his messengers to take him away to Paataal, that dreaded netherworld, read him the list of his sins and condemn him to an eternity of torture.

16

The next two years were good for business on account of the war. Jute soared, sugar was rationed, petrol coupons were in short supply and dhotis were scarce. Even the grain shop, which had long ceased to be profitable, did well. Garib Das's oil depot in Rangpur thrived. A mattress was laid in the office and a servant hired to cook, so Garib Das could occasionally spend the night in Rangpur.

Although their relations were somewhat strained, Tribhuvan began to send postcards from Calcutta again—Tagore Babu had died, Netaji Subhas Bose had disappeared, and Marwaris in Calcutta had given more than three crores to the war relief fund. Some Marwari young men had even volunteered to fight. This made Hari chuckle: whoever heard of Marwari banias being recruited into the army?

'No one thinks the sahibs can hold out,' Tribhuvan wrote. 'If people see two dogs fighting in Harrison Road, the winner is immediately named Hitler, and the loser Churchill.'

In the hot month of Aashaadh there were riots near Bogra, followed by a flag march by the army. Without warning, a whole procession of soldiers came marching down the road. Shops were quickly closed. Garib Das arranged the children in a line in the verandah, from where they watched in wonder. Gayatri stood slightly behind them so she could see the soldiers without exposing herself. Possessing no such modesty, Lakshmi's Ma stared shamelessly, and even grinned. Hari pulled ajar the doors of Harilal & Sons to peer out. These were English soldiers, real sahibs from England, large and strong, dressed in impressive khaki. The dust kicked up by their boots hung over Sat Matha. No one stirred for minutes after they were gone.

There were reports of the army swooping down on villages to take young men away, because many had died in the war and more were needed. A tonga ran through Marwari Para. Three Bengalis sat behind the driver and shouted slogans, calling men to the army. They stopped at Sat Matha. Two of them jumped off and the third stood up in the tonga. He was neither man nor woman but a hijra. He wore a sari, like a woman, but his blouse hung loosely over a flat chest and a moustache sat on his upper lip. A crowd gathered. Using the tonga as a stage, the hijra sang and danced in Hindi, clapping as hijras do, thrusting his hips lewdly to the amusement of the crowd.

Come join the army, my dear recruit
Here you get a torn shoe, there a strong boot
Here you get dirty clothes, there a new suit
Here you get dry rotis, and there fresh fruit

The two men circled the crowd, pulling the young aside and offering eight-anna coins if they would come to the tonga to get their chests measured. A few did; the hijra's song continued. Hari watched from behind his cash box, aware that Fakir Chand was also watching from the cigarette store. Gangadhar had heard the news and come from Bara Gola. Ishwar Das and Mohan Lal had run to the tonga as soon as they saw the hijra.

Fakir Chand stepped into the road to get a better look. Hari hissed at him. 'Go back into your shop!'

Then he called back Ishwar Das and Mohan Lal too. The sahibs would not kidnap such young boys for their army, but hijras were known to be child-lifters.

'I want to get my chest measured,' eight-year-old Ishwar Das said.

'We want to become recruits,' said Mohan Lal, who was seven.

Hari chuckled. Everyone in Shekhavati knew the story of Jagat Seth, the richest Marwari in Bengal, who had financed Robert Clive's war against the Nawab of Bengal two hundred years ago. That was how a bania fought a war—by paying for it. 'The war will end,' he said to Mohan Lal, 'but you will still have a shop to open every morning.'

Early in 1942, a new sales tax was slapped on jute. The press had become increasingly difficult to maintain. Its pulleys, screws and hammers, bought second-hand more than thirty years ago, were in disrepair. The hydraulic chamber leaked and the ropes snapped often. Since the riots, the kyals—all Muslims—had become restive. Although the price of jute had risen, profits had shrunk. Hari wanted to sell off the whole press. Tribhuvan had said that Japan was certain to win in Asia, so this would be a good time to invest in silver with the money freed up by selling the press.

There were two more weddings. Gopi married off his second daughter—as before, Hari sent four gold ginnis to Santahar—and Hari finally found a bride for Garib Das, who was now past twenty. The girl's family lived in Assam; the bride's beauty was vouched for by the matchmaker, a business contact of Hari's who often travelled to Jorhat. This was important because Garib Das, man of Manchester dhotis, would not have settled for a girl who was not fair-skinned. He had already turned down all matches Hari had attempted, which was why he was unmarried at twenty-one.

The wedding party went by train. There being a shortage of passenger cars because of the war, they hitched a ride with a goods train. Someone slipped the guard a few rupees, blankets were spread out in a windowless car, and they went to sleep while the train chugged eastward. Holi was still weeks away and it was very cold. When they woke up, two cooks, sent to Bogra by the bride's father and now travelling back with the wedding party, served them hot tea.

The bride was almost seventeen. This was not unusual these days, more so because Garib Das himself was well past the marriageable age. She came to her father-in-law's house directly after the wedding. Mohammad Ali Bogra's driver was waiting with the Opel at the railway station in Bogra. Garib Das and his fair bride were driven home in the car, which took a circuitous route through Raja Bazar and Fateh Ali Bazar before coming to Sat Matha, so everyone could see the Opel and comment on the bride's beauty, though of course, no one got to see anything because her face was hidden behind her wedding shawl.

For a week after his wedding, Garib Das did not go to Rangpur at all, but engaged Mohammad Ali Bogra's driver to teach him how to drive. The children went along in the back seat, and the Opel was often seen lurching about in Marwari Para. Once, after Garib Das had subjected the car to particular abuse and caused it to stall repeatedly, it would not start at all. He ordered Fakir Chand, Ishwar Das, Mohan Lal and Gangadhar to step out and push the car. Everyone complied except Fakir Chand, who bundled himself up in the seat, shivered and said he was not well, reminding his brother of the astrologer's prediction, by which he had only five more years to live. Garib Das taunted him.

'Raamji meant to make you a girl, which is why he gave you light skin.'

After a week of lessons, the driver declared that Garib Das was competent to drive the car all by himself. By then the petrol tank had run dry again, and Hari refused to spend more money on coupons, which could only be had from the black market. The Opel returned to its usual resting place—outside the grain shop, under the verandah at Sat Matha—and Garib Das resumed his train trips to Rangpur, while his bride, Sumitra, began to help Gayatri in the kitchen.

When Tribhuvan came to Bogra for Holi, he said that the Japanese had captured Singapore and entered Burma, and Marwaris from Burma were running north into Bengal. Some had managed to reach Calcutta but had left much money and property behind. 'It is only a matter of time before they come into Bengal.'

'What kinds of sahibs will the Japanese be?'

'Worse,' said Tribhuvan. 'Much worse than English sahibs.'

'English or Japanese. Both need grain. Both need cigarettes. Both need oil.'

'Yes,' said Tribhuvan, 'but both do not pay the same amount.'

This was a situation that Hari found himself unable to understand. Whether in Shekhavati, Calcutta or Bogra, there had never been any uncertainty about the structure of the world. The thakurs in Shekhavati were Rajputs, the nawabs in Bogra were

Bengali Musalmans. He knew how to address them and get on their good side; he knew what rates to quote when they pawned their jewellery, and how to be firm without offending their pride when a debt was to be collected. Above this world of thakurs and nawabs was the administration of sahibs, who themselves were largely invisible, except in Chowringhee in Calcutta. In Bogra, no one saw them, but everyone knew they were there. Sometimes, a superintendent of police might visit the mofussil area, or a Christian missionary might pass by, but the sahibs' presence was both unobtrusive and constant. It was reassuring to know that they were there—policemen and judges and commissioners and governors, and of course the Lat Sahib—to take notice and action if Musalmans should burn down a shop, or a beel should overflow its boundaries to flood Raja Bajar. Now, if English sahibs were to be replaced by Japanese sahibs, would the old rules still apply? Would it still be safe for a bania to live in a Musalman town like Bogra? And would the police still come when a bania was robbed?

Before he left for Calcutta, Tribhuvan assured Hari that there was no need to panic yet. 'I know many sahibs in the law courts. Even those over fifty have left their positions and returned to England to fight the war. If not allowed to fight because of their age, they will do whatever is asked of them—drive trucks, cook meals, tend to the wounded. Go to any sahib's house in Calcutta and his memsahib will be knitting sweaters, mufflers and socks to send to England for the army. Do not worry about Bogra. The sahibs in Calcutta will take care of it.'

'Even sahibs cannot defy the will of Raamji,' Hari said.

'But it is the will of Raamji that the sahibs prevail.'

17

In the winter of 1942, Tribhuvan found a match for Fakir Chand in Calcutta and a wedding was quickly arranged. Ishwar Das and Mohan Lal had never been to Calcutta. Garib Das and Fakir Chand had told them stories of Tribhuvan's wedding eight years ago—the crowds in Chowringhee and Bara Bazar, Grand Hotel and the earthquake—but this Calcutta was very different. Buildings were wrapped in black cloth for protection against Japanese bombing raids. Trams and buses ran empty, except in the Park Street area, which was full of sahib soldiers who spoke strangely and walked with a swagger, their arms thrown around full-grown girls who were at least twenty and still unmarried, and not ashamed to be seen with men who were neither their fathers nor brothers. Chinese shopkeepers followed the soldiers with crates of cheese, bread and bottles. They bought much, paying in wristwatches, rings and cameras, so each shopkeeper would soon have a dozen cameras slung over his shoulders, and would then signal his partner to take his slot, calling, 'American! American!'

They saw stalls selling brass pots, Gurkha knives and gems that the shopkeepers swore were rare whenever a soldier passed by. Little boys ran after the soldiers, calling them 'you American raja' and saying, 'No food, no money, no poppa'.

Gangadhar turned to Garib Das. 'That beggar just spoke in English.'

Being the oldest, Garib Das was called upon to translate the beggar's call. He shrugged. 'That is gibberish. See, even the sahibs don't understand it.'

They saw sahib soldiers who wore short pants like children—Bansidhar laughed—and others whose trousers were tucked into thick boots. Peering through windows, they saw sahibs drinking tea in expensive china, and then bought tea from pavement stalls, feeling smug about not wasting money on appearances—it was the same tea; did it matter what kind of cup it was drunk from? And they also saw habshis from America, men whose skin was so dark that the darkest servant in Bogra would have regarded them with contempt. And they were amused to see that habshis regarded themselves as sahibs, joked with sahibs in English, and indeed had those same shameless girls on their arms.

'What kind of water do these people drink,' Gangadhar asked, 'that some become pale as paper and others black as coal?'

Once, a habshi stood so close to the children that Murlidhar began to cry loudly. They had to leave the area quickly before any of the sahib soldiers—with their guns and menacing manner—questioned them.

Trenches had been dug all over Chowringhee. 'This is where the sahibs spend nights with those girls,' said Gangadhar in disgust and wonder.

They themselves spent nights in Tribhuvan's flat. He lived on the top floor of a tall building. Because there were only two rooms, large mattresses had been laid in the balcony, and they slept packed together. The windows had been taped over with black paper to prevent the glass from shattering during air raids. The building itself was draped in black, and a wall of sandbags rose in the front to absorb shrapnel from bombings. Having never climbed so high in a building before, they spent their mornings standing in the balcony and looking down at the road, commenting on how small the cars and trams looked.

Hari found living in the flat embarrassing, especially because he knew it was owned by Tribhuvan's father-in-law. The strain in their relations had been partially repaired by Tribhuvan's efforts on behalf of Fakir Chand, but he still found it difficult to look his son in the eye, and anxiously waited for the wedding to be over so he could return to Bogra.

Meanwhile, arrangements had to be made for the wedding, and he found that prices of everything had increased—from the tea in Cotton Street to the rice the cook bought on Harrison Road, even to the fares charged by rickshawalas in Bara Bazar. Everything had been commandeered by the army, and the rates it paid—considerably higher than Hari would—were now being demanded of others. At the bridal shop, he was annoyed when told that the rent for Fakir Chand's shervani had doubled on account of the war. 'No one in the army is getting married.'

The shopkeeper shrugged. People kept renting shervanis even as he kept raising the rent. Everyone wanted to get married before the Japanese came. Who knew if they would permit weddings? To mollify Hari, he said, 'Land is cheap nowadays. No one is buying.'

'I have come to marry off my son, not to buy a house.'

Fakir Chand's bride was from a wealthy family, even wealthier than Tribhuvan's in-laws, though not as well established in the Marwari circles of Calcutta. They had acquired wealth in the last ten years, and were now doing exceptionally well supplying the army with regulation blankets. It was said that their blankets clothed the soldiers in all of Singapore and Burma. The bride herself was an only daughter, sister to four brothers who had never allowed her to cook or sew or knit. Tribhuvan had warned Hari about this but he had overlooked the fact, thinking that a girl of good temperament—Tribhuvan said she was one—would be able to learn all these, especially with Gayatri as tutor. Moreover, the dowry would be generous, and this would help Fakir Chand expand from the cigarette store into more substantial trade, perhaps something connected with supplying the army, given the contacts his in-laws had.

On the night before the wedding, a strange wail rose in the distance as they prepared to go to bed. Tribhuvan recognized it instantly as an air raid siren. 'Run downstairs.'

This caused panic among the children. Bansidhar began to cry, and Gangadhar to console him. Tribhuvan quickly brought out bags, handed one to each child and one to Hari, then grabbed a pot of water sitting outside the kitchen. His wife Kusum was the first to leave, carrying two-year-old Arjun in her arms. Hari and the children went next. The staircase was crowded—everyone in the building was going to the basement. Once there, they huddled together. Hari opened his bag. It contained a block of black rubber—to bite into, said Tribhuvan—a bottle of Vaseline, a bicycle lamp, a pencil, a notepad, a whistle, a gas mask, cloth bandages and tubes, and a bottle of smelling salts.

Ishwar Das and Mohan Lal put on their gas masks, spoke hoarsely through them, laughed and joked. Gangadhar wanted to know if they would be able to see the planes from the basement. And would they also see Japanese men inside them? Murlidhar sniffed the bottle of salts and began to feel faint.

Hari sat through the ordeal silently, turning over in his mind the horror of death. As a child, he had heard stories of Marwari men returning from Bengal with bags full of jewellery for their wives. Camel caravans would shimmer on the horizon, and soon the traders would be surrounded. Everything would be taken—the reward of five years' labour in Calcutta, Assam or Bombay. Who was a trader to put up a fight? He had learned arithmetic, not swordplay. The robbers would also take his camel, so he would have to trudge through the desert and crawl pitifully into Rampura or Sikar or Jhunjhunu. The ones who resisted—for there were some foolhardy enough to make a pass at chivalry—would be left dying among the tibbas, a blade between their shoulders. Nowadays, one just took the Addha train to Sikar; the caravans were long gone. Having survived those perils and come to safe Bengal, what had he now stumbled into? He did not understand the cause of this quarrel between the sahibs and the Japanese, and wanted nothing of it. If it was a dispute over rates, surely the sahibs were sufficiently good banias to resolve it themselves. What turn of events had caused Raamji to trap a poor bania underground so he could be burnt to cinders in a quarrel between sahibs?

He saw the frightened faces of his sons. In the darkness of the basement, Garib Das looked like a shrunken black grape, all his flair had vanished. The dhoti he wore might as well have been cotton, given how crumpled it was. Gangadhar was consoling Bansidhar, and Murlidhar sat in a daze, recovering from the smells of the bottle.

The most pitiable was Fakir Chand, who trembled for the entire three hours, moaned softly, and hid his face between his knees whenever there was a loud report outside. The poor boy had been thinking of his wedding the next day, no doubt, when that siren tore into his heart. And now he had visions of being buried under rubble. By the astrologer's prediction, he had less than five years to live. This gave Hari curious comfort: if Fakir Chand was to live for another five years, the building would not be bombed.

They waited for three hours until another siren announced the all clear. Later that night, after Garib Das had scanned the sky and assured everyone there were no planes, the children went to sleep in the balcony. Tribhuvan said to Hari, 'It is only a matter of weeks before those planes reach Bogra.'

Hari shook his head. 'Kalkatta is a large city so they bomb it. The Japanese have not even heard of Bogra.'

'Send everyone to Shekhavati for a few months, until the war ends.'

'We live in Bengal,' Hari said stubbornly.

'But our home is Shekhavati.'

Remembering something his father had told him, Hari said, 'A bania lives where his shops are, or he will lose both his home and his customers. What has Raamji given to Shekhavati? Sand and sky.'

'The days of famine are gone. They have canals now.'

'You have been born in Bengal. You have not seen the Chhappaniya or walked through sandstorms. You do not even speak Marwari the way they do in Shekhavati.'

'But the Japanese are sure to come to Bogra.'

'Look at the sahibs you meet in your law courts. They are like Marwari banias—they have come to Bengal from afar to buy cheap and sell dear. Like Marwaris, they belong elsewhere. Do you see them running from the Japanese?'

'But we are not Rajputs. We do not fight, we add and subtract...'

Hari did not want to tell his son, who would certainly not understand, that he was not meant to return to Shekhavati, that a son had been taken from him when he once attempted to defy providence. Finally, it was agreed that Hari, Garib Das, Fakir Chand and Gangadhar would stay in Bogra while the women would be sent to Shekhavati with the children.

The wedding was subdued. A bank building had been struck by a bomb, and the gaping wound on its top was plainly visible from Fakir Chand's in-laws' house, where the ceremonies took place. Hari noted that the bride's complexion was dark, and was intrigued by the ways of fortune: dark Garib Das, sampler of Manchester dhotis, had won himself a fair-skinned bride, while fair Fakir Chand, whom his brothers taunted for being a delicate girl, would make do with a dark-skinned wife.

After the ceremonies, everyone returned to Tribhuvan's flat, and Hari disclosed the plan—the children would go to Shekhavati right away with Tribhuvan. The women would be sent shortly after Hari returned to Bogra.

'Am I to go to Bogra, then?' asked Fakir Chand.

'All the men must,' Hari said stubbornly.

Fakir Chand trembled and turned away, and Hari realized that the boy had sunk into despair. His bride sat in the next room, dressed in her bridal skirt, and he already imagined her a widow, seeing himself turned to ash by a Japanese bomb over Bogra. He clearly wished to be with his bride, who would go to Shekhavati. It is this new trend, Hari thought, of bringing brides to their father-in-laws' home immediately after the wedding, that has caused this attachment that husbands developed for their wives. In his days, when both bride and groom were much younger and the bride returned to her father's house to await her youth, no one paid much attention to the bride or groom in a wedding. But he would have to make allowances, both for the times and for Fakira's weak constitution.

'It will help to send one man to Shekhavati,' he said. 'Fakira could go with the children.'

Fakir Chand's relief was plain even as he protested for the sake of appearance. 'What of Harilal & Sons? Who will mind the cigarette store?'

'Do not worry. Harilal & Sons will remain open.'

They packed trunks and bedrolls and set off for Howrah Station. Fakir Chand's bride sat in a ricksha with a cousin. Fakir Chand sat on another ricksha, bedrolls all around him. The children kept looking up at the sky, expecting a swarm of planes any minute. The rickshas clattered over the pontoon bridge, which would soon be closed now that the new bridge was complete. It was the new Howrah Bridge that the Japanese planes had come to destroy, Tribhuvan said.

Howrah Station was crowded. Everyone wanted to leave Calcutta after the bombing.

As they threw their bedrolls into the train, pushing them through windows—the doors had been barred by passengers inside—Hari regarded Fakir Chand's bride with some concern, and wondered if he should have let her stay in her father's house for a few months. A new bride needed the comforts of a home, not the ordeal of a long train journey into dry Shekhavati. She stood silently, laden with jewels, sari pulled low over her face. Hari knew exactly what she had on; he had received a full accounting of her jewellery from her father, who omitted no detail in his zest to advertise his wealth and generosity: a gold cummerbund, pearls, panna and pukhraj stones on her fingers, gold hansuli round the neck, diamond earrings and necklaces, a diamond clove in the nose, a gold mangtika with the sun and the moon as pendants, a gold arm-band, gold bangles inlaid with shellac, gold ankle bracelets... It was time to say farewell. Ishwar Das and Mohan Lal were already inside the carriage. Bansidhar and Murlidhar were being pushed in through the windows. Fakir Chand was now ready to take his bride inside. For her, a passage would have to be created through the door. A cry of 'didi didi' went up and men squeezed this way and that to let her pass through. A vision of wind-swept Shekhavati rose in Hari's mind, full of sand dunes and camel carts and gazelles on the horizon. He said to Fakir Chand, 'Tell the daughter-in-law to remove her ankle bracelets before she enters Rampura. Women do not wear gold below the waist without permission from the thakur.'

'Which thakur?' Fakir Chand asked.

'The Thakur of Nawalgarh.'

'Where is Nawalgarh?'

Hari looked at his delicate son with a mixture of disappointment and wonder. 'Go. The train has whistled.'

Fakir Chand vanished through the door.

Hari, Garib Das and Gangadhar took rickshas to Sealdah Station for the train to Santahar. The electric lights on Harrison Road had been turned off as a precaution against another air raid. Amidst the crowds at Sealdah, a general gloom descended on them. They barely remembered that they were members of a wedding party.

18

Prices rose throughout 1942. During Fakir Chand's wedding in December, rice had reached sixteen rupees to a munn, starting from as little as four at the beginning of the year. By Holi the following year—Hari did not celebrate because Manki, Gayatri, and the children were in Rampura—it had risen to twenty-five. By summer, it was thirty, forty and even sixty rupees in Bogra, and rumoured to be selling for a hundred rupees in Calcutta. Hari quickly dispatched a few bags with Nanuram, but he was able to sell them only at seventy. After accounting for the expense of sending him to Calcutta, Hari calculated that he was better off selling in Bogra. However, few in Bogra had the money to buy. His warehouse in Bara Gola began to fill with sacks. Some stock went bad during the rains. More than once, someone attempted to break in. He installed larger locks and posted a guard outside.

Mangiram came to Sat Matha to discuss rising prices, and to seek Hari's help in marrying off his twin daughters, who were now fourteen.

'This is a good time to find sons-in-law,' Hari said. 'There is a shortage of brides. Most Marwari girls have gone to Shekhavati because of the war.'

Mangiram said,'My daughters will not go to Shekhavati even if the Japanese come. Neither will my wife. We have lived in Bengal for 150 years. We will not desert it now.'

Hari sensed an accusation. 'Beef-eating English sahibs are fighting beef-eating Japanese sahibs,' he said coldly, 'and their bombs fall on beef-eating Musalmans. Where do you find such sympathy for them? Has the Nawabzada turned vegetarian? Have his butchers stopped taking cows to the Nawabbari? Or does the bellowing of those cows no longer reach your ears in Fateh Ali Bajar?'

'I have come to find a match for my daughters, Hariya, not to quarrel with you. You have married off many children and your sons are doing well. I have heard that Garib Das's profits in Rangpur are almost as high as Gopi's in Santahar.'

This softened Hari, as Mangiram had hoped it would. 'Gopi runs seven oil depots, they tell me, up and down the broad-gauge railway line that goes to Kalkatta.' He had heard of five depots a year ago, but added two to allow for any expansion in the last year. Also, he thought it best not to mention that Harilal & Sons in Santahar was not owned by him.

Mangiram began. 'If Durga had lived...'

'You know what they say in Shekhavati: Raamji calls those dearest to him first. The boy could have let those trains collide, but his sons would get hurt in a collision. So he stood between them and *pushed them apart*. But then Raamji sucked the breath out of him. He saved our lives. Durga was like that...'

'I have heard that Tribhuvan spends too much time in the Congress Party offices in Kalkatta. They say he wrote a pamphlet, saying girls should not be married off until they turn sixteen. How old was his sister Shanti when you found her a husband?'

Hari chuckled nervously, wondering why the conversation had taken this turn. 'He is just a boy.'

'I would like to buy that car outside your shop, Hariya'

Hari was dumbfounded. That was why Mangiram had come, and that was why he had put Hari on the defensive: to get a good price. He could not know, of course, that Hari was desperate to get rid of the monster. After being declared fit to drive the car, Garib Das had shown no interest in doing so, both because he spent his time in Rangpur and because his wife was in Rampura. The car sat at Sat Matha all day, blocked Hari's view of the street, collected dust and bird shit—which a servant cleaned every day at Garib Das's insistence—and was an eyesore to Bengalis, who saw it as a symbol of profligacy in a time of scarcity.

'The car?' he asked, feigning indifference. 'It belongs to Gariba.'

'If the father were to sell, the son would not object.'

'These are uncommon times. Sons are no longer compliant, as they were in Shekhavati. You know what they say—once a boy has slipped from your hands, he will never return.'

They fell silent as they contemplated the intransigence of sons. Having no sons, Mangiram was unable to summon a solution, so he mentally added a hundred rupees to the offer he had brought. 'I can give you two thousand.'

Hari expressed shock. 'You know the car belonged to the Nawab of Bogra. It has an all-steel body…' He was unequal to the task of extolling the virtues of the car. 'Perhaps we should wait until Gariba returns from Rangpur. He could tell you more, and teach you how to drive it.'

'Why would I drive it myself? Let someone else do that. I will pay him.'

'It was bought for 2,400,' said Hari. He remembered a number nearer 2,200, but thought it wise to err on the safe side.

'I go the Nawabbari often,' Mangiram said pointedly. 'The retainer showed me an entry for 2,200 when you bought the car.'

Now Hari was embarrassed. He muttered vaguely, 'Gariba knows the numbers, Mangi. Let us discuss this tomorrow.'

Garib Das refused to sell the Opel. A compromise was struck. Half the ownership of the car was transferred to Mangiram for nine hundred rupees. The car was to spend two days at Sat Matha, followed by two outside Mangiram's shop in Fateh Ali Bajar. Mohammad Ali Bogra's driver was engaged for one rupee per month to drive it from one spot to the other every second day. Before the transfer, he was also to polish the windshield with a cloth.

Hari heaved a sigh of relief. On the days the car was absent, he felt light-hearted. His dread grew as the hour of its arrival approached, and he sensed hostile glances all over Sat Matha whenever it drove up. Garib Das preferred the opposite—he timed his arrivals from Rangpur to coincide with the car's presence at Sat Matha. Meanwhile, Mangiram easily found two grooms, both in Dhaka, for his two daughters, because Marwari girls were in short supply, and also because the Opel parked outside his shop increased his status in Bogra. 'My daughters will live in a big city,' he said, 'and the sisters will comfort each other in times of distress.'

Shanti was now sixteen. Hari sent her off with gifts to her father-in-law's house in Kushtia. The children being in Rampura, it was Garib Das who travelled with her, spent two days in her father-in-law's haveli on the river Gorai, and returned with dazzling tales of her in-laws' wealth. Apparently, Nagar Mal and his father spent their time in the sitting room of their mansion—a hall facing the street—and entertained friends and associates from the Congress Party. They had no shop and nothing to do all day, because rent from their many properties was more than sufficient. Their servants cooked in large kitchens, kneaded dough in silver plates and served mango water in gold tumblers. Every morning, Shanti's mother-in-law took a silver watering can to the temple—her own temple, constructed in the mango orchard behind the haveli. Even in these hard times, they sent Garib Das back with gold cufflinks.

Garib Das himself was doing very well in the oil depot at Rangpur. Along with grain, the price of oil had soared during the war. He spent much time in Rangpur so as not to miss the opportunity. Being certain that the rupee would plunge once the Japanese had driven out English sahibs, he had begun to convert his profits into gold ginnis, which he stuffed into a mattress in the Rangpur oil depot.

Everywhere in Bengal—in Bogra, Rangpur, Dhaka, even as far as Calcutta—money was being earned on a scale not seen before. Whatever a bania put his hand to would turn into gold—grain, cigarettes, cotton, oil, jute. Even as prices rose, there was no end to demand, and sales were limited only by a man's capacity to sell. Hari thought Fakir Chand had been a fool to go to Shekhavati. He could have sat in the cigarette store and earned himself a treasure. Instead, he sat in Rampura in his bride's lap and was pampered by Gayatri and Manki, eating rotis soaked in ghee and fussing over his health, all because of an astrologer's prediction. Everyone seemed to think the Japanese would win. Very well, Marwari banyans in Hoare Miller and Andrew Yule would become banyans for Japanese firms; they would learn a few words of Japanese as they had English; they would salaam Japanese sahibs, read *their* newspapers, send fruit baskets to *their* memsahibs and line the streets for *their* Lat Sahib. Why would a Marwari bania shrink from profits? Why else had he left his home in Shekhavati and come to Disavar?

'I sleep on gold every night,' Garib Das boasted to Hari. 'When I turn over in my sleep, I find coins digging in my back. What a sweet pain it is!'

Hari admonished him to find a safer hideout for his treasure, knowing very well there was no such place. Who trusted banks at a time like this? He himself had hundred-rupee notes buried inside sacks of grain at Sat Matha.

'Lower your voice. Better still, do not speak at all. A wise man loudly mourns his losses but is indifferent to profits. Have you not heard the stories from Dhaka? A Marwari must lie low, open his shop every morning and shut it in the evening.'

His warehouse overflowed with sacks of rice. He lay awake at nights thinking of his stock, remembering the men in Rampura who had come looking for bajra in his house and dug up the floor. In Munshiganj near Dhaka, Marwaris had been attacked and their stores looted. Hari thought conditions in Bogra were slightly better, but no one could be certain. He had noticed that the beggars passing through Marwari Para looked thinner than usual. They staggered about with vacant eyes, muttering 'phan, phan', asking not for rice—no one would give rice that cost seventy-five rupees to a beggar—but the starch that was thrown away after the rice had been boiled. Lakshmi's Ma collected the phan in large buckets whenever she cooked. Every morning, a servant walked down a line of beggars, ladling phan into their pans. They drank it greedily, licked their lips and asked for more. Watching them, Hari had a sense of foreboding. The lines were getting longer. What would happen when even the phan ran out? What did men do when there was absolutely nothing to eat?

He knew, of course. He had seen it all in the Chhappaniya. If anyone in Bengal knew what famine was, it would be a Marwari bania from Shekhavati. He remembered the dogs feasting on camel carcasses, the women who had sold their children for bajra. Yet the plight of Bengal was difficult to understand. Shekhavati was dry. Nothing but bajra grew among the tibbas, and it grew but once a year. The sky was a clear white. If the rains did not come by the second fortnight in Aashaadh—they often did not—everyone prepared for a drought. This was Bengal, where the earth yielded three types of rice—how he had marvelled when first told of Aman, Aush and Boro—and three crops in a year. Everywhere the eye looked, there were rivers and beels and ponds and pools of water full of lilies...What right did Bengal have to famine? You only had to see the Karatoya, swollen after the rains, and the Jamuna and the Padma, and the thousand rivers criss-crossing lush countryside. Why was rice at seventy-five rupees? And why was wheat twenty-four, oil fifty, ghee one-hundred-and-forty... There was a mistake somewhere, and it had to do with the war in England.

The government had started langarkhanas. Skeletal women clutching children with large heads and protruding bellies lined up to receive spoonfuls of khichuri. He heard stories of men who had eaten nothing for days devouring so much khichuri that their stomachs swelled up like balloons and their skins stretched like rubber. They died, writhing in pain, calling on the gods to restore them to the arms of hunger, to suck out the accursed khichuri from their bellies.

There were wild rumours afloat. The government had added poison to the khichuri so it would not have to feed the same beggar more than once; sahibs had hidden away thousands of munns of rice for the military; all the rice had been sent to Burma to feed the army, which was now retreating before the Japanese advance; Calcutta had filled up with beggars and its railway stations were closed; the new Howrah Bridge had collapsed as soon as it opened under the weight of beggars sleeping on it; if one stood on the Howrah Bridge and looked down, one could see corpses floating down the Hooghly river; the women in Calcutta had become prostitutes and were demanding payment in rice; in Noakhali, Musalmans who starved had been buried in mass graves with a Namaaz-e-janaaza but Hindus had been thrown into rivers, where they were eaten by crabs, which were caught and eaten by fishermen who then died too.

Meanwhile, he had been receiving news from Rampura. Manki spent her days as she had in Bogra, filling her Raam Raam books, which had travelled with her. Ishwar Das and Mohan Lal had been recruited into the project, and each had filled a sixty-page notebook with twelve thousand 'Raams'. Manki had become even more foul-mouthed—this Hari gleaned from a hint by Fakir Chand, who had written the letter—and Gayatri had taken over the household, as she had in Bogra. The old house needed repairs—it had lain vacant since Duli Chand had locked it to go to Bogra. It had had to be cleaned and aired, and two servants had been engaged. Prices had risen in Rampura, too, and servants there demanded more money than the ones in Bengal, wrote Fakir Chand, which was odd considering the banias in Rampura had much less to give. Lastly, Fakir Chand assured his father that though his health had suffered, he was taking good care of himself.

Hari received other reports about Fakir Chand's fads and obsessions. The boy was only eighteen, yet behaved like an old man with fatal afflictions. In Rampura, he had taken to an ayurvedic treatment called parpatti, to treat a disease no one knew existed. A vaidya arrived every day to wrap cloth bandages—soaked in water, mud, clay or the juice of the bel fruit—around his head, wrists and waist. He lay undisturbed for hours, waiting for the parpatti to cure him. When not lying covered with bandages, he offered his pulse to anyone who could count, assuring the person that it had raced ahead, that the astrologer's prediction was about to come true four years too soon. Where in Bogra Garib Das had sometimes pulled him up for worrying too much about his health and too little about the shop, there were no such pressures in Rampura, where Manki defended her fair-skinned son whenever someone suggested that a married man of eighteen should not lie in bed all day.

In the month of Aashaadh, there was news that Garib Das's wife had had a daughter. In Ashwin, Fakir Chand's wife gave birth to a girl. My family grows in Rampura, Hari thought with satisfaction, in spite of this war.

On receiving news of the births, Gangadhar counted his cousins—starting with Pushpa, Hari's oldest granddaughter, and himself, the oldest grandson—and reported that Hari now had eleven grandchildren—four boys and seven girls—and one great-grandchild, Pushpa's son, born two years ago. Hari beamed. 'There will be many more. I will live to see Mohan Lal's children, perhaps marry them off...'

'How old are you, Dadaji?'

'Fifty-six, but I have never been sick a day in my life. Never a cough or a cold or a fever, and the pox avoided me even as it took my older brother. That is what Shekhavati bajra does to you.'

Gangadhar chuckled. 'Your brother ate Shekhavati bajra too, didn't he?'

'You are a smart one, Ganga. Do not taunt your elders.'

'Did the letters from Rampura mention Bansi or Murli?'

'They both appear to be much improved in Rampura. A stranger would not be able tell there was anything wrong with them.'

Fakir Chand had said nothing about Bansidhar or Murlidhar,

but this had become Hari's usual response when asked about either boy. Months would pass without an epileptic fit, and he would convince himself that Bansi had been magically cured when a seizure would shatter the illusion. No such pretence was possible with Murlidhar, though it did take a stranger a few minutes to guess that something was not quite right with him.

On the night before Diwali, Hari was sitting in his shop, his doors shut. There was gloom in Bogra. Most houses were dark. The beggars had gone to sleep. Many would not wake up the next day. Hari chewed on a lump of jaggery—he had stopped buying sugar because it could only be had through expensive coupons. Gangadhar had closed the hosiery store and was with Hari. The Opel was heard outside. A door slammed. Mohammad Ali Bogra's driver had brought it for its two days at Sat Matha. He knocked. Hari opened the door with some consternation because it was not yet the end of the month, when the driver would expect to be paid. Perhaps he wanted a bonus for Diwali. Even a Musalman marked Diwali when it brought him a bonus.

'I will not celebrate Diwali this year,' he said to the driver. 'My children are in Shekhavati, and you have seen the state of Bengal.'

'Salaam, Babu,' the man said. 'Nawabzada Sahib has sent a request.'

This was unusual. Although Mohammad Ali was a friend of Tribhuvan's, Hari had little contact with him. Perhaps the driver meant Mohammad Ali's father, Nawabzada Altaf Ali.

'Which nawab, the old one or his son?'

'The son, Babu. He asks that you send six bags of rice to the Nawabbari.'

Hari had never supplied to the nawab, and the driver had not mentioned a rate. Did the nawab want the rice as a gift? If so, it was improper to ask for it through a servant—he should have come himself. Thinking that perhaps this was a simple sale, he said, 'The rate is seventy-five for a munn, but the Nawabzada is a friend of my son's, who is a barrister in Kalkatta—the first Marwari to be so honoured. For the Nawabzada, I will quote fifty rupees. You may come tomorrow and take the bags.'

'I could take them right away. The Nawabbari is not far.'

'How will you carry six bags?'

The driver pointed to the Opel. He plans to take my rice in my car, thought Hari bitterly, and he does not even ask my permission. Such impertinence in such a young man! It was time to be stern with him. 'Tell the Nawabzada to come and see me tomorrow.'

'The Nawabzada wishes you well,' the man said ominously. 'In Bengali Para, they say that outsiders have hidden away stocks and caused the rice shortage, that they come from Shekhavati with a lota and a blanket and take away our rice.'

Hari looked hard at the driver, a Musalman boy no older than twenty. *I opened a shop in Bengal before this boy was born, and he calls me an outsider*. He knew that line, of course. He had heard it many times, from Janardhan, from Tribhuvan, and from the Bengali who had written the book that caused Tribhuvan to lose his dowry to earthquake relief.

'The rate is fifty rupees,' he repeated.

There was another knock on the door. Hari started. Had the Nawabzada himself come to ensure the success of his little scheme? But it was Nanuram, and he was out of breath.

'There are three men in Bara Gola—Bengalis, government inspectors. They want to enter the warehouse.'

'Do not let them in.'

'They have a policeman with them.'

Hari saw a smile on the face of Mohammad Ali's man, and wondered if the Nawabzada had something to do with this. He ran to Bara Gola, followed by Nanuram, Gangadhar and the driver, who had the temerity to follow him in the Opel car.

Within ten minutes, the inspectors had counted the bags, determined there were too many and confronted Hari, who stood with hands folded, enraged but panicked. 'Do you know that there is a great famine in Bengal? That men are dying of hunger just outside your Marwari Para?'

Hari raised his folded hands higher. 'This rice is for sale, Babu. Anyone may buy it for sixty rupees to a munn.'

'Who in Bengal can pay sixty rupees?'

'I did not determine the rate, Babu. It is what the market says it is. I am merely a poor bania.'

The men regarded Hari with contempt. 'We will confiscate this stock. The warehouse will be locked and sealed.'

Hari's face fell. 'I have a shop,' he pleaded. 'I buy and I sell. Will you not buy the stock from me? Perhaps at fifty? Or even forty rupees to a munn?'

'You cannot confiscate these bags, Babu,' Gangadhar said.

Hari turned to him in panic. Why had the boy chosen to talk back to these men? Did he not know they could lock the hosiery store too? A Marwari had to lie low…

'These bags have been sold to Nawabzada Mohammad Ali Bogra,' continued Gangadhar. 'His man has come to take them.'

This had an instant effect on the inspectors. They asked for verification. Mohammad Ali's driver asserted that this was true. His word was believed because he was clearly not a Marwari.

After the inspectors had left, Hari turned to Gangadhar with grudging respect. 'That was well said, but it is not wise to engage such men.' Turning to Mohammad Ali's man, he said, 'Take six bags and load them into the car.'

They sat on rice bags—Hari, Gangadhar and Nanuram—while the driver struggled with the loot. Watching him, Hari was suddenly filled with grief. The young man was a Musalman, but a poor one. Not yet twenty. Not one grain of this stolen rice would pass his lips. It was for the Nawabzada or his father, who brought a new memsahib from England every time he went there. Or it was for the dozen retainers of the nawab, or the hundreds of fawning associates who lived on the nawab's largesse, or the children of Mozelle Cohen, the Yehudi woman who had been mistress to Altaf Ali's grandfather. Such a man was this nawab. Why would he throw a crumb at this boy of twenty, even one who was a Musalman like the nawab himself? Look how he carried those bags on his skinny back, which seemed as if it might give any moment! And look how he stood now to catch his breath, watching the six bags he would never taste sitting in the back of the car!

'Do you have children?' he asked the man.

Because of exhaustion, or perhaps because the heist was now complete, the man had lost his self-assurance. Standing pitifully with eyes downcast, he nodded. 'Three girls.'

The Chhappaniya rose again in Hari's mind, along with the eyes of children looking for tamarind bark among tibbas. He pointed to a sack of rice. 'Take that.'

The man looked at the bag, then at the car, trying to determine if he had forgotten to take six.

'For your daughters, not your nawab' said Hari. Then he turned away. It would not do to let any of them—the man, Nanuram or Gangadhar—see tears in his eyes.

19

Through winter and spring, there were daily reports of Subhas Bose's advance through Burma with the Japanese army. He had routed the English sahibs in Manipur; he had turned them back with half the forces they deployed; he had unfurled an Indian flag in Imphal; the retreating sahibs were packing in a hurry to get out of Bengal; it was a matter of weeks, not months, before the Japanese became the new sahibs. Now and then, a boy would shout 'Subhas Babu zindabad!' at Sat Matha, but the vast majority of Marwaris in Marwari Para did not think the English sahibs would let Subhas Babu enter Bengal. Hari exercised an abundance of caution, making no comment and taking no sides, after having forbidden Garib Das, Gangadhar and Nanuram to say a word on the subject.

By early 1945, it became clear the sahibs would prevail. In summer, Tribhuvan sent a postcard from Calcutta, saying that large 'V' signs had been hung in Park Street to mark the victory of the sahibs in England. Japan was still advancing in Burma, and a black market still existed for cloth and grain, he said, but there now seemed little chance that the sahibs would run from Bengal. 'If they can defeat Hitler, they can defeat the Japanese.'

Hari dispatched Gangadhar to Shekhavati. In a week he received a postcard saying everyone had started for Bogra, and three days later they were all at the Bogra railway station. The first things he noticed were that Kaushalya, his second daughter, was now sixteen, and that Manki, at forty-four, had become an old woman. The fruits of her Shekhavati labours were visible—another steel trunk had been added to the three that had accompanied her to Rampura. The coolie groaned under the weight of the Raam Raam books until it was decided to split the load between two men. Fakir Chand appeared prim and in good condition, his face permanently set in self-pity. Next came the two girls, now two years old—Garib Das's daughter and Fakir Chand's—in their mothers' arms. Finally, after all the bundles and steel trunks had been loaded on to the heads of coolies, Gayatri emerged from the train. Her head was uncovered, and her eyes did not flinch when they met Hari's. Indeed she smiled to acknowledge him, not bothering to touch his feet or fold her hands. The two and a half years in Rampura had aged her very little. In a startling white sari with no jewellery, she looked younger than her thirty-six years, and stood erect like a man among women, surrounded by them and commanding them through mere gestures.

Gayatri re-established the household at Sat Matha. The coal oven was fired, the smell of rotis wafted down to the shop, and sugar was bought again—the war had nearly ended but rationing was still in place. Late every morning, when it began to get hot, she sent down sharbat to Hari, as she had before they went to Rampura—cool sharbat flavoured with rose water and sweetened with two full spoons of sugar.

Hari applied himself to tasks that had been postponed by the flight to Rampura. A match was found for Kaushalya. Because she was already sixteen, it had to be explained to her in-laws that the delay had been caused by the war and nothing else. Her father-in-law dealt in cloth in Jalpaiguri, west of Bogra, on the

Teesta river. Hari spent almost twenty thousand rupees on the wedding, after having heard from Tribhuvan that men in Calcutta thought nothing of spending fifty thousand.

After Kaushalya left Bogra, two problems occupied her father: because Ishwar Das was only twelve and men married late these days, he had no more children to marry off for years, and Shanti had not had children even five years after going to Kushtia. Gopi's daughter Pushpa already had two sons—Hari's great-grandsons—and she had been married only a year before Shanti. Was something wrong with his daughter, or had her children escaped his notice amidst the profusion of weddings and births? But he would have remembered Shanti's children, because they would be the first to call him 'nana'. Indeed, he was fond of saying that 'dada' rang in his ears all the time but he longed to hear a child call him 'nana'. Gangadhar happened to come by the grain shop. Hari asked him, 'Do you know if your aunt in Kushtia has any children?'

Gangadhar smiled. 'No. And you are only fifty-eight, Dadaji. Not old enough to start forgetting such things.'

Amongst all his grandchildren, Hari was closest to Gangadhar. Every evening, they ate dinner together; and Hari trusted him with a hundred other tasks—aside from minding the hosiery store—that Garib Das or Fakir Chand would have turned down. When a son died, perhaps his son became more of a son than a grandson. Indeed, Gangadhar was less inhibited with Hari than any of his sons had been. Yet he could not let this banter go unchallenged in front of customers and clerks, so he said sternly, 'Watch your tongue. You are not old enough to start speaking thus to your elders.'

'I am nineteen. The twentieth is upon me.'

Hari started—he had overlooked a grandchild again. With Pushpa, the neglect was excusable, but Gangadhar stood in plain view. Hari saw him night and day. Perhaps a grandfather did not look as closely as a father would. If Durga had been alive... To cover his guilt, he said playfully, 'It is time to find you a bride.'

As it happened, he received a postcard the next day: Gopi was marrying off his third daughter. Hari quietly sent four gold ginnis to Santahar. He did not inform his sons—he was not certain they would approve—and he could not employ Nanuram for the task, because Nanuram had not forgotten his quarrel with Gopi, so he asked the only other man he could trust both to deliver the gold and to be discreet—Mohammad Ali Bogra's driver. Of all the men at His disposal, he thought, Raamji gives me a Musalman.

The match Hari found for Gangadhar was unfavourable, and it took him until the summer of the following year. It had proven difficult to convince people that the hosiery store would eventually be owned by Gangadhar alone. Everyone looked at Hari's six sons—even Mohan Lal, who was only eleven—and saw six claimants, amidst whose assertions the rights of the seventh, only a grandson, would be denied. They saw a boy sitting in a hosiery store as caretaker until his uncles, much younger than him, had reached manhood.

Gangadhar's father-in-law had a kerosene shop in Gobindganj. He bought his stock from Gopi's oil depot and sold retail to Muslim customers. He had three daughters, and this was his third. Two costly weddings had left him nearly destitute, so he proposed to provide very little by way of dowry. The wedding was short and spare. Hari nearly cried in embarrassment when the wedding party reached Gobindganj and he saw the kerosene shop. For a brief moment he considered selling the hosiery store and settling that money on Gangadhar, but the thought of his sons raising objections held him back. Word would travel to Santahar, and Gopi would suddenly remember his patrimony; Tribhuvan would recall that, for all his barrister ways in Calcutta, he was a boy from Bogra. It was better not to force the issue; he would continue to believe that his sons bore no ill-will towards one another.

Gangadhar's bride joined the household. So far, Gayatri had supervised sisters-in-law and, in the case of Manki, a mother-in-law. Now she had a daughter-in-law of her own, and it occurred to Hari that Gangadhar's bride was fortunate to have found a woman such as Gayatri as her guardian.

Meanwhile, his concern about Shanti's children had grown. Because both her husband Nagar Mal and his father had been adopted, there had been whispers during the wedding about a curse. A family in which children had not been born for two generations was marked so by Raamji, some said, but Hari had brushed the thought aside. Now, those whispers rang loudly in his ears. He resolved to travel to Kushtia, and had Gangadhar send a postcard to Shanti's father-in-law asking his permission.

He set out by train with three baskets of mangoes from his orchard, taking Ishwar Das and Mohan Lal—the boys would be overjoyed to see their sister, and their presence would reduce some of the awkwardness of the meeting. From Santahar they boarded the mail train towards Calcutta, crossed the Padma on the Hardinge Bridge, took a bullock cart to Kushtia, and then a boat across the river Gorai, which branched off from the Padma a few miles north of Kushtia. Shanti's father-in-law had constructed his forty-room mansion outside town on the banks of the Gorai. It loomed across the river.

Approaching the bank, the boat encountered a sudden current that knocked both Ishwar Das and Mohan Lal off their feet. They fell on to the mango baskets and laughed. Hari remained standing, transfixed by the mansion that rose before him. He had seen such a haveli before, many years ago in another land. It was a monument to hubris, they said in both Calcutta and Rampura, or a sign of approaching senility. He remembered its name—Daulatram's Grave. And he saw, again, the frescoes on the walls before him—a train cutting across rice paddies, jute stalks and flooded beels, engine spewing a column of smoke, sahibs and memsahibs waving from first-class carriages. Dark clouds obscured the sun. A barber shaved a boy's head on a riverbank, a pandit chanted, and a chandal stood nearby to collect his bones after he had died and been cremated. In the foreground, a motor car bounced along mud-banks with its top down. The man at the wheel looked like Garib Das. Two cows stood in the backseat, their eyes on a butcher flying behind the car on a pair of wings. It was only then that he saw the second train, which was so far away that he had to strain his eyes. It was jumping out of the picture, coming straight at the first train. It was clear to him, though not to the sahibs inside, that the two would collide.

'Babuji!' Ishwar Das called. 'Have you gone to sleep?'

The boat was moored along the bank, and the mango baskets had already been transferred to a cart. Hari fumbled in his kurta for money to pay the boatman. Handing him an anna, he said nervously, 'That haveli is my daughter's home.'

Turning to look at the mansion again, he saw that the walls were bare and the windows without adornment. There were no frescoes anywhere.

Shanti's father-in-law was seated in a room facing the river, awaiting Hari. Ishwar Das and Mohan Lal ran inside, looking for Shanti, calling 'Bai! Bai!' Coolies carried Hari's trunk and the mango baskets into an adjoining room. He stopped at the doorsill, undid a knot in his dhoti, extracted a twenty-rupee note and held it out ceremoniously. Shanti's father-in-law raised an arm in protest, then took the note with an air of wounded dignity and folded it away in his dhoti. This was Hari's payment for the hospitality he would receive. It was all right for Ishwar Das and Mohan Lal to eat in their sister's home—they were younger than her—but no one in Shekhavati would have dreamed of visiting his daughter in her father-in-law's house without payment. However small, a payment established Hari as a paying visitor, not a guest.

He spent the day in the house. Shanti's father-in-law regaled him with stories of his Congress Party activities, lists of properties owned by him in Dhaka, and the virtues of his son Nagar Mal, whom Hari saw only briefly. He had hoped to bring up the matter of miscegenation in the cow shed, but was too intimidated, especially when informed that Gandhiji would pass the Kushtia railway station the next day, and would be welcomed by the local Congress committee led by Shanti's father-in-law.

'They burnt down one of my shops in Munshiganj, near Dhaka,' he said, 'and there has been some trouble in Kushtia.'

Out of habit, Hari replied, 'Conditions are much better in Bogra. Our Nawabzada is Hindu-minded, as are our Musalmans.' Saying so made him feel secure. Everyone in Bogra—Mangiram, Chaman Lal, traders in Raja Bajar and Sat Matha—had said this for years. Indeed, amidst reports of violence in Munshiganj, Kushtia and Bihar—where Hindus had killed Musalmans in retaliation for the killing of Hindus in Noakhali—there had been no 'incident' in Bogra.

'The trouble-makers are not Musalmans but the men who incite them,' said Shanti's father-in-law.

'My son says that too,' Hari said vaguely, hoping not to offend by expressing his doubts about the thesis. What if the men who incited them were Musalmans too? 'Like you, he is in the Congress committee. In Kalkatta, where he is a barrister.'

Shanti's father-in-law expressed surprise and admiration, though of course, he had known that Shanti's brother was a barrister in Calcutta.

In the afternoon, Hari spent fifteen minutes with Shanti. She asked about her brothers and sisters, and especially about Manki. He did not bring up the subject of children. He did not know how.

The next morning, they accompanied Shanti's father-in-law to the railway station, where they found good spots in front of the crowd on account of Shanti's father-in-law's position in the Congress committee. Gandhiji was on his way to Noakhali to stop the Musalmans there from killing Hindus. His train arrived amidst much uproar. Gandhiji was seated at a window. Expressionlessly, he lifted his folded hands. Only those standing nearby were able to see him. A cry went up, 'Gandhiji ki jai!'

Silence fell; everyone waited for Gandhiji to speak.

Mohan Lal said, 'He is old.'

'Do not say that aloud,' Hari said. 'And fold your hands.'

The crowd was suddenly prostrate—men had thrown themselves on the ground and were applying dust to their foreheads. Shanti's father-in-law asked in a voice loud enough for everyone to hear. 'Would you like some milk, Bapu?'

Gandhiji grinned and nodded. A young woman's face appeared behind him. 'Bapu is not thirsty.'

But eager hands were preparing a pitcher of goat milk. Shanti's father-in-law said, 'Bapu, this is Harilalji Tibrewal, my daughter-in-law's father.'

Hari tried to peer through Gandhiji's spectacles. Was he indeed looking at him? Should he ask him for assurance that the Nawabzada was indeed Hindu-minded? Should he mention the cows that were led daily to the Nawabbari by butchers?

'My son is a barrister in Kalkatta,' he said.

20

The next day, Hari and his sons were on the Gorai again, on their way back to Bogra. The trip had been a failure—Hari had not raised the matter of children at all, or even the other issue of German bulls. Ishwar Das and Mohan Lal were in high spirits at having seen Gandhiji—that was some consolation. He sat in the boat with his back to the haveli, determined not to turn around, fearful of the visions that would follow. It was Mohan Lal who pointed at the shore and shouted, 'Babuji! There is a fire.'

Hari turned around. Half a mile to the left of the haveli, a column of smoke rose in the sky, losing itself quickly among dark clouds. The boatman identified it as Nagar Mal's orchard—everyone in Kushtia knew Shanti's father-in-law and his son. Hari turned to him in disbelief. 'But Gandhiji was in Kushtia yesterday. Hindus saw him, Musalmans saw him…'

'Wherever Gandhiji goes, he leaves behind a fire.'

Hari trembled, reminding himself of all the reasons Bogra was safer. The Nawabzada was Hindu-minded; Mangiram's family had lent more than one lakh rupees to the nawab's family; Tribhuvan was a friend of the Nawabzada's son. Indeed, this had become a source of great consolation to Marwaris in Bogra: when Tribhuvan came to Bogra, they made a point of being seen with him. They paid visits to the Nawabbari on the flimsiest of excuses, vied with each other to lend money to the nawab at half the market rate, and cheerfully swallowed insults that the nawab's retainers flung at them.

On reaching Bogra, he went to Fateh Ali Bazar to tell Mangiram about the fire in Kushtia. Mangiram was unfazed. 'Bogra is not Kushtia. Our Musalmans are Bengalis who have lived with us for a hundred years—they know us very well. Kushtia, on the other hand, is full of Bihari Musalmans, who cause all the trouble. They have come recently from Bihar. They are not our Musalmans.'

'But in Noakhali...'

'Noakhali is far from Bogra. I will share a secret with you. The Nawabzada has sent word that he does not want trouble in Bogra. Trouble-makers may go to other towns—Mymensingh, Dhaka, Rangpur, Narayanganj or Munshiganj, where five hundred Marwari families live—but have been warned to stay away from Bogra.'

Hari heaved a sigh of relief. 'A bania must lie low, and the troubles will die down.'

'As soon as the troubles die down in Dhaka, I will send my daughters to their husbands.'

Hari had forgotten—Mangiram's twin daughters had been married for nearly four years and were almost eighteen, yet had not gone to their husbands' homes in Dhaka. 'It is their misfortune to come of age at a time like this,' he said, 'but Raamji brings everything to an end—war, prosperity, profit or loss.'

And then Mangiram began to sob like a child. Astonished, Hari drew the shutters of the shop. What could make a grown man cry thus? Had the nawab declared his inability to pay back his loans? But that had been obvious for years. A great loss in trade? No, Mangiram was a seasoned bania—he understood adversity for what it was: an interval of suffering imposed by Raamji on his devotees, to be followed by an uptick in fortunes. Had the cows bellowing in the Nawabbari finally rent his heart?

'A great curse has fallen on my head, Hariya.'

Hari remained silent.

'My daughters cannot go to Dhaka. Their fathers-in-law will not take them...'

'But the weddings were completed, were they not?'

'The weddings? Yes...'

'Was the dowry insufficient?'

Mangiram shook his head. Hari searched his mind for explanations. A ghastly thought reared its head: was it conceivable that the daughters—Marwari girls of good breeding—were immoral? Was it even possible in Fateh Ali Bajar, where girls rarely left their homes, except to go to the temple with their mother? He had heard no rumours, and he would not start one. It was clear Mangiram was struggling with the disclosure. Not wishing to prolong his agony, Hari rose to go. 'Raamji gives and Raamji takes.'

'There is a problem. A medical one...'

Hari hesitated. It was improper to pry, and doubly so when the girls were Mangiram's daughters. 'There is Dr Saha. He saved Durga from yellowness three days after birth. And Tribhuvan speaks of a Dr B.C. Roy in Kalkatta. His fee will be high, but what is money? The dirt on one's palm...'

'I have already been to Kalkatta with my daughters,' said Mangiram. 'This is not something a doctor can cure.'

'Have you tried homoeopathy?'

'Their monthly ritual...'

'What do we know of such things?' Hari said uncomfortably, hoping to end the discussion.

'My daughters have not had their monthly ritual.'

Startled by the frankness, Hari rushed into reassurance. 'That is a matter of time...'

'The eighteenth is already upon them.'

They sat silently, Mangiram sunk in gloom and Hari in confusion. A demon had laid siege to Bogra—amidst talk of fires and killings, here was a new affliction he had never seen before. For it to visit Mangiram, who had already seen his son die of the pox! How many more arrows remained in Raamji's quiver?

By early 1947, all doubts about Bengal were laid to rest—there would be a Pakistan, no matter what they said in the newspapers. And Gangadhar's wife was with child. Hari awaited this birth with uncommon zeal. Although he had two great-grandsons—Pushpa's sons—she lived in Watsonganj in Bihar. He had not seen the boys, and Gopi would have disapproved if he had travelled to Watsonganj to see them. Gangadhar's child would be the first great-grandchild he would hold in his arms.

'Will Bogra will be in Pakistan?' Gangadhar asked. 'My son will be a Pakistani.'

'We are neither Indians nor Pakistanis; we are banias. If Jinnah wants two countries, let him have two. We will open shops in both.'

Two days later, Tribhuvan came to Bogra to suggest that everyone should go to Calcutta until the matter of Pakistan had been settled. Hari refused.

'Bogra is not our home,' said Tribhuvan.

'A bania lives where his shop is. He merely asks for tolerance, not love; he wants to buy cheap and sell dear, and he wants to remain invisible when doing so.'

But he had heard the rumblings—they had been present ever since he came to Bengal but had now become louder. Marwaris had raped the golden land of Bengal; a Marwari comes with a lota and a blanket and steals the land; a Marwari is like a mosquito—he feasts on people's blood; a Marwari will go where a dog will not...

'Everyone believes there will be trouble,' said Tribhuvan.

'In Mymensingh or Dhaka, not in Bogra. The nawab will see to that. It seems I have more faith in your friend than you do.'

'Mohammad Ali is a good man, but he is a Musalman,' Tribhuvan said. 'And he is only a nawab—not everyone in Bogra does as he says.'

'Our Musalmans know us,' Hari said half-heartedly, thinking of Mangiram. 'It is the Musalmans from Bihar who cannot be trusted. There aren't many of those in Bogra.'

'I do not blame Musalmans at all,' said Tribhuvan. 'Gandhiji has said…'

'Gandhiji was in Kushtia for a mere fifteen minutes. How could he know whom to blame? I have lived here for forty years.'

'I do not want to argue over who is to blame. Come to Calcutta for a few months.'

'They do not want us in Kalkatta either. When I lived in Bara Bazar forty years ago, they called a Marwari "kaiyan", sometimes to his face. The bhadralok scorned us even when pawning their wives' jewellery with us. And you certainly remember that Bengali who wrote that book…'

Tribhuvan left for Calcutta, disappointed. Hari had a second reason for not wishing to go to Calcutta—he was uncomfortable living with Tribhuvan in the flat after the rift between them.

Gangadhar's son was born a week before Holi, just as the cold weather was easing. Beside himself with joy, Hari held the boy in his arms for much of the day, sat with him in the grain shop and showed him to all his customers. When they asked if this was a new grandson, he laughed. 'My great-grandson. The third. And Gariba's wife will have her second child soon. Another grandson. Raamji had it declared from the sky that Harilal shall have many sons, and they shall have many more, and those in turn will beget many…'

He was determined to get on as if nothing strange was happening in the world around him. Yes, an orchard had been burnt in Kushtia and there had been riots in Munshiganj, but no doubt the troubles would die down soon as men returned to the task of living—earning money, arranging weddings, giving birth and disposing of their dead. With that in mind, he settled on a plan that had been bubbling in his head for six months, since Mangiram told him about his daughter's afflictions. The two girls were eighteen; Bansidhar was twenty and Murli nearly sixteen. Neither would find a bride. When Raamji had placed two such boys and two such girls on this earth, he surely meant them to find joy with each other. What harm could possibly come of it?

The girls' weddings had been voided, and indeed had never been formalized. Their husbands had never seen them, nor they their husbands. They were as good as unmarried, and unmarriageable, and they were the daughters of Mangiram, his dearest friend in Bogra. This would be a suitable way to tie loose ends, to settle the matter once and for all. True, no children would bless these marriages, but that would be no tragedy. Murli and Bansi would find partners for their old age—when Gangadhar's children would likely turn their backs on their uncles—while Mangiram would find a home for his daughters. And who knew: if Raamji had chosen to dry the wombs of those girls, he might plant a seed once they were married!

Mangiram broke down when told of the plan and clasped Hari's hand. 'You will have many, many grandsons, Hariya, and they will have grandsons of their own.'

'Raamji hatched the plan,' Hari said modestly. 'I am only the instrument.'

'You are throwing away your boys on good-for-nothing girls. Did you not say that Bansi's seizures are now infrequent? Months go by, you have told me, and nothing happens. Maybe the responsibility of a wife will eliminate them altogether. And if they do not happen for years, does it matter that they ever happened? As for Murli, I have seen him cry when looking at the cows in the Nawabbari, and I know him to be a saint. My daughter will marry a devotee of Raamji. Who can say with certainty that anything at all is the matter with him?'

'I will treat your daughters as my daughters.'

'And I your sons as my sons. Why, they will sit in my shop—for they will inherit it—and I will tell my customers: here are my two sons. Harilal raised them, but I am the one who enjoys them in the evening of my life.'

When Hari climbed to the verandah that evening, Lakshmi's Ma was in the kitchen, Gayatri at the spinning wheel and Manki inside her room. The children having gone to bed, he sat down on his cot and announced, 'I have found matches for Bansi and Murli.'

As was his habit, he had addressed Manki, speaking loudly so Gayatri would overhear. The spinning wheel stopped squeaking. He quickly explained the rest, saying only that the girls had a medical problem but were beyond reproach in their morals, and that Mangiram had accepted. From inside the room, Manki said, 'Balanjogi, Balanjogi…'

She was perhaps addressing her new granddaughters-in-law. The girls would be in Gayatri's care, he thought with some relief, so Manki's demeanour toward them would not matter.

'We will have a double-wedding next week, so the granddaughters-in-law can be at Sat Matha to celebrate Holi.'

He lay down on the cot, satisfied—another two had been married off. At first, he almost did not hear Gayatri, but she repeated herself. 'They are my sons.'

He sat up in confusion. She was looking straight at him, as she usually did, and had made no attempt to cover her head. They spoke but rarely. He was in the shop all day, and it was Lakshmi's Ma who attended to his dinner, with Gayatri hovering nearby. Since Shanti's wedding, he had been plagued by the suspicion that Gayatri had divined his thoughts that morning, and found reasons to avoid the verandah when he was the only one present. But he also knew her to be proper, prudent and restrained, so her outburst took him by surprise.

'Your sons, of course,' he repeated. 'And Durga's. And my grandsons.'

'My sons will not marry such girls.'

It had not occurred to him that anyone but he had authority over Durga's sons. He was irritated. 'Ganga's mother. This is not your place to speak.'

He found himself trembling. He had never addressed Gayatri in the presence of others, and knew that a breach had been made. The incident would be narrated by Lakshmi's Ma, elaborated upon, and find its way around Sat Matha, perhaps even to Mangiram in Fateh Ali Bajar. He had to say more, if only to cover the wound left by his first words. 'I have the boys' welfare in mind. They are of age, and Bansi will soon be too old. Who will take care of them?'

'Their mother still lives,' said Gayatri. 'After her, their brother lives. Gangadhar has taken an oath to look after his brothers...'

Hari marvelled at her boldness. Seated behind her spinning wheel, with head uncovered and without the slightest trace of deference, she looked almost like Gandhiji... When had she gone about extracting oaths from Gangadhar? Which other plans had she made for his family without his knowledge? And what was he to tell Mangiram now?

'I have given my word to Mangiram,' he pleaded.

'Your word is not like Raamji's pledge to his father. It may be broken.'

He fell silent. Gayatri went into her room. Lakshmi's Ma went to sleep in a corner. Manki's mutterings ceased. He lay awake all night. *She sits calmly like the goddess Saraswati while the calf sucks at her teats, but turns into the fierce Kali when you approach the calf*, Master Bholaram had said. No doubt she knew everything. She had read his thoughts on the night of Shanti's wedding, and she had also peered into Tribhuvan's mind when he had made his ghastly proposal after Durga's death.

Two days before Holi, a Marwari was stabbed in Rangpur. Bihari Muslims were blamed by those who received the news in Bogra. Hari forbade Garib Das from going to Rangpur. The next day, a Marwari in Bara Gola was hit from behind with a steel rod while he was shutting his shop. Fortunately, he had little in his pocket, and the men ran away without robbing the store.

The celebration during Holi was perfunctory. The hill of cowdung cakes that was usually built at Sat Matha was smaller this year, and its incineration attracted fewer revellers. The following morning, it was still smouldering when the children began their games with paints and sprays. They were forbidden to leave Marwari Para. A few cries of 'Holi hai!' were heard here and there, but these quickly died. There was a sense that this might be the last Holi for many years—would it be allowed in Pakistan?

Darkness fell. After the children had bathed and washed, Ishwar Das and Mohan Lal were allowed to go and greet their teacher, who lived behind the government school. Gangadhar went to the hosiery store for a puja—the store was closed for the day.

Hari opened the grain shop. A pandit busied himself with the annual Holi puja. There was a glow in the sky beyond Marwari Para, which Hari took to be a smouldering cowdung hill at the next crossroads. That was unusual. Hindu Bengalis did not build these hillocks, and the few who needed the sacred fire for their kitchens came to Marwari Para to take cinders. But the sky was certainly aglow, while the dung at Sat Matha sat before Hari's eyes like a dark mountain, fully extinguished.

Faint cries could now be heard. Men came running into Marwari Para. The glow was from a house on fire, not a Holi celebration. Hurriedly, Hari shut his doors and tried to compose himself. Should the puja go on or should he dispatch the pandit, who was trembling even as he continued to chant? A sharp knock startled him.

'Dadaji!'

He opened the door. Gangadhar stood outside, kurta splattered with blood. Hari grabbed his shoulders and shook him hard, forgetting that he should bring him inside. 'How did this happen? How...'

'A minor wound.'

Gangadhar stepped inside, and Hari's initial shock melted into grief. The wound was indeed minor—he had been struck on the head with a bamboo—but with the stains on his kurta he could have passed for a blood-soaked corpse. Hari shuddered.

'There is trouble in Bara Gola, near the railway station. I saw houses on fire. But I think the men did not come into Marwari Para.'

Hari wondered who 'the men' were. Our Musalmans or Bihari Musalmans? Did it matter? Were these the Musalmans who pawned their wives' jewellery with him, or the ones who came to Gangadhar to buy lungis, or the ones who bought their grain at Sat Matha?

'Nawab Sahib is Hindu-minded,' he said mechanically. 'There will be no trouble in Bogra.'

'Have you accounted for everyone?' Gangadhar asked.

That was when Hari remembered: Ishwar Das and Mohan Lal had gone to their teacher in Bengali Para. His mind ran through terrible images before dismissing all of them. 'It will blow over. A couple of trouble-makers, that is all.'

Garib Das was upstairs—he had had the good sense to listen to Hari and had not gone to Rangpur. Fakir Chand was in bed with a parpatti around his waist. All the children and women were upstairs too. The only ones outside were Ishwar Das and Mohan Lal.

Hari and Gangadhar sat in the shop for two hours, afraid to go upstairs where they would be asked about the two boys. Also, Gangadhar could not enter the verandah in his blood-soaked kurta—that would set off a panic. Every few minutes, they opened the shutters and peered out. Sat Matha was deserted. The glow in the sky was dimmer; the cries had died down. Eventually, they saw Ishwar Das approach. Gangadhar called out to him. He ran into the shop and they shut the door behind him. He stared at Gangadhar's kurta, then chuckled. 'I thought you were too old to play Holi, Ganga.'

'Where is Mohan Lal?' Hari asked him.

'He stopped to play Holi with his friends.'

'Why did you let him go alone?'

Ishwar Das appeared confused. 'He goes there every day.' When told of the trouble near the railway tracks, he broke down crying, certain that he was responsible for causing his brother harm. Hari found himself offering assurances he himself did not believe.

They waited for another hour. 'I see someone,' said Gangadhar, peering through a crack in the door. It was Chaman Lal, leaning heavily on his stick yet walking briskly. Hari rarely went to the jute press—its profits were negligible now that the war had ended—and had not seen Chaman Lal in months. In

Shekhavati, they said it was inauspicious to end your day with a glimpse of a buffalo, a donkey, a widow, a cripple or an ass. And his day was now ending with this ignominious sight when he had hoped to see his son!

Gangadhar opened the door to let Chaman Lal inside.

'Why have you come?' Hari asked irritably.

'I am frightened, Hari Babu. The press is like a graveyard. The kyals are gone. I can see the Karatoya from the office, and I think it wants to take me…'

Hari turned away. His son was somewhere in the lanes of Bengali Para, and an old man was muttering about his fears… What right did Chaman Lal have to be living at his age? Had he not already crossed ninety, or even a hundred? What was the purpose of his life anyway? He turned to Ishwar Das. 'Let us go to this friend's house and bring back your brother.'

Gangadhar protested that it was not safe, but Hari had already stepped out with Ishwar Das. They walked out of Marwari Para, crossed the railway tracks, made their way to the school and turned into the lane where Mohan Lal's friend lived. Their arrival caused some commotion—they were mistaken for Muslims. They were told that no one had entered the lane all day; all houses had been locked since the afternoon, when the first fires were reported near the railway station. No one had seen Mohan Lal. They returned to Sat Matha. Hari considered walking to the police station outside Marwari Para, but the policemen were all Muslims themselves.

Gayatri soon noticed Mohan Lal's absence, and a great storm of chest-beating rose in the verandah. Hari made feeble attempts at restoring calm, offering explanations that sounded increasingly hollow. Eventually, the crying subsided and the children fell asleep. He sat up all night with Garib Das, Fakir Chand, Gangadhar and Ishwar Das. Eager to help, Chaman Lal sat up with them, though his body was unequal to the task. They took positions in the verandah and kept watch, their eyes feeding on forms in the darkness. The night was alive with dogs and cats and the scurrying of rats. From time to time, someone would point excitedly and then relapse into gloom.

They saw dawn break over Bogra and heard the first stirrings at Sat Matha. The dung hill had disintegrated into mounds all over the road. A few men walked by, perhaps on their way to their shops. Cows went by, bells ringing. Goats. Carts. A funeral procession for a Musalman. Ishwar Das was the first to spy Mohan Lal. He ran down the steps, opened the doors and pulled his brother inside.

The verandah erupted in joy. The children crowded around Mohan Lal, poking and prodding him to ensure he was still living. His story was interrupted again and again. After having parted from Ishwar Das, he had passed the school and was about to turn into his friend's lane when he had seen a dozen men carrying spades and daggers. He thought it wise to run. When they gave chase, he ran into Marina Cinema. No one asked him for a ticket, and he quietly squatted on the floor in the women's section, next to the curtain that separated it from the men's area. Because it was the evening of Holi, there weren't many in the audience. The few women in the section paid him no heed in the dark. Shortly before the film finished, he walked out of the theatre but his courage failed him in the lobby, so he hid behind the ticket counter, where he fell asleep. When he woke up, it was morning.

'Which film were they playing at Marina?' Ishwar Das asked.

'*Omar Khayyam*.'

Garib Das laughed. 'So you heard the songs of Saigal! Babuji would never have let you spend eight annas on a film.'

'But I did not pay,' said Mohan Lal, now smug.

'A boy of thirteen must not watch films,' Hari said absently.

'The fourteenth is upon me,' Mohan Lal replied, 'and I sat there with my eyes shut.'

'Liar! You were looking at Suraiya,' said Garib Das.

Hari turned away from the boys' banter. He was shaken, more by Gangadhar's blood-splattered kurta than by Mohan Lal's tale. But what was a bania to do? He could not brandish a stick when challenged; he could only open his purse. Whom could he pay to leave him alone? And how much would such payment be?

He counted the members of his family. Manki was asleep. Gayatri stood in the verandah with the boys. Lakshmi's Ma was in the kitchen. Mohan Lal was now describing the plot of *Omar Khayyam*—after having watched it with eyes shut—and the children were rapt, even those expressly forbidden to discuss films. It became clear: very little was needed to shatter this illusion—a stone, a stick, a knife, a spear, a bomb, a bullet. Those with little to lose had little to fear, but he had sons, daughters-in-law, grandchildren, granddaughters-in-law, shops, merchandise, land. A man with many children to guard was weak, and weaker for being a bania.

He turned to Gayatri. 'Bring out all the steel trunks and bedrolls you find. Have them packed and piled in the verandah. Cook rotis and pack them into bundles with mango pickle.'

'Who is going to travel?' she asked.

'We will all go to Kalkatta.'

There was sudden silence. Garib Das turned to Hari. 'We cannot leave our shops, Babuji. They will take all the stock.'

'We will return as soon as we can.'

Drawing Hari aside, Garib Das whispered. 'What of my gold? I have told you about the ginnis buried in the mattress at Rangpur.'

With great effort, Hari said, 'What is money, Gariba? It is the dirt on…'

'I know, I know!' Garib Das said irritably. 'But we could wait a day or two. I could go to Rangpur…'

'The train to Santahar leaves in the afternoon,' said Hari.

'We should seek Mohammad Ali's help.'

'I do not know if he is in Bogra today.'

'But this is our home, Babuji,' said Gangadhar.

Hari looked hard at his favourite grandson. 'This is where you were born.'

All morning, he sat in the shop with Nanuram, who sealed sacks of grain, locked tins, put away the scales and threw account books into cartons. Hari withdrew the hundred-rupee notes buried inside his sacks and tied them into knots in his dhoti. Upstairs, steel trunks were thrown open and bedrolls dusted. Four trunks full of Raam Raam books were extracted from Manki's room. By afternoon, sixteen trunks lay scattered across the verandah. A mound of bedrolls sat near the stairs. Three bundles—each with fifty rotis soaked in ghee and stacked carefully, and three jars of mango pickle—had been arranged next to the trunks, along with a pot of water. Everyone had on their best clothes, especially Garib Das, and the women had worn their jewellery. The children were dressed in silk kurtas and dhotis. Gangadhar's little boy, born a week ago, wore a maroon velvet cap with dark piping. Mohan Lal brandished his cricket bat; Ishwar Das had the radio—the one given by Tribhuvan—in his hands.

The festive mood annoyed Hari. 'We are not going to a wedding.'

'We will not leave Bogra like beggars,' Gayatri replied.

'It is best to wear jewellery instead of packing it,' Garib Das added, 'because luggage may be lost or stolen.'

Resigned to Gayatri's defiance, Hari turned to Nanuram. 'Go to the railway station with Ishwar Das and bring back a dozen coolies.'

'The train will not arrive for two hours.'

'We have many people and much luggage.' It occurred to him that a headcount would be useful. He said to Gangadhar, 'Make a list with everyone's name.'

Gangadhar ran down to the shop, brought back paper and pencil, and called out every name so no one would be missed.

'Babuji Harilal Tibrewal. Manki Devi. Gayatri Devi. Gariba Chachi, Sumitra Chachi, their little girl, the son who will be born soon...'

Hari found such flippancy out of place. 'Count the living, not the unborn.'

'Fakira Cha Cha, Lajwanti Chachi, their girl. Ishwar Das, Mohan Lal.'

Then he came to himself, and Hari was pleased to note that he was discreet enough not to name his wife in public. 'Gangadhar, the mother of his son, and his son born a week ago. Bansidhar. Murlidhar. Have I forgotten anyone?'

'Your sister Savitri.'

'Savitri,' said Gangadhar.

'That makes seventeen,' Garib Das said.

'Eighteen,' said Hari. 'Nanuram will come with us.'

Garib Das inched closer to Hari and whispered. 'He should stay and take care of the shops.'

Hari hissed at his son. 'You want to leave him here to die? He is nearly seventy, and has spent his life in the service of Harilal & Sons. He watched me grow up in Rampura, followed me to Disavar…'

'But the shops?'

'Shops are mere structures. What will happen to them? Bricks torn apart, stock burnt. We will build new ones when we return.'

'The gold ginnis in Rangpur…'

'Raamji gives and Raamji takes,' Hari said stubbornly. 'We will look for them when we return.'

'They will not let us come back.'

'They will. Will they not need grain in Pakistan?'

Gangadhar tugged at Hari's sleeve and asked softly, 'What about Lakshmi's Ma?'

To cover his embarrassment at having forgotten her, Hari professed shock. 'Of course! Did you think we would leave her behind?'

'Lakshmi's Ma,' Gangadhar called.

'Nineteen,' said Garib Das.

'Hari Babu?'

It was Chaman Lal, seated on the floor. He appeared not to have moved since the previous evening, when they had settled down to watch the road for Mohan Lal. Hari pretended not to have heard him.

'You are the only son I have, Hari Babu. Where will I go?'

Hari cringed at the obsequiousness. Why did Raamji choose to leave carcasses walking about? Which divine purpose had been served through Chaman Lal's life? He still had daughters in Shekhavati, perhaps, but they had not seen him for years.

'Chaman Lal,' he said to Gangadhar with a sigh. 'A total of twenty.'

Nanuram returned from the railway station with a gaggle of squabbling coolies who were still negotiating their rates. They climbed up to the verandah, and a look at the mountain of bedrolls set them quarrelling again. After much argument, rates were agreed upon and three coolies left in a huff. The other seven began to transfer the luggage downstairs to the road, where rickshas, scenting prey, had begun to gather. Meanwhile, the rooms upstairs were locked and the keys hidden away in Gayatri's blouse. She paid and discharged the servants. Stooped and walking with difficulty though only forty-six, Manki was helped into a chair and carried down to the road by two coolies. She sat there in a foul mood, flinging abuse that the coolies did not understand.

Hari watched the road anxiously. Everyone in Marwari Para now knew that Harilalji's family was going away. Other eyes would have seen them too. If a man wished him harm, this was a good opportunity, yet there was no way of transporting everyone, and everything, to the railway station without all this commotion. Word would soon travel outside Marwari Para, and his shops would be marked for plunder.

Seated in her chair, Manki turned to him. 'I need Hanumanji's prasad.'

Every morning, Gangadhar went to the Hanuman temple near Bara Gola and brought her sugar crystals blessed during the morning puja there.

'Gangadhar has been busy with the luggage,' Hari said.

'Send him to the temple.'

'It is not safe.'

'No one will dare stop a boy going to Hanumanji's temple. All he needs to do is recite the Hanuman Chalisa, and the most dreaded murderer will flee in fear.'

He smiled wanly. 'There are men in this world who are not intimidated by Hanuman Chalisa.'

Manki set her face and adopted a stiff posture in her chair, as if she was not going to allow herself the indignity of the slightest movement. 'I will not leave Bogra without Hanumanji's prasad.'

Hari gnashed his teeth. His attachment to Manki, such as it had been, had long withered away. She was the mother of his sons and daughters, and she lived in his house and his room. He himself lived in the verandah. On all household matters he communicated with Gayatri, usually through Gangadhar. This was the longest conversation he had had with Manki in months. She hardly spoke any more, to him or anyone else. When she did, her words were usually addressed to the brass statuette of Raamji in her shrine in the kitchen. When she deigns to speak to humans, he thought irritably, it is to throw a spoke in a running wheel. But he knew she was stubborn. He looked around. Gangadhar was busy with the rickshas. Fakir Chand sat timidly on a trunk, looking utterly lost. Finally, his eyes fell on Garib Das. 'Gariba, run to the Hanuman temple and get your mother some prasad.'

'Why now? We could get some in Santahar on our way to Calcutta. There is a Hanuman temple not far from the station there.'

Hari wrung his hands. He could not insist—what if something should happen to the boy? But another look at Manki convinced him that she would rather die than yield. He turned to Fakir Chand, whose eyes opened wide in horror. 'This is the moment Raamji has chosen for my death,' he said mournfully.

'Stop your nonsense!' Hari shouted. 'Get your mother some prasad right away.'

Intimidated, Fakir Chand slunk away. Hari watched him go in disgust. Fakira was his mother's favourite son on account of his light skin. She tolerated and even indulged his hypochondria, sitting with him when he lay in bed swathed in parpatti bandages, running a hand over his forehead, imagining fevers and aches when even he could not feel them. It was fitting that he was the one to suffer for her obstinacy. But, of course, the temple was not far from Bara Gola, and he would be back soon.

He asked Gangadhar to bring the women downstairs and help them into rickshas. They came with saris and shawls covering their faces. Garib Das's wife was seven months pregnant; she had to be helped down the stairs by Gayatri. Gangadhar's wife carried her week-old son, attached to her breast, in her arms. Manki was lifted into a ricksha by Gangadhar. Bansidhar was in good spirits, and Murlidhar looked about curiously, asking Gangadhar if they were all going to watch *Omar Khayyam*. Their sister Savitri, now fifteen, stood between them.

The last to descend was Mohan Lal, whom Gangadhar had assigned the task of ensuring that all rooms were locked and nothing had been left behind. The rotis and mango pickle sat in Gayatri's lap. Six rickshas had been piled high with trunks and bedrolls, and these were to ride in the middle of the party, to prevent the rickshawalas from making off with the luggage. The coolies were to walk with them to the station and help them into the train. Because the train would stop for only five minutes at Bogra, the coolies would stand ready, each with two trunks and a bedroll, and throw what they could into the carriages through windows. The children would be sent in through windows too; the men would call out 'didi didi mashima mashima' to let the women go through the doors before pushing themselves into the train.

'We look like a wedding party,' Gangadhar said anxiously.

Mohan Lal laughed. 'Ishwar Das is the groom! Look how many guests he has invited.'

At fourteen, Ishwar Das would not be married for another three or four years, given the new fashion of waiting until a boy had crossed sixteen, but this had been Mohan Lal's usual taunt for a year.

'Where is Fakira Chacha?' Gangadhar asked.

'I sent him to get prasad from the Hanuman temple. Your grandmother insists.'

Fakir Chand had been gone for almost fifteen minutes. Hari

was anxious; he had been a fool to yield to Manki. 'Let us go to the station. We will send Garib Das to fetch Fakira and join us at the station.'

'I see him,' said Mohan Lal.

Fakir Chand was running and gesticulating. As soon as he was within earshot he shouted. 'There are men at the station!'

'Musalmans?'

'Bihari Musalmans. They have already burnt down the Hanuman temple. They are now waiting for the train.'

Hari's heart sank. Every moment in Bogra now seemed perilous, but how were they to leave town if they could not take the train to Santahar? The women were already in rickshas. A horrible thought crossed his mind: that the rickshawalas were in league with those at the railway station and Harilal's family would be delivered whole to men with sticks and knives...

'Get off the rickshas!'

Gangadhar was bewildered. 'We need rickshas no matter where we go. The women cannot walk...'

Hari wrenched Bansidhar and Murlidhar out of their seats—both were short and frail in spite of their age—and set them on the ground. Gangadhar helped the women down. Manki was deposited back in her chair. She was muttering 'Balanjogi Balanjogi' at no one in particular. Garib Das's and Fakir Chand's wives stood uncomfortably in the road, saris hiding their faces.

'Take the trunks off too. Lock them inside the shop.'

'Dadaji, we cannot stay here,' said Gangadhar. 'We must go somewhere, anywhere!'

'We will.' A strange notion had taken birth in his mind. Once born, it seemed obvious—he would seek refuge in the Nawabbari. He would reason with the Nawabzada, or his retainer if the Nawabzada was in Calcutta; he would speak of Mangiram's loans; he would promise everything he possessed; he would mention Tribhuvan's friendship with the Nawabzada's son; he would plead in the name of humanity.

Their luggage was quickly locked away. The rickshawalas

were dismissed. They protested about their lost fares. Bitterly, Hari handed them four annas each—better to be robbed than be delivered to the men at the station.

'Count everyone again,' he said to Gangadhar, 'and let us walk to Fateh Ali Bazar. We will see how a Hindu-minded nawab greets a Hindu in peril.'

A car horn burst through the air.

'Get out of the way!' Garib Das shouted. He was sitting behind the wheel of the Opel. His steel trunk and bedroll were next to him in the car. His pregnant wife and four-year-old daughter were in the backseat. He had put up the convertible top and was now trying to start the engine, which had stalled.

'Where do think you will go?' Hari demanded, blocking the path of the Opel and directing Gangadhar to stand behind it.

'This car can go 125 miles in an hour,' shouted Garib Das. He had rolled up the windows and locked the doors. 'I will be in Rangpur in forty minutes. After I have loaded the mattress that has my gold, I will reach Calcutta in two hours.'

Hari stared at his son. Was it possible that a grown man, and one who earned so much in his oil depot, could be such a fool? The Opel had never been driven beyond Santahar. No one knew if it could go much faster than a ricksha, and Garib Das had never driven it by himself, his claim of being a driver notwithstanding. It was not clear he could even navigate the roads around Sat Matha, or that there was sufficient petrol in the car.

'Get out of this car immediately!' Hari shouted.

'Clear the way!' Garib Das shouted back. His wife could be seen snivelling in the back, and his daughter set up a wail.

'Drive over my body if you dare. And Ganga is standing behind the car.'

In frustration, Garib Das pressed the horn again and again, until shopkeepers all over Sat Matha came out of their shops. Windows opened on upper floors. 'Whoever did not know we were leaving has now heard the news,' Hari said angrily. 'And there are men with knives at the railway station, on their way to Sat Matha…'

His eyes fell on the cricket bat in Mohan Lal's hands. Grabbing it, he swung at the car, smashing the windshield. Its pieces landed in Garib Das's lap, who buried his face in his hands. 'Now you have killed your own son!'

'Get out of the car, Gariba. Raamji dislikes you too much to call you to himself.'

The smashed windshield had knocked the wind out of Garib Das. Subdued, he slid out of the seat and brushed glass shards from his dhoti—Manchester, but now without pleats and arranged anyhow. His crying wife and daughter were helped out by Gangadhar and his trunk and bedroll transferred into the shop—it had to be unlocked and locked again.

'I will keep this,' said Hari, grabbing the car key from him and slipping it into his kurta pocket.

Approaching his father with a mixture of fear and admiration, Mohan Lal asked for and received his cricket bat. Garib Das surveyed the ruined windshield mournfully and turned to Hari. 'Mangiramji will ask you to pay for the damage.'

'Let us go to the Nawabbari,' said Hari.

'You should not have sent away the rickshawalas,' said Gangadhar, pointing to Manki. 'How will Dadiji walk all the way to Fateh Ali Bajar?'

'The rickshawalas would have taken us straight to the men at the station,' said Hari. Walking over to Manki, who sat in her chair in a trance, he announced loudly so she and the others would hear. 'We will go to the Nawabbari. Everyone will walk.'

She came to. 'Where are my books?'

He was startled by her sudden alertness. 'All trunks have been locked away in the shop. When we return...'

Manki put her hands over her ears. She would not listen, and she would not budge. If they were to leave Sat Matha, her Raam Raam books would go with her. Knowing her well, Gangadhar shrugged, pulled the brass key from his waistband and opened the shop again. Manki's steel trunks—four of them—were identified and pulled out.

'Who will carry them?' Hari demanded. 'The coolies have gone to the station.'

'Gariba will,' said Manki. 'And Gangadhar. Ishwar Das is almost a man now.' Turning to her favourite son, she added, 'And you, Fakira. Do not worry—Raamji gave Hanuman the strength to lift a whole mountain. Chant his name, and the trunks will become light as feathers on your shoulders.'

'Why not Nanuramji?' Fakir Chand asked.

If Fakir Chand showed no compassion for a seventy-year-old munim, thought Hari, what would he do with his sixty-year-old father if given the chance?

Manki regarded her favourite son with amusement. 'He is your father's munim, not a servant.'

'But two of us are needed to carry you, Dadiji,' said Gangadhar. 'That leaves only two men to carry your trunks, unless you want Dadaji to lift a steel trunk at his age.'

'Why must you carry me?' With astonishing vigour, she stood up and took three confident steps. It was as if she had never been bedridden at all.

I have just witnessed a miracle, Hari thought, even as he wondered at the strange ways of Raamji. He could breathe life into a woman's atrophied legs, so why could He not make the men at the railway station disappear? One must take what He gives when He gives it... They set off, Hari leading. Manki walked with him. He was amazed, both because she kept pace with him and because no Marwari in Bogra had ever seen a wife walk with her husband. It was improper, of course, but this was not a time for propriety. Bansidhar and Murlidhar walked with Mohan Lal between them, holding hands. The women scrambled to keep up, unused to walking briskly in the dirt. Each carried a bundle of rotis or a jar of mango pickle. The goitre at Lakshmi's Ma's throat swung this way and that as she struggled to keep up with the men, carrying Garib Das's daughter in her arms. Being a new bride, Gangadhar's wife had put on an embroidered skirt that swept the road as she walked, so she had to lift its hem with one arm while holding her infant son in the other. He had begun to cry. Nanuram followed her, awkwardly tying to comfort the infant and offering to hold him in his arms. Garib Das's wife had the most difficulty, being seven months pregnant. Chaman Lal limped along with quick jabs of his walking stick in the dust. Garib Das, Fakir Chand, Ishwar Das and Gangadhar brought up the rear, each weighed down by a heavy trunk full of Manki's books.

They passed Mangiram's shop. Hari noted it was shut, and the windows in the house above it were barred—Mangiram was taking no chances in spite of his faith in the nawab. He headed for the yellow pillars framing the cast-iron gates to the Nawabbari. They were shut. There was no keeper.

'Push the gates,' said Manki.

Hari found himself obeying her, and was surprised to see the gates swing open. Manki murmured, 'Raam Raam Raam…' and they walked in. They saw two Alsatian dogs to the left.

'Do not be afraid,' said Manki. 'Raamji has muted them.'

The dogs did not interfere. They went through the gardens, where large guavas hung from overloaded branches, and turned toward the mansion. Near the cow shed, Hari tried to hurry past but Bansidhar tugged at his kurta. 'Stop, Dadaji. Why does the nawab have cows?'

'It is a goshala,' Hari replied. 'The nawab keeps them here until they die. In winter his men throw blankets on them; in summer, they wash them with water from the Karatoya.'

'But these cows do not look old.'

'Twenty of them,' said Murlidhar, who had counted the cows through his tears.

Hari faltered. In the goshala outside town, cows usually sat, chewed cud, dozed or flicked off flies with their tails. Here, they stood almost to attention. He even fancied they were looking at him. Why did Raamji throw so many obstacles in a man's path?

'We must hurry,' he said roughly. 'There are men with knives about.'

They entered the mansion. The children marvelled at the

ceiling in the audience hall, and stopped before the pictures of Lat Sahibs and memsahibs. Through the corner of his eye, Hari saw Mozelle Cohen beaming at him. He could hear his sons tear through the billiards room as he approached the retainer's office with Bansidhar and Murlidhar. On his first visit to the Nawabbari forty years ago, he had wondered why the nawab kept his retainer's office inside the mansion instead of locating it near the gate. Why allow the riff-raff to walk through his mansion? Why let banias gaze on the face of his mistress? He now understood—the nawab *wanted* his creditors to walk through the audience hall, so they would be cowed when coming to collect on debts. Even Manki looked daunted by the ornate ceiling and the portraits.

The porcelain filter sat where it had for forty years. Bansidhar began to play with it.

'Do not touch that!' said Hari.

The office was locked. He banged on the door. His cries echoed through the audience hall, and mixed with Mohan Lal's laughter in the billiards room.

'There is no one here,' said Manki. 'We must go back to Sat Matha.'

'But we will be safer inside the Nawabbari,' Garib Das said.

'Let us explore the grounds. We could hide in the grove of guava trees until it is dark.'

They crossed the audience hall again, now with growing urgency. Behind them, a great crash sent them diving for cover. Had Bihari Musalmans already entered the nawab's mansion?

'Run!' Gangadhar shouted.

'Wait.' It was Murlidhar. He stood alone at the far end of the hall, near the retainer's office, and pointed to the floor, where Bansidhar was writhing in a pool of water. Pieces of porcelain lay around him.

'Raam Raam Raam...' intoned Manki.

Gangadhar held his brother down until the fit had passed, then helped him up.

'We must go,' said Hari.

They emerged from the mansion. Because the building stood at the top of a staircase, they had a full view of the grounds. The Karatoya wound its way lazily along the eastern boundary, shimmering in the late afternoon sun. The nawab's mansion cast a long shadow on the river. On its opposite bank was the main mosque in Bogra, and around it was Musalman Para.

'We will go to the river,' said Manki, standing next to Hari with a familiarity that surprised him.

'We cannot swim,' said Gangadhar.

'Raamji floated stones on the ocean to build a bridge to Sri Lanka. He will make a bridge for us too.'

She set off. Hari and the others followed helplessly. He was reminded of something Mangiram had said: that Nawab Sobhan, Altaf Ali's grandfather, had his own steamer on the Karatoya, which joined the Jamuna and then the Padma. He would take the steamer, get off at Damookdeah Ghat and board the train to Calcutta. This was in the days before the Hardinge Bridge was built, when a ferry was required to cross the Padma.

They reached the nawab's ghat. Steps led down to the Karatoya. Three boats lay moored; only one appeared large enough to hold all of them. Hari made for it. With a foot on the boat's prow, he paused. He was a man from Shekhavati. He could keep his balance on a camel as it sat down and shield his body from a sandstorm, but after fifty years in Bengal he did not know how to steer a boat. Neither did his sons or grandsons. Indeed, Master Bholaram would have said, 'When a bania needs to row a boat, he hires a boatman.'

'Have you have come for a bath in the holy river, Harilalji?'

Hari gasped. A man was seated in the boat furthest from him. He was in the shadows.

'Take everything,' Hari pleaded. 'Every last nose-ring…'

The man stepped on to the shore. It was Mohammad Ali Bogra's driver, wearing a lungi and kurta, and a turban that obscured much of his face. Heart pounding, Hari folded his hands. 'My children have done you no harm. Strike me down and let them go.'

'My daughters have grown up,' said the man. 'The oldest will soon be married off. She still remembers the sack of rice I brought home.'

In his state of confusion, Hari was slow to recall the great famine from four years ago. Had Raamji really responded to Manki's cries? Were those steel trunks an armour around his family?

'Help your women into the boat,' said the driver.

'We will help ourselves,' said Manki. Lifting her sari, she strode toward the largest boat, jumped in like a man and stood erect, seeming not to notice the ground rocking beneath her feet. 'What is your name?' she asked the driver.

Hari was aware of the impropriety, yet conscious that these were not ordinary times.

'Naseer.'

'You are the *kevat* who took Raamji across the river,' she declared.

Gayatri climbed in, followed by the wives of Garib Das, Fakir Chand and Gangadhar. The children went next, except Murlidhar, who stood calmly with Hari on the shore. Chaman Lal and Lakshmi's Ma found places in the stern.

Garib Das sidled up to Hari. 'Should we leave the four trunks behind? Ma will not notice. Once we are on the river, we could say it is too dangerous to go back for them.'

Horrified, Hari delivered a silent prayer skyward, knowing Raamji had heard but hoping he would overlook it. 'Place those trunks in the boat, and guard them with your life.'

Soon, everyone but Hari and Murlidhar had boarded. Naseer jumped into the stern and called. 'Climb aboard, Harilalji.'

Hari felt a sudden pressure on his hand—Murlidhar had squeezed it. 'I will be back,' he said, and walked up the bank with Murlidhar.

'Babuji!' Gangadhar called. 'We must hurry.'

Hari and Murlidhar rushed to the cow shed near the front wall. One by one, they undid the ropes that tied the cows to stakes.

There was much mooing and kicking as the cows were herded towards the river. Once on the bank, Hari had to use Chaman Lal's walking stick to goad the beasts into the water.

'Babuji,' Fakir Chand said, 'the dogs at the gate are growling.'

The Alsatians had been roused from apathy, and men could be heard near the Nawabbari gates. The last of the cows was in the river. Hari called out to Gangadhar, 'Count.'

'Twenty.'

Hari stepped into the boat with Murlidhar and said to Naseer. 'We are ready to leave Bogra.'

They flowed downstream. There was no need to row. Manki sat in the bow, as if commanding an expedition. Hari sat in the stern with Murlidhar and Naseer, who was manning the rudder, and looked back. Instead of flowing south with the current like them, the cows had chosen to cross the river. On the other shore was Musalman Para, where they would probably be slaughtered. He looked away.

The Karatoya was nowhere too wide, so they were clearly visible from both banks, where sullen forms watched them. Naseer found Hari's story about Nawab Sobhan unconvincing. Even if he had really gone to Damookdeah Ghat by steamer, the Karatoya was much shrunken since his days, and it was inconceivable that they would be able to make the long journey to Damookdeah Ghat in a small boat. Their only route to Calcutta lay through Santahar. They would have to land ashore once they were sufficiently far from Bogra, then somehow make the 25-mile journey westward to Santahar, as they would have by train.

The sun set. It was the night after Holi, so the moon was nearly full. Waves glimmered in the Karatoya. Naseer said that the boat was taking water: something had to be thrown overboard. In the last hour, all of Manki's senses had become acute. She missed nothing, and was the first to hear Naseer's remark. She said aloud, 'If the Raamji books go into the waves, so will I.'

'Mohan Lal will fill out a thousand books for you,' Hari said, weakly.

She did not respond.

'The books will not sink,' he pleaded, now aware of grave sin. 'The Karatoya would not dare. Stone sinks, they say, yet Raamji floated a stone bridge...'

A splash was heard. Gayatri had thrown all three bundles of rotis into the river. They were not as heavy as the trunks, but Naseer seemed satisfied.

They drifted in moonlight for an hour. Hari noticed glints of jewellery every time the women moved or the boat heaved. He turned to Gayatri. 'The women must take off their jewellery. There will be thousands of Musalmans in Santahar.'

Being a widow, Gayatri herself wore no ornaments, not even a nose-ring. But the other women were suhagins—their husbands were living. 'A suhagin cannot be seen without jewellery. She lives and dies in all her finery.'

'Well, hide the finery away until we find a train at Santahar.'

Gayatri gave instructions. Bangles, hansulis, mangalsutras, mangtikas, necklaces, earrings and nose-rings made their way to her; a heap lay in her lap, gleaming in the moonlight. She arranged the jars of mango pickle in a row and dropped everything into them, one by one, shaking the jars to let the gold settle. When she was on the last earring, Hari said, 'Give that to me,' and stowed it in his kurta pocket.

Ten miles south of Bogra, Naseer brought the boat to the right bank of the Karatoya. After long negotiations, a bullock cart agreed to take them west. Naseer sat with the driver and the rest huddled together in the back. As they passed rice paddies, Hari thought of his first trip eastward forty years ago, from Santahar to Bogra, when he had marvelled at the Aman crop glistening at sunrise. Now he was going west, and the same crop looked menacing—strange shapes formed themselves in the dark, sometimes looking like men armed with sticks and knives, then melted away.

Three miles from Santahar, the bullock cart came to a rude halt. Its axle was broken. The cart driver created a ruckus—part lament and part diatribe—which ended when Hari gave him the earring in his pocket. The gift also secured a promise not to alert men in the surrounding villages.

'We will die here, Babuji,' said Gangadhar mournfully. 'Our women cannot walk three miles. And Chaman Lalji is past ninety...'

'Stop snivelling,' Manki said. 'I can see the lights of Santahar. Follow me.'

She set off along a mud-bank and they scrambled behind her. Hari turned to Naseer. 'I will not forget this.'

'As I have not forgotten,' he said.

'If I ever return to Bogra...'

'You will never return, Harilalji.'

Hari paused. The earring given to the cartman had been meant for Naseer. He dug into his pocket again and brought out the keys to the Opel. 'I can offer you half a car.'

In the dark, he could not see Naseer's expression when he took the keys. As he walked away, Hari called, 'Tell Mangiram that I will pay to replace the windshield. He may send the bill to my son Tribhuvan in Kalkatta.'

Then he walked briskly to catch up with the rest. Garib Das, Fakir Chand, Gangadhar and Ishwar Das were carrying Manki's trunks as before. Chaman Lal hobbled along with difficulty. Lakshmi's Ma was now carrying Gangadhar's infant son. Garib Das's wife was in pain, and walked with Fakir Chand's wife, who held her hand, while Nanuram carried her daughter in his arms.

A train passed them on the right, on its way to Bogra. This was the train they would have taken to Santahar; it was now returning to Bogra. At this distance, Hari could not tell if the men inside were living or dead. He marvelled that it was still running—did it not matter that its passengers were perhaps corpses?

The rice paddies were flooded—they found themselves wading through water that came to their waists. They trampled on rice plants underneath. Their slippers stuck in the mud and had to be wrenched free after every step, and Mohan Lal had to be lifted on to Gangadhar's shoulders because the water had reached his chin. The lights of Santahar guided them, as did the moon, which bathed the field in an eerie glow that reminded Hari of a desert marked by tibbas.

The women had begun to cry, except for Gayatri, whose face was set, and Manki, who murmured 'Raam Raam' as she marched ahead fiercely. Hari had fallen behind so he could keep everyone in sight, especially Chaman Lal, whose stick sank every time it touched the soft mud underwater. The beel was not quiet—they were passing villages that had not yet gone to sleep. There were songs, cries, the clattering of pans and the barking of dogs. Someone was singing far away. The song was in Bengali, but sounded curiously like the Peepli sung by women in Shekhavati. He was seventeen again, lying under a peepul tree in Rampura, watching women grind bajra through a lazy afternoon. Their skirts were crimson and their sequined shawls covered their faces as they sang to the rhythm of grindstones.

Do not go east seeking profit, my love,
Come back, son of my mother-in-law

The women of Shekhavati had known of the dangers that lurked in the east. There were robbers among the tibbas—whole caravans of death that made a bania tremble—and there were men armed with sticks and knives somewhere in Bengal, ready to turn the bania out after fifty years. Yet men had gone east to Bengal for as long as anyone could remember. They had all gone—Daulatram, Janardhan and Harilal—to lie low, buy cheap and sell dear. They had ignored the Peepli, thinking it to be a women's song, a poem of love and longing, when it really was a warning and a frantic call for help against those who rode horses and wielded knives. And now those who had been so reckless were trudging their way west—as the women of Shekhavati had always implored—making for points of light on the horizon through dark waters, surrounded by unknown horrors. Why had he ever left Shekhavati for this Bengal? Had he not learned as a child that his very name,

Tibrewal, was derived from the tibbas of Shekhavati? The ojha had been right—Harilal had seen pools of water full of lilies. Indeed, he was wading through them, his dhoti torn, his kurta in tatters, and his children crying from hunger and pain.

They could now see the Santahar railway station. To get on to the platform, they had to cross the train embankment. At the top, standing on the rail track, Manki paused.

'We have no time,' Hari said, impatiently.

She scolded him. 'I must rearrange my sari and cover my face. Do you want me to expose myself to the whole world? That station is full of Musalmans.'

The women looked pitiful—their saris were plastered to their bodies, and they were using the pickle jars they carried to shield their modesty. No such device was available to Garib Das's wife, seven months pregnant. She carried nothing, and now stood as if naked, her belly fully exposed in a drenched sari. Among the men, kurtas were ripped and dhotis were caked with drying mud. Manki's steel trunks sat on the tracks while the four men who had carried them caught their breath. Some were barefoot—their slippers had sunk in the soft ground and were lost. Hari watched his bedraggled family shivering in the breeze and thought: a wedding party when they left Bogra, a funeral procession when entering Santahar.

They found some comfort in the crowds at the railway station and formed a cluster under a bridge. There were a few Marwaris on the platform, but most were Hindu Bengalis. All seemed to be in a hurry. He had been wrong to think that he had seen the Bogra–Santahar train, because the train from Bogra had not yet arrived, and neither had news of what was happening there. *No one in Santahar knew*. He trembled to think what might have happened if they had been on that train. But here they were, and if they could somehow find a train that ran south-west on the broad-gauge line to Kalkatta, they would probably be safe. The broad-gauge line passed large towns. There were likely to be policemen on board. The further west they went, the less they would have to fear from Musalmans in the east.

Then he remembered Gopi, as he always did when in Santahar. If Bogra went to Pakistan, so perhaps would Santahar, being only 25 miles to its west. Did Gopi plan to stay on? Would it not be wise to take his family to Kalkatta with them? He could stay in Tribhuvan's flat until arrangements were made. Among brothers, all would be forgiven at a time like this. Why, his depot was only a short walk from the station! He could pack quickly and bring his whole family right away. If he found nowhere else to go, surely his daughter Pushpa would help him? Watsonganj was in Bihar, certain to remain in India when they carved out a Pakistan.

Gopi's absence from the station became unbearable. Hari looked around for help and his eyes fell on his youngest son. 'Mohan, come with me.'

'Where will you go?' Gangadhar asked. 'The Darjeeling Mail is not due for an hour. It is best to sit here under the bridge where no one will notice us.'

'I am going to fetch Gopi.'

Gangadhar stood up. 'You cannot leave the platform, Dadaji. We are safe here, amidst the crowds.'

'I will not go to Kalkatta without Gopi.'

'But there has been no trouble in Santahar.'

'There will be soon,' said Hari.

'We will send him a telegram from Calcutta.'

Hari was torn between his desire to see Gopi and his reluctance to leave his children. They were right: it was not safe to leave the station, and he did not even know if Gopi was home or would agree to join him.

'Hari Babu. I will go if that is your wish,' said Nanuram.

Hari was shocked. It was Nanuram on whose account Gopi had left Bogra, after all. He should have been the last to seek such an assignment.

'You are my brother, Nanuram. I know that Gopi…'

'Your son is my son.'

Hari looked at his munim in wonder. Who was this Nanuram? He had never married. He had no family that Hari knew of. He rose every morning at four for his puja—never forgetting that he was a brahmin—and he had never been sick, like Hari himself. He had been by his master's side for so long that Hari noticed him no more than his own hands. And he was ready to put himself in danger for a boy who had slighted him.

'Bring my son to me, Nanuram. When we are safely in Kalkatta, punish him as you would your own son. Should you want to whip the ingrate, it is I who will hand you the whip.'

As Nanuram walked away, Hari realized he had made a mistake and called out. 'But you do not know where the depot is.'

Nanuram stopped only briefly to say, 'I have been to the depot many times.'

Then he was lost in the crowd, leaving Hari to wonder what his relationship with Gopi had been. His thoughts drifted to his daughters: If there was any trouble in Kushtia, Shanti would hopefully be protected by her father-in-law's position in the Congress committee. Kaushalya was perhaps safe in Jalpaiguri, which had many more Hindus.

There was a scramble as word spread that the Darjeeling Mail was only half a mile north of Santahar. People rushed to grab spots on the platform, so as to be the first to enter the train. Those behind them tried to push closer, and some of the first ones were thrown on to the tracks, to be pulled back to safety just as the train glided into place, its progress arrested by thousands of hands that slapped it, grabbed its bars and reached into its windows.

Hari watched helplessly. These men were Bengalis and Biharis—more aggressive and desperate. Their women were hardier and knew how to push their way through. Even their children seemed sure of themselves. How were banias to compete? At one point, Garib Das and Gangadhar gained entry to the train, but were forced to jump off when they saw the rest would not be able to follow them inside. Then, the men formed a circle around the women and tried to move toward the train, holding hands. But the circle was broken at the first push and they retreated in panic. In dismay, they watched as those who had secured entry barred the doors. Hari said to Gangadhar, 'We will wait for the next train.'

'There may not be another one today. And who knows what will happen by tomorrow?'

The platform was suddenly empty. Almost everyone had managed to squeeze into the Darjeeling Mail. *The strong get to live*, thought Hari, as he looked at his sons and their wives. Fakir Chand sat against a pillar, fanning himself with his dhoti. Garib Das's wife squatted in discomfort—he no longer remembered when her child was due—and Gangadhar's wife struggled to feed her week-old son. Murlidhar watched attentively as the infant sucked, making no allowance for his sister-in-law's modesty as a man of sixteen should. Fortunately, she took no offence—a saint was beyond shame. Chaman Lal lay sprawled on the ground, and Lakshmi's Ma crouched beside Garib Das's wife, comforting her. Manki had gone back into a trance. No, they would not be able to leave Santahar amidst these crowds. He now saw it: they would all be killed. They would present themselves to the Bihari Musalmans as willing victims. Harilal Tibrewal from Rampura in Shekhavati, killed with his family at the Santahar railway station because his children could not push their way into a train... Trains had never loved him. One had filled his eyes with coal; another had taken his beloved Durga; and this one was going to leave him to die on a railway platform. *We are like cows awaiting butchers*, he told himself as he sat down on the floor. Somehow the thought comforted him. It did not matter any more.

That was when he saw Mangiram. He stood with his wife at the far end of the platform, carrying a bundle in his hands. The whole platform was now empty except for two groups of Marwaris—a cluster of twenty at one end and a couple at the other. Mangiram had seen Hari in the same instant. For a minute they stared at each other, pretending not to see even as each knew that the other had seen him. What was Mangiram doing in Santahar? Had the nawab forsaken him? Of the Marwaris in Bogra, few were on such good terms with Musalmans.

Garib Das saw Mangiram, ran to him and brought him to Hari. He appeared to be in a daze, making no attempt to answer Hari's questions, offering no explanation. Then he began to cry silently. His shop had been attacked. He and his wife had walked all the way from Bogra.

'But where are your daughters?'

Mangiram stopped crying. Hari asked no more questions. He never learned how the girls had been taken away, or why Mangiram had not sought help from the Hindu-minded nawab—surely he had other ways of reaching him than by looking in the Nawabbari as Hari had done?—or whether those men had been 'our' Musalmans or Bihari Musalmans. A silence fell, even on the children, as if they were at a puja where the pandit had forbidden cross-talk.

The Darjeeling Mail began to creep away from the station. Hari had heard no whistle, but perhaps it had been drowned by the din. There was contentment in the eyes inside the train, peering out at him in pity and contempt. 'We lived and you died.' Mohan Lal pulled at Hari's kurta. 'The next train will be cheaper, Babuji. Gangadhar says the tickets in this one cost more than a rupee.'

Hari turned to his youngest son. 'Yes, the next one will be cheaper. Wherever we go from here, we will be able to say: we bargained hard and did not pay a pie more than necessary.'

Gangadhar's eyes filled with tears. He placed his head on Hari's chest. It was a strange gesture—he had perhaps meant to embrace his grandfather but, because Hari was taller, his head came to rest against Hari's chest. Hari rarely expressed affection in this manner. Once a boy had passed his tenth year and a girl her eighth, he had treated them as adults and expected the same of them. Even in his most tender moments he had merely softened the tone of his voice with Gangadhar, no more. Now he put an awkward hand on his favourite grandson's head.

Gangadhar looked up. He was about to say something when a roar shattered the wooden boards of the platform. Shards of glass rained on them. Dust swirled all around, and cries were heard faintly before all sound died and the station was silent. The fog cleared. The Darjeeling Mail stood a hundred feet from them. Three of its cars had been ripped apart. Their charred innards were now exposed, strung with mangled human limbs. Smoke billowed from the first car. The platform was strewn with debris. The cries of those who had lived began to rise from the rubble. Hari shook splinters from his clothes, dusted Gangadhar's kurta and clasped him around the shoulders.

'Count again, Gangadhar.'

There were twenty-one, including Mangiram and his wife. The women were sobbing. Fakir Chand sat in a pool of his own urine. Garib Das's wife looked like she might give birth right there. Only Murlidhar appeared unfazed, staring fearlessly at the morgue in front of him. *They are all unhurt*, thought Hari with relief, *and Nanuram will be back soon with Gopi*. Strange indeed were the ways of Raamji, who had made him too weak to force his way inside that train.

They waited all night. Hari saw many more Marwari families, none of whom had been able to board the train. The platform—at least those still living on it—looked almost like one in Shekhavati, with its Marwari turbans and caps, and women with shawls covering their faces. Men had arrived to extricate those trapped in the shattered cars. Bansidhar helped lay out bodies, Murlidhar covered them with sheets—dhotis torn into pieces—and counted them. Garib Das and Gangadhar found their way inside the cars with shovels. Gayatri stood outside, distributing mango pickle to those who could chew. Hari marvelled at their forbearance—they were banias, averse to conflict, who had never seen a bloody body, yet now thought nothing of walking through mangled corpses. It was the bomb—by destroying the train, it had made the station safe.

Gangadhar wanted to go and look for Nanuram but Hari forbade it. He had already made a mistake, why compound it? The station was a safe haven, but Santahar was a dark hole around it—it would swallow anyone who dared leave the platform.

Fakir Chand wailed all night, convinced that this was the astrologer's prediction come true. Even if the rest somehow survived, he would not leave Santahar alive. Hari scolded him—how did he know that the astrologer had been a holy man? Was he wearing a proper rudraksh garland? How many faces did the rudraksh beads have? If less than five, there was no truth to his predictions...

Early in the morning, a relief train arrived from Siliguri. Bodies were piled into its cars. Hari and his sons found space amidst mountains of the dead and the dying. Manki's trunks were pushed under a bench. The sun came up. When the train finally inched forward, Mohan Lal asked, 'Where is Nanuramji?'

Hari's relief turned to dread. He stood up. Did trains not have a cord that one could pull in such a case? He knew little about these things. They had already left the platform. The station master would laugh at him, if he did not choose to stab him first. They sat surrounded by hundreds of corpses, they were carrying a whole morgue to Calcutta. Who would mourn a munim from Shekhavati in this city of the dead? He sat down, took off his turban and laid it in his lap. Tears rolled down his cheeks.

The train picked up speed. He now saw that there were other families in the carriage—most of them Marwaris who had been too timid to take the Darjeeling Mail. Some had lost sons, some had left grandmothers behind, some fretted about daughters who had just been married off in the east. *I am going west*, thought Hari. He wanted to tell them about Nanuram but did not—did a man ever mourn his munim in public?

Chaman Lal squatted near a window, staring. Lakshmi's Ma cradled Gangadhar's infant in her arms. The ball at her throat seemed to have grown overnight. Mangiram sat next to him, mute as a stone. Why is he going to Kalkatta? Hari wondered. He knew no one there—his family had been in Bogra for 150 years. He had no sons, and his daughters had been taken away. What awaited him in Kalkatta? Should he not have returned to Bogra to look for his daughters? Why had he left Bogra at all?

It was a dreadful thought—that a man had fled to safety even as his children were in grave danger. Shaken, he studied Murlidhar, seated beside him, dozing—a man of sixteen who would never sit in a shop, marry or have children. He put an arm around him. *For you*, he whispered to his sleeping grandson, *I will give away my shops, my life, my Raamji. For you, even if not for my sons.*

In an hour, hunger and thirst assaulted them: they had not eaten since the previous afternoon. It would be six hours before the train reached Calcutta. It would stop at stations on the way but they would not dare venture out. Gayatri opened her last jar of pickle. Hari dipped a hand in it and grabbed a slice of mango between thumb and forefinger. Oil dripping from his finger, he took the slice to Murlidhar's mouth and popped it in. The boy chewed hungrily with eyes shut. Hari watched him in awe.

4

WATSONGANJ

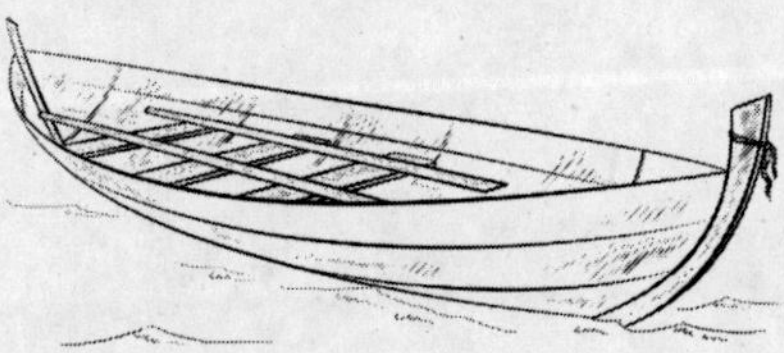

1

They lived in Tribhuvan's flat in Calcutta for eight months—men and children slept in the balcony, the women all together in one room, and Tribhuvan, his wife and son in the other. Hari's discomfort was acute, both because of his relations with Tribhuvan and the presence of Gayatri, who could not be avoided in the small flat. There was much talk of the troubles in Bengal. Tribhuvan would hold forth—the riots were not to be blamed on the rioters but those who egged them on from the shadows. He was vague about who these inciters were. Most Musalmans had been Hindus a few generations ago, he explained, and the ties—of language, culture and shared history—between Hindu Bengalis and Musalman Bengalis were too strong to be broken by the mere partition of a country which, too, was blamed on unnamed villains. Hari would be intimidated by such oratory. The image of a distraught Mangiram would cross his mind, and he would begin to say something about Bihari Musalmans but find himself proven wrong again. Although Tribhuvan was a member of the Calcutta Pinjrapole Society, Hari did not tell him about the cows swimming across the Karatoya to go to Musalman Para. He no longer understood Tribhuvan and was afraid to be faulted again—perhaps it had been a crime to release those cows, considering they belonged to Tribhuvan's friend Mohammad Ali Bogra?

Garib Das would complain about the discomfort of being squeezed into a two-room flat with twenty others. Hari would scold him: a Marwari always got by, he never sought comfort. Had Garib Das not heard of the great banias of Kalkatta who slept on mattresses with dozens of others, lined up for latrines and travelled third class all the way to Shekhavati? The difference between a rich Marwari and a poor one was not in clothes or living arrangements but in the number of jute bales leaving his warehouse every day.

He sent Gopi a postcard, asking about Nanuram as well as the situation in Santahar, but received no reply. He did get news of Shanti. She and her husband had decided to stay on in Kushtia. After the burning of their orchard, there had been no trouble in Kushtia. He sent a message to Shanti's father-in-law.

'Raamji has not yet blessed you with grandchildren, so it will be easy for you, your son and daughter-in-law to slip out without being noticed. Your property will be safe because no one will know you are in Kalkatta. And you could return to Kushtia if, after partition, it goes to India.'

Shanti's father-in-law sent a terse reply. 'Our haveli is in Kushtia and our orchards lie here. We will live in Kushtia whether it goes to India or Pakistan.'

Hari wondered if he had erred in mentioning the lack of grandchildren, which was certain to be a source of great grief in Shanti's family. The whispers about the 'adoption curse' had become louder. Shanti and Nagar Mal had made a pilgrimage to Ganga Sagar, where they had paid for a large puja that was certain to grant them a child. A year had passed—it was now futile to pretend the puja would bear fruit.

When they had been in Calcutta for a month, he received a postcard from Watsonganj in Bihar. Gopi had sent a response, but indirectly through his daughter. Pushpa wrote that her father planned to remain in Santahar. And Gopi did not understand why his father had inquired about a munim at such a time—he had not seen the munim since he left Bogra twenty-five years ago.

'Gopi is probably buying land around Santahar now that prices are depressed,' Fakir Chand said. 'What will he do if Santahar goes to Pakistan?'

'Speak respectfully of your brother,' Hari said out of habit. 'He is old enough to be your father.'

His mind was on Nanuram, who had been swallowed by the dark night in Santahar. What demon had impelled him to volunteer for the task? After a lifetime of serving Harilal, he had given his life away for Harilal & Sons.

There was no news of Mangiram, who had said farewell when they arrived at Sealdah Station. Mangiram had no contacts in Calcutta. He bought nothing from Calcutta and sent no goods there. All his trade had been with jute cultivators and the tenants of the nawab. Where would he go? But Mangiram was adamant. Hari saw him walk away with his wife and vanish in the Calcutta crowds.

There was trouble in Calcutta, too, but it was possible to avoid it. Tribhuvan went to his chambers every morning; the rest of the men took long walks on the road. The news from Bogra was encouraging: after the initial troubles, the whole Rajshahi area was calm. Hari sent Garib Das and Gangadhar back to wind up the shops. The hosiery store was sold at a loss to a Musalman; the warehouse in Bara Gola was given up; a friend of the nawab agreed to buy the mango orchard—land prices were depressed, but Hari had little choice. A buyer was found for the oil depot in Rangpur—both the agency and the building—but backed out at the last minute. The house at Sat Matha, the grain and cigarette shops found no buyers. Before returning to Calcutta, Garib Das was able to extract his gold ginnis from the mattress in the Rangpur depot. They brought back the gold, as well as cash from their sales, strapped in belts around their bodies.

Meanwhile, Mohan Lal and Ishwar Das were furiously filling up new books for Manki. She could not read, write or count, but years of looking at the word 'Raam' had taught her to recognize the letters, and she understood that a thousand was less than a lakh, which was less than a crore. When numbers failed her, she measured progress by holding notebooks between thumb and forefinger and gauging their thickness, and her sons would have to submit to a harangue if the notebook they had filled up was not thick enough.

In May, Garib Das's wife gave birth to a boy. Jokes were told about how the boy would be spoilt because he had been born in a large city. Everyone marvelled at the doctor who arrived to supervise the delivery. Hari had frowned when Tribhuvan suggested a doctor. 'Lakshmi's Ma brought all my children into this world. The only one a doctor tampered with was Durga, three days after his birth, and you see the fate Raamji wrote for him.'

'Durga should not have stood between those carriages,' said Tribhuvan.

Hari was enraged. 'He was trying to prevent an accident! If he had not given up his life, I would not be standing here before you.'

The doctor arrived. He was male—Hari had hoped for a woman. When the boy had been born, washed and brought into his lap, he inspected his skin, counted his toes and thrust a finger into the little mouth. 'He looks like a healthy city boy. And he is fair-skinned like his mother, not dark like Gariba. Lakshmi's Ma could not have done better.'

In June, what they had known for months became a certainty: there was going to be a Pakistan. Nehruji announced it on the radio after Mountbatten, the Lat Sahib, said something in English. Jinnah spoke next, ending with a declaration that sounded familiar.

'What was the last line?' Hari asked.

Gangadhar replied uncertainly—his English was even worse than Garib Das's. 'It was in English, and it said "Pakistan is in a bag".'

'Perhaps he meant "Pakistan zindabad",' said Garib Das.

'If there is going to be a Pakistan,' said Hari, 'it is better for one of us to become Pakistani. Why keep all your money in one country when there are two?'

He hoped that Garib Das or Fakir Chand would agree to return to Pakistan. It made sense for Garib Das to live in Bogra—he would be released from the chafing restrictions Hari still imposed on him. No one would object to his Manchester dhotis or gold chains, or extravagances like the Opel car. Besides, the

Rangpur oil depot was very profitable. But Garib Das showed no inclination to go back. Fakir Chand flatly declined—he was still in wonder that he had defied the astrologer's prediction and lived through Santahar, but the year 1947 had not yet ended, and he fully meant to cocoon himself in a safe place until it had. Hari advanced many reasons why this was foolhardy: the astrologer's prediction would have been for the Hindu calendar—he could not have known English dates—and the Hindu year had already ended in the English month of March... But Fakir Chand would not be persuaded. He hugged his four-year-old daughter and swore he would never live in Pakistan.

'Our country is neither India nor Pakistan,' said Hari. 'It is Shekhavati. Do we not call it *desh*, which is what Congresswalas call India? This India is just a piece of land that surrounds our country.'

'I do not want to go to Shekhavati either. I want to live in Calcutta.'

'How do you know it will not go to Pakistan?'

Finally, Hari turned to Gangadhar, hoping the boy would say no. But as he had for most of his twenty-one years, Gangadhar agreed right away. Hari was to lose his beloved grandson, on whom he leaned far more than any of his sons, and Gayatri, on whose shoulders his household rested. It was settled that Gangadhar would re-open the grain and cigarette shops in Bogra, which had remained unsold, and find a buyer for the Rangpur oil depot. Bansidhar and Murlidhar would go with him.

Hari cried freely when their trunks were packed and taken to Sealdah Station. 'In India or Pakistan, I am your grandfather,' he said. 'I will find brides for Bansi and Murli. Let people say what they will about them, I will find them the most beautiful girls from the best families. Then I will marry off your son.'

Bansidhar and Murlidhar climbed into Hari's arms and would not let go. They were full-grown men—Bansi was twenty, barely younger than Gangadhar, and Murli was sixteen—but thought nothing of jumping into Hari's lap. Their bodies, too, were not fully formed, so they looked like awkward boys of twelve.

At the last moment, Hari faced Gayatri, who stood erect, face exposed, meeting his eyes without flinching. 'When the wives of Gariba and Fakira, and the ones I will find for Ishwar Das and Mohan Lal, break a dish in the kitchen or forget to cook moong on the night of Diwali, I will tell them about you. "You should have seen Durga's wife," I will say. "She would never have been so careless".'

Since Shanti's wedding, he had rarely looked Gayatri full in the face. Of those leaving Calcutta, it was her absence that would create the greatest void in his home and heart. There would be no one to churn milk in the morning, no one to keep track of festivals and death anniversaries, no one to serve cold food on the day meant for the goddess Sheetla, and no one to prevent the children from eating tamarind on the day meant for the goddess Santoshi. Who would protect them from the wrath of these goddesses, and who would bring down the grace of Raamji through her puja? Manki had retreated into a personal shrine with her brass statuette of Raamji, and what she mumbled was between the two of them. That god did not cast a look this way; he had no interest in Hari's children.

'Should you find Gangadhar deficient in his duty towards you,' said Gayatri, 'you only have to send a message to his mother.'

She climbed the ricksha—brushing off the helping hand Gangadhar had extended—and was gone. Gangadhar and his brothers followed.

On Bhadwa badi 14, everyone gathered around the radio to listen to Independence Day ceremonies in Delhi. Late in the night, Mountbatten made a speech; Mohan Lal tried to translate but failed. Hari asked Ishwar Das to prepare his bed in the balcony.

'Nehruji will speak at midnight,' said Mohan Lal. 'Do you not want to stay up?'

'The speech will be in English,' said Hari.

'The sahibs will leave for England while you sleep.'

'Do not wake me up too early.'

The next morning, a cry of 'inkalab zindabad!' woke him

up. Crowds had poured into the road. Everyone was wearing Gandhi caps. Men embraced, sprinkled gangajal on each other and shouted slogans. The new flag—saffron, white and green—was everywhere.

'What is the English date?' Hari asked Tribhuvan.

'August 15.'

He looked down at the road. A fruit-seller stood under the balcony, holding two large mangoes. As he had done every morning, Mohan Lal lowered a basket; the man deposited his mangoes in it; it was pulled up.

'Not yet ripe,' Hari commented.

Mohan Lal said, 'I know this one. His mangoes are never ripe.'

'Everything looks the same,' said Hari. 'Have the sahibs really gone?'

Ishwar Das barged in, excited. In Dharamtolla, the film *Jugnu* was being shown for free on account of Independence Day. Hari reluctantly allowed him to go and watch it with Mohan Lal.

In the month of Kartik, two months after the sahibs had left, Gangadhar sent a postcard from Bogra. The jute business had collapsed. The best jute was grown in the east—in Mymensingh and Faridpur—while the mills were in Calcutta. Now, after partition, this jute could not cross the border from Pakistan to India. It lay rotting on boats and barges—no one would buy it because there was no mill to send it to. What would Pakistan do with its mountains of jute? Gangadhar was negotiating to sell the jute press at a steep discount. The grain business had survived, as had cigarettes. A buyer had still not been found for the Rangpur oil depot. The Opel car had been further damaged in the riots that followed their flight from Bogra. It still stood outside the grain shop, all its windows broken—Hari noted that Mohammad Ali Bogra's driver had not claimed it. There was a shortage of hands—Gangadhar alone had to manage the grain shop, the cigarette store as well as the Rangpur depot. Bansidhar could not be left in charge by himself, and Murlidhar could not leave the house unattended.

So many sons, thought Hari, *yet so few hands to run my shops.*

At the end of the month, Pushpa wrote again, asking if Hari would like to visit her in Watsonganj. It was a small town, smaller than Bogra, but there was the possibility of a jute baling business there now that the balers in Pakistan were cut off from Calcutta.

'Watsonganj is three-hundred miles to the north,' Tribhuvan said. 'You will have to take a train to Sahibganj, cross the Ganga by boat, then get there by bullock cart.'

'I cannot take the children that far. Gariba has a little boy.'

'How long will Ishwar Das and Mohan Lal spend their days watching films? They need a shop.'

Hari was stung. Was there not a note of impertinence in Tribhuvan's voice? After eight months, had his presence become burdensome to his son? But whom could a man lean on if not his son? He wished Gangadhar had been by his side—he needed a steady hand, not the self-absorbed Fakir Chand or the impulsive Garib Das, whom twenty-six years, marriage and two children had not mellowed down. Unable to confide his anxieties to either, he turned to the most unlikely source.

Manki was sitting next to her shrine in deep contemplation. She had an explanation right away. 'That is his wife, speaking through him. She does not like me.'

Hari was baffled. He was unaware of any discord between Kusum and Manki.

'And he is no saint himself,' she continued, referring to Tribhuvan. 'I do not know him; he is your son.'

She had never referred to Hari's previous marriage, or indicated that she did not regard his first three sons as her own. She showed so little affection towards her own sons that her indifference to the three eldest ones had gone unnoticed. Very well, he would take Tibhuvan's hint. The next morning, he announced their departure for Watsonganj.

There were cries of dismay. Watsonganj was a small village, an obscure outpost, a backwater in the poor state of Bihar. After eight months in Calcutta, a move there seemed like a step backward.

'You speak as if you have always lived in Kalkatta,' he said to his sons. 'What do you know of this city? Could you find your way around Bara Bazar? Could you speak in English with a sahib sergeant?'

'The sahibs are gone. And we speak Bengali as well as Bengalis do. In Watsonganj, we will have to speak in Hindi.'

'We will learn Hindi in Bihar, as we learned Bengali in Bengal.'

'But Watsonganj is not our home.'

'Bogra was not your home and Kalkatta isn't either. A bania goes where he may buy and sell. Even a bird goes south in winter. It has no attachment to its home in the north.'

'We could go back to Shekhavati,' Mohan Lal said.

'And what will you do there? To whom will you sell what in the desert? Will you find jute to press, dhotis to fold, rice to weigh?'

Two days later, they took a train to the town of Sahibganj in the north. Lakshmi's Ma and Chaman Lal went with them, the one ever useful and the other a relic. Tribhuvan was solicitous—*because I am leaving*, Hari thought bitterly—and came all the way to Sealdah Station to help load their trunks into the train. At Sahibganj, a boat took them across the Ganga. There were at least fifty passengers with them. The rains had not been heavy, so the river flowed well below its mark and the boat found itself stuck on a spit. Three men pushed bamboos into the shallow water and pushed hard against the bed. The hull came unstuck and slid into the current, and the passengers burst into cries of 'Jai Ganga Maiya!' Hari ran a hand over thirteen-year-old Mohan Lal's head and said, 'We lived near the Karatoya and imagined it to be as sacred as the Ganga. Now, we will live near the Ganga herself. Watsonganj is only a few miles from the other shore.'

'The name sounds English,' said Mohan Lal. 'I thought the sahibs had left.'

'We too have left Bogra, but Sat Matha still has a shop called Harilal & Sons.'

They hired a bullock cart on the other side. Near Watsonganj, they came upon another river, the Kosi. Skiffs lay upturned on the riverbank, and a few launches—motorized boats with giant wheels on their sides—ploughed the water. Garib Das fingered the gold ginnis strapped round his waist.

'I will buy one of those launches.'

'You are not in Watsonganj yet,' said Hari, alarmed that his extravagant son was already thinking of ways to spend. 'And you do not have a shop.'

They reached Watsonganj early in the morning, having waited all night for a launch to take them across the Kosi. As soon as the first hut was seen, Garib Das expressed his disgust. 'This is a mere village, not a town. Do they have a single pakka house here?'

It was easy to find their way to Pushpa's home. Her father-in-law owned one of the largest jute presses in town and part of the jute mill. The house stood inside a great courtyard filled with jute strands—sada jute of low quality, Chaman Lal whispered to Hari. Kyals loitered about. A sudden desire to be back in his jute press overwhelmed Hari. Ah, to be sitting with Chaman Lal next to the cash register, watching kyals sort through loops of sada and mesta, with Gopi and Durga playing next to the press! Then he was reminded of the agonizing moments in the Nawabbari and bitterness replaced nostalgia. No, he did not want to return to Bogra. Had he not said a hundred times that it was not his home?

Pushpa's father-in-law received them with great warmth. Hari, Garib Das, Fakir Chand, Ishwar Das and Mohan Lal sat in his office, along with Chaman Lal. Hari was filled with wonder—as Pushpa's grandfather, he could hardly claim to be a close relative to her in-laws. No doubt the effusive welcome owed its sincerity to Pushpa's agency. Suddenly reminded of propriety, he placed eleven silver rupees at the cash box. Pushpa's father-in-law made the customary protest, but Hari reminded him that Pushpa was his granddaughter, in whose house a man must not ever be a guest.

'You have just left your home and your shop,' Pushpa's father-in-law said. 'You may pay me in a few months.'

'But I have seven sons, of whom Raamji has spared six,' said

Hari. 'Four of them sit before you with eight hands among them. They will earn.'

'They will, indeed. What else is a boy good for? How old is this one?'

'This is Mohan Lal,' said Hari, turning to his son. 'Do not sit there, staring! Get up and touch Dadaji's feet.'

Although Pushpa was nine years older than Mohan Lal, she was his niece, so her father-in-law was Mohan Lal's equal in social standing, not the 'grandfather' that Hari had called him, but Mohan Lal knew it was inopportune to point this out. A benefactor was a grandfather, no matter what his relation to the supplicant. He leaned forward, let his fingers graze the old man's toes—they were all sitting cross-legged—and brought his fingers to his forehead. His father had not yet answered the question, so he said meekly, 'Thirteen. The fourteenth is upon me.'

'Old enough,' said Pushpa's father-in-law.

In the next three months, they rented a courtyard near Pushpa's house and built three rooms in it. Hari and Manki moved into one, Garib Das into the second, Fakir Chand into the third. Ishwar Das and Mohan Lal spent nights in the courtyard. With money they had brought from Bogra as well as Garib Das's gold coins, they were able to open a grain shop. A wooden board was painted and stuck above the door—Harilal & Sons. Ishwar Das, Mohan Lal and Chaman Lal now spent their days in the shop.

Manki had fallen ill on the day they arrived in Watsonganj. Because she had spent the last twenty years sitting next to her shrine, her illness was not noticed for a few weeks. Indeed, it was still not clear what was wrong—a vaidya called by Hari was unable to determine anything—except that she complained of an unspecified ache, and was unable to say which part of her body was afflicted. It came from 'within', as far as the vaidya had been able to diagnose. An ojha ruled that the spirit of the goddess Sheetla had taken residence in her body, but she refused his prescription—to eat nothing but the cold, stale food beloved by Sheetla for one hundred and one days—and the illness persisted.

No one paid much attention to it, and she herself seemed resigned to pain until her death, to which she referred often, though she was only forty-six. A few weeks after they moved into the three rooms, she had her bed transferred to the courtyard, where she sat all day with her idols. Her Raam Raam books lay in steel trunks under the bed.

The household was now run by Garib Das's wife, Sumitra, aided by Lakshmi's Ma, whom age had slowed down. Hari knew that Ishwar Das and Mohan Lal did not like Sumitra very much, but he found nothing wrong in her manner towards himself. Perhaps the two boys were intimidated because Sumitra was light-skinned, or maybe they missed Gayatri, who had been the only mother they had known after leaving Manki's womb. Fakir Chand's wife, Lajwanti, had never learned to cook properly in her father's house in Calcutta, where a dozen servants had looked after every need. In Bogra, Gayatri had quickly divined her shortcomings and learned to ignore them. Now, under Sumitra's indifferent tutelage, she learned how to pile wooden logs in an oven so it would not give off smoke, and how to throw water on the pile late at night so the wood could be re-used. Hari stayed away from the corner of the courtyard where the women cooked—he did not like looking that way and noting that Gayatri was not among them.

2

The grain shop was unable to employ all four of Harilal's sons. It was Fakir Chand who spent his days next to the cash box. Ever grateful for the kindness shown to him, Chaman Lal sat in the shop all day, breathing heavily, saying nothing and doing little—a moribund presence that annoyed Fakir Chand but comforted Hari. When his son complained, he pointed out that Chaman Lal imparted gravity to the shop and made the business look older and better established. Ishwar Das and Mohan Lal made deliveries. Garib Das found himself with much leisure, and promptly turned to the pursuit of his interests. With the last remaining gold ginni, a motor launch was bought and a pilot engaged. While Fakir Chand weighed out rice and wheat, Garib Das could be found reclining on the deck of a launch puttering along the Kosi, its wheels chugging noisily within sight of the shore—he had a fear of rivers and would not let the boat go midstream. Sitting on the riverbank on a piece of jute sacking, Hari watched the sun set on the Kosi and thought of the Karatoya. When the launch returned, he would say, 'You could open a jute press, Gariba. Or an oil depot. You should talk to the Standard Vacuum Oil Company—Gopi is an agent for them in Santahar.'

'A depot needs capital,' Garib Das would respond. 'Let us wait until Gangadhar finds a buyer for the Rangpur depot.'

'Pushpa's father-in-law is willing to lend at 6 per cent.'

'We must not borrow from Gopi's relatives.'

Hari would pull out a Berkeley cigarette and strike a match. All the restraint he had shown in Bogra—where he sat next to cartons of Berkeleys—had now melted away. In a bania like him that was odd, considering he now had to buy his cigarettes. Since coming to Watsonganj, he had settled into the routine of semi-retirement, spending his days without complaining and paying little attention to what went on in the grain shop. A Marwari was not meant to live in the abundance of Bengal, he reasoned. This Watsonganj, named after an English collector who was long dead, was suitable for a bania from Shekhavati. It was poor and unlovely, and a bania could make a living without attracting notice. His sons had begun to adapt to Watsonganj. Bogra was rarely mentioned. The ordeal of their departure had now lost its terror. When they re-lived that day, they laughed about how they had carried the four trunks through beels, how Manki had stood to adjust her sari on top of the train embankment, and how Murlidhar had helped count bodies at the Santahar railway station. And they never failed to mention the smashing of the Opel windshield, which had come to occupy a central place in their narration of events.

'You should have seen how Babuji swung that cricket bat,' Mohan Lal said. 'Like Lala Amarnath!'

Garib Das would interject angrily and everyone would laugh. Even Hari would allow himself a chuckle, though he did not know who Lala Amarnath was. He had begun to enjoy the deference due to a man who has crossed sixty. Every morning, he walked with Pushpa's six-year-old son—his oldest great-grandson—to school, where he sometimes stood in the back. No one minded his presence, thinking him to be the gatekeeper. He went because of the class in English. Over the last year, he had worked up some nostalgia for the days of sahibs, and taken to boasting that, although he could not read or write it, nor understand a word when spoken, he somehow *felt* the English language, and *knew* what an English telegram said, as one understood a picture without being able to name its parts. This understanding was the result of his friendship with Sir David Yule, he said, and those who grew up after 1947 could not hope to achieve it, their English prattle notwithstanding. It filled his heart with pride when his great-grandson stood with others to sing,

God save our gracious King
Long live our noble King ...

When Pushpa grumbled about the song—had not the sahibs gone? Why was her son still being asked to sing this?—he would reply, 'They have gone from Watsonganj too, yet you call it Watsonganj.'

This happy state of affairs was disturbed by news of Mangiram. He was employed as a broker in one of the firms in Bara Bazar in Calcutta, toiling in the ever-declining jute market. His daughters had been located in Dhaka, not in their husbands' homes but in a brothel. The revelation had caused his wife to swallow something and take her own life, and Mangiram had foresworn any relationship with his daughters, made a trip to Ganga Sagar, fed hundreds of pandits, and was now living in perpetual agony.

Hari was heart-broken for days, both at the news and at

Mangiram's reaction. When Gangadhar had been attacked in Bogra, he had feared the worst but known it was in the nature of men, whether Bihari Musalmans or 'our' Musalmans, to do such things. But when Mangiram had walked to Santahar and taken the relief train to Calcutta, leaving his daughters behind, Hari had been troubled. True, a bania did not pick up a stick and fight back, but would not a father's agony spur him to do what was wrong? Should it not? How, then, had Mangiram left his daughters in Bogra and climbed passively into the relief train at Santahar? And now, was it possible for a man to abandon his daughters, no matter what their state? There was much darkness in the world, and not all of it sprang from Bihari Musalmans.

Manki's health was deteriorating, as was her speech. In Bogra, she had kept to her room while Gayatri ran the household. In Watsonganj, she sat on a cot in the courtyard, so her abuse was no longer contained inside a room. Daughters-in-law scurried by, eager to go from room to kitchen, trying to avoid the gale of bile and hatred blowing in the courtyard. Because she rarely left the cot, her meals had to be brought to her, a tent had to be erected to shield her from the sun, and daughters-in-law took turns helping her to the latrine.

Hari spent ever more time on the banks of the Kosi, watching buffaloes sunning themselves in the river, writing on his slate in Modhiya, as he had in Bogra. A cow brings wealth, Master Bholaram used to say, while a buffalo brings nothing but misfortune. He wrote, 'If the cow is the mother, the buffalo is surely the foster mother, the one your father has foisted on you through a second marriage, who feels neither love nor sympathy for you. Where the cow is good-natured, silent and industrious, the buffalo is obstinate, loud and lazy. A bullock will plough twenty acres without complaint. A buffalo will plop down in the furrows after an acre and let the tongue hang out of its dirty mouth. In England, the sahibs drink nothing but cow milk, while Biharis and Bengalis prefer the milk of the buffalo because it is richer. Is it any wonder that the one reigned over the other for two hundred years? If the government in this new country cares about the health of its people, it should send female buffaloes to Madras and males to Shekhavati, so the two may never meet and the buffalo may become extinct in one generation.'

In the spring of 1948, Chaman Lal died. He had been withering away for so long that his death seemed like a natural progression into the next state. The end came in the shop, seated cross-legged in a corner with his back against a sack of wheat. Since morning, he had neither moved nor said a word, as was his habit, so Fakir Chand went about his business, weighing grain, making small talk, even joking with the corpse until it was closing time. When asked to stand up so the shop could be shuttered, Chaman Lalji did not respond.

He was cremated on a ghat near the Kosi. Hari's sons did not attend—Fakir Chand had the shop to look after, Ishwar Das and Mohan Lal were making deliveries and Garib Das was off in the launch. Hari made the arrangements. It was he who cracked the skull, and was the only one standing by the pyre after the pandit had departed and the chandal had picked at the bones to look for gold teeth—there were none.

The sun was setting across the Kosi. The pyre was now nearly extinguished. In its soot-covered limbs it was possible to still imagine a gnarled human form. Hari did not know where Chaman Lal's daughters lived in Shekhavati. Any friendships he may have struck in Bogra had long frayed. He had earned no fortune in a lifetime spent away from Shekhavati, and now no one but Hari stood at his pyre to mourn his passing. It was as if he had never lived. Why had Raamji created a life whose only purpose was to emphasize the futility of all existence? Indeed, it would not have mattered if a dozen crying children and grandchildren had surrounded Chaman Lal's pyre, considering they would soon be dead too. And here he was, worrying about Mangiram's daughters or Garib Das's launch, or a match for Ishwar Das!

He could not sleep that night, and sat down in the dirt beside Manki's cot. Winter had eased—Holi was approaching. The moon sailed through cloud patches. He was reminded of the ride from Chirawa after his wedding. He had pushed a corner of Parmeshwari's shawl from her face and watched her moonlit face. The cart had jumped on a tibba. He had hastily let the shawl fall back. The nevgan had stirred in her sleep and he had quickly shut his eyes, pretending to be in deep slumber. For fifty years he had found comfort in this memory. Now it failed to move him. Something had died with Chaman Lal's death. He spent the night looking at the moon.

The next morning, he announced his intention of going to Rampura. His sons were astonished, 'You used to say you would never go back.'

Yes, thought Hari, I feared that Raamji did not want me to return, until I stood at Chaman Lal's pyre and realized that I do not understand His ways, that men live meaninglessly and die for no cause, that He pushes the moon through the sky with no end in mind.

'Will you go alone? Who will take care of you?'

No one takes care of me now that Gayatri is gone, he thought. I will be no more lonely in Rampura than I am here in Watsonganj.

He left immediately after Holi. Watsonganj was on the main railway route between Delhi and Assam, so there was no need to go through Calcutta. He took a passenger train to Patna, then a mail train to Delhi. A day later, he was sitting quietly in the Addha train, watching the land turn grey as he approached Shekhavati. He wore a large turban—he had given that up in Bogra when he saw other Marwaris do so—and his dhoti and kurta were immaculately white. His foot rested on a steel trunk; a small bedroll sat under his bench. They passed Chirawa. The train had already crossed the spot where Durga had been killed. A curious detachment possessed him—where he should have trembled, he merely turned away from the window. They were now deep in Shekhavati. He recalled the carcasses Hemraj and he had passed on their way to Delhi. The land looked much the same—grey tibbas dotted with khejra trees, stacks of hay scattered on the plain, wisps of smoke from cooking fires. There was the same blinding heat, even though Holi had just passed and summer was yet to come. A grey-black ribbon of road ran alongside the tracks, broken here and there by a bullock cart. Aside from the road, it was as if he had never been away. Raamji had not turned his attention to Shekhavati for fifty years. Nothing but bajra would ever grow here.

The Addha train reached Sikar. He looked about anxiously, half hoping that someone would recognize him. Then the absurdity of this struck him. Those he had known were dead, and those remaining had gone to Disavar. Indeed they no longer called it Disavar, but Calcutta, Bombay or Assam. Sikar was now a large city. No one on the crowded station spoke Marwari. Men had come from Delhi and Punjab and Gujarat, and he was the only one with a conspicuous turban on his head. But for the large signs all over the station, one might have taken this to be a town anywhere between Delhi and Calcutta.

He took a bullock cart to Rampura. Late in the evening, they crossed Nawalgarh and reached the riverbed. As the cart climbed over the other bank and the first houses of Rampura came into view, the sun sank behind the dunes. He watched breathlessly, having forgotten the sunsets of Shekhavati, where nothing obstructed the view for miles and one could watch the shadows lengthen for an hour until they melted into darkness.

I am in Rampura, he told himself in wonder, *and Raamji has not struck me down.*

'Whose house do I take you to?' the cartman asked.

Heart pounding, he replied, 'Duli Chandji's.'

'Duli Chandji of the grain shop? The one whose son is a seth in Disavar?'

'Yes.'

'The shop has been closed since Duli Chandji died in Disavar.'

'I know.'

When he was twelve, Thakur Saheb Roop Singhji had become the Thikanedar of Nawalgarh and, on ascending the throne, had come to Rampura. Homes were decorated, water was sprinkled so the dust would settle—no one knew the Chhappaniya was about to strike—and men lined up to pay nazar to the thakur. A bania who had just returned from Disavar presented three thousand silver rupees. Seated on a silver stool, the thakur had granted him the title of 'seth'. The only other man in Rampura entitled to the honour had been Daulatram himself, and his firm was said to have paid a cess of ten thousand to the previous thakur. That was how men came to be called 'seth' in Rampura. In Bogra, on the other hand, Bengalis always called Hari a 'seth' when pawning their wives' earrings—they used that term for every bania from Shekhavati. And now the title had followed him back to Rampura. We are all seths now, he thought ruefully, yet not one of us is contented.

He unlocked the house. It was in disrepair. He had to bend over to pass the door, which would not close properly—the lintel beams were warped. Inside were bare earthen floors covered with sand dunes—sandstorms had found their way in—that made the house look like an extension of the desert outside. He had forgotten how small the three rooms were, and how low the ceilings had been. From the distance of Bengal, the little house looked scarcely capable of habitation, yet Hari had spent twelve years in it and never noticed the mud walls. The yard in the front—where the cow, Tara, had stood with the camel—was overrun with weeds and khejra bushes.

For eight annas, he was able to spend the night in the courtyard of a public house, where he recognized the owner as the son of the previous one. The man showed no signs that he knew Hari. The bed was too short—his legs protruded over the edge. He lay on his back and looked at the desert sky. The moon was in its waning phase. There was not a wisp of cloud; every star sparkled alone. In Bengal he had never seen such a clear night.

The next morning, he walked to the Hanuman temple to look for the only man in Rampura who might know him, if he still lived. The room behind the temple looked the same. The door was open. Master Bholaram sat on a bed, reading. Hari held his breath. How old was Master Bholaram now? Eighty, perhaps, or ninety, or even older. His hair was gone; his face was a mass of wrinkles hidden behind gargantuan spectacles. The mouth hung loosely—he had no teeth—and his whole frame had shrunk. But this was Master Bholaram, once the strongest man in Rampura, who had grabbed a twelve-year-old boy in his powerful arms and raised him high above a mare so he might strike a toran with a branch of neem and claim his bride.

Overcome, he stepped into the room. Master Bholaram had been arranged carefully on the bed; his dhoti was flared around him so his legs were not visible. Someone had placed a book-stand and a pot of water within reach. He seemed to have sat in that position for hours.

'Pranaam, Masterji,' said Hari.

Masterji nodded. He can hear, thought Hari.

'Do you remember Duli Chandji?'

'The one of the grain shop?' asked Master Bholaram, his voice surprisingly clear. 'He died in Disavar a long time ago.'

'I am his son.'

Masterji's mind appeared to reach backward and exhume the memory. 'Hariya? Go get your slate, and don't let me catch you sitting idly or you will feel the back of my hand.'

Hari smiled. 'I am sixty-two. The sixty-third is upon me.'

'Oh,' said Master Bholaram, disappointed, as if he had just become aware of the passage of time. 'You have grown very tall.'

'That is what they tell me.'

'I heard you were a seth in Disavar.'

'I am, by your grace. If you had not taught me my Modhiya and my tables…'

Master Bholaram chuckled. 'You were never very good.'

He is confusing me with another boy, thought Hari.

'Why have you come back?' Masterji asked. 'There is nothing but sand and sun here. A man cannot cook a meal on tibbas.'

Hari sat down cross-legged by the bedpost so he could look

into Masterji's spectacles. Why had he come to Shekhavati? His sons had asked the same question, as had many men in the Addha train. He had not told them, of course, about the meaninglessness of Chaman Lal's life. He also knew what Masterji would say about that, having taught that lesson fifty years ago. This was nothing but *shmashaan vairagya*, the detachment that comes over one who has seen another burn to ashes in the cremation ground. One wondered what possible meaning there could be to existence, when it must end in such ignominy. But it was a detachment limited to the cremation ground. On the way home, a man remembered debts, spendthrift sons, cantankerous wives and long festering wounds, and sank back into maya, with every little tangle as important as it had been before the cremation.

Yet Chaman Lal had been dead for days and his gloom had not lifted. If this was not *shmashaan vairagya*—what was it? That was why he had come to Shekhavati—to ask Master Bholaram, the only man in Rampura who knew the English calendar, and who could squeeze thirt-five lines of Modhiya on to a postcard.

He said, 'I have seven sons—of whom Raamji has spared six—and two daughters. All but two have been married off and been blessed with children, giving me thirteen grandchildren and six great-grandchildren. And the number may have risen in the last few weeks because Gopi's third daughter was with child when I left... Raamji has given me shops and orchards, gold ginnis and silver rupees; I am thrifty and modest; I do not waste water; I sit on the gaddi and watch my sons count silver; my grandchildren play in my lap; my daughters-in-law look after my comforts. Yet a gloom has descended on me. What have I omitted to do that Raamji should plant this restlessness in my heart?'

'Have you given to pandits in proportion as Raamji gave to you?'

'Yes, pandits, beggars and sadhus. When Raamji gave me a child, I raised it lovingly. When He took a son away, I consigned him to the flames. When He turned grandsons into saints, I treated them with reverence. When He caused my children to come of age,

I found them matches. Shops were opened, profits made, losses borne, pujas conducted, death anniversaries marked, brahmins fed, goshalas visited, cows paid for. Should I have done more?'

'You have lived as a Grihastha should—without introspection or imagination.'

'Why, then, has this gloom descended on me?'

Master Bholaram fell silent, as if asleep, before continuing. 'Did you say the sixty-third was upon you, Hariya?'

'Yes.'

'The table, please, for that number.'

Hari was taken aback, but habit reasserted itself and he recited mechanically. '63, 126, 189...'

'Apply a 3 per cent discount because your customer asked for five.'

Hari smiled. '61.11, 122.22...'

'Good,' said Master Bholaram. 'You remember your tables, but not the last lesson I gave you.'

By this he must mean the discourse on the way to Chirawa, Hari thought.

'A man lives according to the Varnashram Dharam. That was how Raamji intended it; that is what the Shastras say.'

'Yes,' Hari said uncertainly.

'How old were you when you left Rampura?'

'Twelve.'

'Your years in Rampura were the stage of Brahmacharya: a time of study, play and preparation. You were married off then, were you not?'

'Yes, to Narayan Dasji Nangaliya's daughter in Chirawa. But she...'

'Your next stage was Grihasthya. You lived as a householder, accumulated wealth and gave away, both in moderation.'

'That was how I lived in Bogra.'

'When you have married off your children and seen the faces of your grandchildren, you advance to the third stage of Vanaprastha.'

'I have nearly reached that stage in Watsonganj.'

'Withdraw from the entanglements of your Grihasthya life, and reflect.'

'Must I give up my sons, then?'

'Your attachment has weakened but not died. Sit in your shop but do not bargain with customers; cradle your great-grandson in your arms but half-heartedly.'

'I was a Brahmachari in Rampura, a Grihastha in Bogra, and am now a Vanaprasthi in Watsonganj. What of Kalkatta? I spent five years there, between the first two stages.'

'The pull of Brahmacharya is strong—a man would like to play forever. Kalkatta was where you struggled before yielding to Grihasthya in Bogra.'

'Do they not have a name for this stage?'

'Some call it youth. It is not mentioned in the Shastras.'

Hari stood up.

'And the pull of a Grihasthya life is even stronger, Hariya. You will struggle much before you enter Vanaprastha.'

At the door, doubt assailed him again. 'Is there not a fourth stage, Sannyas, when a man loses all attachment and becomes a spirit trapped in a worthless shell?'

Master Bholaram giggled toothlessly. 'I sit before you, do I not?'

'But you never married.'

'There are many ways to reach Sannyas.'

'Will I attain Sannyas after passing through Vanaprastha?'

'You are not a brahmin, Hariya. Most banias do not even attain Vanaprastha. They die seated by their cash boxes, counting silver and contemplating matches for their granddaughters. Have you not seen Daulatram's Tomb? It was built by an arrogant Grihastha who should have entered Vanaprastha instead. He died an anxious man, calculating his amounts receivable, with the final inventory still incomplete inside his head.'

Hari rushed out of the temple yard, his mind in turmoil. He had known that Raamji laid out the path a man was to traverse before sending him into the world. But did he mark it so clearly? Was every twist and turn taken by him preordained, when he thought he was acting on his own behalf? Had his joys been no more than prescribed moments of relief, and his sorrows mere counterweights arranged by a master architect?

He would go to the one place in Rampura that still held meaning—Daulatram's Tomb—to see what came of hubris. He ran to the end of the lane and turned left, and was suddenly lost. How was this possible? To not know his way about in Rampura! Age was playing tricks on him. Seth Harilal Tibrewal from Disavar, with gold ginnis tied at his waist and hundred-rupee notes in his kurta pockets, was lost in the lanes of Rampura.

He asked a man seated in a doorway—a low door, he noted, as in his father's house—the way to Daulatramji's haveli.

'Which Daulatram? Banwari Lalji's son?'

He had not imagined a day when a man in Rampura would not know of Daulatram. He asked the way to the riverbed and made his way there.

The haveli was in ruins. Standing under the kitchen window, as he had fifty years ago, he looked for the fresco. It had completely faded away. Part of the boundary wall had collapsed. Moss overran the sides. The gate was open. The desert had reclaimed the courtyard. The upper floors still stood but looked weather-beaten. No one had entered the haveli for years, and perhaps its upkeep had been stopped after the collapse of Daulatram Gulabchand.

Here stood Daulatramji's monument, he thought sadly. When they called it Daulatram's Tomb, there was some awe mixed with their contempt—awe that a man might build a grand haveli and never choose to live in it. But he had overreached. A man may not build a monument to himself. Here it stood: wind buffeted it by day, jackals howled at night. One day, it would crumble like the firm that Daulatram had created. Some might say it was never built.

Suddenly, he understood why Daulatram had built his haveli.

Like Hari, Daulatram was sixty-two when he started the

haveli. He had been a Grihastha for fifty-one years, since he had walked from Jaipur to Mirzapur. In those years he had lived as prescribed: married off his sons—the ones who did not become fakirs—conducted the Satyanarayan Puja, paid for Ramayan recitations, been to Benares and Ganga Sagar, built a public house in Haridwar—where his son Jainarain now lived, if he still lived—observed the anniversaries of his ancestors' deaths, fed brahmins, built a great temple in Calcutta, and created a firm that earned crores of rupees, employed thousands of clerks, and had dealings with sahibs in England and Germany, even in America.

A man such as that is never profligate. Did they not say he died in a simple vest and dhoti, at a time when his firm shipped five thousand jute bales every month? They were wrong to think he was making a display of his wealth. He was already considered a Birla by the people of Rampura. Every family had a clerk in his firm—in Calcutta, Bombay, Assam or Kanpur. Every father had a son who had started his career in Daulatram Gulabchand. Such a man feels no need for ostentation. No, the haveli was not meant to be his house but a temple to Raamji. But it would not do to put an idol of Raamji inside, because he did not want people to *know* it was a temple. Had they known, he would be celebrated as a great devotee of Raamji, thus defeating his purpose. Here is the wealth you have granted me, he said to Raamji. I give it back to you. I am building a ruin, a temple without an idol, a house no one will ever live in. It will never serve a purpose. And that is the rightful purpose for the silver you have granted me.

In Rampura, it was held to be a great misfortune that Daulatram had never lived in his haveli. He never saw it, did not even come for the inauguration, and succumbed to the curse of the haveli the next day. But Master Bholaram was wrong. They had all been wrong. There had been no curse. What prevented Daulatram from seeing the inauguration was his own will—he built the haveli *because* he would never live in it. At sixty-two, Daulatram had entered the stage of Vanaprastha.

He looked again, and now the haveli was magnificent. The

setting sun threw a shaft of light on its ramparts. Its walls rose majestically in the desert, painted in the seven colours of the rainbow. The train was visible again, winding its way from left to right, with its minuscule cars becoming larger as it came closer. The sahibs were there, too, as were the memsahibs. Motor cars flew, chariots bumped along tibbas, clouds rained flower petals and cows swam across the Karatoya. A woman in a white sari, her head uncovered, her manner frank as a man's, sat at a spinning wheel. She wore no ornaments and wielded no weapons, yet the goddess Kali stood with hands folded before her. Behind her lurked Yamaraj, Lord of Death, straddling his mount, the buffalo. And the whole panorama rested on the giant hood of Sesnag, the king cobra who holds up the universe.

Hari rushed back to Master Bholaram.

'Masterji! Do the masons from Sikar still come to Rampura every week?'

'They are all dead, Hariya.'

'Do their children still live in Sikar?'

'Some. But they are clerks in government service now.'

'Perhaps one learnt his father's trade?'

'You would have to ask in Sikar.'

'And the chitera who made the paintings in Daulatramji's haveli? Where would I find him?'

Masterji giggled. 'Time does not stand still for others, Harilal. That chitera died soon after the haveli was completed. His sons went to Jaipur in your father's time. Perhaps his great-grandsons can be found there, but no one paints gods or trains on walls any more. It is not the fashion.'

'I am going to Sikar to talk to the masons. Meanwhile, find me the great-grandsons of that chitera in Jaipur.'

'Why? Have you returned to Rampura to repair Daulatram's Tomb?'

'No. I will build a haveli next to it.'

3

Hari sent a telegram to Tribhuvan, asking him to transfer the money that Gangadhar had brought from the orchard sale in Bogra—it lay in a Calcutta bank—to a branch in Sikar. The masons were soon located in Sikar, too. They were Shekhavati Rajputs who had fallen on hard times, and did not require much inducement to be brought to Rampura, where Hari installed them in his father's house. Their family boasted of seven havelis built all over Shekhavati—in Nawalgarh, Sikar and Jhunjhunu—but none had been raised in the last twenty years. Marwaris who had gone to Disavar and become wealthy—the ones who built all the havelis—no longer built anything in Shekhavati. Instead, they raised mansions in Calcutta and Bombay and Jaipur, or built temples in Benares and Haridwar.

The masons examined Daulatram's Tomb and declared that its plinth was sinking because poor drainage had eaten away at the foundation.

Only the works of Raamji are permanent, thought Hari.

All of Rampura came to see the ground-breaking. Word had travelled to Nawalgarh, from where large crowds came across the riverbed to find work on the site. When digging began on the riverbank next to Daulatram's haveli, there were celebrations.

While the men dug deeper, Hari walked about the lanes of Rampura, picking his way through camel carts, goats, dogs, children and women carrying pots. Some knew him as the seth from Disavar who was building a haveli, most did not. He sat at the dam—now almost levelled by age—and measured the depth of the water with his fingers, as he had as a child. He walked past old havelis—much smaller than Daulatram's, and too modest to attempt frescoes—which now bore advertisements for hair oil. On one, he even saw a poster for *Hunterwali*—showing Nadia Hunterwali in leather leggings with her whip raised, ready to strike—which was playing in a cinema hall in Sikar, a full twelve years after its first shows in Bombay.

Outside his father's house, he lay on a cot and thought of the Peepli, dozing off in the shade of the peepul tree that had given the song its name. In a corner of the kitchen, he dug up the floor and found eleven clay figurines—the ones they had been looking for during the Chhappaniya. All day, the men of Rampura came to him seeking work on the haveli site, asking about Bengal and Assam, demanding to know how much a hard-working bania might earn on a good day in Kalkatta. Their ignorance sometimes annoyed him; at other times he smiled and indulged them, watching their eyes grow in wonder as he mentioned ever larger sums—hundreds, thousands, lakhs...

It was now the hot month of Jyeshtha. By late morning, the sun was a white ball baking the tibbas, yet Hari sat without food or water to watch the men work. Because the masons had built nothing for years, they used the same lakhauri bricks and stone chips that their fathers had used fifty years ago, and fixed them with burnt lime as they had been taught during apprenticeship. Like plants nourished by rain, walls sprouted in the desert. Hari had told the masons what he wanted with no particular regard for architectural consistency: an arched gateway in the front, a balcony that overlooked the arch and projected into the street, carved wooden doors and windows, ornamental pillars, narrow staircases, brackets under the eaves, and two courtyards, an outer one for men and an inner one for women.

When he gave the masons their first fee—one-rupee notes—they seemed disappointed, not with the amount but with the mode of payment. In the world of Shekhavati Rajputs, paper money was still suspect. They preferred coins they could flip in the air. Until the music of silver hitting the ground had reached their ears, they did not trust the money. Hari sent a man to Sikar to turn his notes into coins.

Meanwhile, Master Bholaram had located the chitera's great-grandson in Jaipur. He made a living by painting the many houses of the Maharaja of Jaipur, and came to Rampura, which he had never heard of and regarded with disdain, very reluctantly.

He took one look at Hari's bare haveli—its walls were not yet plastered—and said, 'No one paints frescoes any more. It is not the fashion in Jaipur.'

'I have built my haveli in Rampura, not Jaipur,' Hari said.

'I will need samples to draw from.'

Hari pointed to the boundary wall to his left. 'Look at Daulatramji's haveli.'

'Who is Daulatramji?'

'The only man in Rampura worthy of being called "seth". Look at his walls.'

'I see nothing.'

'Look closer. The paintings have faded and the plaster has peeled, but the sketches can still be made out.'

The chitera examined Daulatramji's walls, ran his finger along the faded train, scraped off a fleck and crushed it between thumb and forefinger. 'This is the *ala gila* method—very expensive.'

'What is money? The dirt on one's palm.'

Problems arose as soon as the chitera began. Because they were Shekhavati Rajputs, the masons refused to share the house with him—he was a kumhar. The men who came from Jaipur to assist him were kumhars too. Hari was forced to rent rooms for them. Then, on the very first day, the chitera said, 'No one uses natural pigments these days but synthetic ones from Germany.'

'They used natural pigments in Daulatramji's haveli.'

'To do that, you must plaster and paint at the same time because the plaster must be wet when you paint. With synthetic pigments, you could finish the plaster, let it dry, then paint what you wanted, so the paintings could be more intricate. You could add layer upon layer in different colours. With this oleography, you could create shadows and thicknesses. When Radhaji stands with Krishna Bhagwan, do you not want to see the glorious fullness of her body?'

'Did they use this oleography in Daulatramji's haveli?'

'No. But *ala gila* makes the haveli look cheap. That is why the seths in Kalkatta have stopped using it.'

Hari smiled. 'I am not a seth. My haveli is not in Kalkatta. I want *ala gila*.'

The chitera drew up a list of pigments. Some were easily available—lime for white, sediment from the iron-rich riverbed for green and yellow, crushed sandstone for red, saffron for orange, clay for ochre, indigo for blue, lamp black for black—while some required much preparation. A cow was bought and fed mango leaves, which had to be brought from Sikar, where they had come from Bengal. A bag was attached between its legs to collect its urine. On drying, it left behind a brilliant yellow powder. Seated under the peepul tree, Hari watched the cow guiltily. For two days it had eaten nothing but mango leaves. Its mouth appeared distended and it sat lazily on the ground, like a buffalo. He thought of Master Bholaram's words:

'The urine of a cow is as valuable as her milk, and more so than her flesh. No puja is complete without panchagavya, which contains five elements, all derived from her—milk, curd, ghee, dung and urine. In Shekhavati, men let cows loose in their fields during the hot month of Aashaadh, so that cow urine and dung may fertilize their fields before they plant bajra. When a seth builds a haveli, urine and dung are smeared on its floors to keep insects away. And when Krishna Bhagwan dances on those walls wearing a yellow dhoti, the yellow comes from cow urine. Truly, she is a mother even to Bhagwan—he uses her waste to clothe himself.'

The chitera's passion for the project grew when he saw his pigments collect in clay pots. Warm, earthy, honest colours, he called them. On the first day in Aashaadh, he began to paint the walls. Early in the morning, he prepared vats of paste by grinding jute fibre, jaggery, daal, acacia gum and the pulp of the bel fruit in a trench, mixing it with water, and using a pair of bullocks to pull a roller over it. Hari smiled on seeing the bales lying in the courtyard. Jute had paid for much of the haveli, so it was fitting that jute fibres would melt into the frescoes and become one with the walls.

At noon, after the pandit had done a puja, the mason plastered a portion of the wall—as much as could be painted before the plaster began to dry—according to the chitera's instructions: two layers of fine clay followed by a third of clay mixed with lime and the paste prepared by the chitera. A fourth coat was applied—lime and brick dust—followed by a fifth layer of marble dust. A sixth had fine lime dust, jaggery, sour buttermilk and powdered sea shells, which caused the wall to glisten like oiled skin. Before the sixth layer could dry, the chitera began. He dipped a hand in yellow paste and stood next to the wall, fingers poised.

'What shall I draw?'

Hari had not given this much thought—he had been immersed in the paints, sea shells and jute bales. But he knew what was to come first. 'A train as long as the wall, with a black engine and a dozen red cars. Let the engine send up smoke. Draw sahibs looking out of the windows, smoking cigars and pointing at the tibbas of Shekhavati. Draw a memsahib too. She leans out, one hand on the edge of the window, the other pressing down on her hat so it will not fly off. And she smiles.'

The chitera frowned. 'I have not seen a memsahib.'

'I will describe one to you,' said Hari, thinking of the portrait of Mozelle Cohen in the Nawabbari in Bogra.

'I must draw quickly before the plaster dries.'

'Start with the train.'

The chitera ran a hand along the wall, depositing paint in a line that was not quite straight. He drew in quick motions, using the thumb for thick lines and little finger for fine ones. Three men filled in the lines with colors, as directed by him. Both plaster and picture were nearly dry by the time the patch was covered. The chitera's men brought out coconuts, conch shells and pieces of agate, and rubbed the picture vigorously to burnish it, fix it in the wall, and disinfect it, as protection from flies and mosquitoes.

The chitera turned to Hari. 'There it is, Sethji. The wall may crumble but the fresco will never peel.'

'But it will fade.'

'That is in the nature of things,' said the chitera.

The mason prepared to lay plaster on another section of wall, the chitera dipped his finger in paint again, and Hari began to describe the memsahib in his mind.

Through the month of Aashaadh, he flew on the wings of imagination and the chitera drew. Pictures of Krishna and Radha—put them in a motor car!—in amorous play. But they are gods: give the car wings and send them into the sky! Here is a balloon floating above the desert, there an aeroplane suspended in the sky. A sewing machine stabs a ream of cloth. Jesus sniggers at praying sahibs, Victoria scowls at a couple in embrace, soldiers brandish swords at banias, Yule Sahib reclines in a boat on a river being dug by his men even as he sails downstream… There were many walls to paint and none were spared. The frescoes outside were beaten with stone and polished with tempera, gum and camel fat; those inside, being protected from rain, received coats of varnish and shellac. The chitera worked day and night, and Hari was always there, asking him to redden lips, draw mehendi on hands, put creases on foreheads, add flounces to skirts, insert another diamond into Victoria's crown. A girl of sixteen sat on her bed, head adorned with a hat too large for her and a coin with Victoria's head in her lap. A dark boy in a spotless dhoti leaned out of an Opel car. A frail man of twenty-eight stood transfixed between two railway carriages. Two boys sat on a tree branch—one drooled, the other regarded existence with a saintly expression. A boat laden with jute sailed on the Karatoya. A woman squatted on her cot, filling books with the name of Raam. A ricksha was pulled over cobblestones by a Chinese man.

Once the walls had been covered, they painted everywhere else—ceilings, banisters, railings, balusters, under the balustrades, around railings, on the risers of staircases and under the arches. Where only a narrow ledge offered itself, a chain of lotuses was hastily drawn; a pillar was ringed with garlands of champa and chameli; a wide wall invited an aeroplane or a tea party of sahibs on a Calcutta lawn, a long one called for a flowing river; a ceiling was adorned with demi-gods and celestial figures: kinnars, gandharvas and maruts. Around door-frames and windows were sahibs in sola topis, memsahibs wearing parasols, Shravan Kumar carrying his blind parents on a pair of scales, Raamji smoking a cigar, Sitaji watching him in a bowler hat, Raamji and Sitaji in a car chauffeured by Hanuman, cows with calves, kyals at a jute press, a boy standing in the womb and a woman in the agony of childbirth. The warm colours in balconies and courtyards gave way to cobalt blue and dull green in bedrooms, where couples lay in loving embrace while servants stood in the background. At first, Hari was shocked to see these paintings, but the presence of servants somehow made them acceptable.

In the largest room in the haveli, the chitera turned to Hari with a twinkle in his eye. 'This will be your bedroom, Sethji. Here I will draw pictures meant only for you and your wife. Some you will be able to see only with the door shut; others, on the ceiling, will be visible only when you place a lamp in a spot I will show you.'

Hari smiled. What would Master Bholaram, suspended between Brahmacharya and Sannyas, make of that?

The chitera covered the ceiling with memsahibs wearing low-cut blouses and milkmaids bathing in the Yamuna, watched by a playful Krishna. The wall hidden by the open door received a memsahib, naked in her bathtub. Standing beside the chitera, Hari laughed, thinking of the Nawab of Bogra and his mistresses.

In the month of Saavan, the frescoes were complete. Hari sat in the courtyard. A tulsi plant stood in the centre. Like all available surfaces, its plinth had been painted with little ducks. A few drops of rain fell in the dirt—the first of the year. The chitera looked at the sky and sighed.

'Just in time, Sethji, and not too soon. The paintings are all dry, beaten into the wall and burnished. We have learned how to work with Indra Bhagwan. Believe me, he can be manipulated far more easily than some men.'

Hari started. He had heard this before, outside a crowded court in a Calcutta lane paved with cobblestones. 'You will soon learn how to work with Indra Bhagwan,' Janardhan had said in Cotton Street. 'Believe me, he can be manipulated far more easily than some sahibs...' Five years had passed before their agreement with Indra Bhagwan came undone. They had come to Harrison Road, where Hari turned left to go to Sealdah Station while Janardhan turned right for Howrah, across the old pontoon bridge that was now gone. Hari had left for Bogra and Janardhan for Shekhavati, each running from an English sergeant...

'Why do you tremble, Sethji?' the chitera asked. 'The rain can do you no harm—your haveli is complete and your frescoes safe.'

Hari stood up. 'Raamji speaks in many voices. Some we understand, some we do not.'

'Will there be a puja? Will you not bring your grandchildren to live in the haveli?'

'I am going to Chirawa.'

He hired a camel with a keeper and climbed on to the saddle. The camel rose, rear feet first, and he was nearly thrown to the ground. The keeper chuckled. 'You have spent too many years in Disavar, Harilal Seth. Take a camel cart. It will cost more, but you are not short of silver.'

He set off in a camel cart. The few drops had not been harbingers of rain—they rode through scorched earth for fifty miles. The sun lingered directly overhead. Both camel and driver were listless when they reached Chirawa early in the evening. They passed the public house where guests had stayed for his wedding. At the Hanuman temple, he asked about Janardhan. The pandit did not know. He was loath to go to Narayan Dasji's house, so he directed the cart into an alley and had the camel-keeper make enquiries. The sun had set when they finally stopped before a small house—mud walls, khejra trees in the yard—and Hari walked in, bending over to pass the low door.

Janardhan had aged gracelessly. He was only four years older than Hari—he would be sixty-six now—but his skin was grey and his body had wasted away. The kurta hung loosely about his shoulders. He had let his beard grow. He was sitting in a chair and looking at the door as if expecting someone. 'Raam Raam,' he said without warmth.

He did not ask why this man, whom he clearly did not recognize, had entered his house. Hari was moved, remembering the Janardhan Kedia with oiled hair, well-pleated dhoti and neatly pressed kurta. 'I see you have not paid the dhobi to get your sleeves crinkled, Johnny.'

Janardhan stirred. A smile formed itself. 'You have grown very tall, Harry.'

'So they tell me.'

'What are you these days—a lagayival or a khayival?'

'I take rain when Indra Bhagwan sends it. I do not complain when he does not.'

'You look like you have become a seth, jijaji.'

Hari was embarrassed at being called jijaji. 'You perhaps know that your sister...'

'Yes, everyone in Chirawa heard of Parmeshwari Bai's departure. I also know that you re-married.'

'But you are still my...'

Janardhan held up a hand to stop him. Hari noticed how thin it was. 'You need not explain. Chirawa is no longer your sasural, and Narayan Dasji will not welcome you with mango water, but I will still call you jijaji.'

Hari was overcome. Renewed love for Janardhan gave way to outrage at his present condition. Summoning up the authority that a jija possesses, he demanded, 'Where is your wife? Where are your children? And why are you sitting in this state all alone? I had expected a warmer welcome from a sala. I had imagined him dressed in a clean kurta, hands folded, smiling in good health. Where is my mango water?'

'I went to Howrah Station, jijaji, while you went to Sealdah. That was my mistake. I should have gone east with you—to Bogra.'

'But you returned to Chirawa, to your children! Did you not have three hundred rupees in your dhoti? Three hundred went far in those days, especially in Shekhavati.'

'A man who has left Shekhavati should never return.'

'Your father had a shop in Chirawa, did he not? You had no brothers to demand their share.'

Janardhan's eyes filled with tears. 'My father lived to see the shop shut down. His last words to me were, "Make peace with Indra Bhagwan." Because I never did, jijaji.'

'What do you mean? No one knew about 67 Cotton Street in Chirawa.'

'Everyone did. They laid bets on the rain every morning and afternoon in summer.'

'But there is no rain among the tibbas.'

'They wagered on rainfall in Calcutta and Bombay even while living in Chirawa. They had all been to Disavar, earned thousands and returned to build havelis. Men who had seen the rivers of Bengal could not reconcile themselves to the dunes of our desert. And Johnny from Calcutta—under-broker at Andrew Yule & Company, lifelong associate of Indra Bhagwan—could not resist. You see the result before you.'

'Where were the bets registered?'

'In 67 Cotton Street, Calcutta, just as if we had been standing in Bara Bazar.'

'It took three days to go from Shekhavati to Kalkatta in those days.'

'But the sahibs had built a telegraph office right here in Chirawa. Bets could be telegraphed to Calcutta and rain measurements sent back, all in seconds. So you see, it was sahibs who enabled me to gamble in Bara Bazar while sitting in my father's shop in Chirawa. It was they who ruined me. And when the seths in Calcutta sent men to collect on their debts, they came by trains that the sahibs had built. Everyone gathered around my father's shop to watch my creditors humiliate me. My father watched too. Raamji took his spirit—he died the next day.'

Shocked, Hari sat down on the floor. 'Why did you not write to me?'

'You had told me you would never return to Shekhavati.'

'But for you...'

'Parmeshwari Bai had given birth to a son the day you left for Bogra. I remember—a telegram had been received. I did not want to lead you astray. A man has to look after his sons, not his sala.'

'For you, Johnny...'

'What is the boy's name?'

'Gopi Chand. He is almost forty-five now. He has five grandsons, perhaps six.'

'Ah, I had forgotten. Has it really been forty-five years? No matter what men do with their time, Raamji turns the wheel. Did you have other sons?'

'Six more, of whom Raamji spared five. And two daughters. And thirteen grandchildren and six great-grandchildren. These numbers are from a year ago, and have perhaps risen.'

'Raamji grants a large family to a man in good health, jijaji.'

'It is the Shekhavati bajra,' said Hari. 'Never a sick day in my life.'

'So why have you come back?'

Hari looked at Janardhan: Johnny K, seated in a chair like a sahib but with legs folded under him. Johnny K in an old dhoti and crumpled cotton kurta. Johnny K alone in a crumbling house without grandchildren around him.

'Why have you come back, Harilal?' Janardhan asked again.

'To take you to Rampura.'

'And what will I do there?'

'You will live in a great haveli.'

Three days later, Hari received a postcard from Watsonganj. He was sitting with Janardhan in the haveli. Servants had swept the yard and sprinkled water to keep the dust down.

'Is the news good or bad?' Janardhan asked.

'Both. In the last one year, there have been four births—a grandson, a granddaughter and two great-grandsons.'

'And the bad news?'

'In Pakistan, a great-grandson has died at birth.'

'You should go back, jijaji. The haveli will be in order when you return with your children. Johnny K will guard it as his own.'

Hari had been shaken by the news. Gangadhar's son had been stillborn. That misfortune should strike his favourite grandson seemed cruel and inexplicable. Had Gangadhar cried over the child's body? Had he stood on the bank of the Karatoya, as Hari had, to watch boats laden with jute after they had buried the child? Among his children, had not Raamji found someone more worthy of punishment? But that was a vile notion.

He had given no thought to his children for almost a year—to Garib Das's launch or Fakir Chand's afflictions or Manki's books. Now their images flooded his mind. The pull of a Grihasthya life is strong, Masterji had said, and the man entering Vanaprastha resists it with all his strength...

'I will leave for Disavar tomorrow,' he told Janardhan.

4

Arriving in Watsonganj, Hari declared his intention to retire by not going to the grain shop and not asking Fakir Chand about sales in his absence. Instead, he installed himself near the Kosi. Every morning a servant placed a cot there and he lay sprawled on it, watching the river. A pot of water sat under the cot. Fakir Chand's seven-year-old daughter played nearby. Hari had not mentioned the haveli to his sons. Once a month, a telegram arrived from Janardhan, saying cryptically that there was no news.

Garib Das's motor launch had acquired a measure of fame in Watsonganj. It was frequently rented to other Marwaris; the income from it began to accumulate in an account of his own. Land had been bought for a house next to the courtyard. Although it had been meant for everyone, Garib Das insisted that he alone would live in the house on account of his growing family. Both Fakir Chand and he had three children each, but Fakir Chand was too weak to protest. When not in the shop, he lay wrapped in parpatti next to Manki in the courtyard, where they spoke softly for hours about their mysterious ailments.

The house was ready in a year. It was pakka—of brick—and

its walls were finished with plaster. A railing on the upper floor looked down into the courtyard. Garib Das quickly had a pandit do a puja and moved his wife and children to the upper floor. In the days that followed there were many quarrels between Sumitra, Garib Das's wife, who stood at the railing, and Lajwanti, Fakir Chand's wife, who stood in the courtyard below. Raised in a wealthy family in Calcutta, Lajwanti had never learned to cook or even assert her will. Now she found herself in-charge of the kitchen—Manki being bedridden—and there were moments of great confusion: meals were not cooked on time; the children, including Ishwar Das and Mohan Lal, had to go hungry on some mornings.

Hari paid scant attention to these goings-on. The acrimony between Garib Das and his younger brothers had made him more conscious of his remaining responsibilities—the weddings of Ishwar Das and Mohan Lal—and of a throbbing pain in his heart on account of Shanti, who was still childless in Pakistan.

Shanti visited often, arriving with three attendants and a dozen steel trunks, having travelled two days over rivers in Pakistan and India, changed three trains and two bullock carts. She told stories of her husband's associates in Kushtia who had left for India in 1947. They had returned to find that their houses had been declared 'enemy property' by the Pakistan government, to be seized and re-distributed to Muslims who had come to Kushtia from Bihar. She warned of a similar fate for properties Hari had left behind in Bogra, and urged him to return. He reminded her that Gangadhar still lived in Bogra, and that a house would have to be abandoned to be declared enemy property. She responded with dark tales of Marwaris taken away in the middle of the night so their property could be considered abandoned.

But she came to Watsonganj with a far deeper wound in her heart. 'I have forty rooms in my haveli. From the upper floor I can see boats on the Gorai—many of them belong to my father-in-law. I open every window; I sit in each, in turn, to watch the river. It brings me no peace. What do I do with forty rooms if not one resounds with the cries of children? The haveli is a tomb in which four gloomy spirits lie buried—my father-in-law, my mother-in-law, my husband and myself.'

Hari would hear her lament and sigh. He could not say what everyone knew: the family was accursed. For two generations they had extended their line by adoption. They were fated to adopt again. Yet it was possible that Raamji would relent—Shanti was not yet twenty-five, and she had done everything in her power to make Him change His mind: consulted every pandit in Kushtia and Watsonganj and everywhere in between, called ojhas to cast spells, taken herbs prescribed by vaidyas, and hired midwives who could sniff pregnancies much before the pregnant woman could. And Hari had heard about the three sadhus who had arrived in Kushtia and cast a spell on Shanti while her husband and father-in-law were away in Dhaka. She had willingly given them her jewellery—everything she could find in the haveli—and been promised a child in her womb. A family retainer happened to come by before the sadhus could make off. They were accosted and the jewellery was retrieved. Had he not arrived, there would have been a great scandal.

Once, when Shanti had finished one of her tales—a pandit had given her a talisman that had not worked—Manki turned over in her cot and said, 'Raamji places the fault with the woman if she is a sinner. But you have done every puja, been to Ganga Sagar, and observed every fast. Perhaps the fault lies with my son-in-law.'

Delivered loudly and clearly, Manki's suggestion threw the house into confusion. In the kitchen, Fakir Chand's wife stopped slicing potatoes. Seated upstairs in the balcony of her new house, Garib Das's wife pulled a corner of her sari over her face. Everyone had heard, and it now fell to Hari to quell such irresponsible talk. 'There is nothing wrong with Nagar Mal. A fine boy, a gentle boy. And nothing is wrong with my Shanti either. It is the curse of the family.'

Manki grunted in disagreement, and Shanti looked away. Ishwar Das happened to walk into the courtyard. He had come for his lunch before returning to the grain shop. Hari beckoned him and, placing a hand on the boy's head, said to Shanti, 'Here stands your brother, seventeen years old—aren't you seventeen? He will be married off soon. With Raamji as my witness, I declare that the first son his wife bears him will be yours.'

Ishwar Das shifted uncomfortably under the attention, embarrassed at this talk of his children. Worse, Shanti Bai turned to him with burning eyes. 'Do you take an oath, Ishwariya?'

'Yes, yes,' he said quickly before running into the kitchen, where Fakir Chand's wife was waiting to feed him.

That night, Manki let Shanti write Raam Raam in her books. A childless woman being inauspicious, she had never before allowed Shanti to touch the books, but a woman who was almost expecting—it was only a matter of months before a bride was found for Ishwar Das, and then another nine before a son arrived—was endowed with the divinity of motherhood. From being a pariah in Manki's religious ritual, Shanti had suddenly become an auspicious presence.

Ishwar Das had been going to a government school where he had failed his matriculation examination. Manki said that this was a sign he was ready to be married off. Because Hari's long meditations at the Kosi bank were now well-known, the duty of finding a bride devolved to Garib Das, as the eldest brother in Watsonganj—a difficult task because they had come to Watsonganj only three years ago and did not have a network of associates there. A suitable girl was eventually found, and Garib Das summoned her with her family to his new house for an inspection. When told, Hari was horrified. 'Whoever has heard of this inspection ritual? I have married off five sons and two daughters and seen a dozen grandchildren married, and no one ever saw the bride before the wedding.'

'But Ishwar Das will not see her at all,' said Garib Das. 'Shanti Bai will.'

'What does Shanti have to do with this? Will she come all the way from Kushtia to see a girl's face? What would a face tell her?'

'It is because of the oath that Ishwar Das took,' Garib Das said.

Hari recalled, and understood. Shanti was taking an interest in the girl because she would bear her child. Yet it was improper for a family to send a girl to her in-laws' house before the wedding. 'Her father does not understand the bounds of propriety, but I do. A bride cannot enter her husband's house before the wedding.'

'But she will come to my house, not Ishwar Das's. I will not let her stand in the balcony. She will not even get a glimpse of the courtyard.'

This assumption—that the new house belonged to Garib Das alone—irritated Hari, but he acquiesced grudgingly. In any case, the invitation had already been sent to the bride's father, and Shanti was already on her way. Garib Das had not waited for Hari's permission to set his plans in motion.

Shanti arrived with her attendants and her dozen trunks. The next day, the girl crossed the Kosi in Garib Das's motor launch, chaperoned by two aunts. She entered Garib Das's house from the back so she would not come near the courtyard. She wore a simple sari and was carefully wrapped in a shawl. Shanti sat by her in Garib Das's room and examined her closely. 'How old are you, Bai?' she asked.

'Seventeen. The eighteenth is upon me.' The girl spoke faintly, in a voice that combined modesty with awkwardness.

The girl's manner pleased Shanti, as did her advanced age—she was ready for motherhood. She pressed on. 'They say girls wear English skirts nowadays until they are eight, or even ten. When did you start wearing a sari?'

'Five' said one of the aunts. 'We forbade English skirts after that.'

'But of course she will wear a Shekhavati skirt in the wedding,' said another aunt. 'Unlike the English skirt, it is modest.'

'Show me what you have in your ears, Bai.' Shanti inspected the earrings, the bangles, the nose-ring, and the silver bells on the girl's ankles. 'Can you cook daal-bati without having the bati crumble in ghee?'

'Yes,' said an aunt. 'She makes halva and churma too.'

'And the Bhagavad Gita?'

'She can recite half of it.'

Needle and thread were produced. The girl demonstrated her ability to thread a needle to Shanti's satisfaction. The aunts sighed in relief. Everything was going well. Shanti said, 'I have heard that girls are born with saap-saapini nowadays.'

'What are those?' asked the aunts, suddenly worried.

'Snake-like birthmarks on the back. They are inauspicious.'

'But this is a fair-skinned girl,' said an aunt. 'Why would she have those marks?'

The girl's blouse was unbuttoned and her back exposed. After careful inspection, Shanti turned to Manki, who sat in a corner, and nodded. Manki crawled forward—she was too weak to stand up and walk by herself—and slipped a gold ring on the girl's finger.

'Panditji will fix a date for the wedding,' said Shanti.

The wedding was swift. Guests were given tours on Garib Das's motor launch. Pushpa's father-in-law helped with arrangements. Hari had half-hoped that Gopi would come to see his brother get married but he did not. Gangadhar expressed his inability to come from Bogra—there had been riots in Santahar again, and Marwaris were afraid to leave their shops.

The final ceremonies was marred by an importunate Garib Das, who took it into his head that the whole wedding should take place on his launch. He thought himself the master of ceremonies, and the image of seven circles around a fire in the middle of the Kosi had seized his imagination. His suggestion was ignored until a few hours before the wedding. Opinion on both sides—the bride's and the groom's—was arrayed against him. Ishwar Das expressed the tentative hope that the motor launch would be stable enough for his seven circumambulations, but was shouted down by Hari.

Garib Das prevailed. Bride and groom clambered on to the launch. Hari, Manki, Shanti and the bride's father followed. Fakir Chand refused to leave the safety of land. The pandit was helped aboard. Garib Das climbed into the pilot's cabin with Mohan Lal and two of the bride's brothers. At his signal, the pilot took the boat midstream and dropped anchor. There was much fussing over the bride's bejewelled shawl, which flapped around her in the breeze and had momentarily exposed her face. It proved to be difficult to sustain the wedding fire in the wind. The pilot fanned the flames furiously with his cap, and at one stage it looked like the whole launch might catch fire. The seven circles were interrupted by a sudden wave during the fourth that sent the wedding party reeling. Garib Das stood happily in the pilot's cabin and looked down at the deck, where Hari sat cross-legged next to the fire, resigned.

That evening, Shanti made much of the new bride, braided her hair, fed her sweet curd, adorned her with a mangtika and performed a jhaar-phunk to protect her from the evil eye. Before leaving for Kushtia the next morning, she gave the new bride one last hug and walked out of the courtyard, beaming. Her attendants loaded a bullock cart with her trunks. 'I will be back in nine months,' were her last words before the bullocks felt the whip.

In the next two years, sons were born to Garib Das and Fakir Chand and to their sister Kaushalya in Jalpaiguri, but Ishwar Das's wife showed no signs of impending motherhood. Shanti sent a messenger every month until she was obliged to make a trip to determine what had gone wrong. Perhaps the ceremony should not have been held in the middle of the Kosi? Her wrath was now directed at Garib Das, who hardly ever stepped into the courtyard, spending his time on the upper floor of his new house. Hari counselled restraint. It was not unheard of for a woman to bear a child three or even four years after her wedding, and Ishwar Das had been married for only two. Secretly, he wondered if Ishwar Das's wife was accursed—prey to the same fate that had stalked the family of adoptees—because her child had been promised to Shanti.

As befitted a married man, Ishwar Das did not participate in these discussions, and indeed was seldom seen in the house. He had immersed himself in the new undertaking that had come his way: the agency of Lever Brothers, a soap company once owned by English sahibs that needed distribution partners in towns all over Bengal and Bihar. Every week, soap cartons arrived from factories beyond the Ganga, fifteen miles from Watsonganj. Ishwar Das crossed the river, engaged boats and coolies, and supervised the loading of the boats, which were stacked six high with cartons of Lifebuoy and Sunlight soap. A flotilla would set off across the Ganga, arriving in time for coolies to transfer the soap to bullock carts, which would find their way to a warehouse in Watsonganj. The next morning, Ishwar Das would be up early so the cartons could be taken to the railway station. There, a whole carriage would be commandeered and coolies would throw the cartons inside. A clerk would hop in, and the cartons would go all over Bengal, and even as far as Delhi.

Hari did not like this line of work because much capital had to be invested in buying the cartons from Lever Brothers, recoverable only a month later when far-flung customers sent payments. Every week, soap worth tens of thousands sat precariously on boats in the Ganga. Should a boat sink—and that was common enough—it would take down the whole Lever agency with it because Ishwar Das could not afford to buy insurance. Our fortunes ride on the Ganga, he would say to his son.

'The Ganga is our mother,' Ishwar Das would respond. 'She will not look away.'

When the cold weather had eased, Tribhuvan arrived from Calcutta. He crossed the Ganga in one of Ishwar Das's boats, where the boatman set a chair for him between columns of soap cartons. His black coat and neat dhoti intimidated the coolies on the ghat, and caused a flutter in Watsonganj, where everyone knew that he was a barrister in Calcutta. He had come with good news. Mohammad Ali Bogra, his friend and the son of the Nawabzada, had become the prime minister of Pakistan. Hari was overjoyed; his first thoughts were of Gangadhar.

'He can now help Gangadhar find a buyer for the Rangpur oil

depot, and recover the warehouse in Bara Gola that was declared enemy property. With a prime minister behind him, Gangadhar need not fear anyone in Pakistan. They will fear him now—both Bihari Musalmans and our Musalmans.'

Tribhuvan was not so certain. 'Mohammad Ali is a prime minister, not a district magistrate. When he meets Nehruji, they speak of America, Russia and Non-Alignment, not of Gangadhar's troubles.'

'What good is a friendship if it cannot be relied on in such matters?'

'Besides, I have had no contact with him for twenty years,' Tribhuvan said.

'You have been careless,' said Hari. 'A man should keep up his contacts even with Musalmans. Who knows when he might need one?'

Tribhuvan had come to Watsonganj to ask his father for Mohan Lal. He needed a protégé in Calcutta. Who better to fill that role than his own brother?

Hari did not like the idea. 'The boy does not understand English. He was unable to translate the Lat Sahib's speech on the night the sahibs left for England. Unlike you, he has not studied in Kalkatta. What could a boy from Bogra do in a big city?'

'I need a clerk.'

'My son will not become a clerk. He has a father. His brothers have a grain shop and a Lever Brothers agency. He is a bania. Trade is in his blood—he will open his own shop.'

'But this position will be temporary. I will send him to college in Calcutta. When he finishes his studies, he will become a barrister himself.'

Hari peered into his son's eyes to try and read his mind. How much did Tribhuvan love his brothers? How much could he, considering they were not born to the same mother? But here he was, offering to take under his wing a younger brother who, Hari's claims notwithstanding, did not have bright prospects in Watsonganj. The money brought from Bogra had been exhausted in setting up the grain shop and in gaining the Lever Brothers agency, not to speak of Garib Das's launch and new house. Where would the capital for Mohan Lal's shop come from? Perhaps this was all for the good. But there was another little matter.

'He is already nineteen. If he goes to Kalkatta now, when will I marry him off? No one will give his daughter to a boy who is still a student.'

'Men in Calcutta do not marry until they are past twenty. Among Bengalis, it is not uncommon for a groom to be twenty-five…'

'We have our ways, Bengalis have theirs. I was married off at the age of twelve, your brother Gopi at fourteen, Durga at seventeen. You were given a bride at twenty-five, like a Bengali, but only because of your studies. And see how slow you have been to produce a son. Gopi already has eight grandchildren, while your son Arjun is merely… How old is he?'

'Thirteen.'

'You see,' said Hari, assured that his point had been made.

'I will find Mohan Lal a bride,' said Tribhuvan. 'Marwaris in Calcutta do not mind a student for a bridegroom.'

Hari assented, as he usually did nowadays to all schemes hatched by his sons. The next week Tribhuvan returned to Calcutta, taking Mohan Lal with him, and Hari sent a postcard to Gangadhar in Bogra.

'Go to the Nawabbari and pay your respects. Nawabzada Sahib was always Hindu-minded, and the troubles in Bogra cannot be blamed on him. Remind the Nawabzada, if he does not remember, that his son, the prime minister, is a close friend of your uncle Tribhuvan Lal,' he wrote.

Hari let it be known in Watsonganj that his son knew the prime minister. On receiving the news, Pushpa's father-in-law came to see him. 'Could I meet Nehruji the next time he comes to see Barrister Sahib?'

In a few days, everyone found out that Hari had meant the prime minister of Pakistan, not India, and admiration turned to indifference and even mild hostility. He found himself explaining that his son had not spoken to his friend for twenty years, and they were no longer even friends. Why, Hari thought it unlikely that Mohammad Ali Bogra so much as remembered who Tribhuvan Lal was.

In the month of Aashaadh, Manki informed Hari that Ishwar Das's wife was pregnant. A telegram was sent to Shanti, who arrived within the week. The next few months were spent in anticipation. Shanti spent her time fussing over Nirmala, Ishwar Das's wife. She was up early in the morning, cooking ghee-soaked rotis for the expectant mother, supervising the milking of the cow—so she knew that the milk had not been diluted with water—and standing over Nirmala as one did over a child to ensure she drank the milk and ate the rotis. Midwives were brought, pandits were called. During afternoons, with the men out in shops and Hari by the riverbank, it was considered safe for Nirmala to lie down on a cot in the courtyard for a two-hour nap, before the sun became too hot. While she slept, Shanti sat next to her with two midwives to examine her swelling belly. The midwives told her that the child 'rode high' and the bump was abrupt and pointed, all of which indicated a healthy, happy boy.

The baby arrived in the bitterly cold month of Magh. The men were in the courtyard and the women with Nirmala. Hari heard the child cry and saw Shanti emerge from the room. A look at her face told him all. It was a girl. She strode past him, trembling with rage.

'A first daughter is the goddess Lakshmi,' he said. 'She brings wealth.'

'Not if she is the only one I will ever have,' Shanti retorted. 'I need a prop for my last years, not a burden who must be married off with a large dowry.'

She left for Kushtia the next day. Ishwar Das had never said a word about the adoption plan, but Hari saw relief in his eyes when Shanti's bullock cart was gone. No doubt Nirmala was pleased too. What good would it have done them if Raamji had granted them a boy, only to be given away to Shanti? Perhaps it was all for the best.

But he could not overlook Shanti's pain. How many more years would she have to wait to hear the cry of her own child? And there were not many men as dutiful as Ishwar Das. Indeed, he knew of cases where a child once promised had not been given on account of the mother's sudden attachment. If Shanti had once said no to Ishwar Das, would any of her brothers make such a promise again? And a woman who could not secure a child from her own brothers stood no chance of finding one elsewhere. You have seven brothers and a sister, her relatives would say, why not ask them? Your father has dozens of grandchildren, can he not spare one?

He gazed daily at the Kosi, now reduced to a trickle in the cold weather, and realized that he had slipped back into the role of a Grihastha. Worrying about a childless daughter, he would soon begin to comment on Garib Das's extravagance, perhaps even go and sit in the shop. He must tear himself away. But what excuse would he give to his sons?

The excuse soon suggested itself. This happened to be the time for the Kumbh Mela at Prayag. He would go to Prayag and bathe in the Ganga, then continue to Rampura to see Janardhan and his haveli.

His sons raised the usual objections: he was too old—he reminded them that he had never been ill—he would be lonely, and the Kumbh was a crowded festival, too dangerous for a man on his own. Fakir Chand offered to accompany his father to Prayag. Given his regard for his own health, this was a generous leap, but Manki would not hear of it. How would her delicate son wrestle with the crowds in the Ganga, given the bitter cold? Hari thought the offer rash—Fakir Chand minded the grain shop, so profits would suffer if he were to be away.

He left for Prayag in the dark fortnight of the month of Magh, alone. The fifteenth night being the Mauni Amavasya—there would be no moon—was the most auspicious date for a dip in the Ganga at Prayag. Crowds gathered by the riverbank early in the morning. Hordes of naga sadhus had assembled, covered from head to toe in ashes, wielding tridents, spoiling for a fight with aghori sadhus carrying human skulls. Hari had heard of these orders but never seen them, and was too intimidated to try and gain the riverbank in their presence. Retreating to a high embankment, he watched the river. From time to time, a cry of 'Ganga Maiya ki jai' broke out. This was drowned out by a refrain of 'Nehruji zindabad'. Word spread that Nehruji had come to watch the bathing crowds, and a cluster of boats appeared on the Ganga where no boats would normally be allowed. It was difficult to recognize him at this distance, and there seemed to be English sahibs and memsahibs in the boat with him.

Hari was reminded of a joke doing the rounds in Watsonganj—Harilal Tibrewal's son called daily on Nehruji to discuss jute prices in Bogra. He chuckled without mirth. His reverence for the Ganga had suddenly vanished. It may have been the naga sadhus, or the crush of the crowd, or the sight of Nehruji in a boat with sahibs and memsahibs. He did not want to bathe any more; he no longer knew why he had come to the Kumbh Mela. From the embankment, he saw that a stampede had broken out on the riverbank. The naga sadhus were trying to force their way to the river using tongs and tridents. There were scuffles and cries. The boats on the river had turned back. Harilal left Prayag.

Two days later he was in Rampura, sitting in the haveli with Janardhan, listening to the rhythmic drip of a tap. The chitera had been called again. On the arch under the main door, he painted over some lotuses and drew a mother with a child in her arms. A woman sat next to her, eyeing the child wistfully.

'Someone has forgotten to shut a tap,' said Hari.

'It leaks,' said Janardhan. 'I will have it replaced.'

It was an unseasonably warm and cloudy day. A few drops of rain fell in the courtyard. Hari said, 'I hope you are a lagayival today, Johnny.'

Janardhan chuckled. They raised their faces to the sky. No

one had ever seen rain in February. The courtyard resounded with hisses as the rain soaked through hot, dry dirt, filling the air with the soft smell of slaked mud. A telegram arrived from Watsonganj.

'Your sons will not let go of you, Harry,' said Janardhan.

News of the stampede at the Kumbh Mela had travelled east to Bihar. There was panic in Watsonganj because Hari had not returned home: the worst had been assumed. As a precaution, Garib Das had wired Master Bholaram—the only contact he had in Rampura—to ask if he knew of Hari's whereabouts, and Bholaram had forwarded the telegram to the haveli.

'I must return,' said Hari with a sigh. 'Again.'

5

The Kumbh Mela stampede removed from Fakir Chand's mind the last shred of doubt about the astrologer's prediction. He had offered to go to Prayag with Hari, and it was quite clear to him that the whole stampede, including the arrival of Nehruji and English memsahibs, had been arranged for the purpose of taking his life. He had survived 1947 only because Nanuram had died in his place. Who would take Nanuram's place now? It was only a matter of months, weeks or even days before fate took its course. He began to behave unpredictably, locking himself inside his room, refusing to eat or allow his wife entry, demanding to be treated like a dying man. Manki watched impatiently from her cot as her favourite son hurled imprecations at Yamaraj, Lord of Death, whose men had come to take him away.

Hari called pandits and ojhas. After receiving suitable compensation, they raised doubts about the astrologer's competence: there were a dozen such men at every corner, claiming that meditation in the snows of the Himalaya had granted them powers of divination. Most were quacks, and Calcutta was full of them. Indeed, now that his first prediction about 1947 had been proven wrong—was not Fakir Chand still living?—there was good reason not to trust the man.

Fakir Chand would not be dissuaded. His descent into paranoia coincided with a strange transformation in his manner. Except when swatting off the messengers of Yamaraj, he became kind and considerate, a man who was about to receive judgement in the next world and, therefore, watchful of his behaviour in this one. He no longer complained, as he had for years, that his rotis had gone cold or that they needed more ghee. He did not insist that he would eat dinner inside his room, forcing his wife to make a dozen trips to the kitchen on the other side of the courtyard. Instead, he presented himself meekly in the kitchen, sprinkled a few drops of water to purify the floor, sat down at the doorsill and ate from a steel plate, which he then proceeded to wash himself. His wife would rush forward to prevent such an outrage, and Manki would call from her cot,

'You have a wife, Fakira. And three sons and a daughter. Are all five dead that you should wash a plate?'

Fakir Chand's daughter was now twelve. As compensation for previous neglect, he showered her with gifts—dolls, a clay cart, a sewing kit, a silver statuette of Hanuman, a gold chain and silver anklets. His three sons, used to greater attention than their sister, grew resentful. On learning this, he took them for a trip in Garib Das's motor launch—he had never set foot on the launch before—and bought them crushed ice soaked in syrup.

Finally, his quest to chalk up good works before his departure brought him to his sister Shanti. It had been a year since Shanti left in a huff after refusing to adopt Ishwar Das's daughter. Fakir Chand reflected on this for a week and, without consulting anyone, sent a postcard to Kushtia. On it he wrote in Hindi in a neat hand: *Raamji has blessed me with three sons. Take the one you want.*

There was an uproar in the house when Shanti arrived. It had been easy to promise an unborn child to her, but to give away a living boy was a different matter. Fakir Chand's wife Lajwanti set up a wail of the type reserved for mourning the dead. Manki ruled out the adoption and turned on Fakir Chand for the first time in his life. He was unmoved. 'I may not live long. At least one of my sons will have a father if Nagar Malji accepts him.'

After having watched helplessly—torn between his love for the boys and his desire to see Shanti happy—it was Hari who came around to the idea and prevailed on the others. 'Raamji has given Fakira three sons. One will take over the shop, the second will provide insurance. Why not gift the third?'

'All right, take Fakira's youngest son,' Manki said to Shanti. 'He is only two—he will soon forget his mother, and will grow up thinking you gave birth to him.'

'I want the oldest one,' said Shanti. 'I do not have many years to waste. He is already seven. I will marry him off as soon as I can, and my daughter-in-law will look after me.'

A pandit was called. He checked their horoscopes and pronounced them well-matched, so Fakir Chand's eldest boy was given to her. She promptly left for Kushtia with her son.

For two months, it seemed to work. Every week Shanti sent a postcard, in which she reported that the boy was overjoyed to live in a forty-room haveli. He had been given a roomful of toys; a servant and a playmate had been assigned to him; a boat and a boatman had been placed at his disposal, and he spent much time drifting on the Gorai. His slightest suggestion was treated as a matter of utmost urgency. Indeed, he hardly remembered Watsonganj. And he had once called Shanti 'Ma' instead of 'Bua'.

Fakir Chand was unmoved by the postcards. He had relapsed into self-pity now that his charitable work was complete. His wife Lajwanti was dismayed that a seven-year-old boy could be bought off so easily. Because she dared not discuss this with Manki, she asked Sumitra, Garib Das's wife: Was there nothing called mother's milk? Did not a bond exist between a boy and the woman who brought him into the world and suckled him at the breast? Sitting in the kitchen—where Lajwanti invited Sumitra, who now lived in her new house—they talked for hours about her great loss, keeping their voices low lest someone hear them and berate them for insensitivity to their sister-in-law, whose world had been brightened by her new son.

Eventually, Lajwanti prevailed on Fakir Chand to arrange a visit to Kushtia to bid a final farewell to her eldest son. Along with their three remaining children, they went by train to the India–Pakistan border, then by bus and finally, by boat across the Gorai. The haveli was grand beyond their imagination—none of them had been to Kushtia before—and they were cowed by the dozens of servants, the mango orchard in the backyard and the temple deep inside it.

Shanti Bai's postcards about the boy's transformation had apparently been truthful. He embraced Lajwanti—now his aunt—with great warmth, played with his new cousins, and said not a word about the adoption. Lajwanti was devastated. After two days in the haveli, she begged Fakir Chand to take her back to Watsonganj. Servants carried their trunks and bedding to a tonga. Shanti and Nagar Mal stood at the door with their son. Shanti's tears flowed freely. She clutched Lajwanti tightly to her and would not let go. 'You have given me your jewel. You are my sister, you are my mother, you are my Lakshmi, Durga, Saraswati. I will never forget, I will never forget...'

Nagar Mal looked embarrassed. His eyes were moist. In great discomfort, he turned to his son. 'Go on. Touch your aunt's feet before she leaves.'

The boy bent over. His fingers grazed Lajwanti's toes. Suddenly, he wrapped his arms around her thighs, buried his face in her sari and began to scream. Nagar Mal watched in horror. Shanti seized the boy roughly around the waist and tried to pull him away. 'Let your aunt go! She must return to Watsonganj before the sun sets on the Gorai.'

But the boy would not let go. Face bathed in tears, he stuffed his mouth with his mother's sari until he could barely breathe. Lajwanti placed a hand on his head—how soft his hair was!—and tears rolled down her cheeks. There was triumph in her eyes.

They returned to Watsonganj with the oldest one. Three days later, Fakir Chand sent another postcard to Shanti.

The youngest one is two. He will not remember.

Shanti did not respond.

When Mohan Lal had been in Calcutta for four years, Tribhuvan reported that he had found a match for his brother, who was now a clerk in his office and training to become a barrister. The girl's father was a wealthy jeweller. Hari was relieved: Mohan Lal was twenty-three, almost too old. The disparity in wealth between the two sides both pleased and troubled him, but Garib Das fingered his new diamond ring and said,

'Harilal and his sons are not beggars either.'

Indeed, in the years since Mohan Lal left for Calcutta, Garib Das and Fakir Chand had prospered. The grain shop had expanded, the Lever Brothers agency—now called Hindustan Lever—was flourishing, and Garib Das had set up a beedi factory where men rolled tobacco leaves into bidis, arranged them in bundles of ten and stuck a label on each—Harilal & Sons. These bundles travelled up and down the railway route between Delhi and Assam, enabling Garib Das to buy many more gold chains, silk dhotis, a new motor launch and, finally, a Landmaster car.

'A man considered wealthy in Watsonganj is just another trader in Kalkatta,' said Hari cautiously, afraid to offend Raamji.

In Calcutta for the wedding, they admired the four-storey building in which the jeweller's large family lived, saw his showrooms and toured his silver refining laboratory. Being of the groom's party they were given much attention, and they returned satisfied. Mohan Lal remained in Calcutta to complete his clerkship, and his wife, who was renamed Radha Devi at Hari's insistence, came to Watsonganj with them. At Sealdah Station, Ishwar Das joked with Mohan Lal. 'You will come to Watsonganj more often, now that there is someone waiting for you.'

Mohan Lal looked away, embarrassed. Hari addressed himself sternly to his son. 'Nothing must interfere with your studies.'

In Watsonganj, Manki was waiting. As soon as they entered the courtyard, she asked, 'Where is my daughter-in-law? Show me her hands.'

Radha was brought to her. Manki took her hands in her

own and said, 'What pretty hands you have. How old are you, my daughter?'

'Sixteen. The seventeenth is upon me.'

'Take good care of me. I do not have many years to live.'

Pushpa's father-in-law came to see Hari that evening. 'You have completed your duties, Harilalji—your last child has been married off.'

'Yes, but there are grandchildren—dozens of them. And great-grandchildren. Who will find matches for them?'

'I have seen large families in Shekhavati,' said Pushpa's father-in-law. 'In Sikar and Jhunjhunu, I know men with eleven sons, each of whom has a dozen children of his own. I have seen three hundred live under the same roof. Here in Disavar, no one hears of such families because they eat rice and wheat. Their grain is not nutritious like our bajra, their water not pure, their people not sturdy. Yet here you are with a family of almost fifty. That is astonishing in times as sinful as these.'

'Shekhavati blood,' Hari said, wishing to end the conversation.

'But now lies the task of marrying the grandchildren off.'

Hari sighed. 'A man's work never ends.'

To celebrate Mohan Lal's wedding, Garib Das declared that everyone, even the women, would go to a theatre to watch the film *Mother India*. Hari was vehemently against the plan. 'Let the children go. The women will stay home.'

But the women went. Hari went too—this was the only film he ever saw. He resisted until the last moment, and was finally persuaded by the argument that this was not any film but *Mother India*—without obscenity, foul language or improper relations between men and women. He sat uncomfortably on a bench and shielded his eyes whenever the screen showed licentious images, and noticed that his sons took no such precaution. Those who have seen *Hunterwali* will naturally take no offence at *Mother India*, he thought with resignation.

He was not enjoying the film, nor following the plot. He saw the heroine sink into despair and felt no sympathy—she had brought Raamji's wrath on herself. He was softened somewhat by the image of her crying children. Then, he heard the song. Suddenly, he was alert.

Chundariya katati jaye re
Umariya ghatati jaye re
Kaam kathin hai jeevan thoda
Pagala man ghabaraye

But of course this was true. He had sensed this all along—*the dupatta gets shorter, there are fewer years to live, there is much to do but little time, the mind is anxious*... Who could fail to notice the decline in morals? And who did not know that men lived less and less these days, dying ignominiously before their life's work was complete? Women were no longer concerned about modesty, children no longer respected parents, and the cow was being murdered wantonly. The world had been getting darker all along and his sons had not noticed, because they had not seen the sunny days of his childhood when men lived to a hundred, women were wrapped carefully in skirts and shawls, bajra was nutritious and disease was rare. At this rate, what would it be like when Mohan Lal's children grew up? Would morality survive? Would a man live long enough to father children?

'Dadaji is crying,' Garib Das's son whispered to him.

Garib Das nodded in the dark—this was an affirmation of his plan to watch *Mother India*.

Manki took a turn for the worse immediately after Mohan Lal's wedding, as if the arrival of his bride had finally given her the nurse she needed to begin a slow and deliberate decline. Radha was pressed into service right away. Manki's asthmatic attacks were now frequent. She had been abusive for so long that when she called her daughters-in-law 'balanjogi' they did not notice, yet there was new urgency—and new passion—in her imprecations. For much of the day she was inert, unresponsive and withdrawn, meditating on the brass statuette of Raamji that stood in the kitchen. At night, Hari would be woken by a strange babble of words from the cot in the courtyard: *Hare Raam Hare Raam, Raam Raam Hare Hare, Balanjogi, Raam Raam, Balanjogi…*

The words would rise into a wail. Mohan Lal's wife Radha would come running to her side.

'My Raamji is cold,' Manki would say through tears. 'Did you forget to cover Him for the night?'

A small blanket—six inches square—would be hastily thrown on the statuette. Manki would breathe heavily, listen to the words echoing in her head and declare, 'He is comfortable now.'

During her asthmatic attacks, a Bengali doctor who lived behind the courtyard would be called, but she would not let him come near her. He asked questions from a respectful distance. Sometimes she provided terse answers, sometimes did not respond at all. He would write a prescription. Hari would approach Manki. 'The doctor wants you to have these tablets. Will you?'

'You want to poison me,' she would say.

Hari would hand the slip of paper to Sumitra, Garib Das's wife, who was now head of the household. 'Keep this safely. I do not want to waste money on medicines she will throw away.'

Manki had become less and less religious with time. The rosary she had sometimes used to recite 'Raam Raam' had vanished. She no longer paid attention to pujas or pandits. When Hari organized a Satyanarayan Puja, she did not even eat the prasad. Her obsession with Raamji had become personal and private. No one was allowed to mention Him or guess what His current feelings might be. She bathed and fed Him every morning—the only physical activity she allowed herself—with indifferent precision. The bath comprised a silver pot of water turned over the statuette. The meal consisted of balls of rice that were placed around Him, consecrated, then thrown in the dirt next to the cot, where crows descended on them. After His bath and breakfast, Raamji would be carried back to His shelf in the kitchen, to await His nightly blanket.

She turned to her Raam Raam books with a vengeance, casting it as an epic struggle against darkness. All day, books lay scattered around her, their pages blackened with the endless repetition of two letters in Hindi. The first word her grandchildren learned to write was invariably 'Raam', and it was usual for at least two of them to spend a few hours every day, filling books. Sumitra organized relays, ensuring that someone would be at Manki's side every evening, writing, while others would play until it was their turn. This became an evening chore, and the children adjusted to this routine. Manki did not seem particularly grateful. When a granddaughter had finished her shift, she would pick up the book filled by the child and examine the words. No scholar had studied that one word as long as she had. She knew every curve of every letter, and every mood evoked by the word in every light. Occasionally, she would compliment a fine hand, but more often reprove someone for sloppiness—unnecessarily large letters that wasted paper, words cutting through lines, curves that were too smudged, stains that rendered the word illegible. Those who squeezed in two Raams in the space meant for one received grudging pats on the head.

Hari spent his time in the courtyard or, when Manki's rants became unbearable, on the bank of the Kosi. At home, he rarely spoke to his sons or daughters-in-law, or even to the children. Manki kept up a tirade. When he rose to get a glass of water, she said, 'Why must you get it yourself? Do you not have daughters-in-law?'

'They have enough work on your account,' he would respond.

'Not enough, not enough. Not for a mother of seven sons.'

Hari did not retort that only the last four were her own. She did behave like a woman who had raised seven sons: should there be the slightest delay in her meals, she would declare a fast, refusing to eat or drink until one of her sons had been called from the shop to plead with her, and the daughter-in-law accused of negligence had received a tongue-lashing.

When Radha had been in Watsonganj for a month, Manki complained of a great pain in her joints and said she was unable to move her arms or legs. 'My body is dead. Only my mouth lives. Raamji wants me to do nothing but speak.'

Radha had the cot dragged to a corner of the courtyard—the children pulled and pushed, laughing and giggling—until Manki was positioned above a drain. She relieved herself. Radha threw a bucket of water on the drain.

The cot remained there, sitting under a mosquito net that was held up by strings tied to pillars around the courtyard. Every morning, Radha rose early to shake Manki awake so she could relieve herself in the dark before the others woke up. A cloth—an old bed-sheet cut into pieces—was placed under the cot. Manki adjusted her buttocks to find a hole in the cot and emptied her bowels. Radha bundled up the cloth and flung it behind the tin sheds that served as latrines, and threw a bucket of water on the ground under the cot.

Gradually, Manki's cot acquired permanence and a few accessories. Radha sewed dark curtains into the mosquito net, so Manki could remain asleep even after the sun was up. As the cold weather approached, blankets were thrown over the curtains because Manki refused to cover herself, saying the blankets made her asthma worse. Everyone became used to the structure growing in the courtyard, inside which Ma, as almost everyone called Manki, lay with her Raam Raam books.

Mornings were now chilly. After the ritual with the bedsheet, Radha fired a coal oven and set it next to the cot. Dipping a piece of cloth in ghee, she held it over the coals until the ghee began to melt, then massaged Manki's legs with it. As the sun came up, she ground some gold varq—the thin gold film with which sweets were garnished—in a stone mortar, mixed it with honey and a package of Makaradhwaj prescribed by a vaidya, and had Manki lick the paste off a wooden spoon. The varq had come as Radha's dowry—her father traded in it. Aside from the gold, and a bowl of milk, Manki ate nothing all day.

By the next summer, her pains had become acute. She was unable to sit up. Sometimes Radha propped her up in the cot using her own body for support, so she could see her grandchildren writing Raam Raam in her books. This done, she was laid down again, her clothes arranged about her, and an umbrella erected above the cot to shelter her from the sun, because the curtains had been removed from the mosquito net in the heat of summer. Her daughters-in-law, all four of them, took turns asking if she wanted to eat something. She rarely did, aside from milk and gold varq. She spoke little now; the courtyard was quiet.

In the month of Aashaadh, just before the rains, her breathing became laboured. At dawn, as Radha was bundling the soiled bed-sheet from under the cot, Manki suddenly reached out and grabbed her hand. Radha was terrified—her mother-in-law had not shown such alertness for eight months. Trembling, she leaned closer to hear her better. Manki whispered, 'I do not want to go to Raamji in my dirty state. Will you ensure that my buttocks are clean before they take me to the Ganga?'

Radha nodded earnestly. Manki refused the varq and turned away the milk.

Later that morning, Hari called the Bengali doctor. Manki was too weak to resist, or even notice. He wrote a prescription. Tablets were bought, crushed and mixed with water. A bowl of paste was brought to her lips. Some trickled down her throat. She was instantly awake, as if the potion had had a magical effect, and the first word out of her mouth was 'balanjogi', directed at Radha, who held the bowl to her mouth.

'Finally, you have poisoned me,' she said, and swallowed the rest of the potion in one gulp.

That afternoon, Fakir Chand's oldest son entered the courtyard with a box of sweets and approached Radha, who was sitting beside Manki on the cot, massaging her feet.

'This is for you,' he said, popping a laddu into Radha's mouth. By then, Manki had recovered her spirits. She eyed the sweets suspiciously. 'Are you celebrating my death?'

'June 21, 1958,' said the boy. 'A full year has passed since Mohan Chacha's wedding.'

'Only when reckoned by the English date,' Hari explained quickly, to forestall an eruption by Manki.

Radha turned away shyly, but Fakir Chand's son would not leave her alone. 'Show me your hands, Chachi,' he said.

Radha held out her hands, as she had for Manki when she first came to Watsonganj. 'They are dark,' said Fakir Chand's son with a chuckle. 'I wonder what Mohan Chacha sees in you.'

Standing beside them, Hari smiled, but thought it right to reprove the boy for the sake of appearance. 'How old are you? Ten? Your Chachi is seventeen. Speak respectfully.'

Radha pulled a corner of her sari over her face in embarrassment. Meanwhile, Manki had understood the cause of the celebration, and proceeded to find fault. 'We will celebrate when I hear of a grandson.'

'Mohan Lal is busy with his studies,' Hari said. 'He has come home only twice in the last year.'

'I want to see a child.'

'It has only been a year.'

'A year is a year too late,' said Manki, before falling back on the bed.

In the next two hours, Hari called Garib Das, Fakir Chand and Ishwar Das home from their shops. They brought out all the Raam Raam trunks—twelve in number, stored in a corner of Hari's room—set them around Manki's cot and opened their lids, so she could see that they were stacked high with her books. Fakir Chand's son brought out a slate and chalk and added up the numbers. 'There are twelve trunks, Ma. Each has 124 books. Each book has 60 pages. Each page has 28 lines. Each line has 21 Raams. According to my tables, there are five crore, twenty-four lakh, ninety-six thousand six hundred and forty Raams in all.'

Impressed, Fakir Chand said, 'The boy has a good head for numbers. He is ready to sit in the shop.'

Hari wondered what Master Bholaram would have made of this. Unless the tables involved fractions, Masterji rarely expressed admiration. Moreover, no discounts had been applied… But this was not Shekhavati. An allowance had to be made for Bihar and Bengal, and for the times.

Aware of his father's admiration, the boy repeated the number. 'Five crore, twenty-four lakh, ninety-six thousand six hundred and forty Raams.'

'Too few,' Manki murmured. She did not know what the numbers meant, but knew that it should not be considered large, lest Raamji think her arrogant.

Hari reached into the bottom of the oldest trunk and brought out a red-bound book—the type he used for accounts in the shop. 'Here is the first page, the first line, the first Raam, written by Gopi Chand in Bogra more than forty years ago. You were only a child then.' He held the book open in front of her eyes. She seemed not to notice.

He delved into the trunk again and found a broken clay parrot. It was the toy Manki had brought from Gobindganj—the cause of her first fight with Gopi. Its green had faded into dull grey. The clay had been baked twice: first by the potter, then by the heat and weight of Raamji's books over forty years. Again, she did not respond.

Radha brought a brass plate of jaggery, yogurt and ghee, and propped Manki up by sitting behind her. Garib Das broke off a lump of jaggery, dipped it in yogurt and tried to force it into her mouth but could not. Radha then brought pomegranate juice in a silver tumbler, but Garib Das was unable to pour it down her throat. Finally, Radha laid her on the bed and brought out some varq, the same that Manki had refused in the morning. Garib Das brought a finger daubed in gold paste to her mouth. Her lips opened. A gob of gold lay on her tongue.

The courtyard was swept clean. Ishwar Das picked her up in his arms and laid her on the ground, her head in Garib Das's lap. They waited. The afternoon dragged on. Her eyes were still open, and they seemed to flicker. Radha brought an ear close to her lips. Manki whispered, 'Have I passed water?'

Radha discreetly patted the sari between Manki's legs. It was dry. She brought her mouth to Manki's ear. 'No.'

'Check my buttocks.'

'You are clean, Ma.'

Hari turned to Garib Das. 'Shout, Gariba. Shout, so Raamji may hear you. Tell him to keep his doors open because your mother is on her way.'

Early the next morning, the body was taken to the Ganga, fifteen miles away. Summer had been fierce and rains had not yet come, so the river had receded from its banks and now lay more than 500 yards beyond the cremation site.

'We must go to the other shore,' the pandit said.

'Is there no sin in crossing the river with a dead body?' Hari asked.

'This is the Ganga. She washes away all sins.'

'I cannot arrange to cross the river at such short notice,' Garib Das said.

The pandit pointed to three boats that lay moored along the bank. They were laden with cartons of Lifebuoy and Sunlight soap that had arrived the previous day, and were waiting to be unloaded. 'I heard your son say those boats are his. Unload the soap and leave someone on the riverbank to guard it.'

'Unloading will take three hours,' Ishwar Das said.

The sun was coming up: it would soon be too hot to do anything. Also, because Manki had been dead since the previous afternoon and the night had been hot, the body had begun to give off a stench.

'Lay her on top of the cartons,' Hari said.

'What of us?' Ishwar Das asked. 'We must cross the river too.'

'We will sit on the cartons with her.'

The body was laid on the cartons. They arranged themselves around her and set off. The boat swayed dangerously in the current. We sit on stock worth twenty thousand rupees, thought Hari. If we sink, our lives and our livelihood will both be destroyed. He looked at his four sons. Mohan Lal had arrived from Calcutta overnight, having received a telegram when Manki's condition worsened the previous day. Gopi had not come. Tribhuvan had wired back to say that a meeting of the Pinjrapole Society for the protection of cows—he was president of the Calcutta chapter—prevented his coming to Watsonganj.

Hari's gaze fell on the body, wrapped in a white sheet and tied with loops of rope to a column of Lifebuoy soap. She is silent as a cow, Chaman Lal had said of Manki when making the match. As with much else in his life, Chaman Lalji had been wrong. Since his vow of abstinence twenty-four years ago, Hari had not thought of Manki as a wife but a daughter. Parmeshwari's death had been sudden and unexpected. He had cried bitterly. Manki, on the other hand, had approached death carefully and deliberately. She had received a last meal from the hands of a son, she had heard a son announce her arrival to Raamji, and had died with her head in a son's lap. It was odd: Parmeshwari had suffered little and gone suddenly, but Manki, who suffered for most of her fifty-seven years, was the one who had been sent off in the proper way. Was suffering in life necessary for death to be joyous? Why else did a woman crave sons, if not to be sent off by them in her last moments? He was seventy-one. He had never been sick a day in his life. How terrible would his end be?

They approached the far bank. The Ganga was deeper here. Buffaloes lazed about in the water. Hari turned away in distaste, remembering Master Bholaram's words. 'While the sight of a cow or bull is auspicious, who can say the same of a buffalo? The bullock Nandi is the mount of Shiv, Lord of the Universe. And the buffalo? It carries Yamaraj, Lord of Death, and Saturn, Lord of Obstacles. On drinking a cow's milk, the calf becomes frisky—it dances, jumps and runs about. On drinking a buffalo's milk, the calf becomes lethargic and irritable, and sits in a trance for hours.'

They carried the body ashore. The pyre was lit. It began to rain. This was the first monsoon of summer, and it was vengeful. The chandals scrambled to keep the flames going.

'Indra Bhagwan does not want your mother to go to Raamji,' Hari said to Garib Das.

When they returned to Watsonganj that evening, they found it had rained there too. The courtyard was flooded. Because they had left Manki's trunks open around her cot, her Raam Raam books were soaked. Some floated in the yard, some had been washed down the drain. The words had been wiped clean.

5

RAMPURA, 1972

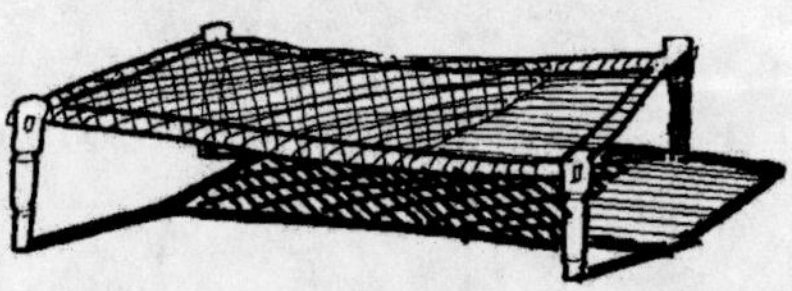

1

Hari sits by the riverbed in Rampura, a hundred yards from his haveli. His legs are splayed out in front of him. He can no longer sit cross-legged—his knees hurt. The sun will rise soon but the tibbas beyond the riverbed are already lit up. For thirteen years, he has sat here every morning to watch the play of light on the dunes. When it gets hot, he is helped up by a servant and taken to the haveli, where he lies in a shady corner of the courtyard. Janardhan pulls up a chair next to him. They talk of Calcutta, Yule Sahib and 67 Cotton Street. Sometimes, Janardhan brings up the subject of repairs to the haveli, and Hari shakes his head.

'If you do not get it painted, the plaster will peel off and destroy the frescoes,' Janardhan warns, pointing in the direction of Daulatram's Grave. 'You see what happens in seventy years; your haveli has already seen twenty-two.'

He has never understood why Hari continues to live in his father's small house, where he has a room and a servant, leaving Janardhan to spend nights alone in a haveli of twenty rooms. He sleeps in a different room every night—the haveli feels like an elaborate tomb.

'I am the ghost who haunts this haveli,' he complains. 'It needs the patter of little feet and the songs of women grinding corn or rolling papad or making pickle. It needs pujas, weddings, births and deaths. It needs whispered conversation and raucous laughter. And it needs the piffle of daily quarrels.'

By now, the sun is slowly appearing from behind the highest dunes. A shaft of light has found its way into the riverbed, casting shadows and creating patterns in the mud, which is caked and gnarled from a bout of flash-flooding two years ago. A Bullet motorcycle winds its way through alleys in the bed, bobbing up and down, disappearing behind hillocks to reappear moments later—two men, in dhotis and kurtas, coming to Rampura from Nawalgarh. As they come closer Hari recognizes them: banias from Rampura, who may have gone to Nawalgarh to check grain prices before opening their shops. They see him too and nod in acknowledgment. Everyone in Rampura knows of Harilal Seth from Disavar, who built a grand haveli but never lived in it. And everyone has an explanation for his odd behaviour. After his death, some witty young man will invent a name that will stick to the haveli—Harilal's Folly, Harilal's Conceit, Harilal's Tomb...

Master Bholaram died ten years ago without seeing the haveli. Two hours before his death, he pressed Hari's hand with his remaining strength and asked, 'Tell me, Hariya. Is the flesh of a woman very soft?' Hari took the body to Sikar for the cremation. When he lifted Masterji up and laid him on a camel cart, he noted how little he weighed. Once the strongest man in Rampura, now his limbs had atrophied. All that remained was the spirit of Sannyas and the curiosity of Brahmacharya.

A servant comes with a tumbler of pomegranate juice. Hari waves him away. He had drunk a glass of water—stale, kept overnight in a clay pot with a lid over it—when he rose, and does not want to ruin the taste in his mouth with the unpleasant tang of pomegranate. The sun now casts a morning glow on the ochre walls of the haveli. As he has done for thirteen years, he turns to look. From this distance he can see only one fresco—the largest—on the right flank: a flowing river dotted with jute-laden boats. Kyals and coolies bustle about; a man in dhoti and kurta, with a Marwari cap on his head, stands with his back to the viewer, watching the boats. His right hand is raised—he is calling out to a boat. In his left hand is an umbrella, still dripping from the rain. Above the boats, in a sky darkened with clouds, hovers an aeroplane... But he cannot see the aeroplane today. It is covered by a loop of marigold flowers. The whole haveli is bedecked in garlands that begin at the top and descend to the ground in cascades—marigolds, champa and chameli, with roses studding the joints where two loops meet.

He has never seen his haveli decorated so. The flowers have been brought from Delhi, Kanpur, even as far as Calcutta. Today, all of Janardhan's wishes will come true—there will be a puja, a wedding, whispered conversation, raucous laughter and the piffle of daily quarrels. There may even be a birth and, if Raamji chooses, a death. And there will be the strains of the Peepli, sung by women who no longer cover their faces before men, at the hour chosen by the pandit. It is the wedding of Tribhuvan's son, Arjun.

Hari had hesitated before giving permission.

'No one has ever seen the haveli,' Tribhuvan had said. 'There has been no puja, no griha pravesh. What better way to consecrate a new haveli than to have a wedding in it?'

It is hardly new. The walls already have a layer of moss at the bottom, where poor drainage has created patches of dampness. Hari found the idea distasteful. 'It is a haveli, not a wedding dharamshala.'

But the concrete in the outer courtyard—the one meant for men—had been poured with a wedding in mind: a block in the centre could be pried loose, exposing a patch of earth into which a pole could be sunk for a wedding pavilion. That was how the mason had built every haveli he had worked on. Standing beside him when the concrete was poured, Hari had noted the loose block and said nothing. Perhaps he had wished for a wedding all along.

'It is his grandfather's haveli,' Tribhuvan pointed out.

Hari knew Tribhuvan did not really need the haveli. He was one of the wealthiest and most eminent barristers in Calcutta. As president of the Pinjrapole Society, he led delegations to the chief minister of Bengal demanding bans on cow-slaughter, and was honoured in countless functions, both Marwari and Bengali. Such a man had no need to bring his son all the way to dry Rampura for his wedding.

He had yielded. Word spread. Garib Das offered himself as master of ceremonies. The decorations were his handiwork.

He had transported a dozen Bengali craftsmen from Calcutta to Rampura for the task.

'The best decorators are Bengalis,' he said. 'People in Rampura have never seen a grand wedding. How will they know which flowers to choose and how to string them together? Bengalis are art-types. They know how to build idols during Durga Puja and decorate houses for Marwari weddings.'

A dozen decorators have worked for four days stringing flowers, which have been shipped by train, bus, jeep and camel cart. Garib Das himself has driven all the way from Watsonganj, a thousand miles away, in his new Ambassador car. The car will now be used in the wedding procession to carry the groom from Duli Chand's small house—where Hari lives, and which will serve as the groom's symbolic home—to the haveli, where the wedding will take place. Like the haveli, the car is being draped in a blanket of flowers.

No one has seen so many flowers in Rampura, especially in winter. Amidst the grey, white and brown of tibbas, their yellow, orange and red is striking, almost jarring. They can be seen from a distance, framing the haveli, creating a colourful halo against the white desert sky.

'A dry morning, Harry. Dry as far as you can see into the future. No chance that rain will mar the wedding tomorrow.' Janardhan has stolen up behind him, unannounced.

Hari looks up at the clear sky. 'You can never tell. Indra Bhagwan is whimsical. There were flash floods two winters ago.'

'Would you like to bet on it?'

Hari giggles. They both know that gambling on the rain still goes on in Sikar and Jaipur. All a man in Rampura has to do is send a telegram with the amount wagered. They have never sent one. 'I take rain when Indra Bhagwan sends it. I do not complain when he does not.'

'They are asking for you in the courtyard,' says Janardhan.

'Why do they need an old man? The boy's father is there, his mother is at hand. His aunts are clustered around him. These are sufficient for any ceremony.'

'They want you to be the first to see the bride.'

'Ah.'

The first, he thinks, after the groom, the father-in-law, the mother-in-law, and half a dozen relatives in Kalkatta. What a strange world, where a bride may speak freely with the boy before the wedding—why, there is talk that they met even before their parents knew of it. And now he, at his age, must suffer the indignity of looking at his grandson's bride. The poor girl will probably writhe in embarrassment. He will be gentle; he will keep his eyes averted.

He tries to stand but fails.

'I would help you, Harry, but you know my condition.'

Hari cannot suppress a chuckle. Janardhan is four years older than him, and the last three have been hard on his worn body. He still refuses a cane—the old Shekhavati grain—but sorely needs one. Were he to sink to the ground to help Hari up, he would likely never rise again. Indeed, he spends much of his day trying to stay a few feet above the ground, never bending, never squatting. For his morning ritual in the latrine behind the haveli, he uses a chair with a hole in it. Hari teases him about that: Johnny has finally learned to shit like Yule Sahib.

The servant approaches again, this time to fetch Hari. He is helped up. As soon as he is erect he refuses the proffered arm. Janardhan sniggers toothlessly to see this stab at vanity. Hari turns to him in consternation. 'Do not laugh. Everyone will see your naked gums.'

'I cannot afford dentures like you on the salary you give me.'

Hari makes an impatient sound. This is Janardhan's usual taunt. Of course, he gets no salary at all. The servants in the haveli cook for him and look after his needs. Every summer, Hari buys him two dhotis and a kurta; every winter, a shawl.

'Let us go,' Janardhan says. 'The bride is waiting.'

The bride is waiting… As if she were a man, a business partner, a customer or a shopkeeper.

'She will grow old waiting if you walk the way you do,' Janardhan says.

'She is old enough already,' replies Hari.

This troubles him, too. The bride is thirty, he has been told. At that age, Manki had had two boys and two daughters, not counting the first two who had died, and was already an old woman. Parmeshwari did not even live to that age. What does a woman do for thirty years if she is unmarried? But of course, Arjun, Tribhuvan's son, is himself almost thirty-two. At an age when a man should be keeping a watchful eye on his sons while they learn to use the scales, the boy is going to get married for the first time. It is all very well that he has become a barrister in England—what kind of an education keeps a boy from getting married? And Hari has never understood why Tribhuvan has only one child. Granted, it is a boy, but does not a man want to fill his home with children? If he was too busy with his law practice to think of his family, what of his wife Kusum? Had she not pestered him as a woman should?

He walks swiftly, even though it hurts his knees.

'The flowers look beautiful on the haveli,' Janardhan says.

Hari does not answer.

When he had announced his decision to leave Watsonganj, his sons assumed he had turned to religion. It had rained for a full week following Manki's death. Much of Watsonganj had been flooded. Shops remained closed. Garib Das's launch had been damaged. An overloaded ferry had sunk on the Kosi, taking dozens of men down with it. I am going, he had said. Do not call me—I will not come. "Babuji has turned to Raamji now that Ma is dead," Garib Das announced. "He lives with Krishna Bhagwan in his heart. He wants to spend his time in Haridwar and Benares, bathing in the Ganga, feeding brahmins, paying for Satyanarayan Pujas and hearing pandits chant the Bhagavad Gita."

But, of course, he had already been to the Kumbh in Prayag and knew there was no devotion in his heart.

He left the waters of Watsonganj for the sands of Rampura, marvelling at the inversion—a bania had left pools of water to watch gazelles among dunes where no customer would ever come. He made no attempt to contact his sisters, who still lived in Shekhavati but whom he had not seen in a lifetime, and he resolutely ignored all postcards from Watsonganj or Calcutta for thirteen years, until Tribhuvan had asked to use the haveli for Arjun's wedding.

A small crowd has formed at the entrance to the haveli—young men, children, girls, even a few women. They are watching him. He pauses to catch his breath—he does not want them to see him winded—and turns to Janardhan. 'Why have the guests come early? The wedding is not until tomorrow.'

'They are not guests. These are your children, Harry.'

Hari is disturbed. He can see their faces now and he is not sure he recognizes anyone. Is that Fakir Chand's boy, the one who was given to Shanti? But he would be much older now. Perhaps that is the boy's son—Fakir Chand's grandson. How many grandchildren does Fakir Chand have? And do they have children of their own?

Everyone has now turned to him. A child shouts. 'Happy New Year, Dadaji!'

Hari turns to Janardhan. 'Today is Pausha sudi purnamasi. How could that be the new year? Or have I lost my mind already?'

'The English year, Harry.'

A young man rushes forward to hold his arm. He brushes him off. 'I have eaten Shekhavati grain, my son. Never been sick a day in my life. The eighty-fifth is upon me, to be completed on Phalgun sudi dwaadashi.' The man appears confused. Hari sighs and adds, 'Two months from now, three days before Holi.'

The man is very fair-skinned, and looks frail and vulnerable, as if used to being constantly sick. Hari is almost certain he knows whose child this is. 'Whose son are you?'

'Fakir Chandji.'

'Which one? Fakir Chand has three, I think.'

'The first.'

So this *is* the one who was given to Shanti. The man now beckons three children between the ages of four and six.

'Come and touch Dadaji's feet.'

Soon a dozen boys and girls—great-grandchildren all—gather around him in various stages of obeisance. Some touch his feet, some tug at his dhoti, some pull his hands, some just touch his kurta with a mix of indifference and amusement.

'What do you deal in, my son?' Hari asks the man.

'I don't have a shop, Dadaji.'

'Ah.'

'I am a doctor. In Calcutta.'

Hari is flustered. Why does the boy not have a shop? Is he not a bania? The children milling around him are becoming tiresome. He gently pulls out a little hand that has snaked its way into his kurta pocket. Someone chases the children away. 'Go on! Babuji, come inside.'

Hari is looking at the ground. He sees silver-lined Jaipuri shoes and the folds of a well-pressed silk dhoti resting on them. It is Garib Das.

'You look no older than me, Babuji,' he says.

But Garib Das looks very old indeed. *How old is the boy?* Fifty, perhaps, but he has never looked young because of his thinning hair. And now his dark skin has acquired blotches around the temples. As if in defiance, there is a gold chain around his neck and diamond studs on his kurta. And he is wearing perfume.

'Gariba.' Garib Das bends over to touch Hari's feet. 'I am told you came from Watsonganj in your car.'

Garib Das beams. '1400 kilometres! And I drove myself all the way.' The Ambassador is parked at the door. Three men hover around it, stringing garlands. 'The latest model. Mark II.'

Garib Das leads him inside the haveli, pushing others out of the way. Hari looks straight ahead, letting his children become an indistinct throng before his eyes. Here is a daughter, there perhaps a daughter-in-law—because she covered her face when he approached—and that certainly is a grandson-in-law: a young man, sitting with his legs crossed, regarding Hari with hauteur.

The Bengali decorators have plastered the courtyard with flowers. Garlands hang from every balcony on the second floor.

As is the custom in Calcutta, pillars are completely covered in rings of marigold that start at the top and wrap around until they reach the floor. Far from beautifying it, the decorations have stained the haveli—the frescoes have been hidden—yet no one seems to mind. Thankfully, the flowers will be gone in two days and he will see Parmeshwari again, seated on the edge of her bed wearing a memsahib's hat that is too large for her.

The bride is brought to him. Kaushalya leads her by the hand. He carefully averts his eyes from her and looks at Kaushalya instead. She and Shanti are a study in contrast. No one would know they were sisters. Married five years after Shanti, she has two sons and a daughter. Now in her forties, she laughs often—her teeth are large, and two protrude over the lower lip—and carries herself with an assurance born of happy matrimony. Age has been kind to her, even as it has been harsh on Shanti, whose childlessness has embittered her with each passing year. Indeed, so little had he worried on Kaushalya's account when in Watsonganj that he often forgot she was his daughter. Now, he does not remember what her children look like, or if he ever saw them at all. And she certainly has grandchildren, who are among the boys and girls running about in the courtyard.

'Touch Babuji's feet,' Kaushalya says.

The bride bends over. Her fingers graze his toes. He steps back in embarrassment, then remembers etiquette and lays a hand on her head, patting her in the lightest way possible. Then she stands up straight and the shawl on her head—it is a Marwari *orhani* of thin cotton, embroidered with gold thread and silver sequins—slips off. He is suddenly looking her full in the face, and she at him. He gasps. She does not avert her eyes. He stutters a second blessing. 'May you have many sons...'

'It was I who wanted my wedding to take place in your haveli, Dadaji.'

He is befuddled. In fifty years, no daughter-in-law, aside from Gayatri, has spoken to him directly. When necessary, messages were delivered by proxy. If a child happened to be around, a daughter-in-law used him as messenger: tell your grandfather his lemonade is ready. If no one was available, she loudly called to the child to tell his grandfather that...and Hari knew that she meant to address him. That is how it has been, and that is how it still is in Rampura. But in Calcutta... He does not understand. The shawl may have slipped off by accident. Will she not pull it back hurriedly and withdraw in embarrassment? She does not. She speaks; he listens wide-eyed. He looks to the left and the right, and at Kaushalya. Like Arjun, she is a lawyer in Calcutta. She names her husband without the slightest inhibition. She actually mouths the word 'Arjun' publicly, amidst a hundred people, in front of Arjun's grandfather—as if the women of Shekhavati did not have a dozen ways of referring to their husbands when their names came up in songs. Why else had Vishnuji given himself a thousand names? The wife of Krishna could substitute that name with Gopal; if Gopal happened to be her father-in-law's name, she could resort to Girdhari, or Murari, or Narayan, or any of the thousand names of Vishnu. Arjun's wife had recourse to Partha, Parantapa, Bhaarat, Dhananjaya... Was not the Bhagavad Gita full of Arjun's many names? In conversation it was even easier, because the husband could simply be called 'he'. But here stands Arjun's wife, blithely telling him 'Arjun and I will work in the same office.' She speaks for a long time, longer than he considers appropriate, and is led away by Kaushalya. He stands rooted to the spot.

A song is playing somewhere in the haveli. A film song, of the type he would not have permitted:

inhi logo ne, inhi logo ne
inhi logo ne le lina dupatta mera
These are the very men who took away my dupatta...

Another woman mourning the loss of her modesty, as in the film he had watched in Watsonganj. These are the two immutable facts of our times, he thinks: ever declining morals and ever shorter lives.

Someone touches his elbow. It is Tribhuvan. 'She will be your most educated daughter-in-law, Babuji. When Arjun returned from England, I knew his bride had to be a graduate… She will earn money like her husband.'

He is jolted. He had heard the bride say something like that but glossed over it. 'No doubt you spent much to send Arjun to England. Can he not earn enough for his wife and children? Why must a woman bear the burden?'

'It is not a question of money…'

'Why else does a man work? Why do you think I sat in a shop for fifty years? And why must a man force his wife to leave the house unless he is lazy or incompetent?'

'It is her decision, Babuji.'

'But are you not her father-in-law?'

Tribhuvan begins to extol the bride's virtues again but fails to mollify Hari. Finally, he says, 'She is a gentle girl, Babuji. Silent as a cow.'

Hari shakes his head. They say that about every girl when making a match. In any case, he has already heard from this girl and knows that is not true.

'I have met her father and her brothers,' says Tribhuvan. 'The family is wealthy. We could have had the wedding in Grand Hotel—where I was married, you might remember. It was she who said it had to be the haveli in Rampura. It was she who asked for all your children to be present. Tomorrow, she will become your daughter too. When you speak to her, you will not be able to tell she has been to college.'

This softens Hari somewhat but he is still suspicious, and annoyed that the whole wedding plan was set in motion by the bride, not her father-in-law.

'By having the wedding in Rampura, we are able to see you. And I am able to see my brothers. I have not been to Watsonganj for years.'

'I know,' Hari says. 'You did not come when your mother died.'

Tribhuvan is taken unawares. 'There must have been good reason... I have invited everyone to the wedding. All your children. And their children. And *their* children too.'

'Everyone but Gopi. Is he not your brother?'

'But I did, Babuji. I sent two telegrams to Santahar, and messages to his four daughters.'

Hari is suddenly uncomfortable. 'Is Gopi here, then?'

'Pushpa has come from Watsonganj with her children. Her sisters are here too. But Gopi and Sharda Bhabhi...'

'I did not want to see him anyway.'

'Pushpa says Gopi is on his way. Perhaps he is in Nawalgarh right now, hiring a camel cart to cross the riverbed.'

Hari shakes his head. He does not believe.

'Pushpa has come with her son and daughter-in-law, and her granddaughter, born three days ago. Did you hear that, Babuji? Pushpa is a grandmother! She was not sure she should travel by train with a three-day old, but I told her she had to so you could see the child. That girl is your great-great-granddaughter. How many men live to see that!'

'Babuji.'

Ishwar Das has bent over to touch Hari's feet. He is trailed by a boy, whom he scolds. 'Do not watch idly. Touch Dadaji's feet.'

The boy complies. Ishwar Das beams. 'This is Tinku. He has talked of nothing else but seeing you since he found out we were going to Rampura.' He turns to the boy. 'Go on.'

The boy looks at the ground and shuffles his feet uncomfortably.

'Go on! You had no trouble saying it in the train.'

In a faint voice that breaks often, the boy recites the multiplication table for one-and-three-quarters until he has reached seventeen-and-a-half.

'He is only six,' says Ishwar Das.

Hari is suddenly tired—he has been standing for a long time. 'Take me into that room, to the left.'

He is led inside. Tinku follows him, saying brightly, 'That

is from the film *Pakeezah*. We watched it in Watsonganj.' He is referring to the film song, which seems to go on forever.

'Leave Dadaji alone, Tinku,' Ishwar Das calls.

Inside the room, a chair is brought. Hari sits down gratefully. The sounds of the courtyard are muted here. The room is full of women. His arrival causes a flutter: faces are quickly hidden behind shawls, saris are wrapped tightly around bodies and their corners pulled over bare heads.

The women are making papad. Large vats lie open, filled with a paste—daal and rice spiced with cumin and asafoetida—that is being mixed. A group of three is rolling papad. A team takes the papad to be laid out to dry on the upper floors of the haveli. A group makes pickle. Oil is being poured, spices measured—salt, cumin, diced chillies, sangar bean, black gram and mustard seeds. The women have to go to great lengths to move their arms while keeping their saris pulled over their faces. He is sorry to have caused so much trouble, but they do not seem to mind. Their hands move mechanically as they sing.

The peepul you planted before you went east
Is now a great, dense tree
I was only a child but am now a beautiful woman
Come back, son of my mother-in-law

He sighs in relief. Some things remain the same, even if the lines no longer mean anything to anyone.

Then he sees the one woman who has not covered her head and who, from her mien, seems to disdain modesty. She has not changed at all, though she is certainly now past sixty. Durga would have been sixty-three… There are strands of grey in Gayatri's hair and folds of skin under her chin, but she holds herself exactly as she did when he last saw her in Calcutta. 'Should you find Gangadhar deficient in his duty toward you,' she had said, 'you only have to send a message to his mother.'

He feels tears in his eyes. This is the daughter he never had, or perhaps the wife he should have been granted. She must not see him or he will give himself away before a dozen women—granddaughters and nieces and the wives of grandsons—and they will talk of how Dadaji wept like a child during Arjun's wedding. Perhaps he should speak to her in private, but how is that possible in this menagerie? Thankfully, she does not appear to have noticed him. She alone of all the women in the room is unaware of his presence—she did not shuffle or scramble to cover herself when he was brought in. Indeed she had continued rolling papad—one a minute—creating perfect discs out of lumps of dough.

He remembers what Tribhuvan had suggested after Durga's death. That would have been an outrage, yet here she is, a silent reproach to him. He is consumed by guilt. If only she had not been sitting so close to him! Her hands stop for a moment. The rolling pin hovers over the dough, then resumes. He has no doubt now—she has seen him. And she knows. She has known all along, even about the thoughts that had stained his mind after Shanti's wedding. He cannot bear to sit near her—such a gentle woman, and such fire emanates from her! She is a Kali whose wrath is expressed without word or deed. He will be burnt to ashes. He must get away.

He tries to get up from the chair but cannot. Panic seizes him. Hands help him up. He stands unsteadily and turns around to admonish the presumptuous fool. It is Mohan Lal. His hair has receded—he could not be more than thirty-five, perhaps forty. Hari tries to hide his disappointment in banter. 'Another barrister. There are lawyers everywhere I turn. Four in this haveli alone.'

Mohan Lal shrugs uncomfortably. 'I am in Watsonganj, Babuji, in Harilal & Sons.'

'But why? You were clerking for Tribhuvan, were you not? He had said that in four years...'

'We had a shortage of hands in Watsonganj. In the grain shop.'

'What of Gariba's sons? And Fakira has three! Ishwar Das has two, I think. How many hands do they need in Watsonganj? You should have remained in Kalkatta.'

'Tribhuvan Bhaiya thought that...'

'Ah.' It had been Tribhuvan's doing, then. He had sent Mohan Lal back from Calcutta, perhaps to focus his energies on sending his son to England. But Mohan Lal was almost like a son to Tribhuvan—he was only six years older than Arjun—and a brother besides... Perhaps the bond of brotherhood does not extend across mothers. Hari feels a great burden on his chest.

'Use my shoulder for support,' says Mohan Lal.

He steps back in consternation. There was no need to feel sad on Mohan Lal's account. There were countless barristers in Calcutta with no cases to fight, while Mohan Lal had his own shop in Watsonganj. A bania needs no more—his place is behind the scales. He will thrive through good times and bad because men will always be hungry. Indeed, Hari has always been suspicious of what Tribhuvan does, regarding it as hollow and meretricious. A law practice is not real work. Real work is in trade—in the buying and the selling of goods—not in capitalizing on a quarrel between two men. Doctors spend their time wishing people would fall ill while a lawyer prays for conflict. That is what they demand of Raamji when they go to a temple. And a bania? He simply wishes for prosperity and well-being. He need not ask Raamji for hunger: there is so much of it already.

'How many sons do you have, Mohan Lal?'

'Three, and a daughter.' As he says this Mohan Lal pushes a child forward. 'Your youngest grandson.' It is a boy of two, small and dark-complexioned, who reminds Hari of Mohan Lal's wife.

'I remember my daughter-in-law very well. It was she who prepared your mother's last gold varq.'

'She is here too.'

But Hari cannot wish away his discomfort at Mohan Lal's return from Calcutta. He points to the two-year-old boy. 'When he is of age, bring him to Rampura—he will get married in the haveli. I see that Tribhuvan's son has been to England. Do they not say that the sahibs in America are richer than the ones in England? This little one will go to America.'

Mohan Lal smiles. The Peepli ends. Hari is caught unawares

by the sudden silence—his words ring loudly in it. To his left, he sees Gayatri stiffen. But she could not possibly know what Tribhuvan had suggested. Unless he told her… He must leave the room right away. The women begin a new song.

Let us go for a walk, my dear,

Let us see Victoria in the cool breeze

'Take me outside,' he says to Mohan Lal. 'I want to see my children.'

The women do not notice his departure. In the far corner of the courtyard he sees Gangadhar seated on a chair. He does not want to speak to him. Even at this distance he can see the boy is tired—he could not be more than forty-five—and he can tell, from the kurta and dhoti, that Gangadhar has not done well. For many years after coming to Watsonganj—until he cut off all contact with his children—Hari had received postcards chronicling the steady decline of Gangadhar's fortunes in Bogra. Marwari families in Pakistan continued to flee west. Those with daughters found sons-in-law in India; those with sons sent them to set up shops in India, then followed their sons there. Gangadhar had stayed, partly on account of Murlidhar and Bansidhar, and seen his wealth dwindle. The oil depot in Rangpur had been sold at a loss, the jute business had already collapsed, the cigarette shop was shut down. All that remained of Harilal & Sons in Bogra was the grain shop—that is where we got our first rupee, Hari had told himself in consolation—which fed a whole family and two invalids.

He compares Gangadhar with his cousin Arjun, Tribhuvan's son, who has come back from England. What does Arjun have that Gangadhar does not? The steady hand of a father over his head. They say Tribhuvan is the best-known Marwari barrister in Calcutta. He takes delegations to the chief minister. Mohammad Ali Bogra, the prime minister of Pakistan, was his friend. When such a man has a son—and he has only one—the son soars like the father. Poor Gangadhar. If only Durga had let those trains collide, if he had not given his life to save his father's, Gangadhar would not be sitting so tentatively in a cotton dhoti. But who can divine the mind of Raamji? Instead of giving Gangadhar a father, he had burdened him with Bansidhar and Murlidhar, both incapable of looking after themselves. Well, at least no one would ever say that Gangadhar had not done his duty by his brothers.

He does not see Bansidhar or Murlidhar in the courtyard. Perhaps they have been left behind in Bogra. But who is looking after them there? He will not ask Gangadhar. The conversation will be too painful.

He is left alone—Mohan Lal has been called away. He feels unsafe amidst the children. Again he tries to identify their fathers or mothers from their faces. They run about heedlessly, using him as a pillar, describing circles around him or resting against his legs. How will he survive the next three days? The guests have not even arrived yet. After the wedding tomorrow, it will be another two days before everyone goes away and the tibbas reclaim Rampura. It is now late in the morning—the hour when he sits quietly wth Janardhan in the courtyard, as he has for thirteen years. There will be no soft banter with Johnny today. He is busy supervising the erection of the wedding pavilion in the courtyard, where the fire will be lit. The concrete slab has been removed. A wooden pole stands tall. A flower tent of sorts is being raised, peaking at the central pole, from which garlands radiate in patterns he finds unnecessarily intricate.

Unnoticed, he enters the stairwell. He rarely goes upstairs—his knees hurt. By the time he reaches the upper floor he is out of breath. The corridors are foreign to him, as are the frescoes here—he has not seen them in years. To his left is the great bedroom where the chitera had painted those embarrassing pictures. Has anyone seen them yet? The door is wide open—the most titillating drawings are hidden behind it, to be seen only when it is shut. He peers inside. There is no furniture in the room; it has never been lived in, except occasionally by Janardhan, who throws a sheet and a pillow on the mosaic floor. But now a mattress has been brought in. Fakir Chand lies on it, prone. He is naked but for a loincloth around his buttocks, looking like Gandhiji. His hands are extended above his head; his legs are fully stretched; his face is buried in the mattress—there is no pillow—and he is covered from the back of his neck to his heels in a dark brown paste. On hearing Hari's footsteps, he turns his head as much as he can without moving his body.

'Do not get up,' Hari says. 'I have come only for a moment to catch my breath. It is too noisy downstairs. '

Fakir Chand goes back to burying his face in the mattress. Hari sits down next to him. The stench from the paste is overpowering. 'It smells like cowdung.'

'It is.'

Hari sighs. No doubt a vaidya in Rampura has recommended this. Fakir Chand has not come to Shekhavati for fifteen years, yet he knows of every vaidya here. He maintains a list in faraway Watsonganj, and accosts vaidyas and hakims from Shekhavati whenever they visit Disavar. For years he has followed their prescriptions, indulging himself with parpatti, bel juice and turmeric poultices. Nothing has changed his frail condition, or that indescribable suggestion of disease that hovers over him. It is perhaps because of his excessively fair skin that he has always looked vulnerable, always in need of consolation. Now past forty-five, with his children married off and grandchildren to behold, he has finally reached the age to which he has aspired all his life—his attitude now becomes him.

'You look very healthy, Babuji,' Fakir Chand says.

Whenever he says this—Hari knows—he expects a very specific reply. He humours his son. 'You yourself look rather weak. Is it indigestion?'

Fakir Chand shakes his head. 'I have been careful to drink stale water every morning, and to take a spoonful of *isabgol* powder before going to sleep. That keeps me regular. But only Raamji knows what he has in store for me.'

'You will get by, Fakira.'

'That was what the astrologer said: you will get by until Raamji strikes you dead. When their time comes, men die without warning. And those whom He has marked for a long life live to be a hundred. Look at Shanti and Nagar Malji. They crossed the Gorai by mounting cows; they walked through beels, in water that sometimes reached the chin, for two days; they nearly drowned in paddy fields; they were chased by Musalmans; yet they live. While I…'

'What on earth are you talking about?'

Fakir Chand pauses. 'Have you not heard about Shanti?'

Terrible thoughts pass through Hari's mind. He is afraid to dwell on them.

'She fled Kushtia. She and Nagar Malji. There were riots. Such terrible stories—shops looted, men murdered, babies burnt, women violated…'

'When did this happen?'

'During the war.'

'I do not know of any war.'

'It ended two weeks ago. Bogra is no longer in Pakistan, Babuji. Bengalis have their own Shekhavati now. They call it Bangladesh.'

Hari feels blinded. He has sat by the riverbed for thirteen years and bantered with Janardhan in the courtyard. What have the others been doing outside Shekhavati? 'Who fought whom?'

'Musalmans fought Musalmans, but it was Hindus who suffered. And Marwaris had the worst of it. Shanti left her haveli, Nagar Malji abandoned everything in Dhaka and Mymensingh—his properties are all gone, they are now in Bangladesh. Raamji spared their lives. They walked through water for two days to cross the border into India, then somehow took a train to Watsonganj. And they came with nothing except the jewellery Shanti had hidden in her clothes. '

'And her in-laws?'

'Raamji took them away ten years ago. Had they lived, they would have been slaughtered—they could not have waded through rivers.'

Hari holds his head in his hands.

'Indira has said there will be reparations. Houses left vacant will be declared "enemy property" and compensation will be paid. But who will pay for a forty-room haveli?'

'Whose daughter is Indira? Gopi's? I do not remember...'

'The prime minister, Babuji.'

'Ah.'

'We saw the war too. Planes flew over Watsonganj on their way to the border. We heard that yellow letters had been painted on Hindu homes. Nagar Malji saw the letter—'H', in English—on his haveli, and knew he had been marked. The trouble was not caused by our Musalmans, but Musalmans in the Pakistani army...'

Hari has heard such talk before. No one is ours, he wants to tell his son, except the banias of Shekhavati. But his thoughts are on Gangadhar. Had there been trouble in Bogra too? Gangadhar had looked glum and defeated. Now he understands—it was not merely the resignation of a man without a father; it was the shrug of a man without a home. Perhaps they have chased him out of Bogra. What of Gopi? And who else among his children still lives in Pakistan? He is afraid to ask, but Fakir Chand guesses his thoughts.

'Gangadhar is safe, for now. There was no killing in Bogra.'

'And in...'

'None in Santahar either. The Musalmans there have had their fill in '47 and '50.'

Fakir Chand turns over. There is no paste on the front of his body. His stomach and thighs look startlingly white after the dark brown of his back. 'I have told Shanti she may stay in Watsonganj as long as she wants. She did not take my children, but at least she can have my second house. It is a small building across the road from mine. What will I do with it? My children have enough. My daughter has been married off. Two of my sons have shops of their own. My eldest son is a doctor in Belle Vue, the clinic Birlaji has started—the best in Calcutta. Raamji has given me enough. And after I am gone...'

'Who is looking after Shanti in Watsonganj? Everyone is here in Rampura.'

'Oh, she came too.'

'Shanti is here? You did not tell me.'

'Gariba brought Shanti and Nagar Malji in his Ambassador car.'

Hari corrects him out of habit. 'Gariba Bhaiya. Do not disrespect your elder brother.'

Fakir Chand replies just as mechanically. 'Only four years separate us, Babuji.'

So Shanti is here, Hari thinks. To the great misfortune of her life was now added another one. He did not see her in the courtyard or in the room where the women were making papad.

'Raamji chooses a curse for everyone,' says Fakir Chand. 'For me an early death, for Shanti childlessness and the loss of her haveli, for Bansidhar and Murlidhar...'

'Are they married yet?' Hari asks, his heart pounding.

'Who will give daughters to them? It is too late now: they are almost as old as I am. It is their good fortune to have a brother like Gangadhar. I know men who have turned such brothers out of the house.'

A great weight descends on Hari's chest. There is Shanti, there is Durga, there is Gangadhar, and his brothers Bansidhar and Murlidhar. And there is Gayatri, who suffers silently unlike Shanti but who causes him the greatest pain. Then he interrupts himself—what would Master Bholaram make of this grief? Still a Grihastha after thirteen years by the riverbed! Tribhuvan should have married his son off in Grand Hotel in Calcutta, after all. Thirteen years of detachment have been undone.

Fakir Chand leans toward Hari carefully, without disturbing the paste on his back. 'My son examined Bansi and Murli this morning. He wants to take them to Belle Vue for treatment.'

'What is wrong with them?' Hari demands.

'The best hospital in Calcutta, Babuji.'

'But they are not sick.'

He gets up. It must be the ache in his heart, because he has never been so tired: the act of raising himself from the mattress has knocked his breath out. As he walks away—Fakir Chand has shut his eyes—he finds every step difficult, as if weights have been attached to his feet. Wherever I go, I drag around the sufferings of my children, he thinks.

'Dadaji.'

It is Fakir Chand's son, the doctor, whom he had seen at the gate. He has come looking for his father, thinks Hari, but the boy wants to speak to him. 'I hope Babuji mentioned Bansidhar Bhaiya to you. I want to take him to Belle Vue in Calcutta. Epileptic seizures can be controlled with a tablet taken once a day. There is no such remedy for Murlidhar Bhaiya's autism, but behavioural therapy is known to...'

Hari does not listen. The pain is now acute. Slowly, he descends the stairs, watching the frescoes on either side. The Bengali decorators have somehow missed the stairwell. The walls are painted with flying demi-gods—maruts, kinnars and gandharvas. One strums a veena, another a guitar, a third blows into a dundubhi and a fourth beats a nagara. A bania sits beneath them, looking up, hands on his ears to shut out the cacophony, brow wrinkled in consternation. Hari chuckles.

He must go back to the riverbed. The sun is now high in the sky, but it is winter. Indeed the warmth will thaw the knot in his heart. He must cross the courtyard quickly before his sons stop him.

He starts. The wedding pavilion sits in the centre. He must take a circuitous route to avoid the pavilion and Janardhan, who has his back to him. Gangadhar is still sitting in the wicker chair. From the room where papad is being made, the sounds of the Peepli flow again. When he was a child, they used to say in Rampura that two things never come to an end, the making of papad and the singing of the Peepli. Far to his right stand three women—heads uncovered—laughing. Pushpa's younger sisters, perhaps. Is their father here yet? The pavilion is now a few feet from him. He turns sharply to the right, and finds himself face-to-face with the ghost of Nanuram.

'I came to the station with Gopi Chand, but you were gone.'

Hari stutters. 'There was a bomb on the train…' The words refuse to fly out. His tongue feels stiff.

From a great distance, he hears a cry. 'Is Dadaji all right?'

It sounds like Murlidhar. Can a saint speak so clearly? He should not shout like this—it is improper in a house where a wedding is being planned.

'Babuji has fallen!'

That one is Gariba, no doubt.

'Stand aside, everyone.'

'Is he all right, Doctor Sahib?'

'Give him some air.'

That sounds like Fakira's doctor son. He cannot seem to get away from that boy.

'Bring a mattress. There is one in the room upstairs.'

No, no, Hari thinks. The boy is a doctor from Kalkatta but does not understand propriety. He must not lay an old man—an old, tired man—next to the wedding pavilion. It is inauspicious. At least take me to the riverbed, away from the haveli where my grandson will circle the wedding fire.

He can see the sun above—it is white and clear. The sky is white too, and there isn't a single cloud. This is the Shekhavati dome, so different from the muddy skies of Bengal, where dark clouds shut out the sun and thunder rolls endlessly. But why has the sky gone dark? And how can anyone see stars twinkling by day in the desert? Is he no longer in Shekhavati? Ah, it is evening. He is on a bed in the courtyard. There is silence. Why have the women stopped singing? You cannot have a wedding without songs. Perhaps they are waiting for him to wake up. That will happen soon enough. He has eaten Shekhavati grain. Never been sick a day in his life.

'Pranaam, Dadaji.'

It is Bansidhar. He looks healthy and cheerful. You would not know that anything was wrong with him. Indeed you would ask him what he dealt in and how many children he had. He could be a shopkeeper sitting behind his scales in Bogra or Watsonganj or Rampura, with his son playing near a mound of grain. And there is Murlidhar, spittle running down his chin, a hand clutching his brother's arm. Gangadhar stands next to them, shorter and sadder. How odd, that Gangadhar—the one who fills his brothers' bellies—looks weak and tired, while the two brothers, each half a man, radiate health and well-being. To Gangadhar's left stands Fakira. He must have washed off the cowdung. They are all here. Both his daughters, and all his sons, except Gopi. Their sons and daughters. And their sons and daughters. The children stand in front, leaning over the bed, watching him. Why do they crowd around like this? He remembers—today is Pausha sudi purnamasi. A full moon will rise today—indeed it has already risen to his left. There is a lantern somewhere on the floor, throwing strange shadows on their faces. *I am a* pret *in the court of Yamaraj*, he thinks mournfully, *and these are my fellow ghosts, awaiting justice.*

Bansidhar says. 'Murli has been eating almonds. They have improved his condition. I have found them to be beneficial too. Months go by and the spirit does not seize me.'

Hari looks at Gangadhar. 'I have not forgotten my promise to you, Ganga. I will find brides for these two. It is not too late. I have heard that men now get married in their forties.'

Gangadhar sobs but does not reply. Hari is irritated. 'Look cheerful! We have a wedding tomorrow. Guests will arrive soon.'

But his own cheer melts away because he sees Shanti, standing to his right. One look at her face tells him that there is no joy in the world. She looks much older than her forty-five years, and from that strange plateau of indeterminate age she radiates bitterness. It is impossible to look into her eyes and not see an accusation. Beside her, Nagar Mal looks lost and uncomfortable. He has added girth—how had he managed to walk through beels for two days?—and somehow his face does not give away his pain as Shanti's does.

Now that she has lost her haveli, Shanti harbours an even greater grievance against the world. He wonders if he is to blame: was he remiss in marrying her into a family of adoptees? But they had a forty-room haveli... That, too, has turned out to be a curse. It was the haveli, and the properties in Dhaka and Mymensingh, that kept them in Pakistan when he and his sons came to Calcutta in '47. Why else had Nagar Mal and his father remained in Kushtia? There stands Shanti now, her eyes on his, fixed in grief, for him or for herself he does not know. She has never been in a house with as many children as she sees today. Her thoughts are written on her face: so many little gifts from Raamji, none hers. There are tears in her eyes even though none can be seen. Perhaps they have dried and set years ago. They are part of her face; no one notices them, the way no one sees old moles and warts.

A child tugs at his sleeve. He turns his face and notes that his body will not follow. It is Ishwar Das's son—what was his name?—the one who had recited those multiplication tables. His face glows in triumph; he can barely contain his excitement as he holds up a slate and chalk. Good boy, thinks Hari, doing his lessons even when far from school.

'Dadaji,' says Tinku, 'I have been adding up the numbers all morning. You have sixteen grandsons, twelve granddaughters, fifteen great-grandsons, seventeen great-granddaughters!'

'Speak softly, Tinku.' That is Ishwar Das. 'Dadaji needs to rest.'

'And one great-great-granddaughter, four days old!'

'Tinku!'

Why has the boy added up these numbers, and why must he announce them? Does he not know it is inauspicious to count a man's sons? Never count aloud, Master Bholaram had said, whether it is money, sons or gold coins. Who knows which ears will hear your words, and what ill they will wish you? The world abounds in misfortune, and only the rash invite it. A bania says sixteen-hundred instead of one-thousand-six-hundred, because men's hearts beat faster when the word 'thousand' is uttered; he discreetly says 'five' when he means five lakhs or five crores; he calls gold 'the yellow one' and silver 'the white one', and you will never catch him saying 'diamond'... And here is a little boy announcing how many children Harilal Tibrewal has. Did his master not teach him discretion?

Twelve granddaughters, fifteen great-grandsons... It sounds like a final tally, the last entry in a ledger, the final inventory of stock at closing time. But the shop will reopen the next morning. Why, he has still to see Arjun's children!

Then it dawns on him: this is closing time. The last customer has gone. The doors have been shuttered. Very little remains to be done: grain has to be poured into bags and their mouths have to be sealed; scales have to be put away and weights arranged in piles. Perhaps a scoop of wheat for the kitchen upstairs...

A bania does not attain Sannyas, Master Bholaram had said. He dies in Vanaprastha if he is fortunate. Most die in Grihasthya, seated at their scales. He becomes anxious. Am I dying in Grihasthya? Should I have been alone with Johnny in this last moment? Or the ghost of Nanuram? Or Parmeshwari? But I have sat at the riverbed for thirteen years...

There is gentle pressure on his ankles. A man is sitting at his feet, massaging them. He is frail and bald, perhaps seventy, and looks astonishingly like Parmeshwari. Hari chuckles. 'You were always the short one, Gopi. We had to put you on a fat English book during your engagement.'

Gopi smiles. 'Sharda is here too, Babuji. She still has an inch on me.'

'I think I forgot to send gold ginnis for your fourth daughter's wedding.'

'It does not matter, Babuji.'

'Gariba will send her four ginnis.'

'Nanuram never came to my house, or I would have joined you at the station in Santahar.'

'Call him Nanuramji. He is ten years older than your father.'

'He died on my account.'

'What do you deal in?'

'Everything, Babuji. Raamji has been kind. There is no dearth of the yellow one in my home. I have oil depots in Santahar, Rangpur and Gobindganj, shops in Dhaka and Narayanganj, fields and orchards all over the Rajshahi division. People buy from Harilal & Sons as far south as Cox's Bazar.'

'Fakira tells me there was a war.'

'Yes, but the rates have never been better. East Pakistan is now Bangladesh, but people still need grain and oil.'

I am dying in Grihasthya, he thinks ruefully. *It is not easy, Masterji*, he says to Bholaram's ghost. His eyes fall on Shanti again. Ah, there lies the unfulfilled task.

Masterji had been very clear: when you have married off your children and seen the faces of your grandchildren, you advance to the third stage of Vanaprastha… Yet there stands Shanti, childless. He must see her children before he goes.

'Tribhuvan.'

'Babuji is calling Tribhuvan Bhaiya,' someone says. Quite unnecessary, he thinks, because Tribhuvan is beside him, holding his hand.

'Where is Pushpa?'

'I am here, Dadaji.' She stands beside him too. In her arms is a bundle of blankets and rubber sheets—her four-day-old granddaughter. Tears stream down her face. She raises a corner of the blanket to let Hari see the infant. 'It is her good fortune that she has seen you, Dadaji …'

'One great-great granddaughter!' Tinku shouts again.

How old is Pushpa? Then he remembers that she is exactly the same age as Fakira—they were born within moments of each other in adjacent rooms. Jokes had been told—how little Fakir Chand was already an uncle, how he should not be wetting the sheets with his niece crying beside him. And he remembers, too, why Gariba and Fakira were named so—well, they have lived, even if Fakira dies every day of his life.

'When we first came to Watsonganj, I borrowed eleven rupees from your father-in-law.'

'He considers the debt settled, Babuji.'

'Gariba will ensure that the debt is repaid, with nau-anna-saikada interest.' There is a sudden silence, in which he hears that song again. *Inhi log ne le lina dupatta mera…*

Have they been playing it all day?

Of course, they do not know what nau-anna-saikada is. 'Six and three-quarters per cent, compounded annually. And an anna was four paisa then, not the new six and quarter paisa. You can work it out with Johnny. He will know.'

Another silence. Someone asks, 'Who is Johnny? A sahib?'

He will not answer this. He is looking at Pushpa, who has now wiped her tears. How lovingly she holds her granddaughter in her arms! The father of this little girl is Pushpa's oldest son—the boy with whom he had walked to school in Watsonganj, the one who used to sing about the English king in such a clear voice. Poor child—only four days old. What will have happened to the world by the time she grows up? Will modesty exist when she reaches womanhood? But of course, he knows. He has been hearing the answer over and over again—it is in that song, which is not a lament but a cry of relief. Pushpa's granddaughter will grow up to be like Arjun's bride. She will speak to her grandfather-in-law without covering her head, and she will work in the same office as her husband… Who is he to understand the ways of Raamji? He fixes his eyes on Pushpa. 'Do you see your Shanti Bua next to you, Pushpa?'

'Yes, Dadaji.'

'Give the girl to her.'

The infant is transferred to Shanti, who holds her awkwardly.

'Take good care of your daughter, Shanti. Do not go back to Pakistan, or whatever country they now call it. Your daughter will grow up with cousins, aunts and uncles, nephews and nieces. You are the only mother she will know. No one will tell her otherwise. Pushpa will be her cousin, not her grandmother.'

He pauses. The words have exhausted him. The sky is clear. Stars shine brightly as they never do in Bengal. Has he gone into Vanaprastha now?

'Switch off the gramophone.' That sounds like Mohan Lal.

Hari thinks of silver tibbas and Parmeshwari's face in the moonlight. He thinks of camel carcasses lying among dunes. The song stops abruptly. He hears it now—water is dripping somewhere. 'I hear a tap.'

'I have had it repaired, jijaji. It is not leaking.'

That is Johnny's voice. Why does he still call him jijaji? 'Johnny, go to 67 Cotton Street tomorrow. Put down two rupees. The morning will be dry.'

'Yes, jijaji.'

How absurd—Johnny is sobbing. They will all see his toothless gums. But there it is again—the drip, drip of water. 'I hear the tap. Someone has forgotten to shut it tightly.'

They do not know about the Chhappaniya, Harilal thinks, as he shuts his eyes.

Author's Note

My grandfather Hiralal Saraf was born in 1880, and died in 1960 of cancer of the throat, apparently brought on by a lifetime of smoking Berkeley cigarettes. Hiralal was already fifty-five when my father—the youngest son by a second marriage—was born, so his recollections of my grandfather were sketchy and impersonal, and restricted to the usual platitudes about long-dead ancestors – his deep religiosity, his obsession with water and his uncommonly good health, which I was assured was the result of a childhood spent eating Shekhavati grain.

It took me many years and dozens of interviews—with relatives in Bangladesh, Kolkata, Mumbai and Rajasthan, many now deceased—to piece together the story of a man whose travels epitomized the peregrinations of his community. Much had to be imagined, reconstructed and situated in context. This descent into personal history revealed family secrets—which shall remain interred—petty quarrels and simmering resentments, and entailed delightful hours spent in obscure Kolkata libraries, evenings spent under khejra trees in desert towns, familiarization with the dead Modhiya script, and the fingering of decayed letters buried inside steel trunks that have not seen light for a century.

In February 2005, someone calculated that Hiralal Saraf's descendants numbered 502, and his great-great-great-great grandchild had already been born. While some had moved to the legal and medical professions and some had crossed the oceans, the vast majority were still busy selling jute, cotton, grain, spices, biscuits, undershirts, saris, bed-sheets, soap and shampoo in towns all over Bengal and Bihar, creating an ever-expanding 'Harilal & Sons'. The story of his business was enmeshed with the story of the family because the two are indistinguishable in a Marwari's world.

Acknowledgements

Just before Hiralal's death, my cousin Chiranjiv Lal Saraf had the foresight to record, on a cassette tape, an interview with his grandfather. Without his enthusiastic support and the benefit of his prodigious memory, I could not have known where to begin. It was his network that made my travels in Bangladesh possible. Additionally, I am indebted to the countless relatives in Mumbai, Kolkata, Rajasthan and Bangladesh whose recorded interviews—preserved in my files forever—provide much of the material for this novel.